TO THE
OUTER BANKS OF NORTH CAROLINA

TO THE
OUTER BANKS OF NORTH CAROLINA

by
Dave Poyer
and
Chris Kidder

Published by Insiders' Guides Inc.
Highway 64
P.O. Box 2057
Manteo, North Carolina 27954
(919) 473-6100

Distributed by
Elizabeth City News
Elizabeth City, North Carolina 27909

REVISED EDITION
11th Printing, revised 1990
Copyright 1990 by Chris Kidder and Dave Poyer
Printed in the United States of America

All rights reserved. No part of this book may be reproduced in any form without permission, in writing, from the Publisher, except by a reviewer who wishes to quote brief passages in connection with a review in a magazine or newspaper.

ISBN 0-912367-25-3

PREFACE

The success of a serious guidebook is measured not by its first reception, but by its service, dependability, and acceptance by the travelling public over a period of years.

This edition marks the eleventh year of our existence, a milestone we may be forgiven some pride in. We're archived by The University of North Carolina and the Outer Banks History Center: We've even been used by the National Geographic.

In short, *The Insiders' Guide to the Outer Banks* has succeeded beyond our fondest dreams. The guide was a best seller from its first year of publication, in 1979. But while many books spring up like weeds in spring and then wither, this one has lasted. This year will see our in-print figure pass 145,000. The many letters we receive from readers tell us why: you rely on us. This means we are doing our job. And this makes us proud.

From the beginning, we designed the book not to sit on a shelf, or in a glove compartment, but to be used, steadily, every day and often every hour. We designed it for the visitor and resident alike. Even a glance will show you the time and effort that have gone into it.

Some people down the years have told us we didn't need to be so thorough. We could reprint press releases instead of doing our own research, or update less often. That we didn't have to improve and expand every year.

We didn't agree. We have an old-fashioned mind set: that painstaking research and careful writing, that solid value rather than glossy paper and bathing beauties would pay off in repeat sales. And time has proven us right.

Not that we, as authors, deserve too much credit. We have to thank our publisher for riding herd on our enthusiasms, or prodding us where necessary; to Banks residents, who are the first to inform us when we've fallen short; and to our readers, who have never failed to write when they don't find in our pages what they needed to know. Thanks to you all!

To our many repeat readers, you'll have no difficulty finding your way in this edition. Our profiles and maps are still oriented north to south. We still cover everything we used to. But you'll find some changes here too, not only updates but new material. We know laurels are nice, but they're too prickly to rest on.

For our new readers, welcome! Here is a brief rundown on what you'll find in the Insiders' Guide.

4   PREFACE

To introduce you to the deep-down flavor of the Banks, we have expanded our "this is" sections and original historical articles over the years to include dramatic but factual accounts of pivotal events in local history. We've also undertaken to help save the fast-vanishing tales of the old days with our ongoing oral histories.

To help you find your way, we included maps and getting around sections. We check and update these yearly. They should be sufficient for most tourists. However, if you're buying a home here, or spending a long vacation, we suggest picking up a large fold-out map of the Banks from the Tourist Bureau, the Chamber of Commerce Welcome Center, or one of the real-estate agencies. This is easier to use in a car, and will also help you orient yourself to the larger-scale (more detailed) maps in the book.

To help you find worthwhile things to do with your time once you're sunburned, we've visited and reviewed hundreds of historic attractions, shops, theaters, and fun spots. Not only have we profiled the usual, and usually heavily advertised and relatively expensive attractions, we've put in many days on the ground to locate the out-of-the-way things to do that may not be evident to a harried family with limited time or limited funds.

To help you choose the best in recreation, we've interviewed local experts on fishing, surfing, hang-gliding, scuba diving, windsurfing, and other sports to give you the best possible introduction to a new sport, or getting the most out of one you already enjoy.

To guide you to the best in lodging and dining, each year we spend hundreds of hours revising, visiting, and updating our accommodations, campgrounds, and cottage rentals sections. We don't sleep at every hotel, or drink at every bar (God forbid), but we visit, inspect, and value-rate them, and we eat at every dining place we profile. If you're in the market for a vacation home, or a year-round one, our real estate listings are a handy and timesaving guide to reputable companies that will give you a fair shake.

Last, but hardly least, our directory section is the first place to look in emergencies, small or large. And the exhaustive index makes getting to what you need a breeze.

The Banks have changed immensely since our first edition. Miles of open beach have become populated areas; empty dunes, shopping centers; the islands themselves have moved noticeably before the sea. The northern Banks have been opened to widespread settlement. Ocracoke has its first condominium. Avon is booming, and the Buxton area (basically the last available land on Hatteras) is being marketed. The central Banks, Nags Head, Kitty Hawk, and Kill

Devil Hills, are still growing visitors. And Manteo is undergoing a face lift downtown and continuing its growth as a service area to the beach.

Though the face of the Banks has changed dramatically since 1979, there are indications that its rate is slowing. A four-day northeaster in March of 1989 damaged or destroyed many beachfront structures in South Nags Head, Kitty Hawk, and Kill Devil Hills, and accelerated erosion in northern Hatteras (including the Bonner Bridge approaches). This, with other problems inherent in rapid growth, is leading to a reappraisal by governing bodies and investors. It now appears to us that the Nags Head of 1999 will not resemble Virginia Beach, as many thought. We have always believed in slow growth, with time for thought and research. Perhaps this period of reevaluation will help save the Banks we knew and loved in our youth.

But some things haven't changed. The Outer Banks is still a vacationer's paradise. It's still home for the old residents and hundreds of new ones. It's still a daughter of the sea, tumultuous with storm in February and placid and glittering in July. It's still dunes and wild ponies, sea oats and yaupon. It's still raucous amusement at Dowdy's and quieter times touring the Elizabethan Gardens. We have had many happy times here, and hope you will too.

Thank you for your support over the years. We've done everything we can to make your time on the Banks a happy time. That was our goal from the beginning. We promise you it will continue to be, for years to come.

-- Chris and Dave --

Acknowledgements: For their help during the updating of this edition, the authors and publisher would like to thank Bob Woody, Kirston Justice, Ray Hollowell, Julie Folwick, Ralph Buxton and dozens of others up and down the Banks.

Staff and Credits for Insiders' Guides, Inc.: Beth Storie, editor and production; Barbara Jaxson, production; Judy Wilson, advertising sales; Michael McOwen, cover art.

Photography: J. Foster Scott; The National Geographic Society; The National Park Service; D. Westner; The Dare County Tourist Bureau; The N.C. Aquarium; The Lost Colony; The Whalehead Club.

Line drawings: Courtesy of Jerry Miller, Raleigh, NC.

ABOUT THE AUTHORS

Dave Poyer is a novelist, naval Reserve officer, diver, and sailor. His contributions to the historical, recreational, camping, and oral history sections of this book represent thousands of hours and thousands of miles over fourteen years of camping, diving, sailing, researching, and appreciating the Outer Banks and their people..

Along with his work on this book, over half a million copies of his novels are in print. Poyer has published *White Continent, The Shiloh Project, Star Seed, The Return of Philo T. McGriffin, The Dead of Winter* and *Stepfather Bank*. He is now engaged in an ambitious sea tetralogy, the first volume of which, *The Med*, was a best seller in 1988. His most recent novel is a sea adventure set on the Banks -- *Hatteras Blue*, St. Martin's Press, 1989; available at bookstores on the Banks.

Chris Kidder grew up in Chicago and the San Francisco Bay area. She attended Knox College and the University of Maryland. After living and working on both coasts, she spent the next eleven years in between, fighting what proved to be an irresistible urge to go to the beach. In 1984 she gave up the struggle, left her career as vice president of a very successful Midwest advertising agency and moved to the Outer Banks. She is now happily settled in Nags Head -- near the beach -- with her good friend and partner, Alan Bell, son Jeffrey and two cats. She works as a freelance writer and graphic designer.

Her years of enthusiastic traveling for both business and pleasure have given Chris a special insight into the information readers want to know about area accommodations, restaurants, shops and services.

☆ 10 rooms with antique furnishings

☆ Private Baths

☆ Color TV, refrigerator and telephone

☆ Moderately priced

☆ Separate Annex

☆ Two pots of coffee in your room

FOR RESERVATIONS WRITE OR CALL:

P.O. BOX 1310

HIGHWAY 64-264

MANTEO, NC 27954

(919)473-3979

Serving lunch and dinner

Authentic German and American cuisine

Outdoor Beer Garden

Watch our Brewmaster as he brews

Five Liter Mini-kegs available to take home

Highway 64 • Manteo, NC • 473-1157

Sales Rentals & Property Management

ROBERT A. YOUNG & ASSOCIATES, INC.

The Young People *since 1950*

Robert A. Young & Associates, Realtors • Box 285 • Kill Devil Hills, NC 27948

Sales (919) 441-4816   **TOLL FREE RESERVATIONS**   Rentals (919) 441-5544
1-800-334-6436
Outside NC

Please call or fill out and mail this coupon to The Young People Realty to receive free information about:

☐ Sales
☐ Rentals
☐ Property Management

ISG90

NAME

ADDRESS

CITY   **STATE**   **ZIP**

PHONE (HOME)   **(WORK)**

TABLE OF CONTENTS

INSIDE THE OUTER BANKS	17
GETTING AROUND	26
INSIDE **THE NORTHERN BANKS**	29
Attractions	38
Recreation	41
Shopping	42
A LIFE ON THE NORTHERN BANKS	49
INSIDE **KITTY HAWK**	55
Attractions	57
Recreation	58
Shopping	59
INSIDE **KILL DEVIL HILLS**	63
Attractions	70
Recreation	74
Shopping	75
INSIDE **NAGS HEAD**	81
Attractions	84
Recreation	89
Shopping	97
INSIDE **ROANOKE ISLAND**	109
Attractions	114
Downtown	129
Shopping	140
A LIFE IN MANTEO	145
INSIDE **BODIE ISLAND**	159
Attractions	159
U-85	166
INSIDE **HATTERAS ISLAND**	177
Attractions	185
Recreation	215
Shopping	219
A LIFE ON HATTERAS	231
INSIDE **OCRACOKE**	241
Attractions	246
Shopping	254

A LIFE IN OCRACOKE	259
OUTER BANKS RESTAURANTS	267
Southern Shores, Duck, Sanderling, and Corolla	271
Kitty Hawk	275
Kill Devil Hills	278
Nags Head	287
Roanoke Island	297
Hatteras Island	302
Ocracoke	310
NIGHT SPOTS	316
OUTER BANKS RENTALS	325
OUTER BANKS ACCOMMODATIONS	341
Southern Shores, Duck, Sanderling, and Corolla	341
Kitty Hawk	343
Kill Devil Hills	344
Nags Head North	354
Nags Head South	356
Roanoke Island	361
Hatteras Island	364
Ocracoke	375
CAMPGROUNDS	385
OUTER BANKS REAL ESTATE	395
GOLD AND SILVER SEASONS	419
OUTER BANKS FISHING GUIDE	423
SURFING, WINDSURFING, AND OCEAN SWIMMING	435
SCUBA DIVING	442
FERRY INFORMATION	444
OUTER BANKS HEALTH CARE	447
SERVICE AND INFORMATION DIRECTORY	451
Emergency Numbers	447
PLACES OF WORSHIP	462
ANNUAL EVENTS	464
PORTSMOUTH ISLAND	469
NEARBY ATTRACTIONS	473
BE AN "INSIDER"	480
INDEX OF ADVERTISERS	485
INDEX	488

the Outer Banks
the natural choice
VACATION GUIDE

Welcome to North Carolina's Outer Banks!,

We are glad that you are here and hope you will enjoy the beaches, fishing, historic sites, restaurants, shopping, and more while you are staying with us.

If you have questions, there are three welcome centers ready to help. **The Aycock Brown Welcome Center is located at Milepost 1 in Kitty Hawk, The Outer Banks Chamber of Commerce is at Milepost 8 1/2 in Kill Devil Hills, and The Dare County Tourist Bureau can be found on Budleigh Street in Manteo. If you cannot visit our office, please feel free to call us at 441-8144 or 473-2138 (If you are staying on Hatteras Island, call us toll free at 995-4213).**

Once again, we are glad that you are here and hope that you enjoy your stay!

Cordially,

Gene O'Bleness, Director
Dare County Tourist Bureau

John Bone, Executive Vice President
Outer Banks Chamber of Commerce

P.S. Please remember...When You Go, Leave Only Your Footprints On the Beach!

Dare County Tourist Bureau
P.O. Box 399, Manteo, NC 27954
(919) 473-2138

Outer Banks Chamber of Commerce
P.O. Box 1757, Kill Devil Hills, NC 27948
(919) 441-8144

DIRECTORY OF MAPS

Routes to the Outer Banks	14
Mileage to the Outer Banks	15
Outer Banks Area	25
Northern Banaks	31
Kitty Hawk	56
Kill Devil Hills	65
Wright Brothers National Monument	68
Nags Head North	83
Nags Head South	92
Roanoke Island	112
Fort Raleigh	116
Dare County Regional Airport	122
Downtown Manteo	130
Elizabeth II State Historic Site	131
Bodie Island	160
Hatteras Island North	180
Hatteras Island South	181
Hatteras Village	182
Cape Hatteras Area	183
Pea Island Wildlife Refuge	186
Ocracoke Island	242
Ocracoke Village	249
Portsmouth Island	470
Cape Lookout National Park	478

A young boy jumps for joy at the sight of the Atlantic Ocean. DCTB

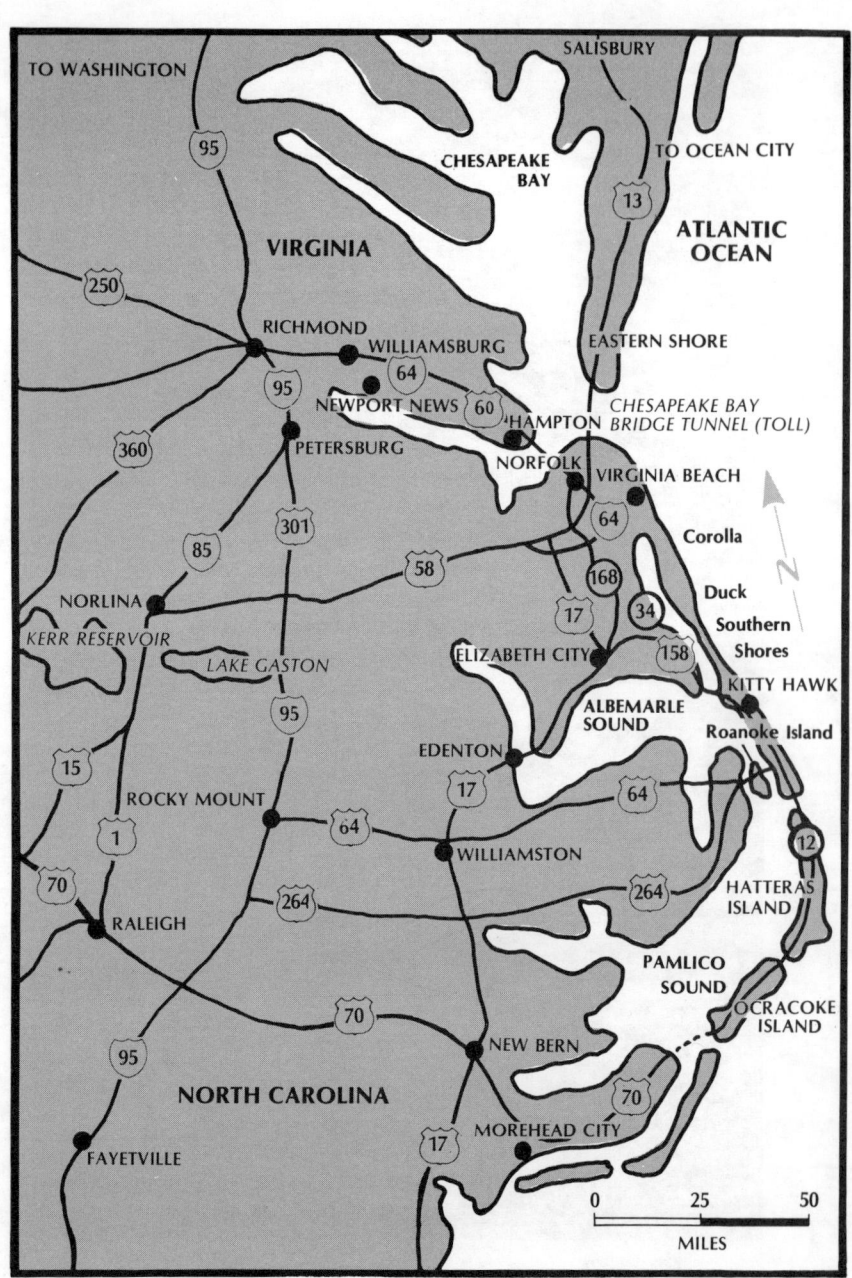

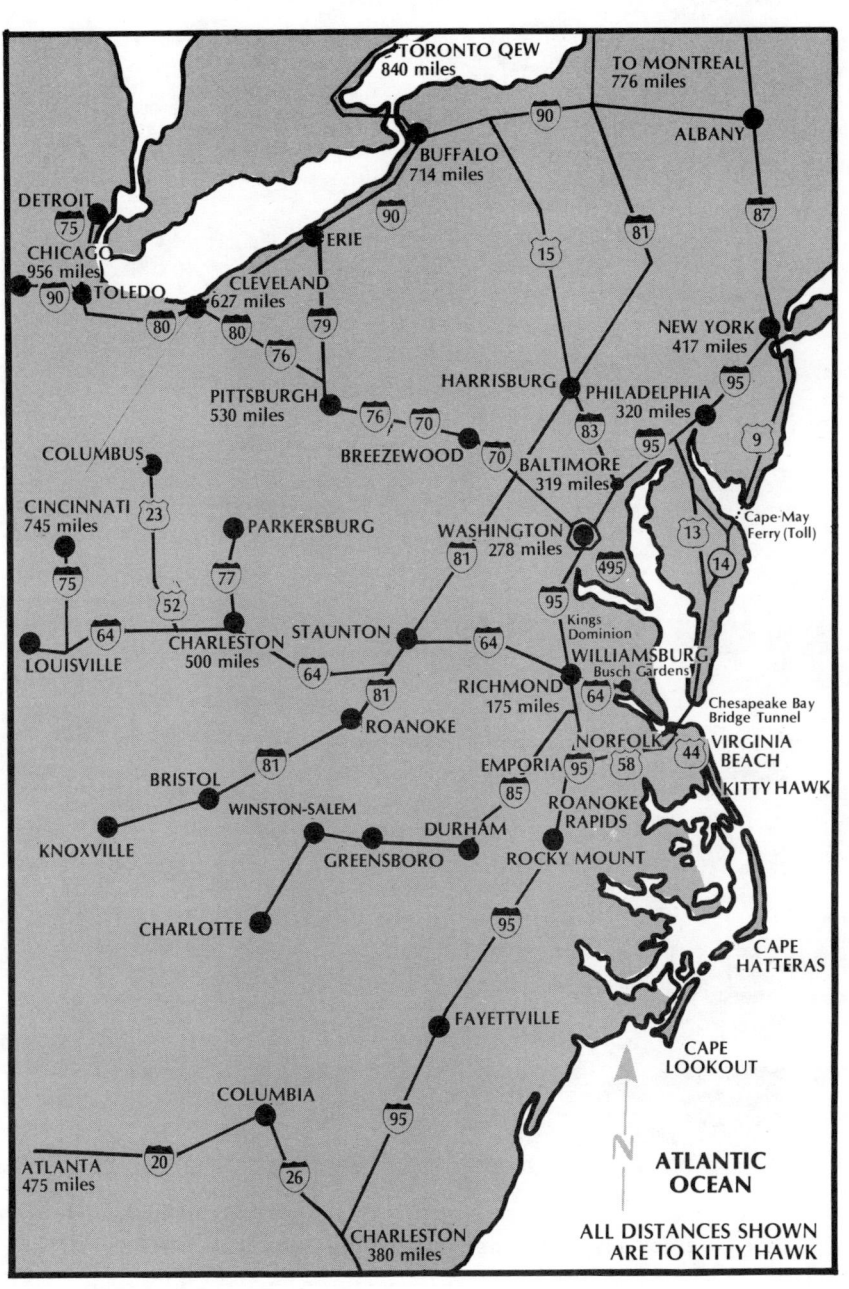

Kids enjoy a typical summer day on the Outer Banks. DCTB

INSIDE
THE OUTER BANKS

What are the Outer Banks?

To the visitor, they are wind, sand, and fun.

To the artist, they are a thin line of beauty drawn at the edge of a blue, blue sea.

To the resident, whose family has lived there for generations, they are, quite simply, home.

How do you describe these lonely, remote, wind and sea swept barriers to the ancient sea?

Let's begin with the land: with geology.

Geologists call the Banks a prime example of the land form called the 'barrier island.' They are made entirely of sand, without the keel of rock that anchors most islands firmly to the earth. It is a fascinatingly evanescent phenomenon in geological terms, a land form so transient that changes are visible from year to year. A phenomenon that is, even now, in the process of passing forever out of existence.

As most people know, the level of the ocean has changed steadily throughout geological history, as a result of water released or stored up in the great polar icecaps. When, during the ice ages, great amounts of water are withdrawn from circulation, the consequent lowering of the sea extends coastlines far out into what is now the ocean.

This is, as most authorities now agree, how the Banks were formed. They are surprisingly recent. As the last great ice age, some 20,000 years ago, drew to an end, the sea was four hundred feet lower than it is now. The area we now call North Carolina extended some thirty miles farther out, to the edge of the North American Continental Shelf. The polar icecaps, warmed by some still mysterious climatic change, then began to melt, and the sea rose.

The Banks must have begun as dunes, at the very edge of that ancient shore. Rivers from inland contributed silt to build them up. But as the sea rose, the dunes were submerged, becoming sand bars.

N · E · W
to the Outer Banks?

For valuable information and free gift package,
CALL

473-2042

We also have gift packages for
new parents and newlyweds.

Nancy McWilliams

Thousands of years passed. The waves kept rolling in, and the bars grew. They also moved, pushed westward and southward by the prevailing northeast winds and seas. The rising sea flooded the low land behind them, forming estuaries that we today call the sounds. The Banks grew, and broke to the surface once again.

A few thousand years later, the rise in the ocean slowed, though it continues today at the rate of about one foot per century. The Banks had a breathing space. Life began to take root as rain leached the salt from the sand. Beach grass and other vegetation helped to keep sand in place, further slowing the rate of migration.

Today the Outer Banks seem, to our short-lived eyes, a permanent land from. We see today a string of narrow, low islands, about twelve feet above sea level, from a few thousand feet to three miles across, punctuated by narrow inlets. But they're not permanent; they are alive, and they are moving even now. Two examples:

1. Oregon Inlet. Note, as you drive across the Herbert Bonner Bridge, the expanse of low, flat land under the northern piers. This land was not there when the bridge was built in 1964. It's new land, more than a mile of it. Bodie Island is extending itself southward. *All the islands are moving south.*

2. If you know anything about shells, examine closely those you find at the surf line at Nags Head or Coquina Beach or Hatteras. You will notice many old fresh and brackish water snail and oyster shells. You may also see large flat chunks of what looks like dried horse manure. This is peat, formed in freshwater bogs. How did these materials get to the sea side of the islands? Answer: they didn't move. They stayed right where they were and the islands have migrated over them. *All the islands are moving west.*

Of course, it's all happening very slowly. Don't cancel your reservations; it will be thousands of years before the Banks rejoin the North Carolina mainland. But it's fascinating to understand how dynamic, moving, living the Banks are.

Within these living islands, five major natural communities have evolved in response to different conditions. The *Ocean Beach* habitat is between the surf line and the dune line. There is little vegetation in this area, but clams, ghost crabs, and a few other small marine animals exist or venture above the surf line. Primarily the Ocean Beach habitat belongs to the birds: willits, sanderlings, plovers, terns, and gulls. All are present, especially during the summer months.

The *Barrier Dune* habitat is manmade, but is a distinctive community nonetheless. The 14-ft. barrier dunes along the Eastern shore were stabilized with plantings of sea oats, beach grass, cordgrass, panic grasses, and such shrubs as wax myrtle, bayberry, and baccharis. These plants are all salt-resistant and have deep, extensive root systems that hold the sand against the wind and sea. Mice, rabbits, small harmless snakes live here, as well as toads, racerunner lizards, and again, many birds.

Behind and partially protected by the dunes is the *Herb-Shrub* habitat. This extends clear across most of the center of the islands, except where submerged by moving dunes. Characteristic plants are wax myrtle, bayberry, yaupon, live oak, cordgrass, and blackberry. Rabbits and mice are more common than amid the dunes, and larger animals (raccoons, foxes, mink) are seen along with toads, frogs, and lizards and their predatory snakes. Land birds live here, including marsh hawks and short- eared owls.

The *Tidal Marsh* habitat is found on the sound side of most of the islands. Its cordgrass, rushes, and other salt or brackish water plants nourish a vast variety of life: waterfowl, muskrats and nutria, falcons and hawks, ducks. Much of Pea Island, a wildlife refuge famous for its birds, is marsh. Amid the sheltering roots of the marsh plants grow many of the shrimp, crabs, mollusks, and fishes that later leave the marshes and enrich the sea.

The last habitat on the Banks, the *Maritime Forest*, is found at its widest points, where shelter from salt-carrying wind is best. Thick forests of live oak, loblolly pine, dogwood, and red bay alternate with freshwater ponds. Gray squirrel, opossum, and white-tailed deer live here, or have lived within these forests in historic times.

The Banks were like this -- wild -- when human beings arrived, and history, properly speaking, began.

The early movements of the Indians are shadowy; little of their lore crossed the gulf that separated their culture from that of the invading whites. Apparently North Carolina was settled between 500 and 1000 A.D. by Indians of Algonkian stock. By the late 1500's these had diversified into various tribes, speaking dialects of the original tongue. The Poteskeets were found around Currituck Sound; the Roanoaks, on Roanoke Island and the nearby mainland; the Croatoans, on what is now Hatteras. They ranged widely along the Banks, living on fish, shellfish, wildfowl, and deer; and cultivating maize, beans, cucurbits (a gourd like plant), and sunflowers.

The first European eye to rest on the Banks may have been Italian, for Giovanni Verrazzano sailed and mapped these coasts in 1524; or may have been Spanish, for Lucas Vasquez de Ayllon and others had learned to use Cape Hatteras as a shortcut from the West Indies back to Spain. But the Spanish, then masters of the riches of the Inca and Aztec, had little interest in goldless forests and sand. They decided not to follow up their explorations and claims with colonies. It was left to the English, relative late-comers to exploration, to step in; and beginning in 1584, they did.

It was on Roanoke Island, where Fort Raleigh National Historic Site is now, that the first English colony in America was planted. It failed; the colony was lost (its complete story is told in the section, 'This is Roanoke Island'). But the English kept trying, and a few years later John Smith succeeded (at Jamestown Island) where John White had failed.

In many ways, residents of the Banks still look north to Virginia as their homes, almost as much as to Raleigh. This may reflect their ancestry, for the Banks were permanently settled by second-generation English who trickled down from Jamestown, Williamsburg, and Norfolk, leavened by fugitives from the King's justice and shipwrecked mariners. These early settlers were the direct ancestors of today's numerous Midgetts, Baums, Grays, Etheridges, Burruses, Tillets, Manns, Twifords, and other old and famous families of the Banks. They settled at the islands' widest points, where forests offered shelter: Kitty Hawk, parts of Hatteras, and Ocracoke, as well as Roanoke and Colington Islands. It was not an easy life they led, as the section 'This is Kitty Hawk' makes clear; but it was a free one, and doubtless healthier than the cramped and plague-haunted cities of Olde England.

There was one part of the Banks that did flourish in those early days, though, and that was Ocracoke. The inlet, deeper then, was an important place of entry for oceangoing vessels. But Ocracoke was also attractive to another sort of seagoing entrepreneur: the pirate. 'This is Ocracoke' tells the story of the career and fall of old Occacock's most notorious citizen, Captain Edward 'Blackbeard' Teach.

The Bankers, independent in spirit then as they are now, sided firmly with the patriot side during the Revolution. Ocracoke was an important port of entry for French war supplies, and the inhabitants had several lively skirmishes with British would-be invaders. But the inlet silted up later, after Oregon Inlet opened in 1846, and in any case the large new steamers drew deeper water than the sounds and inlets of eastern North Carolina could provide. Ocracoke, and its sister village, Portsmouth, began to decline.

The War between the States brought several sharp battles early in the war. At Hatteras Inlet (August, 1861), Chicamacomico (October, 1861), and Roanoke Island (February, 1862), the Federals won their first victories of the war and established a control over the Banks that lasted throughout the conflict. The inhabitants, few of whom owned slaves, were not strongly attached to the Southern cause, and many took the oath of allegiance to the United States.

As if to reward them, the postwar years saw a steady flow of Federal dollars to the Banks, and they were spared Reconstruction. Navigational improvements had become unavoidable, and three fine new lighthouses (Corolla, Bodie Island, and Hatteras) were built 1870-1875. These provided employment to locals as lighthouse keepers and assistants, and a flow of something new to these bare islands -- cash. Seven stations of the U.S. Lifesaving Service were also built along the coast from the Virginia border to Cape Point, Hatteras. (See "U.S. Lifesaving Service.")

Changes were taking place in the Banks' internal economy, as well. Nags Head was becoming the area's first and finest summer resort (see 'This is Nags Head'). Commercial fishing and wildfowl hunting replaced wrecking and whale oil as sources of income.

The twentieth century, destined finally to end the fabled isolation of these low, remote islands, began with a symbolic event: the arrival of the brothers Wright. The history of their failures and their final success, told in 'This is Kill Devil Hills,' is probably the best-known story of the Outer Banks, though the Lost Colony must run a close second.

The boom years began in 1930-31. The rest of the country was in a depression, true, but these years marked the completion of the first road accesses to the 'beach,' the Wright Memorial Bridge across Currituck Sound to Kitty Hawk and the Washington Baum Bridge from Roanoke Island to Nags Head. Paved roads down the islands followed, and development began.

Another milestone was passed in the late 30's, when the Federal Government decided to 'save' the Banks. Six Civilian Conservation Corps camps were established and millions of dollars were spent erecting sand fences and planting sand-binding vegetation along 115 miles of shoreline. The Cape Hatteras National Seashore was officially established in 1953, and now controls most of the land from Whalebone Junction down to Ocracoke Inlet, with exemptions for the villages of Rodanthe, Waves, Salvo, Avon, Buxton, Frisco, and Hatteras and Ocracoke Villages. The National Park Service also administers the other two most popular visitor attractions, the Wright Brothers National Memorial and Fort Raleigh.

The Second World War saw the Banks' isolation end -- with explosions. In 1942 Hatteras abruptly became the war's front line as Hitler's U-boats struck at American merchant shipping. Scores of vessels went down, many in sight of the Beach's horrified residents; but the tide turned here, eventually, and the first U-boat sunk by Americans lies a few miles off the beach of Bodie Island.

The postwar period saw two concurrent booms; short-term visitors, attracted by the National Park Service facilities and the sea, and longer- term summer residents. The now-ubiquitous beach cottage, built on piers or posts in case of hurricane flooding, appeared first at Nags Head and has spread steadily north. Until recently, the permanent (winter) population of the area had not changed much since 1900. That population has grown significantly, however, in the past few years. These permanent residents, many of whom own, run, or work in seasonal retail establishments, now derive most of their income from services to visitors, though commercial fishing is still important in Hatteras and Wanchese.

These independent, clannish Bankers deeply love their home islands. It is for the visitor, though, that the Outer Banks seem to have been designed.

For camping, fishing, swimming, hang gliding, surfing; for tennis and golf; for beachcombing, bird watching, and just lying on a fine sand beach in the sun. For vacationing, honeymooning, winding down, taking it easy, dropping out, goofing off. For learning a little American history firsthand. For getting to know the sea and wind again. That's what the Banks are really for.

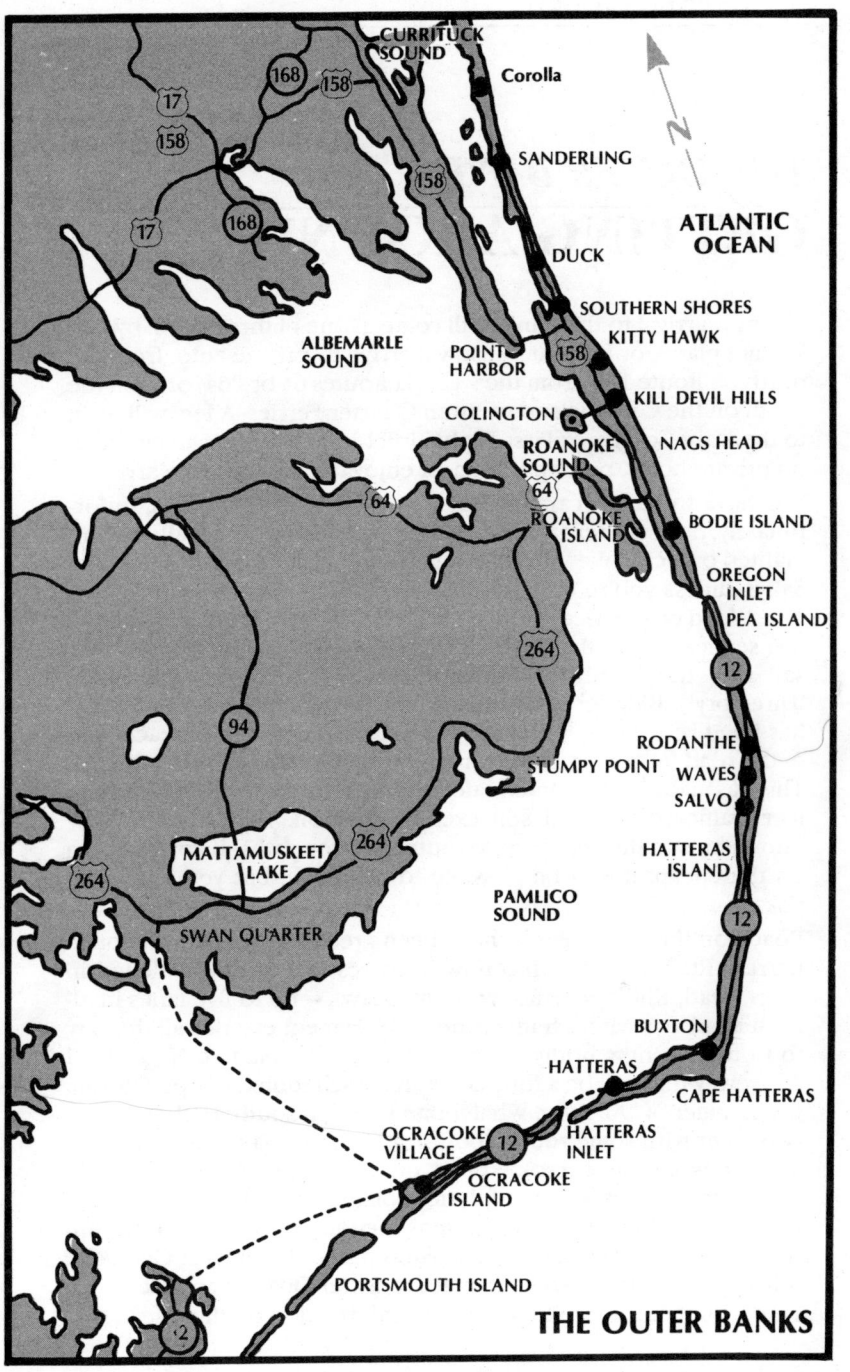

THE OUTER BANKS
GETTING AROUND

The new arrival to the Banks will come in one of three ways: by car, by light plane, or by boat. Most will arrive by private auto, from the north via Route 158, from the west via Routes 64 or 264, or from the south on the Cedar Island or Swan Quarter Ferries. A few will fly in to the Dare County or First Flight airfields. And a few will cruise in on private boats, perhaps the most enjoyable way of all to arrive.

You have to have a car to really enjoy the Banks. There is, unfortunately, no real alternative to the automobile. You can walk around Manteo or Ocracoke Village, but you can't walk from Kitty Hawk to Salvo, unless you're tougher than the authors. There is no regular interisland bus service, though charter busses are available, and the taxi service out of Manteo is reliable (see 'Directory'). If you fly or sail into the Northern Banks you can rent a car (again, see 'Directory'). Bicycle? Over the last few years, while the 158 Bypass has been resurfaced, an extra width has been added on each side of the road from Nags Head through Kitty Hawk to allow for bikers. This has made cycling much safer on the Banks but with all the summer traffic you should still exercise caution. Look for the new "Mountains to the Sea" bicycle route signs for paths. If you're going on the cheap, it may be possible to hitchhike, but you know the risks.

Roads on the Outer Banks have been greatly improved. The once narrow Rt. 158 Bypass has now been resurfaced and widened in Nags Head, Kill Devil Hills, and Kitty Hawk -- up to five lanes in almost all places where traffic is heavy. Pavement extends all the way to Corolla. A new bridge is being built on the Manteo-Nags Head Causeway that will be a four-laner and is scheduled to open during the summer of '90. From Whalebone Junction south, Highway 12, a two-laner with some rough spots, leads all the way to Hatteras Village. Oregon Inlet is crossed by a modern concrete bridge which, incidentally, gives a beautiful view of the inlet. Hatteras Inlet is crossed by a free ferry; see Hatteras section for schedule. Continuing south, Highway 12 on Ocracoke is paved but ends at Ocracoke Village, where toll ferries connect to Swan Quarter and Cedar Island, N.C. See Ocracoke section for information on these ferries.

A note of caution: in storms, the beachfront Highway 12 may be flooded or cut by overwash as heavy seas break through the barrier dunes. Ferry service is stopped during storms and even the bridges can't be called totally safe. Please read the section on 'storms' in the Directory.

One change that seasoned Outer Banks vacationers will note is that in 1988 the state designated "Highway 12" as the name for the entire beach road from Ocracoke through to Sanderling. Though this is the *official* name, in this edition, we will still give locations per the "158 Bypass" or "158 Business" names for clarity. The signs now say "12."

You should also be aware that a gasoline price differential exists between mainland North Carolina and Virginia, and the Banks. We've seen gas on Hatteras as much as thirty cents a gallon higher. So tank up before you come. There -- if you're driving a motor home, we've just saved you the price of this book.

Finally, 1989 saw the inauguration of Outer Banks Airways, a daily local service to Norfolk International from First Flight and Dare County airfields. See entries for these fields for details.

The head keeper's house stands close to the Currituck Beach Light.
© '88 D. Westner

INSIDE
THE NORTHERN BANKS

It used to be that visitors to the Banks thought of Kitty Hawk as the "beginning" of the beach area. This was, after all, where the rental cottages began. Until quite recently it was impossible even to enter large portions of the Northern Banks. First, there was no paved road north of Southern Shores, and second, there were gates and guards blocking access. Unless you were lucky enough to have friends who owned some of the exclusive, private property above Southern Shores, or had a four-wheel-drive that could traverse the beach, you were out of luck.

Well, the last few years have seen dramatic changes in the northern beaches. And, though the age-old struggle of development versus nondevelopment has certainly been played out here as elsewhere, for the most part developers and regulatory agencies have attempted to guide and limit growth north of the Wright Bridge in a way that preserves the natural surroundings that made the Banks beautiful in the first place.

The history of the Currituck County section of the Outer Banks is a repetition of two themes: hunting and government.

Let's begin with the ducks.

One of the least known, least documented (except for the Currituck County Historical Society's excellent efforts) parts of the Banks' long history is the story of rich men, waterfowl, and hunting clubs.

After Currituck and Caffey Inlets closed late in the nineteenth century, the sound, till then salty like those further south, suddenly changed. Marine plants and animals were replaced by those that thrived best in brackish (slightly saline) waters and marshes. The marshes began to attract thousands of ducks, geese, and swans. As the century drew to its close, a few northern businessmen discovered the new sport and began shooting there on a regular basis. The trip down then, though, was far rougher than it is today -- most of them came by boat -- and once they were here, they found it hard to live the way the local North Carolinians did.

The solution? Hunting clubs -- enormous, semipalatial clubhouses, fitted with fireplaces, carpets, Tiffany chandeliers, oil paintings. In the years between 1869 and 1922, several great clubs were built on the Northern Banks, forming perhaps the closest analog to the "Great Houses" of Britain that America offers. Monkey Island was the first. Narrows Island, Whalehead, and Swan Island quickly followed. All were remote, luxurious, rambling houses with great screened porches and plenty of bedrooms and fireplaces. And some are still there, back on the islands that dot the bay, or sited grandly at the edge of the marshes, handy to the duckblinds and boat sheds.

Of them all, the grandest, in some ways the most typical, was Whalehead.

The Whalehead Club began in 1874, when the "Lighthouse Club" (its original name) was formed by a group of wealthy men from New York. They hunted and fished there quietly enough for some fifty years, employing local Bankers as superintendents and guides. In 1922 Edward Knight, a Philadelphia man with interests in sugar, oil, and publishing, bought the property.

Norris Austin, the Corolla postmaster, whose family has lived here since 1891, told us the story of how Knight tried to get his wife, also an avid shootist, admitted into the hitherto males-only club. The other members wouldn't have her. So (much later) he bought the place, renamed it Whalehead, then tore it down. He had in mind a far grander house, in fact a "castle," on what he called "Corolla Island."

Knight's summer home (he had another in Newport, R.I.) was completed in 1925, at a cost of around $383,000. For that kind of money in those days you got a three-story mansion of thirty-six rooms, ten full and two half baths. You got the only basement, elevator, and wine cellar on the Outer Banks. You got a coppered roof, screened verandahs, custom dredging, and arched wooden bridges to your own little island. It was a setting worthy of a Fitzgerald novel.

Knight died eleven years later, and the immense sound front house passed from owner to owner. In 1940 Ray T. Adams, a meat broker from Washington, DC bought the building, all the furnishings, and the 2,000 acres around it for the grand sum of $25,000. During World War II it was leased to the Coast Guard and used as a barracks. After that it was a hunting lodge again, for a time, then a boy's school (Corolla Academy, still active in England), then headquarters for Atlantic Research Corporation, a rocket testing company.

Whalehead's last private owner, (Mr. Adams) died in 1958, and the "Castle" fell on hard times. Too grand for any local resident, too ostentatious for any modern Croesus before Donald Trump, the house

NORTHERN BANKS

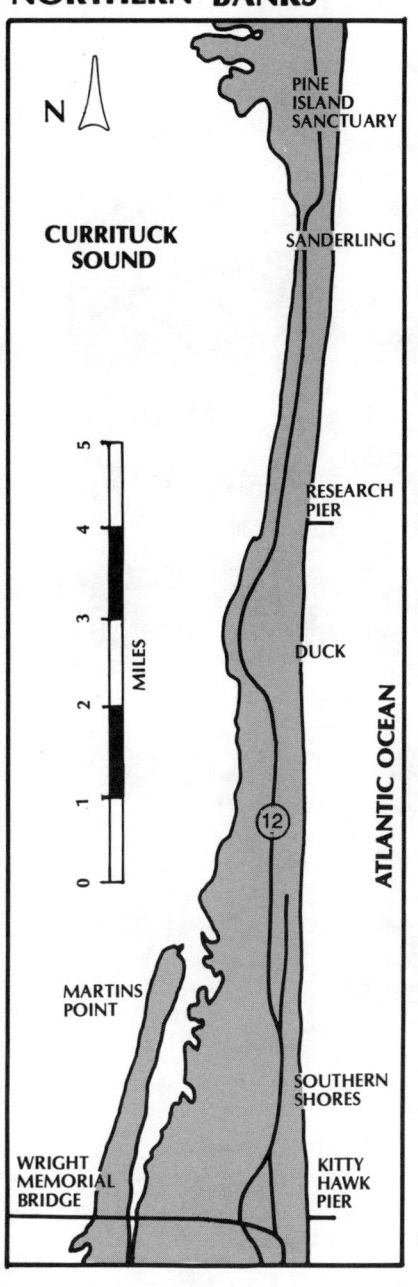

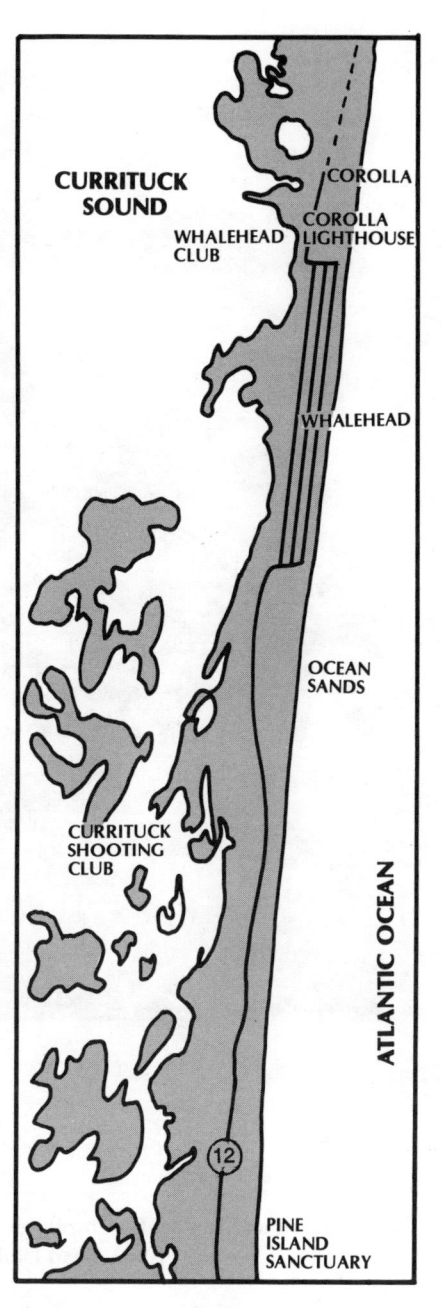

Head stallion of the Corolla ponies, Star, looks regal beside the Whalehead Club. © '88 D. Westner.

WILD HORSE SANCTUARY

CURRITUCK COUNTY HAS ESTABLISHED THIS SANCTUARY TO PROHIBIT THE KILLING, TRAPPING, INJURING, TORMENTING OR TAKING OF WILD HORSES. IF THERE IS AN ACCIDENT, INJURING A HORSE(S) IT IS A VIOLATION NOT TO REPORT IT IMMEDIATELY. THEY SHOULD NOT NEEDLESSLY SUFFER. PLEASE REPORT ANY VIOLATION OF SAME TO THE SHERIFF'S DEPARTMENT OR THE ANIMAL CONTROL OFFICER.

THE WILD HORSES ARE DESCENDENTS OF THE SPANISH MUSTANG AND HAVE BEEN A PART OF THE CURRITUCK ENVIRONMENT BEFORE EARLY SETTLEMENT OF THE BARRIER REEF. IN 1523 THE SPANISH EXPEDITIONS BROUGHT THEM HERE. WHEN COLONIZATION WAS UNSUCCESSFUL, THE HORSES WERE LEFT BEHIND. IN 1584-1589 THE ENGLISH GOT THEM FROM THE SPANISH, AT PUERTO RICO, SANTA DOMINGO, PUERTO DE PLATA AND BROUGHT THEM HERE WITH OTHER LIVESTOCK FOR SIR WALTER RALEIGH'S COLONIZATION ON ROANOKE. THE CHEROKEES, CHICKASAWS, & CHOCTAWS TOOK MANY OF THE HORSES ON THEIR FORCED MIGRATION WEST, CALLED "TRAIL-OF-TEARS". MANY TODAY SAY THE INDIANS SAFE ARRIVAL AND CONTINUED SURVIVAL WAS ENTIRELY DUE TO THESE HORSES. LATER ISLANDERS USED THEM FOR TRANSPORTATION, TO ROUND UP LIVESTOCK, TO PULL FISHING NETS, AND THE U.S. LIFESAVING SERVICE USED THEM FOR BEACH PATROLS. DURING THE DEPRESSION MANY WERE SOLD.

THE EXACT NUMBER IS NOT KNOWN FOR THE CURRITUCK BEACH AREA, BUT THERE ARE 10 LEFT IN THE COROLLA AREA AT THIS TIME, AFTER THE TRAGIC DEATH OF 6 TO CAR ACCIDENTS AT NIGHT. THE LEAD STALLION AND HIS SONS WILL FIGHT FOR MARES. ONCE THE STALLION'S SONS ARE OF AGE TO MATE, HE WILL SHUN HIS MALE OFFSPRING FROM THE MAIN HERD. THE BATTLE FOR EACH STALLION TO CREATE HIS OWN HERD IS ON GOING, SO THE NUMBER WITHIN EACH HERD CONSTANTLY CHANGES. PLUS, MARES FOAL IN SPRING & FALL, SO THERE ARE ALWAYS NEWBORNS. THEY ARE THE ONLY KNOWN TRUE SPANISH MUSTANG HERD IN THE WORLD STILL LIVING IN THE WILD.

HANDLING HORSES PUNISHABLE BY LAW!

PLEASE BE AWARE THAT THESE ARE WILD HORSES. APPROACH THEM, IF AT ALL, WITH CAUTION. DO NOT ATTEMPT TO RIDE, HANDLE OR FEED THEM. THEIR NATURE IS UNPREDICTABLE: THE STALLION WILL PROTECT HIS HERD AS WILL THE MARES PROTECT THEIR YOUNG. ADMIRE THEM FROM A DISTANCE. DO NOT CHASE OR RUN FROM THEM. SPECIAL EFFORTS ON YOUR PART ARE APPRECIATED, AS MOST EVERYONE WOULD LIKE TO SEE THEM ROAM FREE AS THEY ALWAYS HAVE. WATCH WHEN YOU DRIVE, ESPECIALLY AT NIGHT! THEY ROAM THE WHOLE AREA AND YOU WILL OFTEN FIND THEM CROSSING THE ROADS DAY AND NIGHT. THEY TEND NOT TO GO SOUTH OF OCEAN SANDS, AND THEY STAY MOSTLY IN THE COROLLA VILLAGE AREA. EFFORTS ARE BEING MADE TO KEEP THEM NORTH OF THE HARDSURFACE

A NON PROFIT FUND HAS BEEN ESTABLISHED FOR THEIR PRESERVATION. ANY DONATIONS OR QUESTIONS CAN BE DIRECTED TO: "COROLLA WILD HORSE FUND", PO BOX 361, COROLLA, NC 27927 T-SHIRTS ARE AVAILABLE BY WRITING TO THE ABOVE ADDRESS OR STOPPING IN AT TWIDDY & CO., IN COROLLA. JUST MAIL $10 PER SHIRT + $2 FOR SHIPPING PER SHIRT. COLORS: TURQUOISE/PINK/YELLOW, SIZES: YOUTH L, MED., L., XL, (SOME XXL ADD $1).

stood deserted for nearly two decades. Its plaster deteriorated, paint flaked off the fine juniper exterior, windows stared dimly out over the lawns that slope down to the marshy sound. Abandoned refrigerators leaned on the verandahs like ancient guests. It was a white elephant, an Ozymandaic monument to days when the northern Banks were remote, unknown, a land of sky-thronging clouds of ducks, slow-spoken Bankers, and well-dressed millionaires 'roughing it.'

In 1988 that long sleep ended. Whalehead is now being restored, developed as the centerpiece of a controlled-access residential community. See Attractions, a few pages on, for details.

The second "theme" in the history of the northern Banks has been the U.S. Government; specifically, the Coast Guard (formerly the U.S. Lifesaving Service). The two lifesaving stations at Corolla and the three farther south in Currituck County provided employment for the local inhabitants and contact with the larger world outside. The Corolla Lighthouse is still a U.S. facility, beaming its light far out to sea, though most of today's larger ships stay well clear of the shoaling water off the beach. Remnants of these days on the Northern Banks are the Kitty Hawk Station, now moved to Corolla, and the Sanderling Restaurant, formerly Caffeys Inlet Lifesaving Station.

Today Corolla, and all the northern Banks, are undergoing rapid change. Subdivision and development are replacing the old patterns of fishing and soundside dwelling, and displacing or overshadowing the people whose ancestors lived simply here for centuries. But their ancestors displaced the Indians, who had displaced previous tribes too, no doubt. This is what we call "progress."

Today's residents are still isolated, but not for the same reasons. The pattern of development north of the Dare County line seems to be avoiding the obvious commercialism that prevails farther south, but in the process it is becoming exclusive. Many residential developments are guarded and access is controlled. The roadless expanse of Back Bay National Wildlife Refuge to the north also limits access. Only residents are granted permits for transit (Virginia Beach is only 11 miles away), and these too are limited; there's a midnight curfew, and only two round trips a day are permitted through the refuge.

Now let's shift focus from history to the Northern Banks today. To discover these new, rapidly growing towns -- Southern Shores, Duck, Sanderling, and Corolla -- first find Route 12, Duck Road. This winding, scenic two-laner curves left (north) at the stoplight in front of the Aycock Brown Welcome Center, located on the northern edge of Kitty Hawk.

Southern Shores, one of the oldest planned developments on the Banks, is the first area you'll be driving through. There are plenty of summer residential properties here, though there are also substantial year round homes nestled nearby in the sound side woods.

In the last several years, residential neighborhoods with names like Tuckahoe, Nantucket, Chicahauk, and Georgetown Sands have been developed and dot the road from Southern Shores north to Duck. These are primarily cottage-type homes, though more and more are being occupied year 'round.

You're in for some beautiful scenery as you drive along this seaside route. The road winds along for miles, rising briefly for a look at flat, brackish Currituck Sound, then diving to shelter itself between dunes covered with low, scrub woods. An occasional private road leads off to the right, to expensive oceanfront cottages. Despite the growth, the feeling to this area still is much less cluttered than elsewhere on the Banks, testifying to the success of the strict building codes established by the original developer and maintained by the city council. It's worth your time for an afternoon drive to just meander through, continuing on till you find yourself in Duck.

When we first wrote about it Duck was still strongly reminiscent of the villages of Hatteras. It was isolated, and its two or three hundred residents were all of old families, dependent on fishing or waterfowling for their livelihoods.

All that has changed with the explosive growth of the 1980s. Today's visitor will find most of the old-line residents making their living either owning or working in the dozens of new retail shops, real estate agencies, residential developments, sailing centers, and other service-oriented operations formed in recent years. The shopping development especially has been astounding in the late 1980s. If you last came in, say, 1977, you'll find Duck Blind Limited still there, but there's precious little else that hasn't changed. There's Scarborough Faire, a big 28-shop location; Osprey Landing; Loblolly Pines; Duck Waterfront Shops; Wee Winks Square and more. Once it was hard to buy anything but staples up here, but that time is long past.

Still, as you continue north, there are some things time hasn't changed. The sea is quite close to Duck and is worth a right turn almost anywhere near the village. Park and walk over the dunes. Sea oats, wild beans and peas, and a variety of shore birds throng the seaside: loons, cormorants, gannet, the same birds one sees at Pea Island farther south; and of course, terns and gulls, shrieking flocks of them. Climb to the top of a dune and look far out to see. See a stirring in the water, as if silver-blue wheels were rolling just beneath the surface? They're bottlenosed porpoises, *Tursiops truncatus*, common in these fish-rich waters.

Leaving Duck and heading north, you'll see that the explosive residential growth continues with such developments as Barrier Island Station, Sea Ridge, Osprey, Ships Watch, Northpoint, Colony by the Sea, Port Trinitie, Gull's Flight, and others. There's a nice view out over the sound to your left. You'll pass a sign for the U.S. Army Coastal Engineering Research Facility, an 1800-foot-long-reinforced-concrete coastal engineering research pier used by the Corps of Engineers to investigate the forces that create and destroy beaches. Research carried out here is proving essential to intelligent reaction to beach movement and silting at Oregon Inlet and elsewhere. Sorry, the Army doesn't encourage casual visitors.

Moving north still, you'll see lining the oceanfront and sound some of the most beautiful houses on the Banks, built under the tight Sanderling codes. This development set a high standard for the others by creating landscaped areas filled with flowers and greenery indigenous to the Banks. In 1985 the Sanderling Inn and Restaurant opened. Though both are profiled later, they deserve special mention for their architectural and historic significance. The Inn has the Southern charm that characterized the old Nags Head resorts at the turn of the century. It's large and airy, with wide porches that provide room for conversation or drinks. Note the cedar shake siding, natural wood interiors, and English country antiques.

The Restaurant is housed in a Historic Landmark, Caffeys Inlet Station. Designated U.S. Lifesaving Station Number Five, it was built on its present site in 1899, when, along with two at Corolla, one at Ocean Sands, and others dotting the shore every seven miles, it served as a home to the men who patrolled the beaches searching for sign of shipwreck. (Read "A Life on the Northern Banks" for a taste of what it was like. Have you walked the beach in a February storm? These men had something more than courage.) Though abandoned and deteriorating for a number of years, the Station was given a new lease on life with a thorough renovation, first as the Sanderling office, then, in 1985, as the restaurant.

A few hundred yards on a sign will inform you you've left Dare County and are now in Currituck. You're also now in the Pine Island Sanctuary. Until October of 1984, this area was closed to all but property owners, unless you had a four-wheel-drive that could take the beach, or unless you could scam your way past two armed guards paid to be suspicious. (We had to.)

Though the traffic on Route 12 is now vastly greater, the sanctuary will give you a good idea of the way life was on these shores many years ago. The Currituck Lighthouse blinks its warning each night; wildlife roam the undeveloped dunes; and mile after mile of empty beach leads us toward the community of Corolla.

When we first made it to Corolla in 1977, sweating our way over unpaved roads, it had 200 inhabitants and one grocery. Some thirteen miles north of the Wright Bridge, modern-day life began arriving in the mid-eighties in the form of planned communities. Corolla may be incorporated as a town one day, according to Norris Austin, the postmaster (he's getting busier, but he still likes a chat). It's nowhere near as crowded as Kitty Hawk or even Ocracoke, but it's no longer isolated. Tourist traffic is getting heavy; a shopping development has been built.

Modern-day development first came to the area in the form of Corolla Light, a 215-acre sea-to-sound community. Now other developments are selling and building: Whalehead Club, Monteray Shores, Spindrift, and others. Land values in Corolla are still rising rapidly. A semi-oceanfront lot 100 x 200' which sold (closing prices) in 1984 for $30,000 went for $65,000 in 1986, $90,000 in 1987, and is being offered now at around $160,000. And no one expects it to stop there or even slow.

It's a new way of life for an area that for so long stood untouched. Like many long time residents, we greet it, but with feelings of regret for what Corolla once was. (And what was it? Pick up a copy of *Whalehead: Tales of Corolla*, by Norris Austin and Suzanne Tate, a little book of reminiscences you'll enjoy. No, we didn't publish it, but that doesn't mean we won't recommend it.)

Route 12 ends about half a mile north of the lighthouse, though privately maintained pavement lets you go about a mile farther. But there are growing non-road-accessible communities between Corolla and the Virginia border. Reachable only by four- wheel-drive along the beach, they're the subject of intense speculation as rumors fly about possible road extensions and/or a cross-Sound bridge.

SOUTHERN SHORES, DUCK, SANDERLING, AND COROLLA
ATTRACTIONS

PINE ISLAND SANCTUARY
North of Sanderling

Just north of Sanderling as you pass the sign that tells you you're entering Currituck County, you come upon an area that is nothing but open beach to sound land as far as the eye can see. This is, for the most part, Pine Island Sanctuary. The property, which was donated to the Audubon Society by a local man with a deep respect for the coastal environment and the wildlife that lives there, is home to ducks, gulls, sanderlings and other sea birds, racoon, deer, rabbit, and many other animals. Audubon members can arrange with their local chapters to tour the Sanctuary. But for non-Audubon members, the rule is to stay off the property, for the protection of the dunes and the wildlife. Even driving through the Sanctuary, though, on NC 12, is a pleasurable, relaxing experience and one we highly recommend.

OLD KILL DEVIL HILLS LIFESAVING STATION
Corolla   453-2135

The Old Kill Devil Hills Lifesaving Station was built in 1878, one of eleven built along the Banks to rescue passengers and crew from storm-wrecked shipping. Yes, this is the station near which the Wright Brothers used to fly. Their helpers came from here the morning of a windy December 17, 1903. (See "This is Kill Devil Hills.") It was moved to Corolla in 1986 and restored with private funds. Now the office of Twiddy and Co. Realtors, it's nonetheless open for the public to view Doug Twiddy's personal collection of Wright Brothers and Lifesaving Service memorabilia. This includes a Lyle gun, oars, vintage photos, medals, magazines, logs, a piece of the original 1903 airplane, coins and other artifacts. Locate this small white high-peaked building a quarter-mile north of the Currituck Beach Light, on the left (west) of Highway 12.

WHALEHEAD CLUB
Corolla

The old Knight mansion just south of the Currituck Beach Light, described in "This is the Northern Banks," has been restored as the centerpiece of Whalehead Club, a controlled-access residential development. A new gatehouse has been built. The old pool has been demolished and the grounds cleared of rubbish and overgrowth. In their place now is a beautiful new pool with cascading waterfall and a hot tub overlooking the basin, surrounded by tasteful landscaping. The old boathouse has been given a facelift and will soon be a private club for Whalehead Club property owners. The bridge will be restored and the boat basin has been dredged and slips built for homeowners' boats.

Plans call for fifty-eight exclusive homesites. We can think of few prettier places to call home. A model is open daily at the Whalehead Club with staff on hand to explain how to get a piece of this good life.

CURRITUCK BEACH (COROLLA) LIGHTHOUSE AND KEEPER'S HOUSE
Corolla Village

The northernmost of the four lighthouses of the Banks, Currituck Beach Light was put in commission at what was then called Whales Head in 1875. Still active, still U.S. Government property, this 150-foot, 50,000-candlepower red brick tower dominates the Corolla area. But its surroundings of dunes and scrub brush diminish it, unlike the Bodie Island and Hatteras lighthouses, which seem to stand out on the open spaces of the Southern Banks.

The Keeper's house, located in the shadow of the lighthouse, has in the last several years been rescued from certain death by a local historical architect, John Wilson IV. He and other concerned friends worked to get the house designated a Historic Landmark, then went to work restoring it. So far the exterior and porches have been restored and work is proceeding on the interior. The lighthouse is easily accessible from Highway 12. Just when you think you've passed it you'll see a discreet sign at the left pointing down a sandy trail among yaupon and pine. You can park opposite the entrance, pulling off on the berm of Highway 12. Though visitors are rarely allowed inside the building, a tour of the grounds should be on your list. This quiet, dignified architecture, the curving, red-brick walks are the way we'd all like to live. The house is a beauty and a lesson in the value of preserving our historic past. Grounds are open 10 - 6 daily.

WASH WOODS COAST GUARD STATION
North Swan Beach, Corova   453-4000

The Wash Woods Coast Guard Station was built in 1917, just four miles south of the original 1878 lifesaving station. It was named for the hundreds of old stumps that are constantly exposed at low tide on the northern Currituck Beach. Like other stations, Wash Woods was built to aid seagoing vessels in distress and to warn against the dangerous shoals just off the coast.

The station was purchased by Twiddy & Company Realtors in 1989 and went through the first stage of restoration this past winter. Today it is an active real estate office and a museum for United States Coast Guard and lifesaving memorabilia. Among the collections of artifacts you will find a USCG Lyle gun and photographs of the station dating from 1919 to the present. Found under the building during restoration, and also on display, is a surfman's hat with a brass pin bearing the original United States Lifesaving emblem of life ring and oars.

The Wash Woods Coast Guard Station is open seven days a week and is located seven miles north of the last paved road in Ocean Hill, accessible only by four-wheel drive vehicle, or by foot, if you're a hardy walker.

SOUTHERN SHORES, DUCK, SANDERLING, AND COROLLA
RECREATION

COROLLA LIGHT SAILING CLUB
1/2 mile south of Currituck Beach Lighthouse   453-8016

This new fun facility is a spinoff of the Corolla Light community. Parking is to the soundside of Route 12 for catamaran, windsurfer, daysailer, canoe, and kayak rental on the Sound. An eighteen-hole lighted miniature golf course is PGA- approved and harder than putt-putt golf. There is also a small retail shop and snack bar. The pool and hot tub are for Corolla Light residents only; everything else is open to public. Free crabbing and fishing from pier. Open from Memorial Day to Labor Day, Hours 9 a.m. to 8:30 p.m.

BARRIER ISLAND SAILING CENTER
North of Duck   261-6262
                   261-7100

Bill Miles, a sailing and windsurfing enthusiast, operates this sailing center, located at the end of the long pier behind Barrier Island Inn. Here you can rent sailboards, fun boards, catamarans, day sailers and smaller monohulls, as well as Yamaha Waverunners at hourly or half day rates. Bill and his staff of experienced instructors also offer windsurfing and sailing lessons. One of his instructors was even Women's Division winner of the Hatteras Wave Classic. One of the attractions about this spot, apart from its well maintained equipment, is the breezy gazebo at the end of the pier where you not only rent your equipment but also can spend a lazy hour watching sailors, swinging in the hammock, or meeting up with other well-tanned bodies. The Inn is nearby for respites of cold beer and snacks. Open 9 a.m. to 6 p.m. daily.

WATERWORKS, TOO SAILING
Duck   261-7245

There's no lack of places to sail in these parts! This spot offers lessons in both windsurfing and sailing. You can also rent windsurfing boards and sailboats if you're already a pro. Or, if you prefer to ride something that doesn't depend on the wind to move it, you can also rent jet skis or Wave Runners. Waterworks, Too is open from late spring until early fall from 9:00 a.m. till 6:00 p.m. They offer a 10% discount before 10 a.m. on all rentals.

KITTY HAWK SPORTS
Duck   261-8770

A branch of the Nags Head store, KHS/Duck sells windsurfing supplies and boogie boards. Reservations can be made here for windsurfing and sailing at their Nags Head location. Open from March 1 through January 1.

NORBANKS SAILING CENTER
Just south of Britt Real Estate   261-2900

This is the oldest sailing school in the north beach area and still offers instruction in both sailing and windsurfing. They rent equipment by hourly or expanded rates. They're open 9 a.m. until dusk.

SOUTHERN SHORES, DUCK, SANDERLING, AND COROLLA
SHOPPING

Most shops on the northern beaches are not open year 'round, and those that are will probably have shorter hours. We've listed phone numbers: If you're visiting off-season, before you head out for an afternoon of browsing, you might call ahead to see what's open.

COROLLA

Along with residential development in Corolla, shopping needs haven't been overlooked. **The Corolla Light Shops** are beginning to fill up. The **Silk Gardenia**, 453-8863, offering fresh flowers, as well as silk, is open all year. Ed and Ruby Cox, owners of The Silk Gardenia, had a loyal following down the beach at Nags Head Florist, which they sold in 1986. Other shops offer basic vacation needs: rentals, videos, beach supplies and the like.

Wink's, 453-8166, has been in Corolla for seven years, before the road from Duck was opened to the public and, for now, is the only place to buy groceries and other necessities. This is the newest of four Wink's stores on the Outer Banks. The first was built in 1953 on the Beach Road in Kitty Hawk by Miles "Wink" Davis. In the early 70s he built Wee Winks in Duck; a few years later, he opened Three Winks near the Wright Memorial Bridge in Kitty Hawk. The first three Winks stores are now each owned and managed by a Davis son. They jointly own the Corolla business.

Plans are in the works for a retail center at Monterey Shores to be opened in 1991. Food Lion, the region's grocery giant, is expected to be the anchor store.

DUCK

The proliferation of shops in Duck has been mind-boggling. "Stuck in Duck" is an outdated notion: if you run out of other activities, you can always go shopping.

 Duck Blind Art Gallery, 261-2009, offers quality, contemporary fine arts and crafts and hosts several shows for individual artists throughout the season, as well.

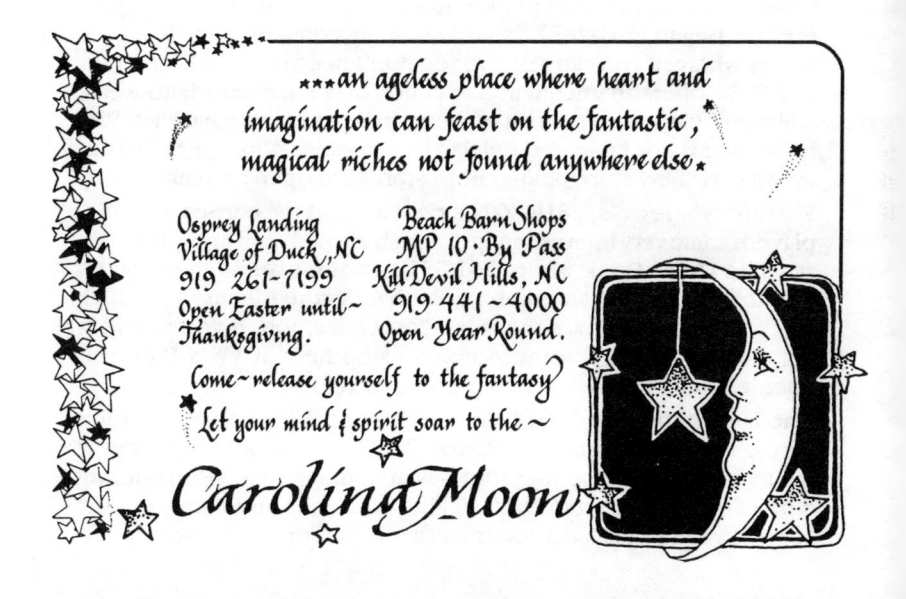

***an ageless place where heart and imagination can feast on the fantastic, magical riches not found anywhere else*

Osprey Landing
Village of Duck, NC
919 261-7199
Open Easter until ~ Thanksgiving.

Beach Barn Shops
MP 10 · By Pass
Kill Devil Hills, NC
919 441-4000
Open Year Round.

Come ~ release yourself to the fantasy
Let your mind & spirit soar to the ~

Carolina Moon

Duck's first shopping center, **Scarborough Faire**, continues to be one of the most inviting spots to shop on the entire Outer Banks. Nestled in the trees, with plenty of benches and gazebos for relaxing, it's a very attractive place. More than a dozen shops offer everything from art to egg beaters, flags to freshly ground coffee. **Bizarre Duck,** 261-8116, is not nearly as bizarre as it is fascinating. Set up like a gallery, objects are identified with information about their history or construction. American Indian masks and shields, Turkish weavings and American handmade quilts were on display this spring. **Gray's,** 261-3514, is beginning to develop some character, and feels like a mini-version of their old Nag's Head store. It's a browsers' delight, packed full with all sorts of nice things. There is also a well-stocked golf and tennis shop here, a full service bookstore, a toy shop, an art gallery. You'll find Judy and John Cammarano, owners of **Gourmet Kitchen Emporium**, 261-8174, ready to assist with your choice of kitchen gadgets, gourmet gift baskets and food, and other specialty items. This is a great spot for those talented in the culinary arts...or for those lucky enough to be on the receiving end. **Trappings,** 261-8113, is an "ooh and aah" shop, offering contemporary and classic objets d'art for the home. **Motifs**, 261-6335, features womens separates -- flowing, wrappy pieces in natural fibers--and wonderful jewelry by Outer Banks goldsmith and designer Sara DeSpain. **Ocean Annie's**, 261-3290, (see the write-up in Nags Head shopping) is another shop you won't want to miss.

Loblolly Pines may not look as interesting as some other shopping centers in Duck, but we think it has the most unique stores. **Just for the Beach**, 261-7831, is an amazingly complete beach supply center where, if you can't find it, you don't need it. **Lady Victorian,** 261-8622, offers an uncommon selection of women's ready-to-wear, children's clothing, and a lot of things in Victorian white eyelet. Victorian decorator items and Belgian lace curtains, too. See the write-up on their new store below. Both stores are open all year.

Yesterday's Jewels, 261-4869, is right around the corner, with displays of some very interesting "previously owned" and antique jewelry. **The Duck Duck Shop**, 261-8555, features ducks in every imaginable form, with an emphasis on handcrafted items. The Duck Duck Shop now houses the Duck Post Office, too. If you're a fishing enthusiast, you'll want to make a stop here at **TW's Bait and Tackle,** 261-8300 (see write up under Kitty Hawk Shopping).

The Lucky Duck, 261-7800, located at **Wee Winks Square** -- right across the street from Wee Winks, 261-2937, Duck's original year 'round, one-stop shopping spot -- is an attractive gift store offering a bit of everything, from nautical gifts, souvenirs and country crafts to wicker furniture, local books and artwork. **Tops 'n Bottoms**, 261-

1282, moved here from its Kill Devil Hills location two years ago. The store is filled with moderately-priced, casual women's clothing, swimwear, great accessories. They have an excellent selection of plus sizes, too. Walk into the newest **Lady Victorian**, 261-1654, and you'll feel as if you're trespassing in an opulent boudoir from a bygone era. Bridal gowns, formals and lacy lingerie are upstaged by extravagant surroundings.

Also in Wee Winks Square is **Kitty Hawk Sports**, 261-8770. They carry surfwear in brands such as Quicksilver, Billabong, Starbus, Raisens and Sommerset plus an excellent men's and ladies' swimwear and t-shirt selection. Lots of accessories, boogie boards, and sunglasses, too.

The Farmer's Daughter, 261-4828, is located at the **Duck Soundside Shops** and no shopping trip would be complete without a visit to this store. Owner Julie Boyd has put together another class act with "folk art collectibles" (her original store is in Nags Head). You'll find a good selection of quilts, needlework samplers, wood carvings and plenty more. Open all year.

At **Osprey Landing**, you'll find **Birthday Suits**, 261-7297, and **Carolina Moon**, 261-7199 (see write-ups in Kill Devil Hills section).

North Beach Sailing at **The Waterfront Shops**, 261-6262, is a very complete shop for anyone who loves sailing and wind surfing, carrying boards by F2, O'Brien, and Tiga as well as Neil Pryde and Calvert sails. You'll also find sailing hardware for boats. A good selection of casual wear, t-shirts, beach toys and supplies get you ready for a day in the sun.

For grocery shopping in Duck, no place is faster than **Wee Winks**. **Tommy's Market**, 261-8990, just up the road, has a broader selection and a deli. For the "big shop," when you need to stock up on enough food to last the whole vacation, you may want to head to Food Lion at The Marketplace in Southern Shores where prices are lower and they carry just about anything you could want. Unless you go to Food Lion real early or very late, though, be prepared to wait in a check out line. In season, peak hour lines can be long enough to make you think twice about saving money. For prepared food-to-go, order ribs or chicken from the **Duck Deli,** 261-DELI. For a more elegant repast, try **Osprey Gourmet**, 261-7133, where you can get dishes like macadamia nut salad or marinated beef tenderloin with pickled cabbage.

You can get fresh seafood to go at **Dockside 'n Duck**, 261-8687, in Wee Winks Square.

The closest drug store is **Peoples** at The Marketplace in Southern Shores.

SOUTHERN SHORES

The Marketplace on Rt. 158 in Southern Shores is fast becoming the "in" place to shop year 'round. **Outer Banks Music**, 261-6334, a Radio Shack distributor with a well established business at the Outer Banks Mall, has bought what was Fender Music. This store does its own buying, so its not a carbon copy of the Mall store.

Two Virginians, Mike Warren and Len Setterlund, left the city and came south determined to make Outer Banks cooks happy. **Michaelen's**, 261-6313, their kitchen shop, stocks an assortment of cookware, kitchen gadgets and small appliances that will make any would-be chef drool with desire. They also sell gourmet foods, coffees and have an excellent selection of wine.

After years at The Galleon, Paige Harrell has opened her own store catering to women who are looking for a little drama in their dressing. **Paige's**, 261-1777, is big on personal service and accessorizing.

CAROLINA CASUAL

Specializing in PVC-Resin & Wood Furniture
Factory Direct Prices · 5 Year Warranty
Affordable Style and Quality
Maintenance free

Visit our showroom

We deliver & ship

Just across the
Currituck Bridge

Point Harbor, NC
919-491-2545

Party stores are popping up everywhere these days, and the nicest one we've been in just happens to be here at The Marketplace. **Party Poopers**, 261-6393, has just about everything you'd need to create a party. Lots of fun stuff.

Daniels', 261-8200, a local department store, has earned a good reputation for attractive, moderately-priced merchandise.

The locals flock to **Food Lion** for grocery shopping and, if you want selection and the best prices, you will too. Be forewarned that lines can be long and slow on weekends. If you're looking for natural foods, **For Goodness Sake**, 261-6480, offers fresh ground spices and herbs, bulk teas, pastas, beans and packaged foods made without preservatives or chemical additives. They have a juice and yogurt bar, too.

For fresh seafood to take home, try **Carawan Fish Co.**, 261-2120, across the road from The Marketplace, next to **Three Winks.**

People's Drug Store, 261-8097, at The Marketplace is the place to go for prescriptions and sundries.

Fishing on one of the many Outer Banks piers nearly always ends up with fresh fish for dinner. DCTB

A Life on the Northern Banks:
Maggie Mae Twiford

The late November sunlight glints off the Nags Head dunes outside the window, and glints again off Maggie Twiford's snow-white hair. It is cut short and pinned up with a brown barrette. Her tiny hands lie softly together in the colorful afghan that covers her lap, except when they twist at the plastic band at her wrist. Outside in the corridor there is the hiss of wheelchairs on tile, the chatter of nurses.

"It was all dirt roads in them days. All such as that. And I remember a lot about it. My mother and my father have been dead for years, and my sisters and my brothers too. And I've got three relatives here, and all my other kinfolks are dead. I've got children -- three, two boys and a girl. And today's my youngest son's birthday, he's 62 years old today.

"I was born in 1900. Our closest doctor was at Poplar Branch, Doctor Griggs. Had to go by water to get him, wa'n't no bridges, you see. Sometimes you died fore the doctor got there. My mother had a doctor, Doctor Newburn. He lived at Jarvisburg. And both of them was with my mother when I was born.

"Most all my people were Service people. My father was in the Coast Guard -- it was the Lifesaving Service, years ago. He was a surfman. I heard him say that his mother died when he was thirteen years old, and he couldn't go to school. He had to go out and work to take care of his mother; his daddy was dead. He had it pretty hard. I never heard him say what he did when he was a boy. I imagine he fished. T'weren't nothing else much to do here. He didn't have no education, that was the reason he couldn't get rated, couldn't get up. Well, he was a big stout man, and he had a red complexion. Oh, he was a wonderful father. And he didn't live too long after he was retired. But he was in the Service 37 years. I heard him say that when he went in the service it was at Number Nine station. That was Poyner's Hill. Then he was transferred to Paul Gamiels. Don't imagine there's anything left there now, they've had so many storms.

"My people come from Kitty Hawk. My people were Beals. B-E-A-L. Some B-E-A-L-E. We call ours B-E-A-L-S. Now my father I don't know where really he come from. Up in the hills...seems to me I've heard him say that his mother was from Columbia or somewhere over that way. Uh huh. My mother's family name is Perry. She was a Kitty Hawk

Perry. They have a lot of Perrys in Kitty Hawk. Used to. There's a few still living but not as many as there was years ago. And my mother's mother, she was a Fisher. I think there were four of them, Fisher girls. My grandmother Betty, and Thanny, Amy, and Lebarcia. I didn't know them, that was before I was born. I didn't have no grandparents when I was small.

"My mother died having my sister, when I wasn't quite three years old. I don't remember what she looked like. I wish I had some faint remembrance of her but I don't. She's buried in Kitty Hawk. All my people are buried in Austin's Cemetery there.

"But my little sister lived to be grown and married. And she died the same way my mother died. And she had typhoid fever along with it, and of course the baby didn't live. There wasn't time for it to be borned. And my sister Martha, she died about the same way my mother died. In childbirth. And then my oldest sister died in 1919 of the flu, when it was raging, you know, so bad? She didn't live but one week from the time she was taken, went into pneumonia and died.

"My daddy was a hard workin' man. And he raised a big family. I had three sisters, and I had one, two, three -- four brothers. There was eight of we children to raise up, and he in the service. He had to have a housekeeper to take care of us. No, not colored, elderly white women mostly. And I'm telling you he had a hard time of it.

"But he was a good father. Didn't make much money, but there was a lot of people didn't make as much as he did. We had something to eat and a place to stay in. He always worshipped we four girls.

"I was a little barefooted girl. In the summer I went barefoot. We had a little one-room schoolhouse in Duck. You wouldn't believe it to go up there now. There's a art gallery there now. And it was history, geography, arithmetic, things like that.

"We had ball games. We had a game we called fifty-oh. And ring around the roses. And a game we called sheepie. You'd be surprised at the silly things we had them days. How do you play fifty-oh? Some would go off and hide, and we'd try to find them. And if you found them and could make the home run before they did we'd win the game. Yes, hide and seek was what it was, and they called it fifty-oh then. We played cat, sure did. It's been so long ago I nearly forgot. And we had a croquet set, young people used to come to our lawn and play.

"And on Sunday afternoon we'd go to this big hill north of Duck. It wasn't as big as Jockey's Ridge, but it didn't lack much. And we'd run up and down it and play until we were so tired we couldn't hardly get back.

"We had one teacher that rang a bell -- it was a hand bell. The teacher would stand in the door and ring, ring, when we children would be playing, for us to come in. And we had to stay in at recess a lot, we'd misbehave and done something we shouldn't. Whisperin' in school, or laughing. There was a lot of laughing. And certain ones had to stay and sweep the schoolroom and put things in order for next day. Went to school in the summertime, hot weather, barefoot -- we didn't have to wear shoes, no.

"The Wright brothers? They flew in 1903. I was born in 1900. Oh, yes, they came back in 1908. I remember that. But there was always something going on that I didn't know about. I didn't really live that close to Kill Devil. I saw them flying around. It looked different from planes they have now. We thought it was something scary, flying around up there.

"My daddy had a horse that he used at the station, and then on his liberty at home. He'd bring the horse home. He didn't have but one day liberty a week, one day and one night. He come home at twelve and left next day at eleven to get back to the station. It was about a hour's ride on the horse because it was sand, it took longer to go. He had to be on time, they were strict them days. The horse was named Fanny. That horse ran away with him. I think he was on patrol and the horse got frightened, something happened that he just ran. And throwed him out of the cart and hurt him pretty bad. Throwed him out on his head. Doctor had to tend him.

"Sometimes he patrolled with the horse, but most times he walked. He had what they call a lay-house on each end. Between the two stations, you know. And most times he had to walk the night. He had a north patrol, sometimes he had a south patrol. If it was a stormy night he'd patrol twice a night. And again he'd just have one patrol a night. He'd walk up and down the beach -- that ocean had to be watched for ships, y'know. And I can remember all the ships come ashore when he was in there and I used to worry when I was a kid when I'd hear talk -- we'd get word from the station there was a shipwreck on the beach, and I knew my daddy had to go. I remember how I used to worry about it, thought maybe he wouldn't make it back. Because then they said go, you didn't have to come back. It was the rule. If it was possible to get to the ship, to get the men off, they had to go. And sometimes you didn't come back. You got drowned. I remember seein' em come ashore. Ships from different countries. Some men got lost, some got saved. Some ships was torn to pieces. I've seen men washed ashore on the beach drowned. That's when I was a little girl.

"There wasn't very much. The houses weren't very well kept up. There weren't very many big homes. There were some hunting lodges, one or two. The people who weren't in the service depended on fishing.

"I'm telling you we had a rough time of it, but them were the happy days. Happier than they are in this day and time. We didn't have a lot, but what we had we enjoyed. And we didn't look for a whole lot. If I got a rag doll at Christmas, and a stocking full of nuts and candy and all that, I was happy with it. Now little children gets everything and in no time it's tore up and gone. We took care of our little things that we got.

"But we were happy people them days. It was almost like one big family. Some of them was poorer than others. And them that had a little bit more they'd always divide. I know my daddy did.

"My daddy never had much money but he always raised a lot of stuff to eat around him. Even guineas. And hogs. He had a lot of hogs. We didn't have to buy no meat, no lard. The hogs went free till the new law, the fence law come in, and he had to get rid of them. The woods used to be full of hogs and cattle. Always had a plenty to eat on Christmas. Wasn't like it is now -- all beefsteak. We raised chickens and raised geese and ducks, we had fowls of all kinds. And then gunnin', you know, you killed wild ducks and geese. No problem 'bout eating. We had a garden and grew beans, and collards, and cabbage, sweet potatoes and horse potatoes, cucumbers, tomatoes, most every kind of vegetable you could raise around here. It wasn't the kind of food people eats this day and time. It was good food, it sure was.

"No, you wouldn't hardly believe how people lived them days. We only went to the city once a year. Elizabeth City, that was the closest city. That wasn't very big but to us it was a big one. It was like goin' to New York. Nobody got nowhere much -- I think I did go to Norfolk once or twice when I was growin' up. Went on a steamboat. The , I think.

"I moved to Chesapeake in 1918. We didn't have no high school. I went there to take a business course. It was in Norfolk, on Main Street. Mr. Wresler's college. He died, and Mr. Keyes took it over.

"No, I didn't get a job then. I married William Twiford, in 1918, and he wouldn't let me go to work. He was from Princess Anne, there's where his people was from. He lived down Corolla. But we lived in Norfolk for right many years. My oldest son was born in South Norfolk, and my daughter was born in South Norfolk.

"Then we moved from Norfolk to Church's Island. He was a guide, for two lodges. White's, and for Hampton. Duck hunting lodges. Oh, yes, I know that's a unpleasant job -- he complained about it. I think we were there a couple, three year he worked for the lodge. From there he put in for the Coast Guard. He decided he'd better when he was younger go in the service.

"And we were stationed in Dam Neck. And we lived there I think two year. From there we moved from one station to the other. And finally settled down in Duck, where I was born. And he was in Caffey's Inlet, and then in Kitty Hawk. And I think in Nags Head too. He was all over. And he went to Florida too, was there a whole winter. But I didn't go, the children was small. And he got transferred back. We were in Wash Woods I think six years. That's up above Corolla. And Caffeys Inlet. I think he retired out of Kitty Hawk. He's been dead -- buried him close to twenty year.

"I remember the worst hurricane up there was in 1933. You can't imagine what a hurricane sounds like. It's terrible -- Whoooo. The water came up and flooded us out of our house. Everybody had to leave their home. First we went to the garage, on a hill, and there was lots of women and children in there. The ocean was between us and the station, and the surf had bursted their lifeboat all to pieces. So the men couldn't come and help us. We were helpless. And the water was rising. There was this old lady who had a big house, and she would take people in. The children wanted to go there. So to please the children I left the garage and was trying to get to it. Wading. But the water was too deep, and it was coming in, and I had to try to get up to the top of a hill. And it was sand, and I had the children by both my hands, trying to get up to the top of that sand hill. And I couldn't do it, and the water was rising. But just then the eye of the storm came and we was able to get to safety at the house.

"Some of the houses was took away -- the ocean just took them away. I was lucky. The sand was hilled up as high as the eaves of my house. The wind was so strong it blew the winter lights and the curtains and the shades and the glass out, and blew some of the roof off. And the sea had eat under my kitchen. But I had my house. That's the reason I don't think much of the beach. I just look on that water and walk away. And I think that was why when I was growing up, my father kept us so far from the shore.

"Oh, yes, I really feel lucky to have my children. I got five or six grandchildren. There's more than grandchildren, of great ones. I don't know how many I got, haven't counted them up lately. And I love the great ones just as good as I do the grandchildren.

"I've been in here for two years now. I'm not getting much better, but my mind seems to be clearer. But I'm a lot better than some of them in here. I'll tell you, this is a pitiful place. You go around and see the sufferin' and the sick people. I'm not bodily sick, but I broke my hip a couple of year ago and something happened that the leg got twisted. They did try to straighten it out, but I think they waited too long. It can't never be back right. And this wheelchair...I'm still not well. And I don't think I've got enough time for this hip to ever heal.

"This is a wonderful place to be. They have helicopters here, they take you to hospitals, to the doctors. I haven't been on them. We have everything here that's needed for this kind of home. And my children take care of me pretty good, they do all they can for me. But I'll be glad if I can get out.

"I've had a lot of trouble in my life, yes I have. I think the unhappiest time was when the children left home. I had two in the war. Clyde was in Germany, right in the midst of the battle there. He got his feet froze there. He still has trouble with his legs. And Tom was in the Navy, on the high seas the times when ships were getting sunk down here. You never knew when word was coming that he was drowned. I had a lot of worry on to me. You're bound to worry about them when they're facing danger every minute of their life. And Tom got rheumatic fever in England, and it still bothers him.

"The happiest time was when I was young -- getting married, I reckon.

"The best way I'm happiest is when I know the Lord's going to take care of me. I know I've got to die. But while I'm living I feel like if I live the right life, which I try my best, then he'll take care of me. Although I'm suffering, that'll be over after a while. I want to be prepared to not have none of these aches and things. No, I'm not afraid, not a bit. I want to live as long as the Lord sees fit for me to live, then when it's time I got no dread. No worry about my soul. I know the Bible tells us a lot, but I still think we got to die and go on to find out really what it's all about. Maybe I'm wrong, but if I am it's ignorance, the Lord will forgive me."

Maggie Twiford sits facing the window, immobile in the waning sunlight, watching as the wind ruffles the beach grass at the top of a dune. If you were eight years old, barefoot, you could scramble to the top in a minute. And see for a long, long ways.

INSIDE
KITTY HAWK

Kitty Hawk (the name is probably a corruption of the Poteskeet Indian 'Chickahauk') is the first commercialized part of the Outer Banks that visitors encounter (Southern Shores is actually the first township). It's a town, or an area, typical of the northern Banks -- that is, a study in contrasts. There's a quaint old Kitty Hawk nestled far back alongside the sound. There's a more recent, but visibly aging, Kitty Hawk Beach, along the sea on Rt. 158 business. And there are booming new Kitty Hawks to the north, incorporated as Southern Shores, and Sanderling, and in the high dunes west of Route 158 bypass. There are stretches of undeveloped dunes and near-impenetrable sound side woods, and there are miles of cheek-by-jowl summer cottages and glistening new shopping centers.

The Poteskeets moved out of the northern Banks about the time the Etheridges, Perrys, Baums, Gallops, Hills, and Twifords moved in from Virginia. There were not many of them. Living in mean dwellings on the sound side, amid forests and mosquitoes, they fished, raised a few scrawny cattle, and scratched in the sand to grow a few beans. It was a hard and squalid way to live and when, as sometimes happened, a ship full of rich merchandise like cloth, flour, rum, or logs blew ashore in a storm, there was a general stampede to the scene. When the government-appointed Wreck Commissioner arrived, if there was anything left, a *vendue* was held, auctioning off the remains for partial compensation of the vessel's owner. The tales that the Kitty Hawkers used to tempt vessels ashore with lights are probably exaggerated. In 1700, however, it was reported that when "his Majesty's ship the *Hady* was drove a shore upon the sands between the Inlets of Roanoke and Currituck, the Inhabitants robed her and got some of her guns ashore and shot into her sides and disabled her from getting off." From time to time dead whales, too, were washed up, and trying (cooking) out their oil was another source of income.

Since the northern inlets (Currituck, Caffeys Inlet, and Roanoke, all now closed up) were shallow and treacherous, the northern Banks never developed the trade that Ocracoke and Portsmouth did, and remained sparsely populated well into the twentieth century. Commercial duck hunting, shrimping, crabbing, eeling, and turtling sup-

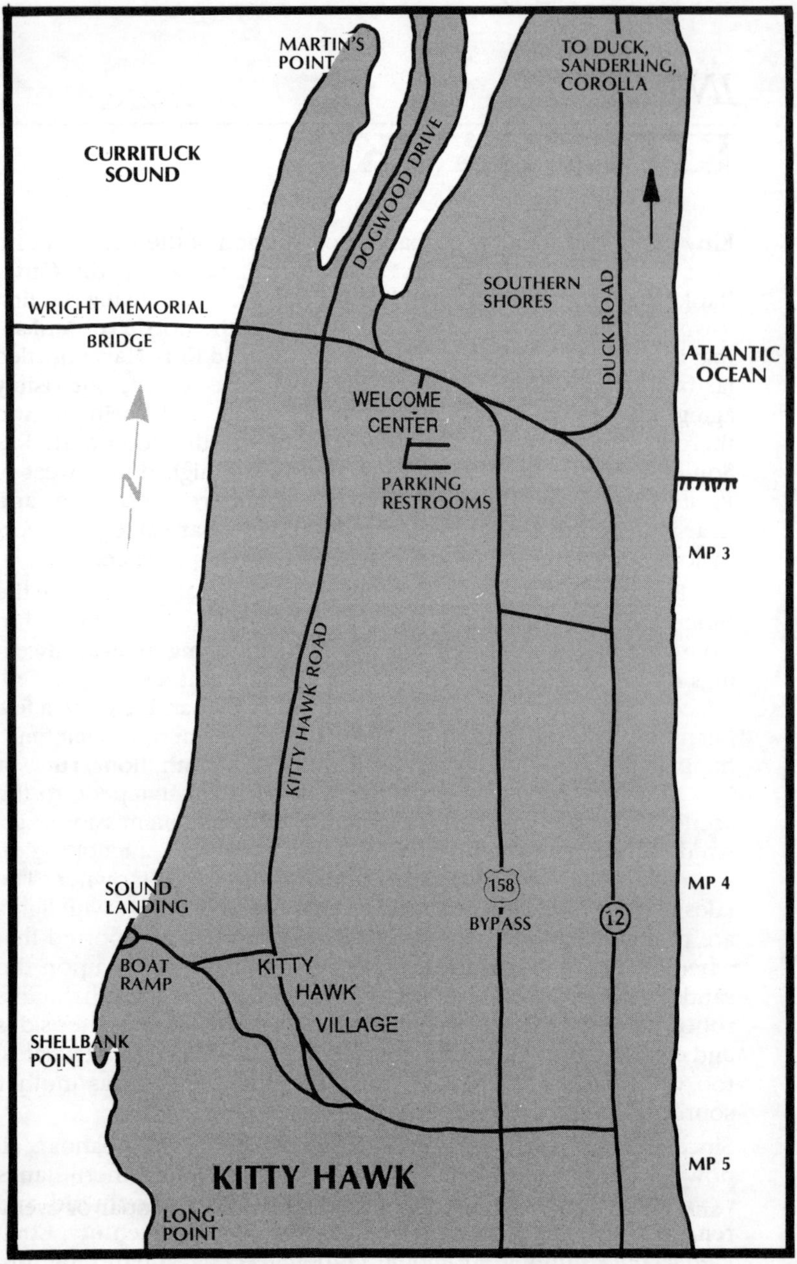
MARTIN'S POINT
TO DUCK, SANDERLING, COROLLA
CURRITUCK SOUND
DOGWOOD DRIVE
SOUTHERN SHORES
DUCK ROAD
WRIGHT MEMORIAL
BRIDGE
ATLANTIC OCEAN
WELCOME CENTER
PARKING RESTROOMS
N
MP 3
KITTY HAWK ROAD
SOUND LANDING
158
BYPASS
12
MP 4
BOAT RAMP
KITTY HAWK VILLAGE
SHELLBANK POINT
MP 5
KITTY HAWK
LONG POINT

plemented the continued income from fishing, and some Kitty Hawkers went to work for the government after 1870, when the Life Saving stations and lighthouses were built.

Kitty Hawk's remoteness and isolation were probably among the reasons the Wrights decided to try out their new flying-machine designs there in 1900. Its steady, strong winds and soft sand were additional advantages. The story of their trials has been covered in 'Kill Devil Hills' section, as that area has since become a separate township. The house on Moore Shore Road where they lived burned in 1928.

With the easy access that the new bridges of '30 and '31 provided, the useless sandy stretches of Kitty Hawk suddenly became desirable real estate. By 1950 the old beach road, now Route 158 business, had become effectively choked, and a new bypass was built. Development now centers around this area, in the high sand hills overlooking the sound and Kitty Hawk is today primarily a permanent year round place of residence. But summer months find the area playing host to weekly and seasonal visitors also. It has the sun, sand, wind and ocean of the Outer Banks, but all of the modern conveniences as well; shops, golf courses, cable television, a $2.1 million medical complex (being built by Albemarle Hospital and opening in 1991) -- things the more remote and romantic section of the Beach lack. Obviously, it's a successful combination, and Kitty Hawk in the future can only grow.

KITTY HAWK
ATTRACTIONS

THE AYCOCK BROWN WELCOME CENTER
Rt.158 Bypass, MP 1 1/2   261-4644

As you drive off the Wright Memorial (Currituck Sound) bridge, keep an eye out to your right. About half a mile east, at the first major intersection, look to the right. You'll see a new building, designed to look like the Banks lifesaving stations of old. This is the Welcome Center. Staffed by the Dare County Tourist Bureau, it offers hotel and motel information, maps, flyers, a monthly calendar of events, changing displays and videos, and other data for the traveler. Open from 8:30 till 5 during the off season, its hours are extended spring, summer, and fall to accommodate visitors. Plenty of parking on the west and south, with ramps for handicapped. Restrooms too.

KITTY HAWK
RECREATION

DUCK WOODS COUNTRY CLUB
Rt. 158 Bypass, MP   261-2744

Duck Woods is the Banks' only private golf course, a green, well sculpted marvel amid the sandy wastes of the beach. Located just east of the Wright Memorial Bridge, to the north of Rt. 158, (behind Kitty Hawk Elementary School), Duck Woods has 18 holes, par 72, overall length 6,700 yards. There are the usual sidelines: a full service restaurant, serving beer and wine; a medium-sized pro shop; electric carts for rent; a driving range; two resident PGA professionals and staff. Not so routine are two unlighted tennis courts and an outdoor pool. To join a private club like Duck Woods, contact the membership chairman through the number above and arrange for payment of initiation fee and dues. Duck Woods is open year round from 8 a.m. to nightfall.

COLONY HOUSE CINEMA
Southern Shores   441-5630

Locations VII and VIII of this longtime Banks movie chain have been built in the Marketplace. They're located about a quarter-mile west of the Aycock Brown Welcome Center in north Kitty Hawk.

KITTY HAWK FISHING PIER
Rt. 158 Business, MP 1   261-2772

Owned by Kitty Hawk Hotel Associates, this is a privately owned establishment. Kitty Hawk Pier was built in 1954. It's 714 feet in length, lighted, and has a small restaurant, tackle shop, bait, ice, and rental tackle. The depth at the pier varies, since the sandbars just offshore are continually moving. Fishing is good here for all the inshore species normally caught off the Banks: bluefish, gray and speckled trout, flounder, spot, king mackerel, and cobia. The state record striped bass was taken here in 1969 and at one time the pier held the world record for bluefish (for state records and citation weights, along with a detailed discussion of fishing along the Outer Banks, see the Fishing Guide section). Kitty Hawk Pier is open April 1 to Thanksgiving. daily adult admission $5.00, child admission $3.50, week pass $25.00, season pass $125.00. Handicapped and blind patrons are admitted free.

SEA SCAPE GOLF CLUB

Rt. 158 Bypass, MP 2 1/2   261-2158

Located amid sandy hills on the sound side of Rt. 158 bypass, Sea Scape is an attractive course, though not as refreshingly green to the eye as mainland courses. The links are Scottish-type, without trees or water hazards -- but what sand traps! The greens, the owner says, are among the smoothest and most level in the state. Sea Scape is an 18-hole course, par 72 (36 front, 36 back), 6200 yards long.

Amenities: gasoline-powered carts for rent, grill, and Sea Scape Club 19th hole. Liquor is available by the drink.

Sea Scape is open from 7:00 a.m. till dark every day of the year. We recommend mosquito repellent in summer, especially after wet weather.

COLONY HOUSE CINEMAS V & VI

Rt. 158 Bypass, MP 4 1/2   441-5630

These two cinemas, located in Kitty Hawk, provide family entertainment year round. Check their marquee or call for the current shows and times.

SHOPPING
KITTY HAWK

Kitty Hawk is better known for its residential areas than its shopping, but a few stores stand out. They are all open year 'round.

Pelicans, once facing extinction, now entertain beachgoers along the edge of the water.

Virginia Dare Hardware, 261-2660, between the 2 and 2 1/2 milepost on the Beach Road, is a friendly place where they might be handing out fresh-picked flowers "for the ladies" or dispensing gardening advice with the authority of folks who know what they're talking about. They also carry a large selection of fine art supplies.

Among the local surf set, **Wave Riding Vehicle**, 261-7952, at Milepost 2 on Rt. 158, is a must-stop shop. They specialize in high performance surf, skate and sailboards and the appropriate accessories and clothing.

TW's Bait & Tackle, 261-7848, next to the Seven Eleven at Milepost 4 is the place to go for fishing equipment and information year 'round. The owner, Terry "T. W." Stewart, has been helping fishing enthusiasts in Kitty Hawk for nine years. His store offers in and off shore charters and bass guides. In addition to the standard fishing tackle, they sell custom rods, live bait, hunting and archery supplies. They do repair work.

You're close enough to grocery shop at the king-of-the-food-chains, **Food Lion**, in Southern Shores (and we have to admit they seem to have the best prices), but you'll find the locally-owned **Food-A-Rama** at Kitty Hawk Plaza to be a well-stocked, pleasant store. It's usually not as crowded, and unless you're buying a lot of groceries, you won't see too much difference in the tab.

If you're shopping for desserts, consider a stop at **Aunt Mary's Kitchen**, 261-8169, at Milepost 2-1/2 on Rt. 158. Ginny Ness (Aunt Mary was an old family friend) is becoming famous in these parts for her homemade cakes and pies. She'll sell you a piece or two (she doesn't sell whole cakes or pies and she doesn't do special occasion cakes) of her delectable coconut cream cake, a heavenly (and cholesteral-free) angel food cake or any of several other desserts she makes daily.

For prescriptions and other drug store purchases, you'll get the best selection at **Peoples**, 261-8097, in Southern Shores.

Surfing in the ocean on a catamaran is a thrill for anyone bold enough to give it a try.

INSIDE
KILL DEVIL HILLS

The early history of Kill Devil Hills is indistinguishable from that of Nags Head and Kitty Hawk. In the old days they were all simply part of 'the beach.' The Kill Devil Hills themselves, a region of large, moving dunes, were unpopulated, though a small community known as Rosepock existed during the eighteenth century in the sound side woods north of Kill Devil Hill proper.

The name? There are almost as many explanations as there are sand hills. Some say that one happy day a cargo of New England 'Kill-Devil' rum came ashore and the Hill region was named in memory of it. Some say the name may be a corruption of 'Killdee' or 'killdeer,' a shore bird once common around the dunes. And there are the legends about bargains with the devil, and even more elaborate explanations undoubtedly made up after the fact in order to answer visitors, who persist in asking "why is it called Kill Devil Hills?"

At any rate, this patch of sand hills south of Kitty Hawk and north of Nags Head has been called Big Kill Devil since at least 1808, and the highest of them, naturally, was called Kill Devil Hill. But it was not until the dawn of the twentieth century that they found their niche in history.

This is the way it happened.

Way out in Ohio, along about 1899, two Yankee brothers, bicycle mechanics, took up building flying-machines as a hobby. No one in those days had yet flown a powered heavier-than-air machine, and therefore many of their neighbors thought their hobby odd.

In August of 1900, Wilbur and Orville Wright had completed and tested some flying models and were ready to build a man-carrying glider. Examining records of mean wind velocities from around the country, they found that according to the Weather Bureau a place called Kitty Hawk, in North Carolina, had strong, steady winds. They did a bit more research and found that it also had bare hills, made of nice soft sand, the better to crash-land into. Writing ahead to the Kitty Hawk Weather Station, they received assurances that the strength of the wind and the nature of the land answered their requirements. Captain Bill Tate, a prominent Kitty Hawker, wrote:

If you decide to try your machine here & come I will take pleasure in doing all I can for your convenience & success & pleasure, & I assure you you will find a hospitable people when you come among us.

Wilbur arrived first, on September 13, after a miserable two-day schooner trip from Elizabeth City, and set up camp near Capt. Tate's home, about four miles north of Kill Devil Hill, in what is now Kitty Hawk Village. Orville arrived two weeks later and they soon had their first glider assembled, flying it for the first few trials with lines, like a kite. Later, they carried it four miles to the ninety-foot high sand hill and made about a dozen glides, taking turns piloting it. Their total time aloft was about 15 seconds. That ended the gliding season for 1900. Their time in the air had been short, but they had learned some important secrets. The lifting power of the wings was less than they had expected, but the wing warping system they had invented to enable them to turn the machine worked beautifully. They left for Dayton resolving to return the next year.

By summer, 1901, they had completed the second glider, a larger model with wings 22 feet wide and of 7 foot chord, with increased curvature to conform to Otto Lilienthal's aerodynamic tables. They arrived at Kill Devil Hill with it on July 10, and put in a few days building a 16 x 25 shed and drilling a well. Between July 27 and August 20 they made several dozen flights. They discovered that Lilienthal's figures were wrong. They decided that a vertical surface was needed at the tail. But in spite of that, they succeeded in gliding farther and more skillfully than anyone had before.

The next winter in Dayton passed swiftly. There was the bicycle business, of course, which was taking off; yet the Wrights found time to build the first scientifically accurate wind tunnel and to carry out their own calculations of wing curvature versus lift. By September 19, 1902, they were back at Kill Devil Hill with a new glider, not much bigger than the old one, but designed now to their own growing knowledge of aerodynamics. And it had a tail.

Over a thousand flights in September and October of 1902 proved that they were very near the 'secret' of flight. The glider soared, remaining aloft for more than a minute and going over 600 feet. When they added a movable rudder to the vertical tail, the basic idea of the airplane was complete.

Satisfied with the glider itself, they went back to Dayton to buy an engine. But none were available that met the Wright's rigorous specifications. So they built one, a four-cylinder, aluminum-block gasoline engine that delivered between 9 and 12 horsepower. Then

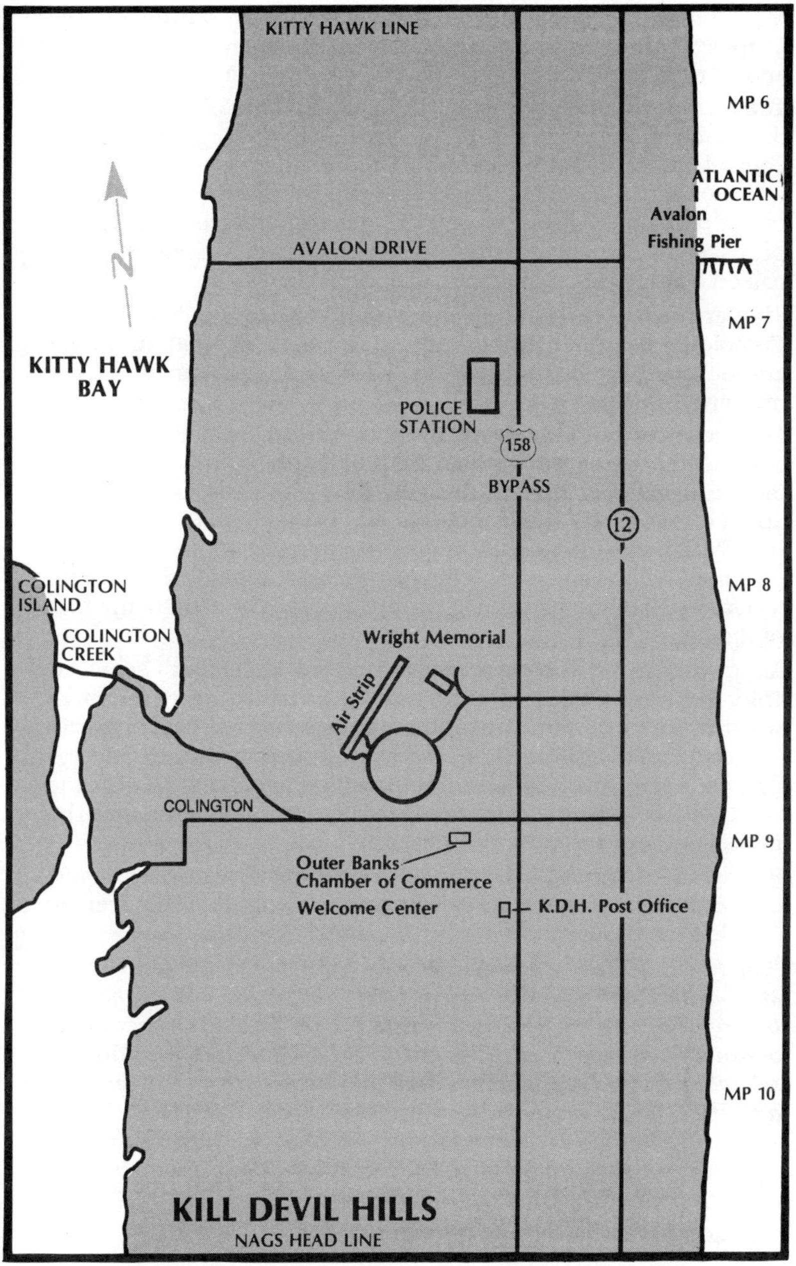
KITTY HAWK LINE
MP 6
ATLANTIC OCEAN
Avalon Fishing Pier
AVALON DRIVE
MP 7
KITTY HAWK BAY
POLICE STATION
158
BYPASS
12
MP 8
COLINGTON ISLAND
COLINGTON CREEK
Wright Memorial
Air Strip
COLINGTON
MP 9
Outer Banks Chamber of Commerce Welcome Center
K.D.H. Post Office
MP 10
KILL DEVIL HILLS
NAGS HEAD LINE

they built a complete new plane. Finally they started on the propellers, discovered that no one really knew how to design one, and learned how themselves. Then they built them.

The final result did not look much like the planes of today, but all the elements were there. A 40-foot span double wing, with aileron control interacting with a movable rudder. Attitude was controlled with horizontal elevators. A gasoline engine, placed alongside the prone pilot on the lower wing, driving two counterrotating pusher props. And a launching system -- a rail down which the plane could roll on a little dolly, which then dropped off.

They arrived at Kill Devil Hill for the fourth time in September, 1903. Completely ignored by the press and the outside world, they built another shed, repaired various breakdowns, and ground-tested the machine.

On December 14 they were ready to fly. A sheet, taken from the bed and nailed to the side of the quarters building, brought several husky men trudging over the sand from the Kitty Hawk Lifesaving Station, about a mile away. The launch rail was set up near the top of the hill; Wilbur won the toss; the engine was warmed up, and the flying-machine slid down the rail. Wilbur, overeager, brought the nose up too fast, stalled the plane, and dropped it into the sand at the foot of the hill.

After two days' work, repairs were completed. December 17 dawned cold and very windy, with 27 mph clocked at the government weather station nearby. The brothers dragged the machine out again and called the lifesavers. With the wind so strong, they decided to fly from a level track, and set the launching apparatus up near the sheds. At 10:35 Orville climbed aboard and started the engine. The propellers began to turn.

Facing a 27 mph wind, the machine started very slowly when Orville eleased the hold-down wire. Wilbur ran alongside. The flyer, in Orville's words later:

...lifted from the track just as it was entering on the fourth rail. Mr. Daniels took a picture just as it left the tracks. I found the control of the front rudder quite difficult on account of its being balanced too near the center and thus had a tendency to turn itself when started so that the rudder was turned too far on one side and then too far on the other. As a result the machine would rise suddenly to about 10 ft. and then as suddenly, on turning the rudder, dart for the ground. A sudden dart when out about 100 feet from the end of the tracks ended the flight.

He had been in the air only 12 seconds.

11:20 a.m.: second flight, Wilbur piloting. The wind dropped for a moment and the machine flew faster, going 175 feet in 12 seconds.

11:40 a.m.: third flight. Orville traveled 200 feet in 15 seconds.

12:00 noon: fourth and last flight. Getting the hang of it, Wilbur flew 852 feet in 59 seconds.

The brothers planned to go for distance on the next flight, perhaps as far as the lifesaving station, but a few minutes later, as the flyer was sitting on the sand, a gust of wind struck. The machine rolled over and over, destroying itself. The 1903 flying season was at an end.

That afternoon, after eating lunch and washing their dishes, the brothers walked to the Kitty Hawk weather station, which had a telegraph connection. Orville wrote the famous message:

SUCCESS FOUR FLIGHTS THURSDAY MORNING ALL AGAINST TWENTY-ONE- MILE WIND STARTED FROM LEVEL WITH ENGINE POWER ALONE AVERAGE SPEED THROUGH AIR THIRTY-ONE MILES LONGEST 59 SECONDS INFORM PRESS HOME CHRISTMAS. ORVILLE WRIGHT.

In 1904 the Wrights shifted their experiments to a farmer's field near Dayton, extending their flights to 24 miles in 38 minutes by the end of 1905. Incredibly, they attracted little attention, even in Dayton. In 1908 they returned to Kill Devil Hill to test new aircraft, engines, and control arrangements, and there, belatedly, the press discovered them. The rest is history.

Kill Devil Hills' meagre population began to grow rapidly when Roanoke and Currituck sounds were bridged in 1920 and 1930. The hill itself, which Army engineers had stabilized with grass in 1928, was capped with the Wright monument in 1932. In 1938 the growing citizenry gained a post office, and in 1953 became an incorporated town...named, of course, Kill Devil Hills. Though it has a large permanent population, it is also one of the most popular resort communities, welcoming thousands of visitors and summer residents each year to enjoy sun, sand, sea, and wind.

Many of them -- especially VIPs -- come to Kill Devil Hills, appropriately enough, by air.

WRIGHT BROTHERS NATIONAL MEMORIAL

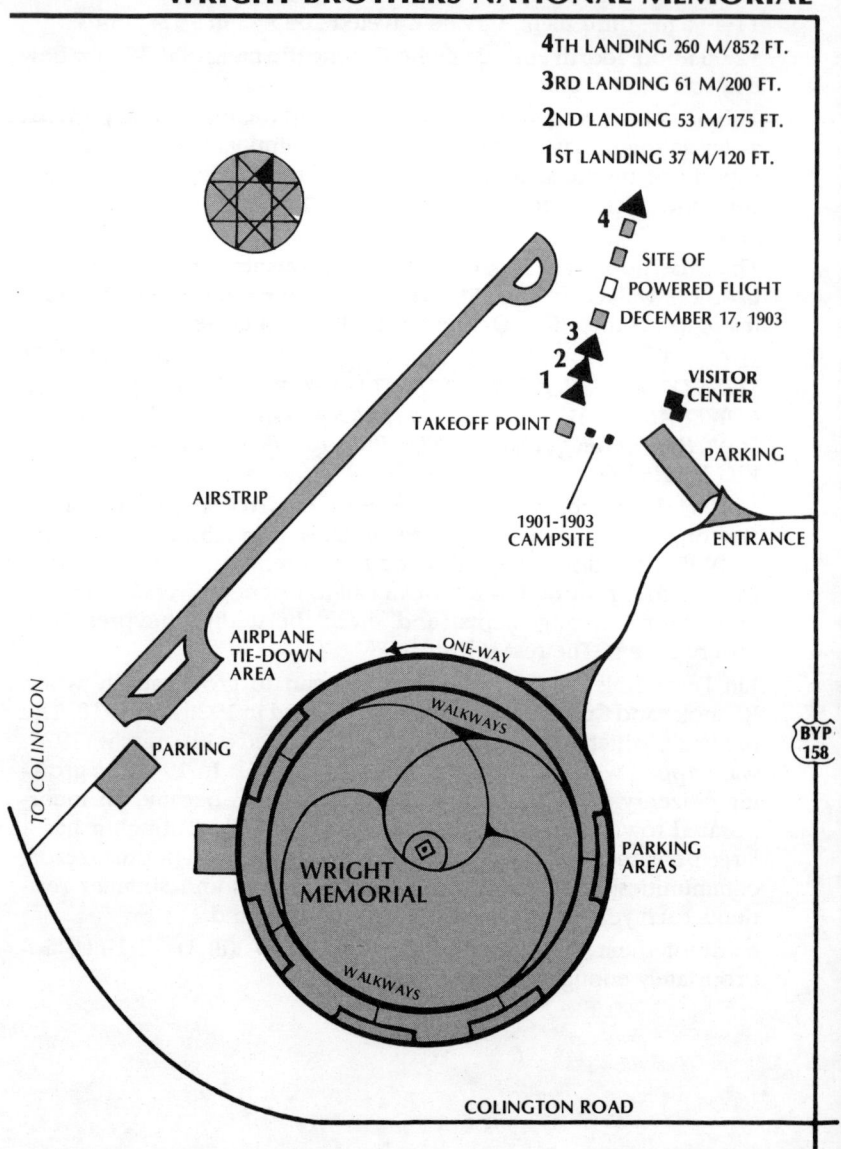

4TH LANDING 260 M/852 FT.
3RD LANDING 61 M/200 FT.
2ND LANDING 53 M/175 FT.
1ST LANDING 37 M/120 FT.

SITE OF POWERED FLIGHT DECEMBER 17, 1903

VISITOR CENTER

TAKEOFF POINT

PARKING

1901-1903 CAMPSITE

ENTRANCE

AIRSTRIP

AIRPLANE TIE-DOWN AREA

ONE-WAY

WALKWAYS

PARKING

TO COLINGTON

WRIGHT MEMORIAL

PARKING AREAS

WALKWAYS

BYP 158

COLINGTON ROAD

The Wright Brothers Memorial in Kill Devil Hills honors the men who made flight possible. DCTB

KILL DEVIL HILLS
ATTRACTIONS

WRIGHT BROTHERS MEMORIAL
Rt. 158 Bypass, MP 8   441-7430

Eight miles south of the Wright Memorial Bridge, the Wright Brothers National Memorial is a complex of activities and reconstruction honoring the men who made flight possible -- and those who followed them into the air.

Looking at the map, you'll see that the first building you come to after turning off Route 158 bypass is a low, domed white structure on the right side of the access road. Parking is available in front of it. This is the National Park Service Visitor Center. It's open daily, except Christmas, and it definitely should be seen. Hours are variable with the season and there is a small entrance charge.

It's well put together. Along with the information desk and restrooms, there's a well-stocked book store as well as a very well-developed selection of displays and reproductions. A small entry fee is now charged. The long struggle of the Wrights to fly is documented in a series of exhibits that explain at the same time the principles of powered flight. Parts of the Wrights' motors and planes, samples of their notes and calculations lend an air of authenticity. In a large, light-filled room to the south, looking out toward the Hill, are full scale reproductions of the 1902 glider and of the 1903 Flyer. On the walls are portraits of aviation pioneers, military and civilian, male and female.

From the Center we suggest a short walk out the door and toward the two wooden sheds you see between you and the hill. These are reconstructions of the Wrights' 1903 camp, built in 1963. They're furnished with tools and equipment like those the Wrights used.

Moving to the east, you'll see a large granite boulder. This marks the takeoff point for the flights of December 17. Looking north, you'll see signs marking where the first, second, third and fourth flights touched down. It doesn't look very far, and it isn't. You might say it was one small step for a man...

The Memorial itself is a good walk, and you may want to return to your car and drive around the circular access road (one way!) to the parking areas that ring Kill Devil Hill. We definitely recommend driving over if it has rained recently, for the area between the Center and the hill is low and you may find your ankles getting wet. No, you can't drive to the top on a motorcycle. And please stay on the paved paths going up; the Park Service has to work hard to keep what is still just a big sand dune from blowing away.

Kill Devil Hill itself is ninety-one feet high. The granite pylon, rising sixty more feet into the air, was erected in 1932 under the supervision of the Army Corps of Engineers. Intended at first to be used as a lighthouse, the beacon was shut down when ships at sea confused it with the Bodie Island and Hatteras lights. Today, floodlit at night, it is visible from as far away as Duck, and from its base -- there's a rampart to walk around on, and bronze busts of the brothers -- you can see the sound, the sea, and most of the northern Banks.

You can also see light planes landing and taking off from a small strip in the woods to the northwest. This is the First Flight Airstrip. It is 3000 feet long, asphalt-surfaced, and has a small tie-down area (stay is limited to 24 hours). No lights, fuel, service, or navigational aids, other than a wind sock are present. If you need a fully-equipped airport see 'Dare County Airport' in Manteo, but this is a convenient strip for a short-term visit.

Grounds close to vehicles at the same time as the Visitor Center (9 a.m. to 7 p.m. summer, 5 other times), but they're open to walkers any time.

The Visitor Center also offers summer programs and kite flying demonstrations at the Center, the Wright's camp buildings, and at the top of the hill. Ask at the Center desk for a schedule.

COLINGTON ISLAND

Just south of the Wright monument, a narrow road leads off to the west from Route 158 bypass, near the 8 1/2 mile marker. This is the road to Colington, or Colington Island, a little-known, seldom-visited part of the Banks that nonetheless deserves a footnote both for its history and for its gem like beauty.

In Charles the Second's great divvying up of North Carolina in 1660s, Sir John Colleton, an English gentlemen, was granted a small island in Roanoke sound, just west of present-day Kill Devil Hills. The flat, heavily-wooded island, protected by the dunes from salt spray and wind, had good soil, and was colonized in 1665 by a party under the leadership of Peter Carteret, making it the first permanent settlement in the Outer Banks. Since then the inhabitants have lived a happy and almost history less existence, farming, raising livestock, and fishing.

The winding, five-mile drive today's visitor takes to and through Colington (the spelling has changed since Sir John's time) will pass small businesses -- Colington Seafood, Joe and Kay's Campground,

Billy Seafood, Endurance Seafood, Cozy Cove, Colington Park Campground, Bridges Bait and Tackle, Nunemaker Fish Company, the Outer Banks Loan Office, with the wonderful slogan "Pockets Bare in Dare? See Jack" -- roll over scenic old arched bridges, twist and turn through forests of oak, holly, and pine. Several private, restricted-entry communities line the shores of the sound. A pretty drive, a nice side trip, and some good photographic opportunities.

Colington is seeing gradual development. New shops and smaller housing units are filling in the remnants of the Colington woods. Still, it's enough off the beach strip to be a quiet place most of the year.

If you plan to camp out on Colington in summer, take one precaution: plan for mosquitoes.

DARE COUNTY LIBRARY KILL DEVIL HILLS BRANCH

Rt. 158 bypass, MP 8   441-4331

The Banks new librarian, Ellen Adkins, runs this 10,000 volume library with books on tapes, overhead projector, videos, VCR's and meeting facilities. They're trying to increase their size to 20,000 volumes, so if you would like to make a "learning" donation, give a book! Hours are M - F 9:30 - 6:30, Sat 10 - 4, closed on Sunday.

OUTER BANKS CHAMBER OF COMMERCE WELCOME CENTER

Rt. 158 Bypass, MP 8   441-8144

Remember the little round red building in Kitty Hawk? The Chamber's welcome center has moved. It's now on Colington Road (corner of Mustian and Colington) in a brand new building. Turn west off Rt. 158 Bypass on Colington (south of the Wright Memorial), and it'll be the second building on your left. Along with information on member businesses, the Center operates as a clearinghouse for written or phoned-in inquiries, and can help you with motel reservations in advance (though they can't make them for you). Mailing address: P.O. Box 1757, Kill Devil Hills, NC 27948. Open 9 to 5 Monday through Friday.

KITTY HAWK AERO TOURS
Wright Brothers Memorial   441-4460

Captain Kitty Hawk (Jay Mankedick) offers several flying tours of the Banks in his seven aircraft. The local tour flies over ocean, shore, down to Oregon Inlet, around the lighthouse at Bodie Island, and back over Roanoke Island covering about 50 miles. The tour is very pretty and gives you a different perspective on how thin and fragile the Banks really are. Mankedick offers other, longer tours north to Corolla and south to Ocracoke, as well as charter services. The Aero Tours operates year round. Rates are $15.00 per person for parties of three or more and the flight lasts about 20 - 25 minutes. You can make your reservations by going to their booth at the Wright Brothers Memorial or by calling.

NAGS HEAD WOODS ECOLOGICAL PRESERVE
441-2525

Not all the land in the Banks is "for" human use (or abuse). Nags Head Woods Ecological Preserve is a Nature Conservancy program dedicated to preserving a barrier island ecosystem. The Visitor Center is located at the end of West Ocean Acres Drive off the 158 Bypass. It is open to visitors Tuesday, Thursday, and Saturday, 10a.m. to 3 p.m. Two loop trails begin at the Center and wind through forest, dune, swamp, and pond habitats. Organized groups may arrange further use of the Center with the staff.

The Preserve is private property, not a park, and should be treated as such. No camping, littering, firearms, alcoholic beverages, or pets. To become a member of Friends of Nags Head Woods, write the Preserve at 701 W. Ocean Acres Drive, Kill Devil Hills, NC 27948. Levels of membership

are $15 for an individual and $25 for a family. These fees give you membership in the national Nature Conservancy, as well, and go to support the Preserve's environmental education and research programs.

KILL DEVIL HILLS
RECREATION

AVALON FISHING PIER
Rt. 158 Business, MP 6   441-7494

Avalon Pier, owned by Charlie Falk, was built in 1960 and is presently 705 feet long. The pier is lighted and has a restaurant, bait and tackle shop, ice, and gear for rent. The catch includes bluefish, gray and speckled trout, flounder, spot, king mackerel, cobia, and channel bass, depending on the season (see Fishing section in Hatteras Island chapter). Avalon is closed Dec. 1 to March 1. Admission prices:
adult $4.75 under 12, $2.75. Weekly pass $28.00, weekend $13.00, season pass $125.00. Handicapped in wheelchairs admitted free.

SEA RANCH TENNIS CENTER
Rt. 12 Business, MP 7   441-7126

The large building you see across from the Sea Ranch is the motel's tennis center and it is open to the public. Open year round from 9:00 a.m. until 9:00 p.m. (hours are often extended in the summer),

---

Shear Genius

A Full Service Salon for Men and Women

- We carry complete retail lines of
  Aveda · Redken · Nexxus
  for hair & skin, including cosmetics
- Free consultations
- Open Tuesday through Saturday, 9-5:30,
  year round. Hours extended in summer.

Non-Smoking

Precision Haircuts	Facials
Highlights	Pedicures
Colors	Manicures
Perms & body waves	Full Body Massage
	Waxing

Sea Ranch II, Milepost 7, Kill Devil Hills   919-441-3571

the Center provides two indoor courts and an observation lounge. Rackets are available for purchase as are balls, sweat bands, and other supplies. The pro, Judi Dixon also provides lessons by appointment. Reservations for court time are required.

NAUTILUS ATHLETIC CLUB
Rt. 12, MP 7   441-7001

Nancy and Stu Golliday have been building bodies on the beach since 1983. The Sea Ranch facility (lower level of the Sea Ranch II) makes available free weights, 12 pieces of equipment, sauna, bikes, Jacuzzi, vitamins and supplements. No aerobics at this location. Open year 'round, Monday through Friday, 7:30 a.m. until 9 p.m., Saturday, 10 a.m. until 7 p.m., closed Sunday. There's a daily fee for nonmembers.

SHOPPING
KILL DEVIL HILLS

Shopping in Kill Devil Hills is on the upswing with the completion of **Dare Centre** at Milepost 7 on Rt. 158. **Belk's**, **Rose's** and a **Food Lion** are the big draws now; only a few of the smaller shops that complete the center are open as of this writing.

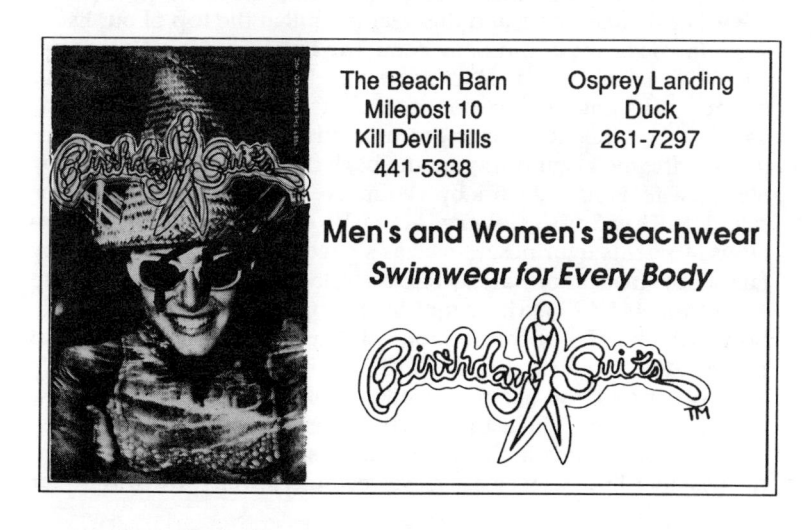

The Beach Barn
Milepost 10
Kill Devil Hills
441-5338

Osprey Landing
Duck
261-7297

Men's and Women's Beachwear
Swimwear for Every Body

> ## Seventeen Shops Full of Fun, Great Service, and Friendly People.
>
> Take a leisurely walk through our unique little village. Enjoy shops featuring clothing, ice cream, gifts, toys, American handcrafts, art prints, kites, bathing suits, home decorations, collectibles, South American fur rugs, nautical gifts, gemstones and hair salon. Come for the fun, stay for the bargains!
> Open daily year round.
>
> ## *Sea Holly Square*
>
> **Located at Milepost 9 1/2 on the Beach Road (across from Ramada Inn).**

Seagate North, at Milepost 6 on Rt. 158, has more than a dozen shops that range from computers to needlework.

Last year, we thought the best shopping was at **Sea Holly Square**, MP 9-1/2, Beach Road, and this year it's still at the top of our list. A long-time favorite of ours has been **Tar Heel Trading Company**, 441-5278. Local owners Mary Ames and John Stubbings travel the country selecting quality American crafts for the shop. At **Bequa**, 441-6834, you might see artist Steve Beunis creating one of his sculptures in the metalsmith shop at the back of the gallery. Paintings by Steve's wife, Fini, and work by a couple other local artists is also for sale. The **King Smith Gallery**, 441-5010, carries Hummels and Precious Moments figurines, as well as signed prints of local scenes by famous art instructor Barclay Sheaks. And, just for fun, there's **Kite Kingdom**, 441-6235, where they'll be happy to teach kids of any age how to fly their fancy contraptions (if they're busy, you may have to come back later in the day). If you're looking for women's sportswear and you like the Catalina look, **Splash Too**, 441-1244, is for you. Owners Linda and Lou Trombley say they have the largest selection of Catalina in the state. They also carry other, more trendy, designer lines as well as cruisewear and jewelry. But swimwear is their forte: No matter what shape, size or style you want, they probably have it. Even in the hard-to-find sizes, they have dozens of suits in different styles, different colors. Service is out-of-the-ordinary, too, especially when you head to the dressing rooms. Trombley is genuinely helpful without being pushy. They also carry a good selection of suits for women who have had mastectomies. In addition to these five shops, there are a dozen more that offer hours of browsing. For those who don't like to browse, there are benches for people-watching.

North Carolina Books, 441-2141, a paperback fiend's paradise, moved from its old quarters on the Beach Road to the Times Printing building at MP 7-1/2 on Rt. 158. The new store feels like a paperback library, which is sort of how it operates: Customers bring in their used paperbacks for credit toward the purchase of other used paperbacks. It's a great way to get some good, cheap beach reading.

The **Sea Isle Gifts and Lamp Shop**, 441-7206, at MP 9-1/2, Beach Road, has a large selection of moderately-priced lamps -- and all the parts to repair or make a lamp, including shades and decorative finials. They also carry all sorts of stands for displaying seashells, rocks or other small curios. If you've picked up beach treasures and don't know what to do with them, take a look here for some ideas.

Photographers -- professional, amateur, reluctant, or otherwise -- will appreciate a stop at **Jim's Camera House**, 441-6528. Jim and Hattie Lee opened their store years ago on the Beach Road. We

---

SPLASH TOO

for the Beach: Swimwear, cover-ups
for play: sportswear, sun dresses
for work: separates, dresses
One of the Largest Selections of
Catalina on the Beach

SPLASH TOO
SEA HOLLY SQ. 9.6 MP BEACH ROAD
441-1244

"Where women of discriminating taste shop for all their fine fashion needs...."

watched this business grow until we thought it was going to burst at the seams! Thank goodness they finally moved to larger quarters at Milepost 9 on Hwy. 158. Jim's sells cameras and accessories (including video). They do one-hour color print processing. They do family vacation portraits, too: You can go to their studio or they will shoot your group at any location of your choice.

Carolina Moon, 441-4000, Milepost 10 on Rt. 158, is an intriguing gift shop, catering to the "new age" interest in crystals and other aura-enhancing diversions. They have beautiful pottery, music, kaliedoscopes, cards, essential oils, gems and stones...you could spend all day just looking at everything. Even if the "new age" isn't your age, you'll appreciate the unique selection of jewelry and decorative housewares. Right next door is **Birthday Suits**, 441-5338, with men's and women's clothing for the 30-something crowd. "Relaxed, California contemporary," is how owner Jill Bennett describes her inventory. This eight-year-old store has a real boutique feel -- you'll find everything from hats to shoes -- with special attention paid to giving good service. Both Carolina Moon and Birthday Suits have stores at Osprey Landing in Duck.

For groceries, the obvious choice is the new **Food Lion** at Dare Centre. But it doesn't seem to matter how many of these supermarkets get built on the Outer Banks, there are always lines! I still vote for **Food-A-Rama** at Kitty Hawk Plaza or **Seamark Foods** at the Outer Banks Mall unless your idea of a good time is standing in a

Snap's Produce Market

- fresh produce
- Bergey's dairy products
- bedding plants
- quality cheeses
- coffees
- beer and wine

Your farm market on the beach!!

M.P. 9 KDH 441-0997

Owned by Donald and Banta Blanchard

Open Daily 9-6   Summer hours 8-8 check-out line. For emergency rations, run into the **Kill Devil Hills Superette**, 441-7283, at MP6 on Rt. 158. They're open 24 hours a day all year.

For fresh seafood, you're close to the place that dozens of our local friends rate the best: **Billy's**, 441-5978, in Colington (there is a Kitty Hawk location, but it isn't open all year and is not as well stocked). If locals drive 20 and 30 miles out of their way to shop there, they must be on to something good.

Petrozza's, 441-1642, at the Dare Centre is an Italian delicatessen offering fresh pastas and specialty items like roasted red peppers and cannoli.

Snaps, 441-8445, at Milepost 9 on Rt. 158, under new ownership and management this year, sells a wide variety of fresh, bulk produce. They also offer some specialty food items, ground-to-order peanut butter, fresh squeezed fruit juices, wines and garden plants.

The **Revco Drug Store**, 441-3633, next to Food Lion in Nags Head, has a big selection and it's convenient.

Shear Genius, 441-3571, is one of the best known full-service salons in this area. Located at the Sea Ranch II building, they offer precision haircuts, perms and body waves, and colors and highlighting. But we like them best for the *incredible* facials and full body massages they offer. How could there be any better way to spend your vacation than being pampered like this!

Jockey's Ridge in Nags Head is the tallest sand dune on the East Coast. DCTB

INSIDE
NAGS HEAD

Most everyone has heard the old story about how Nags Head got its name. How, as legend has it, the early inhabitants of the sandy banks were not above tying lanterns around horses' necks (or their tails, as one variation goes), and leading the animals up and down the beach. Merchant skippers at sea, seeing the bobbing lights, would take them for the anchor lights of ships safely in harbor, and would steer for them. When they ran aground, the Bankers salvaged the cargo to supplement their own meager belongings.

It seems more likely, all things considered, that this narrow section of the beach east of Roanoke Island was named by early settlers after geographically similar features of the English coast. But it *is* certain that some strange things used to take place off Nags Head. The story of Theodosia Burr Alston confirms that. Twenty-nine years old, daughter of adventurer, duellist, and former vice-president Aaron Burr, all trace of her was lost when her New York-bound ship, the *Patriot*, disappeared at sea in late 1812. Later in the century, deathbed confessions were reported of former pirates who said they had seized the ship and murdered all hands, setting the empty vessel to drift. In 1869 a portrait bearing a startling resemblance to Theodosia was turned up in a Nags Head cottage. Its owner, an old woman, said that it had been taken from a deserted schooner that had come ashore in early 1813....

Nags Head first became a resort in the early 1800s, when wealthy planters began the practice of taking ship for the Banks during summer months to escape the unhealthy climate farther inland. The first hotel was built in 1838, and did a good business; excess visitors were quartered in private residences. Summer cottages began appearing about this time, most of them near the sound rather than the sea side. Dancing, fishing, bowling, and sea-bathing occupied the visitors' time while native Bankers kept to themselves in their own sound side village in Nags Head Woods. In 1851 the hotel was enlarged and half a mile of mule-drawn railway laid to make the journey to the sea less wearisome.

In 1862 the Nags Head Hotel was burned by retreating Confederates. Rebuilt in the late '70s, it boomed anew as the popularity of the resort grew and transportation to it became more convenient.

One of the worst disasters in Banks history happened at Nags Head in 1877, when the 541-ton barkentine-rigged screw steamer USS *Huron* went aground in a November storm. The then-new Nags Head Lifesaving Station Number Seven was only two miles away, but Congress had been cutting costs, and it was unmanned. Local fishermen helped the men who made it ashore, but almost a hundred sailors were drowned or crushed as the fearful surf tore the iron ship to pieces. Today the *Huron* lies straight out between mile markers 11 and 12, even with the end of Nags Head Pier. Recent shifts have uncovered the wreck again, and local divers have recovered such artifacts as portholes, rifle rounds, cannonballs, fittings, etc. (see "SCUBA Diving" section).

More recent decades have seen the population of the area (incorporated as a town in 1961) increase slowly. Recent development of a 400-acre ocean-to-soundside community known as "The Village at Nags Head" will bring new residents to the area as well. Construction is underway at The Village, which will feature small clusters of single family homes as well as multi-family townhouses and condominiums. The homes are situated between fairways of the private golf course and clubhouse there. In addition, there is an attractive oceanfront beach club and pavilion. Plans have been approved for a restaurant and lounge; two hotel sites; a commercial area for professional offices; and a low-profile business area to contain a grocery and/or convenience store.

Despite the growth, Nags Head still retains its individuality with respect to Roanoke Island, across the causeway and the Washington Baum Bridge, and the explosively growing communities farther north. A center of recreation (fishing, swimming, boating, hang-gliding), art (the largest collection of studios and galleries on the Banks), and legend, Nags Head still holds to its old title as the premier resort spot of the North Carolina Coast.

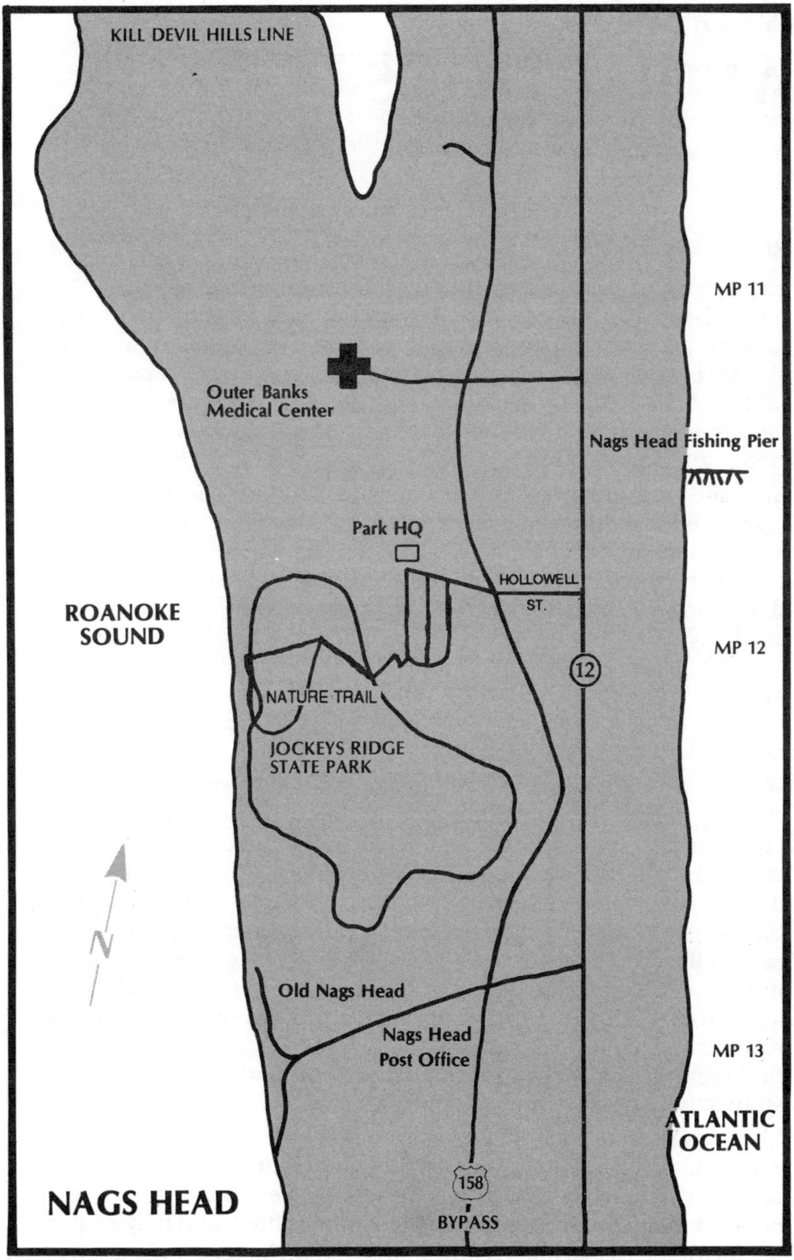
KILL DEVIL HILLS LINE
MP 11
Outer Banks
Medical Center
Nags Head Fishing Pier
Park HQ
HOLLOWELL
ST.
ROANOKE
SOUND
MP 12
12
NATURE TRAIL
JOCKEYS RIDGE
STATE PARK
N
Old Nags Head
Nags Head
Post Office
MP 13
ATLANTIC
OCEAN
158
BYPASS
NAGS HEAD

NAGS HEAD
ATTRACTIONS

JOCKEY'S RIDGE STATE PARK
Rt. 158 Bypass, MP 12   441-7132

Jockey's Ridge has been an attraction for tourist since at least 1851; it was then a Norfolk editor passed on the Banks legend that "...the lady who may accompany you to its summit if not already a wife will shortly become yours." It's now one of the state's newest parks, established in 1975. Contained within its 403 acres are a unique ecosystem of shifting sand ridges, dense shrub thickets, temporary pools, and sound side habitats.

At a mile long and up to 12,000 feet wide, 110 to 140 feet above sea level, the Ridge forms the tallest "medano" (the geological word for a large isolated hill of sand, also called a "transverse dune") on the east coast. It was once thought to be caused by the early colonists, destroying the natural cover of the banks with logging and stock grazing. Today, though geologists still disagree about some points in their formation, it seems certain that these huge bare sand hills have been here for thousands, not hundreds, of years. Today the Ridge is actually two great dunes, one lower to the east, parallel to Rt. 158, and the other, higher, beyond it.

What do you do with a vast hill of sand? We suggest a walk first of all. Park in the lot north of the Ridge (a hundred yards north of the MP 12 marker) and walk through scrub to the dunes. When we first climbed it the day was foggy, and the dunes seemed an endless desert, somewhere unearthly -- Mars, perhaps. When the wind blows, as it almost always does here, long streamers of sand writhe Sahara-like from the crests. You may see the hang gliding confraternity in action, hanging almost motionless or engaging in great kite-like swoops. From the top of the dunes you can see both sea and sound, and far up and down the Banks. It's a great place for photographs, for walking around barefoot, and for studying the strange patterns the wind sculpts in the sand.

The park is run from a small gray shingled building near the northern parking lots. This is where to get you permits, hang gliders; you must check in at the office, but there's no fee. Maps are available here outlining the areas where gliding is permitted, and they're also useful for the casual hiker. During summer, the rangers offer a series

NAGS HEAD 85

Glenn Eure

cordially invites you to experience his
Ghost Fleet ART GALLERY
where tradition and the avant garde converge.

This versatile artist expresses his unique sense of artistic adventure in collagraphs, etchings, woodblock prints, paintings, drawings, and carvings on a variety of themes. The gallery also features one-person shows and special exhibitions, an art lecture series and museum quality custom framing.

From nautical...

to the abstract...

THE PLACE FOR THE ARTS
Glenn Eure's Ghost Fleet GALLERY

210 East
Driftwood St.
Milepost 10½-
Between the
Highways
Nags Head, NC
27959

919-441-6584

of natural history programs here; they last from an hour to an hour and a half. Call 441-7132 for a schedule. There are also roofed picnic shelters for a leisurely lunch.

A self-guided 1 1/2-mile nature trail was dedicated in 1989. The trail starts from the southwest corner of the parking lots. It proceeds to and returns from Roanoke Sound via 14 marked posts. This trail is strong on plant identification (persimmon, bayberry, Virginia creeper, wild grapes, black cherry) and on animal tracks, trails and spoor (fox, raccoon, white tailed deer, racerunner lizard, antlions, opussums, hognosed snakes). It takes about 1 1/2 hours to walk at a leisurely pace. Wear shoes (there are sand spurs). Not recommended for the handicapped. Pick up a brochure at the visitor center to explain and illustrate the tracks.

A new natural history museum is planned for 1990.

A safety feature installed by D.O.T. in 1987 at the Ridge was the crosswalk stoplight. When you're crossing the 158 Bypass to get to Kitty Hawk Kites and other shops, use it. Don't try to dodge the heavy traffic in this area on your own. We recommend approaching the park from the north (visitor center) rather than this way.

OLD NAGS HEAD

Rt. 158 Bypass, MP 12

Like most of the Banks towns, Nags Head was originally a small sound side community, and Old Nags Head is the remnant of that village. Just south of Jockey's Ridge you'll note a narrow road leading west. It's worth a short drive to follow its winding path back to the sound, a five-minute trip to see some classic old-style Banks homes. One is even built on pilings out into the Bay. Beware of the gulls -- there are oyster beds out in the sound shallows, and we once had our car hit with one the gulls wanted to open!

OUTER BANKS MEDICAL CENTER

MP 11, 158 Bypass   441-7111

Okay, so it's not an *attraction* -- that is, until you need it. But we want you to know it's there. OB Medical is a family and emergency medical practice, a not-for-profit branch of Chesapeake General Hospital. Appointments can be made for between 9 and 5 Mon.-Fri., 9 - 12 Saturday, and emergency care is available 24 hours a day at the emergency room on the right side of the building. There's a helo pad for Dare County Emergency Services, flying to nearby hospitals. Laboratory and X-ray facilities; referrals to local specialists. Note: some readers reported difficulty finding OB Medical. Remember it's not on Rt. 158, but down Barnes Street (in the direction of the sound) about 1/3 mile (700 meters) from the Bypass road itself. They've put up new signs and they help.

REARVIEW MIRROR

Between the Highways, MP 11   441-2277

Next to Galleon Esplanade

Think back to the first car you ever owned, the car you took on your honeymoon, the cars you've seen in old movies and wished you had. These are the cars you'll see at the Rearview Mirror, a museum of automobilery that already is becoming nationally known. The white building's head-turning exterior sculpture is by Jude LeBlanc of Kitty Hawk. It prepares you well for the interior! There's a 1904 Caddy, a 1963 Corvette, a 1957 Thunderbird, a 1914 Hupmobile, a 1955 Messerschmitt, to name a few on display at time of writing (the museum frequently exchanges cars with the other location in Ann Arbor, to keep the show new). All told, eight generations of cars are on display with special features highlighted, and information explaining the influence our society had on the cars, and vice versa. It's a place that every member of the family will enjoy. Don't wait for a rainy day to visit -- it's worth a trip any day.

The average tour lasts 30-35 minutes and is guided. The cars are spotless. The mood's enhanced with memorabilia, music, toy cars, a book room, and two video rooms. All are included in the admission fee.

The Mirror is open daily. In season hours run from 10 - 9, Mon- Sat, 10 - 6 on Sundays; and they're open off-season too. Admission is $5.00 for adults, $2.00 for kids aged 6-12, under 6 free. Accessible to handicapped. Special rates for groups in advance (call) and AAA members.

GALLERY ROW

Between the highways, MP 10 1/2

For several years, Gallery Row was a Soho-style covey of artists, with seven or eight studios all within a block or two of each other. We're disappointed that this cooperative effort to establish an art community hasn't held together. Most of the artists that were part of Gallery Row are still on the Outer Banks, and they still successfully make a living from their art...they've just gone off to do it in other neighborhoods. Three studio/galleries remain, however, and they are worth a morning or afternoon of your time if you enjoy art.

Glenn Eure's Ghost Fleet Gallery, 441-6584, is a busy place all year. It's become the unofficial center for many cultural happenings on the Outer Banks. Glenn hosts the annual Frank Stick Show each February and opens his gallery for poetry readings, lectures and one-artist shows throughout the year. Hardly a month goes by without something interesting happening at the Ghost Fleet.

Glenn is an interesting character in his own right. You might find him doing an ice carving in his parking lot or sketching and chatting with visitors. The chances are good, if you spend much time at the Gallery, you'll meet him. The Ghost Fleet is a showcase for his own work, which spans a range of styles, subjects and media, but it often takes a back seat to the interesting -- and frequent -- special shows he allows to take over his main gallery. The Ghost Fleet Gallery is open all year, but hours vary off season.

Right across the street is **Jewelry by Gail**, 441-5387. The name sounds like a conventional retail store, but don't be fooled. Gail Kowalski is a designer-goldsmith who has won national recognition for her creations in precious metals and stones.

In 1987, she opened a new studio and gallery in the same location as her old shop. The gallery showcases a most unusual amethyst crystal chandelier, created especially for the shop by Michael Fornadley, a Pennsylvania artist. It's worth a stop just to see it. Gail and her staff won't mind at all.

While the gallery does offer a few standard pieces, the bulk of Gail's jewelry falls into the "wearable art" category. Everything is created in the studio by Gail and her assistant, Erik Peterson. Closed during January.

The third gallery left in this area is the **Morales Gallery**, 441-6484, now owned by Mitch and Christine Lively. Vivian and Jesse Morales, founders of the gallery, have retired, although the gallery still carries some of their paintings.

The gallery recently expanded. Prints have been moved from an upstairs room to a building on the Beach Road, making more room for original art and photography. The number of artists exhibiting at Morales varies, according to Mitch, but the number lies somewhere around 100, with most being local artists or artists who vacation on the Banks regularly. A few of the better known local names are Jim Wood, Chris Haltigan, Steve Andrus and James Melvin. A photography exhibit changes regularly and features work from well-known local and national photographers.

Beauties & Beasts

Fourteen pure white diamonds, the beauties, woven together in platinum with ten dazzling golden diamonds, the beasts. Wearable art from

JEWELRY BY GAIL, INC.™
Designer Goldsmiths
207 Driftwood Street
Nags Head, NC 27959
919-441-5387

Morales Gallery carries a nice cross section of work and, while subject matter is primarily beach and wild life oriented, the styles vary enough to make for interesting browsing. They offer framing services and duck stamp prints are sold at the Print Gallery. They are open all year and have two other locations to serve the artistic-minded among you, on the beach road at MP 10 1/2 and in Scarborough Faire in Duck.

NAGS HEAD
RECREATION

HANG GLIDING

They swoop, they bank, they dart and dive; they hover, circle, ascend and descend with the easy grace of gulls. The brilliantly-colored wings flash and glow in the brilliant Banks sunlight. Wind, sand, and sun -- that's hang gliding, one of the country's newest sports. And Jockey's Ridge, only a few miles from where men first flew at Kill Devil Hill, is its national center.

Hang gliding's roots go back beyond the Wrights -- perhaps to Lilienthal, who was killed flying a glider not unlike these, or even farther back, to the first person who launched a kite. But its modern revival is a direct spinoff of the American space program. Francis M. Rogallo, a NASA engineer who now lives in Southern Shores, developed the flexible Rogallo Wing in order to bring down space capsules. Though the parachute finally won out, light mylar-and-aluminum-tubing gliders began to appear in the hands of sport fliers in the early '70s, and now the sport is booming.

"Basically, it's flying in its purest form," said John Harris, president of Kitty Hawk Kites. "It's as close as you can get to flying as the birds do. No noise, no engines, and the wind in your face." The novice hang glider begins with the basics, gliding down from a higher place to a lower, but soon learns to make use of the same thermals and ridge lift air currents that birds use in order to extend their powerless flights.

You can't learn to hang glide from a book, but to give you some idea of what the sport entails, here is a brief description of the sequence of events in beginning and controlling a glide.

The flier is attached at his or her waist to the center of gravity of the wing, at its midpoint. In front of him is a triangular metal control bar. The flight is begun downhill into the wind, with a good run to get up airspeed. The glider will begin to lift as it gains speed and will quickly leave the ground.

From here on, its attitude and direction is controlled by the pilot. Shifting the weight of one's body to the right dips the right wing and the glider will turn to the right. Moving the control bar forward or back with the hands causes the center of gravity to move and the kite's nose to pitch up or down. When the pilot runs out of hill or wind, and it's time for a landing, he comes in low into the wind and pushes the control bar out, causing the glider to stall; and, if he's skillful, drops neatly to his feet in a perfect stand up landing.

It's a fairly safe sport, though less so than bowling; the most common injury is a broken arm. Accident rates are about three- tenths of one percent. One fatality has been recorded on Jockey's Ridge as a result of hang gliding. Crash helmets are recommended.

In the mid-seventies, a natural evolution of this form of flying took place when experimenters began attaching chain saw engines to hang gliders. Today complete "ultralight aircraft," weighing two hundred pounds complete with specialized two-stroke-cycle engines, are available for advanced flyers. Still foot- launchable, these unlicensed flying machines are unregulated by the FAA, and offer the same kinds of thrills Wilbur and Orville used to get.

Ultralights, however, are less often seen around Kitty Hawk these days than the "conventional" hang glider.

And the sport continues to develop. The last few years have seen the introduction of truck towing. In this concept, glider and pilot are tethered to the back of a pickup truck. A hydraulically-regulated winch permits the glider to ascend after the truck reaches the glider's flying speed. The pilot can ascend up to 2000 feet and can cut loose from the tow line at any time. KHK has applied this system in tandem training, where student and instructor can ascend together and can do 10-15 flights a day instead of two or three.

According to Ralph Buxton, most hang gliding enthusiasts today tend to be in good physical shape, coming to the sport from sailing, bicycling, backpacking, surfing, parachuting, and other "risk sports." The students are more varied, but tend, he says, to be extroverts, and "a cut above average in intelligence, personality, and fitness." You can take a look or mingle with them year round in the lot back of Kitty Hawk Kites or aloft over Jockey's Ridge.

Season? There really isn't any; people fly here year round. But winter weather is less pleasant (although, as the Wrights found out, the winds are stronger). For that reason, the best weather is considered to be from mid-March to mid-November.

Who said that man will never fly?

KITTY HAWK KITES/KITTY HAWK SPORTS/KITTY HAWK CONNECTION

Rt. 158 Bypass, MP 13   KHS 441-6800

KHK 441-4124

So far, at least, KHK is the only complex to service the hang gliding crowd, and its location across Rt. 158 from Jockey's Ridge makes it the center of activity. The present structure, with its dramatically soaring observation tower, is hard to miss. KHK handles gliders, of course -- all the major manufacturers, new and used, from a few hundred dollars up to $2500 or more for an advanced new machine. The retail stores handle kites, flying toys, art, harnesses and other gear, books, t-shirts and other flying- related items. Windsocks are still popular.

The focus of activity at KHK, though, is on flying, and training others to fly. Hang gliding is self-regulated; you don't need any sort of a license or training or permit. But unless you're after a broken arm (or neck), it's the better part of valor to sign up for a KHK course. The beginning lesson is only $55.00, lasts for three hours, and gives

NAGS HEAD SOUTH

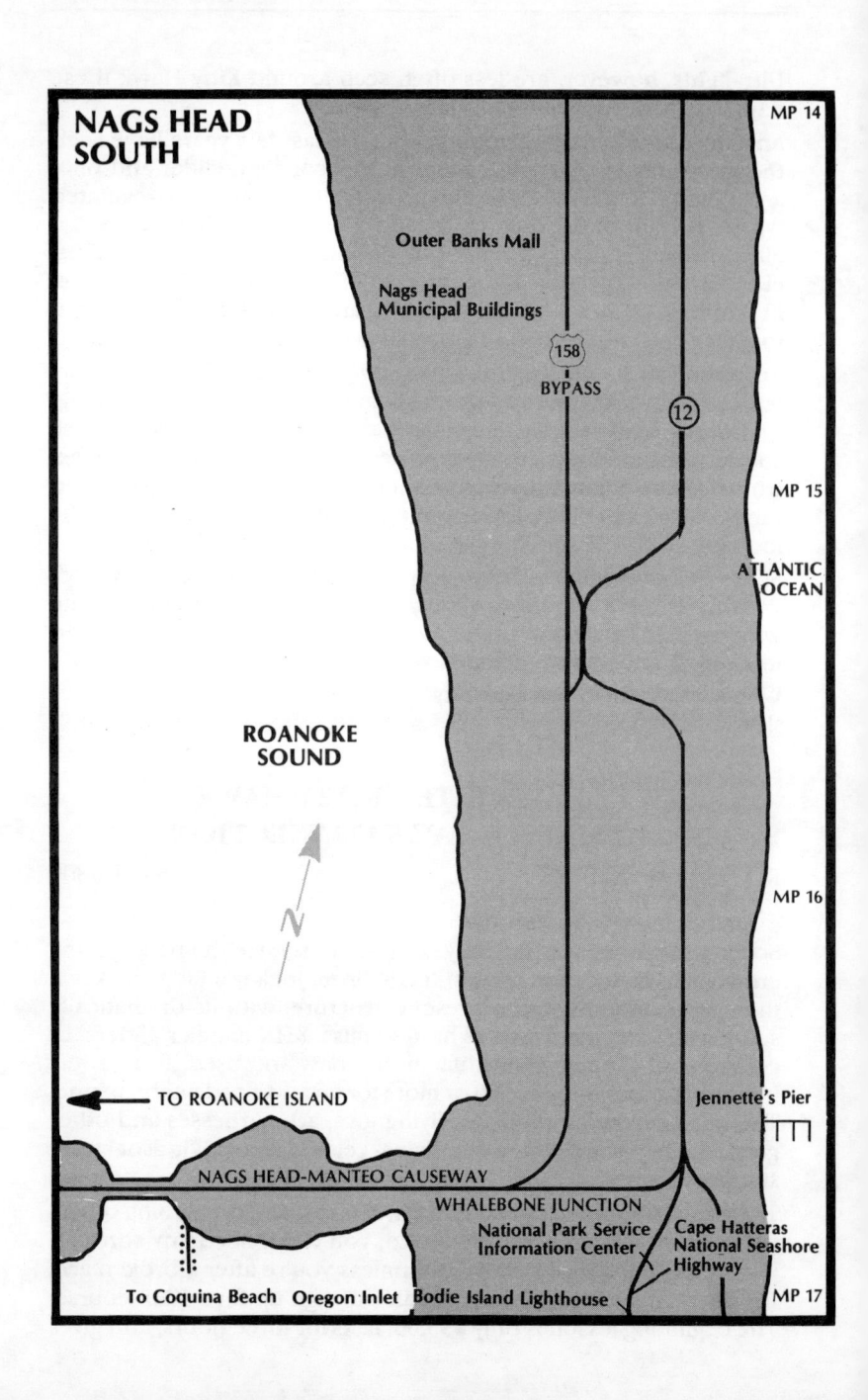

MP 14

Outer Banks Mall

Nags Head Municipal Buildings

(158) BYPASS

(12)

MP 15

ATLANTIC OCEAN

ROANOKE SOUND

N

MP 16

← TO ROANOKE ISLAND

Jennette's Pier

NAGS HEAD-MANTEO CAUSEWAY

WHALEBONE JUNCTION

National Park Service Information Center

Cape Hatteras National Seashore Highway

To Coquina Beach Oregon Inlet Bodie Island Lighthouse

MP 17

you five flights. Advanced and Fledgling courses go farther, teaching you the techniques of flying higher, farther, and more skillfully. Call for reservations; the courses are given year round.

Next door to KHK is Kitty Hawk Sports. This shop concentrates on water and wind sports. Boogie boards, rafts, Prindle catamarans, windsurfers, along with a top line of sportswear, swimwear and t-shirts. Some featured brand names are Quicksilver, Billabong, O'Neil, Garron, Raisins and Sommerset.

An attractive row of shops connect the two buildings, Kitty Hawk Connection. In these shops, all of which open onto a porch-like breezeway, you can find stores such as Nags Head Pro Dive Center, a print shop, and Donna Designs.

The Kitty Hawk Sports sailing site next to the Windmill Point restaurant at MP 16 on the Bypass offers lessons and rentals in windsurfing and sailing as well as jet ski rentals. The Windmill Point site is a popular launching site for experienced windsurfers and an ideal site for learning the sport because of the shallow and sheltered waters. The site ia also an internationally recognized High Wind test center for Mistral and North windsurfing equipment.

The main KHK complex is open from 7:30 a.m. till 10:30 p.m. during the summer, more abbreviated hours during the off season. The KHSports shop is open from 8:30 a.m. till 10:30 p.m. in season, with shorter hours off season. The Connection shops will basically follow the hours of the two main shops. Hours for the sailing center run from 9:00 a.m. till 6:00 p.m. during the season.

NAGS HEAD GOLF LINKS

RT 158 Bypass MP 15   441-8073

The Outer Banks newest golf course, Golf Links, is an 18-hole Scottish links type course. It has par 71, several pros on staff, and an overall length of 6,126 yards. Voted in the top 50 for the South Eastern region by Golf Week magazine, this course is in excellent condition. Call for green fee and cart information and starting times. Open to the public 7:30a.m. - 6:00 p.m.

NAGS HEAD FISHING PIER

MP 12, on the Atlantic   441-5141

This privately owned pier is 750 feet long and carries all the standard Outer Banks pier facilities of tackle shop, bait, and ice. The tackle is reasonable and the restrooms are newly overhauled and clean.

Blues, gray trout, spot, croaker, and flounder are all taken off this pier, depending on the season and the proclivities of the fish. The pier is lighted for night fishing.

There are game tables to keep the kids happy, and the pier's restaurant, whose special fish of the day is yours (you catch 'em, they cook 'em). Nags Head pier is open year round, 24 hours a day April 1 - December 1. Admission is $5.00 a day adults, $12.00 3 day pass, $30.00 8 day pass, season rate $125/$200 for couples, half price for children.

JENNETTE'S PIER

Whalebone Junction   441-6116

Nine hundred feet long, Jennette's is the longest pier north of Rodanthe. It has quite a history -- first built in 1939, it's been repaired and rebuilt time after time since then. All the normal inshore species are available, as well as bait, ice, and tackle. The snack bar has beer on tap; the game room has about thirty video games, plus pool tables. First opens mid-April; open twenty-four hours a day from mid- May to October; closes around the end of November. Rates are $5/day basic, $30/week, $125/season. This is the pier for shark and float fishing, which will cost you $3.00 a day extra. Call 441-7245 for details and reservations.

OUTER BANKS FISHING PIER

S. Nags Head, MP 18 1/2   441-5740

Outer Banks Fishing Unlimited runs this sea front pier, 650 feet long, built in 1959. Lots of parking out front; lots of blues, gray trout, flounder, croaker, spot and channel bass out back. Pier is open 24 hours a day from early spring to late fall (lighted, of course), and provides rental tackle, fresh bait, snacks, and beverages. Admission $5 daily for fishing, $12.50 3 day pass, $25.00 1 week pass, $1 for sightseers. Season admission $90, or $150 per couple. Special rates for handicapped and groups can be arranged.

NATIONAL PARK SERVICE INFORMATION CENTER

Whalebone Junction   441-6644

On the right side of Highway 12 as you leave Nags Head going south, this booth offers information on NPS facilities and activities throughout the National Seashore. Hours 9:00 a.m. - 6:00 p.m. in season.

Fishing is a pastime which can be enjoyed by anyone on the Outer Banks.

KITTY HAWK SPORTS (SAILING SITE)

Rt. 158 Bypass, MP 16 (behind Windmill) 441-6800
  441-2756

Kitty Hawk Sports runs this waterfront recreation business. From April through October, 9 a.m. till 6 p.m., water lovers can windsurf and sail in the sound under the watchful eye of qualified instructors. They also give lessons in both sports. Windsurfer boards and sailboats are available for sale and rental. This is an internationally recognized high wind test center for Mistral and North windsurfing products. KHS is now into windcruising, and has sponsored trips to Oregon Inlet and Portsmouth Island. More trips are planned this season.

SOUNDSIDE WATERSPORTS

Rt. 158 Bypass, MP 16 441-4270

Soundside Watersports provides Jet Skis, daysailers, Wave Runners, JetStars, Hobiecats, and canoes. If you've the notion, you can rent a small sailboat for a week and they'll deliver it to your cottage. Everything that's for rent is also for sale. A good selection of used sailboats is usually in stock. Hours 9 a.m. - 6 p.m. daily.

OUTER BANKS BOWLING CENTER

Highway 158, Milepost 10
in Food Lion Shopping Center

While Here, Enjoy
Our Video Arcade,
Restaurant
and Lounge

441-7077

WATERWORKS
Rt. 158 Bypass, MP 16 1/2   441-8875

This two-story natural-finish building is the office for renting and buying Jet skis, Wave Runners, Scats, windsurfers, cats, and boats. Sailing is right out back. The first floor shop carries t- shirts, wet suits, and other water-oriented necessities. They're basically open April 15 - Oct. 15, depending on the weather.

...AND LOTS OF OTHER THINGS TO DO...

Nags Head is a thronged, sometimes slightly crazy place to be in the summertime. (Just driving down 158 can be an adventure.) There are more things to do every year, it seems, but there are also some traditional fun spots you won't want to miss. Here are some we've enjoyed.

Dare County Tennis Courts, lighted, MP 10, soundside (441-1101)...**Colony House Cinemas** are at MP 10 1/2 Business and at the Outer Banks Mall. Family entertainment year round (441-5630)...**Beach Bowling Center**, a big new facility, MP 10 (441-7077)...**Surf Slide** is on the bypass, MP 11, with multiple curves, changing facilities, snack bar. Open summers 10 to midnight...**Deep Africa Mini Golf** has 36 lighted holes, with an African motif. MP 11 1/2, business side. Open summers 10 am to midnight (441-5151)...The **Footsball Palace** is hot with teens in the summer. Videos, pool, bathhouse, footsball, it's the premier game spot on the Beach (441-6158)...**Forbes Candies and Carpet Golf** is a well-known Virginia-based candy chain; this location also has a nice gift shop and two 18-hole mini-golf courses. MP 12 1/2, business side (441-7293)...**Go-Kart Grand Prix** has a 200-foot winding level course. Adults and kids both are welcome to drive these screaming monsters. Open summers only on 158 Bypass, MP 11 1/2. Have a great time! All we ask is...please don't drink and drive.

SHOPPING
NAGS HEAD

Nags Head may well be the mecca of Outer Banks shopping. There are so many stores here that we can't list even all the good ones!

Gallery Row is an excellent area for shopping and browsing. See the write-up under Attractions.

You'll find just what you're looking for at the Outer Banks Mall.

- Rose's
- Colony House Cinema
- Peoples Drug Store
- Big Dipper
- Games People Play
- Radio Shack
- Everything's $1
- Riddick's Jewelry
- Ocean Annie's
- Reflections
- Cara's Hallmark
- Professional Opticians
- S & S Candies
- Seawitch
- Mule Shed
- Russell & Holmes Shoes
- Specialtees
- T-Tops
- Holidaze
- Yellow Submarine
- Quality Clothing
- East of LA
- Whalebone Surf Shop
- Planters Bank
- Sidney's
- Outer Banks Cleaners
- Hair & More
- Sound Feet Shoes
- Video Andy

- P & G Laundry
- King's Grant Realty
- Mister Donut
- North China Restaurant
- Tropical Tans
- Outer Banks Animal Hospital
- Lady Dare
- Isit
- Hardee's
- Book Scents
- Outer Banks Podiatry
- Seamark
- Pet Dock

OUTER BANKS MALL

Mile Post 14
158 Bypass
Nags Head, NC 27959

At MP 10 1/2 on Rt. 158, you'll find **The Christmas Mouse**, 441-8111, a year 'round shop dedicated to twinkling lights and Christmas carols.

Nags Head Hammocks, 441-6115, also on Rt. 158, MP 10 3/4, sells hammocks made right here in Nags Head. Even if you are sure you don't want one, a visit to their store may convince you otherwise.

On the Beach Road, Milepost 10-1/2, is **Gray's Department Store**, 441-5143, a local institution that has been on the beach for nearly 40 years. Once inside this deceptively small-looking store, you'll be amazed by the selection of clothing and shoes they carry for the entire family. It may be one of the best all-around selections on the beach -- and at competitive prices. Service is one of their strong points, too. The only slightly negative thing we can say about the store is that it's very crowded. But, what the hey, it's got atmosphere. Their new store in Kitty Hawk is nice, but it's not fun like this store is.

On the practical side, make a stop at **Beach Hardware**, 441-6214, MP 10, Beach Road. While the Ace Hardwares on the beach are excellent stores, Beach Hardware smells and feels like an old-time hardware store. Owner Carl Nunemaker and his staff are very helpful when it comes to ordering parts and pieces of things.

Visit the **Yellowhouse Galleries**, 441-6928, MP 11-1/2 on the Beach Road, where you'll find thousands of antique prints and maps, along with some of the striking work of owner and artist Ann Holland

---

UNCLE JACK'S

"Celebrating 21 years in Nags Head"

441-6928

Milepost 11-1/2 on the Beach Road
9-5 Mon.-Sat.
Sometimes Sunday 12-2

· POSTERS
· ANTIQUE PRINTS
· OLD MAPS & BOOKS
· FAST, EXPERT CUSTOM PICTURE FRAMING
· OPEN ALL YEAR
· *FREE* CAT with PURCHASE

YELLOWHOUSE
POSTERS·ANTIQUE PRINTS & MAPS·FRAMING

Sandberg. The Yellowhouse Annex, presided over by "Uncle Jack" Sandberg, is the place to get posters, prints and fast, custom framing.

The Secret Spot Surf Shop, 441-4030, MP 11-1/2, Rt. 158, isn't much of a secret with the locals and serious surfers. Steve Hess, owner of the store, has been shaping custom surfboards here since 1977. He is usually on hand with good, practical advice. He has patience with the younger kids who aspire to be surfers -- and with their parents. That's enough right there to earn the shop a gold star in our book.

Country Time Cycle Shop, 441-0550, has moved across the street; they were previously located in the Outer Banks Mall. The store sells kids bikes, bicycles for touring and racing, biking accessories and clothing. Owner Thomas Burget, who moved here from New York to open the shop three years ago, provides exceptional service. He also does bike repairs.

At **Pirate's Quay, The Source,** 441-5887, is a well-established jewelry store with a mind-boggling selection of watches. They do repairs, too.

Across from Jockey's Ridge, at Milepost 12-1/2 is the **Kitty Hawk Sports** complex, 441- 4124. See their write-up under Attractions.

At Milepost 13, you'll find **Surfside Plaza**, the first shopping center on the Outer Banks, built more than a dozen years ago. It seems to

COUNTRY TIME
2808 S. Croatan Hwy. Nags Head, N.C.
(919) 441-0550

SALES
SERVICE
RENTALS

BICYCLES
ROLLERBLADES
SKATEBOARDS

CYCLE

Chalet Gift Shop

TAKE HOME A MEMORY FROM THE COLLECTOR'S SPOT

David Winter Cottages — Lladro'
Collectible Dolls — Limited Edition Carousels
14K and Sterling Silver Jewelry
-- plus --
Souvenirs -- Tee Shirts -- and Everything for the Beach

Open 7 Days A Week
6406 Va. Dare Trail
Nags Head, NC 27959
MP 15-1/2

Beach Road

Phone 441-6402

Sea Shore Stuffe

Beach Supplies

NEW HEAT TRANSFER TEES, CHOOSE YOUR OWN DESIGN

Panama Jack Products

Noa by Lladro'
Sterling Silver Jewelry
Sun Catchers
Wind Socks
Kites
T Shirts
Hermit Crabs
Shell Jewelry
Gifts

15-1/2 MP on Bypass
OPEN DAILY · 7 DAYS A WEEK
441-8446

do well, keeping most of its 22 storefronts occupied and hanging on to tenants from year to year. **Hobby Craft Harbor**, 441-7407, is the place to go for handicraft assistance and supplies of all sorts. They have an especially good selection of needlework projects, including local scenes. **Southern Exposure Clothing Company**, 441-3371, has funky, fun clothes and accessories for guys and gals, including hand-painted textile fashions. When you're looking for a swimsuit, plan on spending the day at **Surfside Casuals**, 441-7449. That's how long it would take to try on all the different swimsuits they carry. We are talking about rack after rack after rack... They have a store in Duck, too.

Newman's, 441-5791, on the Beach Road, MP 13-1/2 is an Outer Banks landmark with its bright pink building and giant sea shells. It's one of the real old-time attractions, having opened in 1939. The sign on the outside says museum and they do have quite a collection of carefully labeled shells, but it's really a store, full of gifts and shells and whatnots. You can easily pass an hour or two browsing here, especially if you're interested in sea shells.

Souvenir City

Welcomes You

to

the Outer Banks

At Milepost 16, Beach Road, you'll see **Souvenir City**, 441- 7452, located between The Chalet and Farmer's Daughter, mentioned mainly because it has an enormous selection of souvenirs all under one roof. If you're in a hurry to find gifts to take home, this may well be the best place to come. The store is also well-known for its hermit crabs, and the friendly staff will be happy to instruct you on the care and feeding of one of these homely fellows.

The **Outer Banks Mall**, MP 15, Rt. 158, is the only enclosed mall on the Banks, although several of its stores are in the north wing, which is separate and not enclosed. The anchors at this mall are **Roses**, **Peoples** Drug Store and **Seamark Foods** (formerly Safeway and Farm Fresh). It's not as much a browsers' mall as some other shopping centers on the Beach. You'll find a cleaners, an optician and other service-oriented businesses, along with several clothing and shoe stores. **Radio Shack**, 441-2581, has a decent selection of records, tapes and cds, in addition to their usual electronic gadgetry, computers and supplies. **The Mule Shed,** 441-4115, has built an enthusiastic following of locals and visitors, with their chic collection for casual and dressy occasions. **Ocean Annie's**, 441-4500, has expanded this year, offering an even larger assortment of handcrafted gifts from all over the country -- with an emphasis on pottery and jewelry. They have information on most of the artisans whose work they carry, giving your purchases some added interest and value. They also sell ground-to-order coffees. This locally-owned store is going into its eleventh season on the beach (it was at Seagate North before the Mall opened) and is one of three; the others are in Southern Shores and Duck. **Sound Feet Shoes**, 441-8954, specializes in shoes made for sports and comfort, and you'll find brands like Reebok, Nike, Bass and Dexter, for men, women and children, all discounted from the suggested retail price. Next door, women who wear large sizes can find stylish clothing and accessories at **Lady Dare**, 441-7461. Owner Alice Creef goes out of her way to help customers find what they're looking for.

If browsing through a large country farmhouse filled with handcrafted accessories and antiques is your idea of a good time you won't want to miss **The Farmer's Daughter**, 441-3977, at Milepost 16 on Rt. 158. Owned by local Julie Boyd, the store has earned a leading role on the Outer Banks shopping scene. This is country craft and folk art heaven.

The Chalet Gift Shop, 441-6402, at Milepost 15-1/2, Beach Road, is a store with a split personality. One side has an impressive assortment of collectibles and fine gifts, including Lladro and other porcelains, carousel horses, dolls and jewelry. Not beachy, mind you, but a selection you would expect to find in any good city gift shop

Best Prices & Largest Selection of Shells on the Beach

- T-shirts
- Hermit crabs
- Jewelry
- Antiques & Collectibles
- Driftwood
- Gifts & Souvenirs

Blackbeard's Treasure Chest

On Nags Head-Manteo Causeway Next to RV's · Milepost 16-1/2
OPEN DAILY

---

that caters to collectors. The other side, however, is beachy to the max with trinkets and baubles. Maybe it's to keep the kids busy while Mom and Dad do some serious shopping.

Directly behind The Chalet on Rt. 158 is **Sea Shore Stuffe**, 441-8446, a shop dedicated to the Outer Banks tourist. It has stuff to keep the kids occupied, stuff to help you get a sun tan, beachy note cards and picture postcards for writing the folks back home, Nags Head t-shirts and caps, sea shell jewelry, and more stuff to take home to remind you and your loved ones of where you've been.

The Dare Shops, 441-1112, at Milepost 16 1/2 on the Beach Road have been around the beach for nearly 35 years. It's actually just one store that carries a nice selection of sportswear for men and women. They usually have an especially good collection of sweaters. Nice shoes, too. George and Erdena Farah are the accommodating owners.

A new mall is getting ready to open as we're going to press: **Soundings Factory Stores** at Whalebone Junction on Rt. 158. This outlet mall will have a couple dozen shops offering everything from shoes to china.

Every seaside resort has to have one of those places where the kids beg you to stop. **Blackbeard's Treasure Chest,** 441-5772, on the Causeway is the Nags Head spot. The ten-foot tall yellow octopus out in front named J.R. Squidley grabs their attention every time.

This locally-owned store has all sorts of gifts and souvenirs, hermit crabs, baskets, t-shirts, driftwood, antiques and an impressive stock of seashells from all over the world.

When it comes to grocery shopping, this author's philosophy is to spend as little time at it as possible. To that end, her store of preference is **Seamark Foods** because the aisles are wide enough to zip through even when crowded; they stock almost anything you could want; and you hardly ever have to wait in line very long. It doesn't hurt, either, that they keep the place clean and the staff is pleasant and quick.

For bakery goods and carry-out food, go to **The Chef's Corner**, 441-6042. They have deli meats and cheeses, salads they make themselves (the chicken salad is excellent), and fresh breads and pastries. They also do catering and special occasion cakes.

Another good, but totally different, carry-out place is **Ye Olde Ham Shoppe** (441-6803) where you can get ham, of course, buffalo wings and barbecue. If you squeal like a pig when you place your order, they'll give you a free order of fries. They're the best fries on the beach in my book, and worth making a fool of yourself for.

For fresh seafood, **Whalebone Seafood**, 441-8808, run by the Daniels family, Milepost 16-1/2 on Rt. 158, is a personal favorite. The fish is always good and the service is excellent. Another good

---

Seamark Foods

Largest Selection of Groceries and Wine on the Beach

Call 441-4121
Outer Banks Mall
Milepost 15,
158 Bypass
Nags Head, NC

We Accept Mastercard and Visa

Fresh Seafood
Beer, Deli, Salad Bar
Ice, Bait, Tackle
All Types of Beach Supplies

One of the pleasures of vacationing on the Outer Banks is feeding the sea gulls. DCTB

spot and local family enterprise is **Austin Fish Co.**, 441-7412, at the 12-1/2 Milepost. This looks like the gas station it once was, so it's easy to miss. Watch for the handpainted signs.

If it's steamed crabs or picked crabmeat you're looking for, drive down to **Daniels Crab House**, 441-5027, on the Causeway. They've been in the crab business for over 30 years and you won't get bigger, fresher crabs anywhere. The place has atmosphere, too. From the sloping concrete floor to the large steamers out back and the picking room where nimble-fingered grandmas sit culling the sweet meat: you know these people are serious about crabs.

Peoples Drug Store at the Outer Banks Mall, 441-3434, is well stocked and competitively priced.

Open All Year

Plenty of Parking

Since 1967

Every Season There Are New Things To Discover

In a pleasant setting of tall pines and gardens, you'll find five rambling buildings where room after room is filled with shopping treasures... Spring, summer, winter and fall!

the Outer Banks' Original

christmas shop

IS IN MANTEO

The **island gallery**

Representing over 100 local and regional artists... watercolors, oils, decoys, jewelry, pottery, sculpture and more.

at The Christmas Shop in Manteo • 473-2838

INSIDE
ROANOKE ISLAND

Few names in American history awaken echoes as "Roanoke" does. Roanoke Island...this is where, four centuries ago, the curtain began to rise on English colonization in the Americas...then dropped, never to lift again for that brave small first colony.

What happened to them? Where did they go, and why? To understand it all, to see the significance of this small, still-forested island, we'll have to go back -- all the way to the 1580s.

In those days Spain, not England, ruled the waves, and the treasure lands in the New World as well. The Conquistadors had devastated South American Indian empires in their lust for gold. But they had left North America untouched, except for a settlement at St. Augustine, Florida. The French, too, were active, trying (and failing) to establish colonies in Canada and in South Carolina.

England was not in those days the daring seafaring nation she later became; but interest in the new lands was slowly building, fanned by Elizabeth's refusal to bow before Spanish might. It was Humphrey Gilbert, Sir Walter Raleigh's half-brother, who first advocated actual colonization of America, both as an advanced base for operations against the Spanish and to settle"...needie people of our Countrie, which now trouble the common wealth." Gilbert himself was lost on an expedition in 1583, but Raleigh caught the fever for colonization from him.

And fever it was. Raleigh, almost alone among his contemporaries, seemed to have some idea of the possibilities this vast, temperate, fertile land held for permanent settlers; and he was determined that they should be, not Spanish or French, but *English*.

In 1584 Raleigh dispatched his first exploring expedition. On July fourth -- a date later to be commemorated throughout the land, but for different reasons -- Captains Arthur Barlowe and Philip Amadas arrived off the Banks and began their explorations. They landed north of Kitty Hawk to take formal possession, and were astounded at the profusion of cedar, deer, wildfowl, and wild grapes (see 'Mother Vineyard'). They met the local Indians, who had a village on the northwest end of Roanoke Island, and found them friendly. They left after a month, taking along two Indians named Manteo and Wanchese, and their reports caused a stir in England. In fact, by the very next spring Raleigh had outfitted seven ships and 600 men, getting them to sea in April. Again, Raleigh himself could not go; Elizabeth wanted him in England in case of Spanish attack. Sir Richard Grenville was placed in charge of the fleet, with Ralph Lane as 'Lieutenant Governor'.

Grenville had a little trouble at Ocracoke Inlet -- his flagship *Tiger* went aground and was almost lost -- but he freed and floated her and pushed on, into the sound.

He took a week to explore the mainland within the sounds. The English visited several Indian village, and were well received at most. After a visit to one, however, Aquascococke, Grenville found himself missing a silver cup (it is possible there was a misunderstanding about an exchange of gifts). Unable to regain it, he had his men burn the twon, then proceeded on his explorations.

At last he pushed on up the sound, to Roanoke, and after some time decided that this would be the site for the first settlement.

Why did Grenville and Lane choose Roanoke? There were better sites for a colony already known -- the Chesapeake Bay area, farther north, had much better soil, deep rivers, and better harbours. They may have chosen Roanoke because it was inaccessible to large ships -- *Spanish* ships. Or it may have been a simple miscalculation.

The six hundred men spent the summer building a small earthwork fort, Fort Raleigh, and a few houses. In August Grenville sailed with his ships, leaving "Governor" Lane in charge of 107 men.

The winter was not easy, but more ominous than the weather was the worsening of relations with the Indians. Land and some of his men explored up the rivers of the Albemarle, following rumors of cities of gold, but their methods of obtaining food and information quickly turned the inhabitants against them. When he returned, the Governor, alleging conspiracy, then led an attack on the village of the Roanoke weroance (king) Wingina, killing the chief and his advisors. Afterward he tried to set up Manteo, who remained pro-English to the end, as the new king, but it was evident that English and Indian were beginning to regard each other as enemies.

Perhaps that was why, when Grenville was late in returning, Land decided to pull out when Sir Francis Drake stopped by in the spring. Grenville's relief fleet arrived just a few weeks later and he was surprised to find the island deserted. Unwilling to abandon the fort, he left fifteen soldiers there to winter over before sailing again for home.

High dreams were dreamed that winter of 1586-7 in England, for Raleigh was pulling together, at long last, his colonizing expedition. Led by John White, three ships left Plymouth, carrying 120 men, women, and children.

The first mystery met them when they landed. The 15 men Grenville had left were gone; only one skeleton was found, moldering beside the demolished fort.

The new colonists shook their heads, doubtless prayed, but pitched in to clear land and build homes, guarding always against the hostile and shadowy figures in the forest. On August 18 a child was born, Virginia Dare, the first English child born in the New World (though let us not forget that the Spanish had been around, farther south, for almost a century). Governor White, her grandfather, left with the autumn for England to organize more supplies and colonists.

But war intervened, war with Spain, and, with Philip's Armada menacing England, Elizabeth had no ships to spare for Raleigh's dream colonies. It was not till 1590 that White was able to return, and when at last he landed again on Roanoke, the village had been evacuated, and the colonists had gone -- where? On trees nearby were carved the words: CROATOAN; CRO. But on Croatan Island no traces have ever been found.

What happened to the Lost Colony?

Paul Green, in the last scene of his historical drama of the same name, suggests that they abandoned Roanoke because of a Spanish threat, hoping to stay with friendly Indians of Manteo's tribe. As to what happened after that, many theories have been advanced over the years. One, widely believed early in this century but now largely discredited, was that the main body found friendly Indians at Croatan Island (now part of Hatteras), intermarried with them as they wandered about North Carolina, and survived until modern times in the English surnames and blue eyes of the Lumbee Indians of Robeson County. Today most scholars believe that the main body went north rather than south, arriving safely at the southern coast of the Chesapeake Bay. They lived with the Indians there peacefully, but were massacred by Powhatan when the Jamestown expedition arrived in 1607. No one will ever know for sure.

Roanoke was left to the Indians for a long time after, but eventually, circa 1655, the press of whites southward out of Tidewater Virginia reached the Northern Banks, and families still seen today on the island -- names like Gallop, Baum, Meekins, Tillet, Daniels and Midgett -- settled down to stay. The small population was supported by stock raising and small-scale farming through the 17th and 18th centuries.

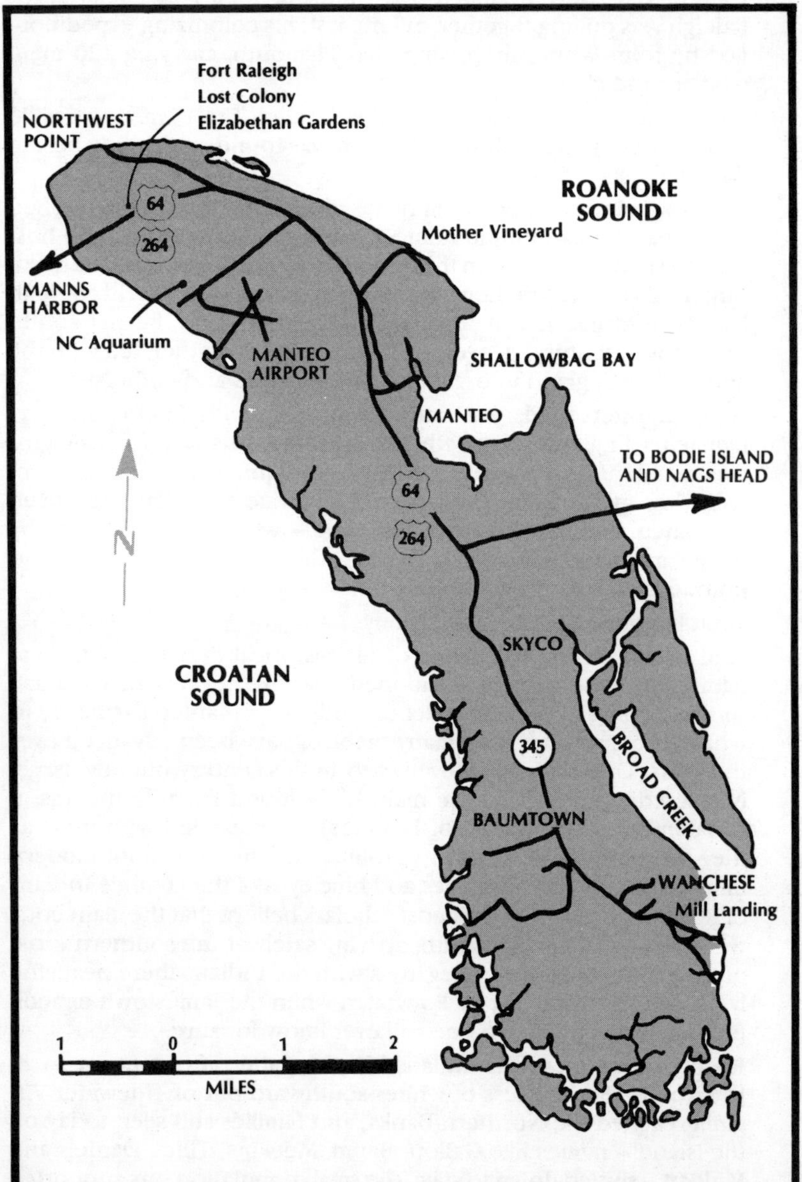
Fort Raleigh
Lost Colony
Elizabethan Gardens
NORTHWEST POINT
64
264
MANNS HARBOR
NC Aquarium
MANTEO AIRPORT
ROANOKE SOUND
Mother Vineyard
SHALLOWBAG BAY
MANTEO
TO BODIE ISLAND AND NAGS HEAD
N
CROATAN SOUND
SKYCO
345
BROAD CREEK
BAUMTOWN
WANCHESE
Mill Landing
1 0 1 2
MILES
ROANOKE ISLAND

The Civil War began the process of the island's awakening with a cannonade. At 10:30 a.m., February 7, 1862, a gigantic shallow-draft Federal fleet, with 12,000 troops aboard, began a bombardment of Confederate shore batteries on the northern end of the island (an overlook at Northwest Point today commemorates this battle). That evening 7500 Federals disembarked at Ashby's Landing (now Skyco). The next morning they moved north, opposed bitterly every step of the way up the island, till a final charge routed the Rebels, who surrendered. The War was marked also by the quartering, on the northern end of the island (west of where the Elizabethan Motel now stands) of some three thousand newly freed slaves, most of whom were relocated off the island when the war ended.

As population increased after 1865, homes clustered around the two harbors at Shallowbag Bay and at Mill Landing. These were referred to respectively as the 'Upper End' and 'Lower End' of the island. Around 1886 the 'Lower Enders' grew understandably tired of being called that and chose the name of Wanchese for their town; Manteo followed suit, incorporating in 1899, shortly after being named seat of newly formed Dare County. Since then both towns have grown slowly, but steadily.

In 1902, Reginald Fessenden, a pioneer in the development of radio, transmitted signals from an apparatus on Roanoke Island to one on Hatteras.

In 1900-1903, the brothers Wright took a ship from Roanoke for Kitty Hawk.

In 1928, a privately-constructed bridge first connected the Island with the Beach at Nags Head, opening the outer islands to development.

In 1937, *The Lost Colony* was performed for the first time.

After World War II, the stabilization of the Banks and the construction of roads and bridges, along with the creation of the National Park, brought modern tourism and real-estate development to the Island.

Today Roanoke Island has two characters. For much of the year it is a quiet, low-key area, where most of the three thousand permanent residents know one another by name, and the principal commercial activity is fishing at Mill Landing. All this begins to change round about May, when the golden tide of tourists begins; and the months of summer are full of activity, especially at Fort Raleigh, *The Lost Colony*, and in the shops and stores of Downtown Manteo and along Route 64/264. Still, though activity is brisk, Roanokers have not yet succumbed to full-scale commercialism. Most of the island is still wild, with forests and marshes covering the land outside the town. The people are still friendly, and beauty still lies on the land during the long humming evenings of summer. As Amadas and Barlowe found in 1584, this might still be said to be "...the goodliest land under the cope of heaven."

ROANOKE ISLAND
ATTRACTIONS

THE ELIZABETHAN GARDEN
Manteo   473-3234

The Gardens are one of the 'must-see' attractions on Roanoke Island. Along with Fort Raleigh and *The Lost Colony*, the Elizabethan Gardens are located on Route 64 north of Manteo.

And they are a sensual delight. From the moment of entry, through the ivy-covered Great Gate, a visitor begins to feel the hurry and anxiety of the twentieth century drop away. As in the formal gardens of the Governor's Palace at Williamsburg, each tree, each flower bed, each jewellike piece of statuary and each gently curving brick or sand path has been designed to a severe and classic discipline of beauty. Horticulturists, gardeners, and history buffs will all appreciate such touches as a replica of a 16th century orangery, an herb Garden, an ancient live oak believed to have been living when Sir Richard Grenville first set foot on Roanoke Island. There is a great deal more to the Gardens than is evident from a quick glance. For example, the bricks of the walks throughout were salvaged over the years from all over North Carolina, from churches and tobacco flues; they are all pre-Revolutionary. The famous Virginia Dare statue, which looks rather preciously and incongruously Graeco-Roman to the modern eye, was conceived after an Indian legend that said Virginia, far from dying, grew up amid them and became a beautiful woman. The statue itself was sculpted by Louise Lander in Italy in 1859, was lost at sea for some years, recovered, then stood in the North Carolina State House before being given to Paul Green to take back to Roanoke. But aside from all the history, the spot we like best was the Sunken Gardens. Its quiet beauty let us contemplate all the tumult of the past in bee-buzzing peace.

The Elizabethan Gardens is at its best in the months of April (azalea, dogwood, pansies, wisteria), May (rhododendron, marcrantha, hydrangea), July (gardenia, roses, magnolia, crepe myrtle, oriental lilies, all the summer annuals) and autumn (geraniums, hibiscus, impatiens, camellias). Hours are from 9 to 7, except that, when *The Lost Colony* is playing during the summer months, the Gardens stay open till 8 p.m. Open Dec., Jan., and Feb. weekdays only (weather permitting). Admission is $2.50 for adults; children under 12, $1.50; call for group, senior citizen, and handicapped rates.

FORT RALEIGH
Rt. 64, north of Manteo   473-2111

The center, historically, of any Outer Banks trip is located some three miles north of Manteo, on Route 64, near the northwestern tip of Roanoke Island. Here are grouped a complex of activities, dramatic, historic, archaeological, horticultural, and just plain fun, all dedicated to those first efforts of the Elizabethan English who found a new nation in the Western Hemisphere.

The Fort Raleigh National Historic Site was designated as a National Historic Site in 1941; its 144-acre expanse of woods and beach includes the location of the settlement sites of 1585 and 1587, a Visitor Center, the (restored) fort that Ralph Lane built, and a nature trail. Nearby are located the Elizabethan Gardens, the Waterside Theatre, and National Park Service Headquarters for the Outer Banks.

The visitor will enter the site by turning north (right, if you came from Manteo) off Route 64/264. A circular drive leads to parking lots located at the Visitor Center; admission and parking are free.

The Visitor Center is a fun place. Probably it's best to start with the displays in the small museum to the right while waiting for the hourly movie to start. Between them, the museum and the 10-minute orientation movie will put you and the kids in the picture as to what you're about to see and experience.

Stroll into the 400-year-old Tudor room from Heronden Hall in Kent. Aficionados will delight in noting the Tudor rose in the mantlepiece, the large eyes and the masculinity of the carved women, the beautiful old oak panelling, the stone fireplace with facings of herringbone-laid brick, and the blown glass in the leaded window lights. The furniture, too, is period.

FORT RALEIGH NATIONAL HISTORIC SITE

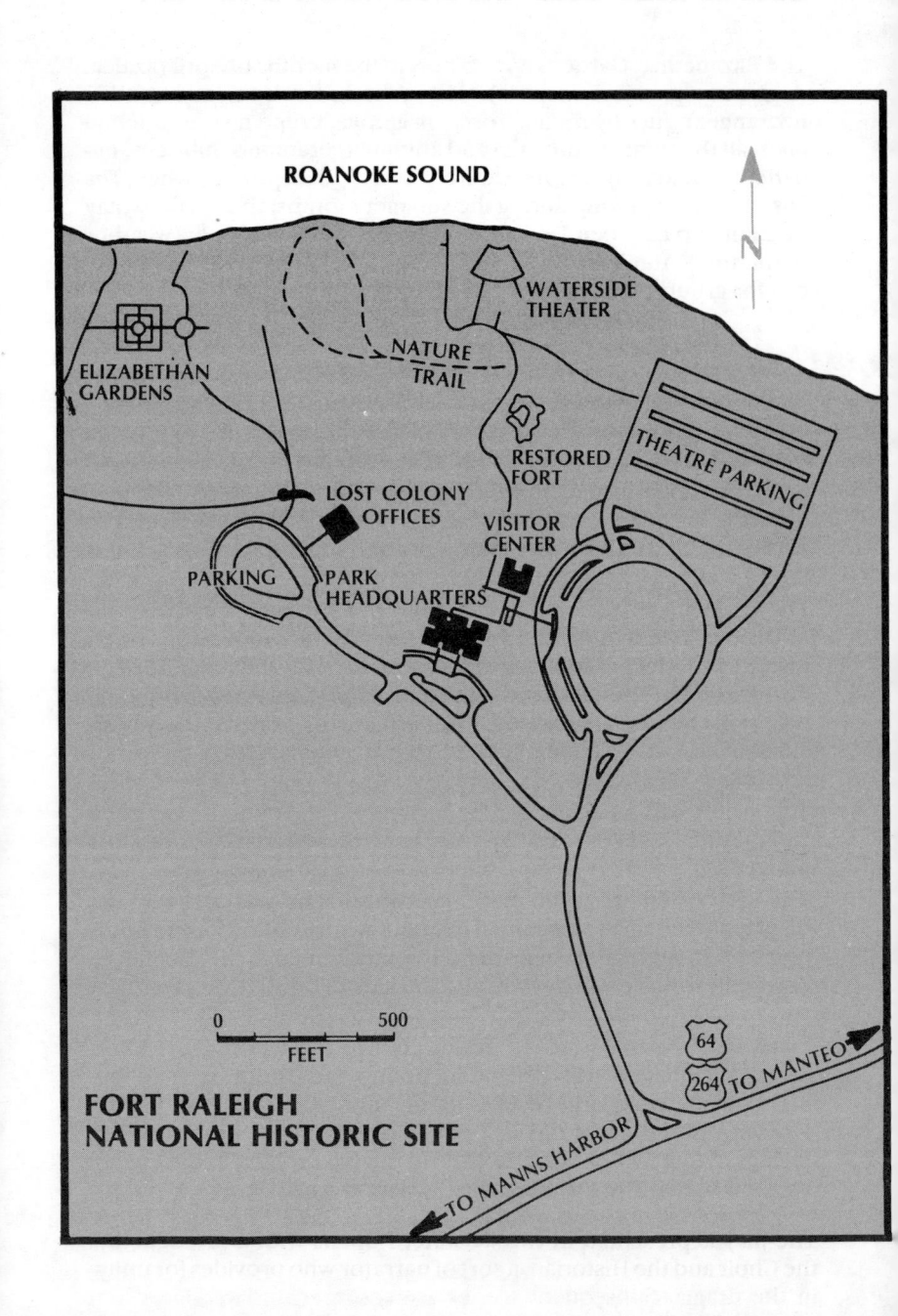

ROANOKE SOUND

- WATERSIDE THEATER
- NATURE TRAIL
- ELIZABETHAN GARDENS
- RESTORED FORT
- THEATRE PARKING
- LOST COLONY OFFICES
- VISITOR CENTER
- PARKING
- PARK HEADQUARTERS

0 — 500 FEET

64 / 264 TO MANTEO

TO MANNS HARBOR

That complete, join one of the guided tours around the Fort area. Depending on the time of day and season of the year, you'll be treated to living history programs on such topics as "Food and Farming in 16th Century America," "Life on Roanoke Island," or "Pikes, Powder Flasks and Petronels."

Sometime on your pregrinations, you will encounter the Fort. It is only partially a reconstruction, for it's on the exact site of the original, and is pretty much as it must have looked after the colonists disappeared and slowly, slowly, the pines and grasses began to take over the scarred earth again. It's a strange feeling standing inside the fort; it's so small, and the woods are so close. After the Indians turned hostile, the abandoned colonists must have felt themselves at the ends of the earth.

Just past the Fort, to your left, you'll find the Thomas Hariot Nature Trail. This is a short self-guided trail, with a soft fine pine-needle surface and gentle gradients. Plaques along the trail point out the native plants that the colonists encountered and tried to put to use. The lower part of the trail leads to the sandy shore of Roanoke Sound, quite near the spot where Sir Richard Grenville first stepped ashore on Roanoke. Swimming is permitted here, but it's quite shallow. There are no lifeguards.

Back at the Center, you might want to drop by the Lost Colony Craft Shop before you leave.

The Fort Raleigh National Historic Site is open on the following schedule:

Mid-June -- Late-August: 9:00 a.m. to 8:00 p.m. Mon-Sat; Sundays, 9:00 a.m. to 6 p.m.

Remainder of year: 9:00 a.m. to 5 p.m., including Saturdays & Sundays.

THE LOST COLONY

Near Fort Raleigh, Manteo   473-3414

The Lost Colony is, in a few words, a must-see.

It has been since 1937 -- over fifty years now. What is it? It's a marriage of drama, history, dance, choir, costume, and music, carried out in an expansive outdoor theatre on the shores of Roanoke Sound. Called 'historical drama,' *The Lost Colony* was the first such work ever produced, the brainchild of Pulitzer Prize-winning author Paul Green.

The play is presented in two acts. Act I opens with a prologue by the Choir and the Historian, a sort of narrator who provides for unity in the drama. Subsequent scenes are set in an Indian village on

Roanoke, 1584; in England, in the court of Elizabeth; again, on Roanoke, a year later; and on a street in Plymouth, England, as the colonists embark, filled with fear and hope. Act II is set, for the most part, in the 'Cittie of Raleigh' on Roanoke -- which was somewhere within a quarter-mile of where the Waterside Theatre now stands -- and follows the web of circumstance that led to the final tragedy: the disappearance of the colonists, into...legend.

It's great entertainment, but it's more. The ending is powerful, and sad. You may find yourself weeping.

The Waterside Theatre is the semicircular bowl where the play is presented. It's just north of Fort Raleigh; bear to the right as you enter from Route 64 to reach the large parking area. As you walk in you can see the waters of the sound over the backdrop. Things to be aware of at the Waterside are: the wooden seats are uncomfortable; bring blankets or pillows (pillows can be rented at the Theatre). It gets cold in the evenings, when the wind blows off the sound, so bring sweaters along even in July and August. Finally, mosquitoes can be vicious, especially when it has rained recently. The woods nearby are sprayed, but this is only partially effective; bring repellent. There are special accommodations available for the handicapped in the uppermost row at the entrance and in the first row.

And with all the creature comforts taken care of, settle back and enjoy a thoroughly professional, well-rehearsed, technically outstanding show. The leads are played by professional actors, and most of the backstage personnel are pros too; and it shows. Supporting actors are often local people, and some island residents pass from part to part as they grow up...but they are all good. The colorful costumes, the choir, the tension inherent in the play itself make it a combination of delights that you won't soon forget.

Now: tickets. All shows start at 8:30 p.m. The show season runs from mid-June to late August and is presented nightly, except Sunday. Adult tickets are $10.00, children 12 and under $4.00, active military, senior citizens, and handicapped in wheelchairs $9.00. Accompanied children are free on Monday night performances. Groups of 15 or more can call for a discount.

This is probably the most popular event on the Banks in the summer, and we recommend you make reservations, though you can try your luck at the door if you care to. You can make paid mail reservations by writing *The Lost Colony,* Box 40, Manteo, NC 27954; or make phone reservations starting in early June by calling (919) 473-3414. These reservations will be held at the box office for pickup until 7:30 p.m.

A scene from *The Lost Colony*, presented in Manteo nightly except Sunday. Lost Colony Photo

NORTH CAROLINA AQUARIUM ON ROANOKE ISLAND

(Formerly Marine Resources Center)
Rt. 116 (Airport Road)   473-3493

Tucked away northwest of Manteo on route 64, by Manteo Airport, is a surprising place called the North Carolina Aquarium. It's one of the 'sleepers' of the Banks, a place you won't want to miss if you have the slightest interest in the sea, the Banks, or the life that thrives in this unique chain of barrier islands.

The Aquarium contains labs, for the use of marine scientists; and a reference library, on marine-related topics. But these aren't what attracts visitor. The display section and aquarium -- that's what you'll want to see.

Once in the door, you'll walk among changing displays on such topics as underwater archaeology and marine ecosystems; children love the "shallow observation tank" with live marine creatures you can feel. The aquarium is surprisingly beautiful. Set like jewels in a long, darkened corridor, the lighted tanks display sea turtles, longnosed gar, ugly burrfish and sea robin, lobster, octopi, and a three-tank shark exhibit. The aquaria start out with fresh water species, shading through brackish to salt water. The biggest is 3000 gallons, holding salt water. The fish are fed every day at 3:30 and you might want to make a special point to be there then.

And there's still more. Feature films on marine and biological topics are shown at different times. There's a schedule of daytime programs for all age groups, including field trips, bird walks through Pea Island, and more; check at the desk for a current schedule. The Aquarium caters to groups of any kind, and can even supply meeting facilities in its conference room, seminar room, or 240-seat auditorium.

It's a surprising place. To reach it, drive north from Manteo on route 64. Turn left on Rt. 116, following signs to airport; the Aquarium will be on your right. It's open from 9 a.m. to 5 p.m. Monday through Saturday, 1 p.m. to 5 p.m. Sundays. Admission is free!

WEIRS POINT AND FORT HUGER

N. end of Roanoke Island

Another of the improvements for the 400th was the development of Weirs Point, at the northwest corner of the island, where the Route 64/264 bridge arrives from Manns Harbor. Empty shoreline as recently as fall of '83, it is now a pretty, easily accessible public beach. Parking is available at the first turnoff after the bridge.

About three hundred yards out (the island has migrated quite a bit in a hundred and twenty years), in six feet of water, lie the remains of Fort Huger, the largest Confederate fort on the island during the Union invasion of 1862.

A few years later, from a hut on this beach, one of the unsung geniuses of the electrical age began investigating what was then called "wireless telegraphy." Reginald Fessenden held hundreds of patents on radiotelephony and electronics, but died without credit for many of them.

For most people, though, swimming and fishing in the sound will take precedence over vanished forts and disappointed inventors. The beach is sandy and shallow, and shoals very gradually, except under the bridge, where currents scour a bit deeper. If you approach in a boat, watch carefully for stumps and old pilings. Picnic benches, a Dare County information kiosk, and restrooms are also available at Weirs.

DARE COUNTY REGIONAL AIRPORT

Rt. 116, next to the N.C. Aquarium   473-2600

Dare County (formerly Manteo) is the major airfield serving the Outer Banks, and the only one with fuel and services (the others, at Kitty Hawk, Hatteras, and Ocracoke, are paved strips only). Manteo has two runways, both asphalt-surfaced; orientation as shown in map. Runways 16-34 measure 3290, and runways 4 - 22 measure 3300, with 500-foot stopways. (Runways 10 - 28 were closed permanently in 1986.) Fuel: 100 octane low-lead and jet "A" fuel available. Equipment: VOR and DME, NDB, VASI, REILS, Unicom U-1 122.8. For runway lights key 122.8 five times in five seconds.

Dare County is the point of arrival of most of those who come to the Banks by air, including some VIPs, and it has the services to match. There are rental cars by B & R, a local company; a limo service; hot sandwiches and drinks from machines; and restrooms. There are also taxi services (see Directory).

Dare County Airport is operated by the Dare County Airport Authority and managed by Mr. John Price. It provides light aircraft rentals, flight instruction, sightseeing tours, and charter services out of Dare County. Call the number above to make arrangements.

Dare County Airport provides service and minor maintenance from 8 a.m. until 8 p.m. during the summer and from 8 a.m. until 6 p.m. during the off season.

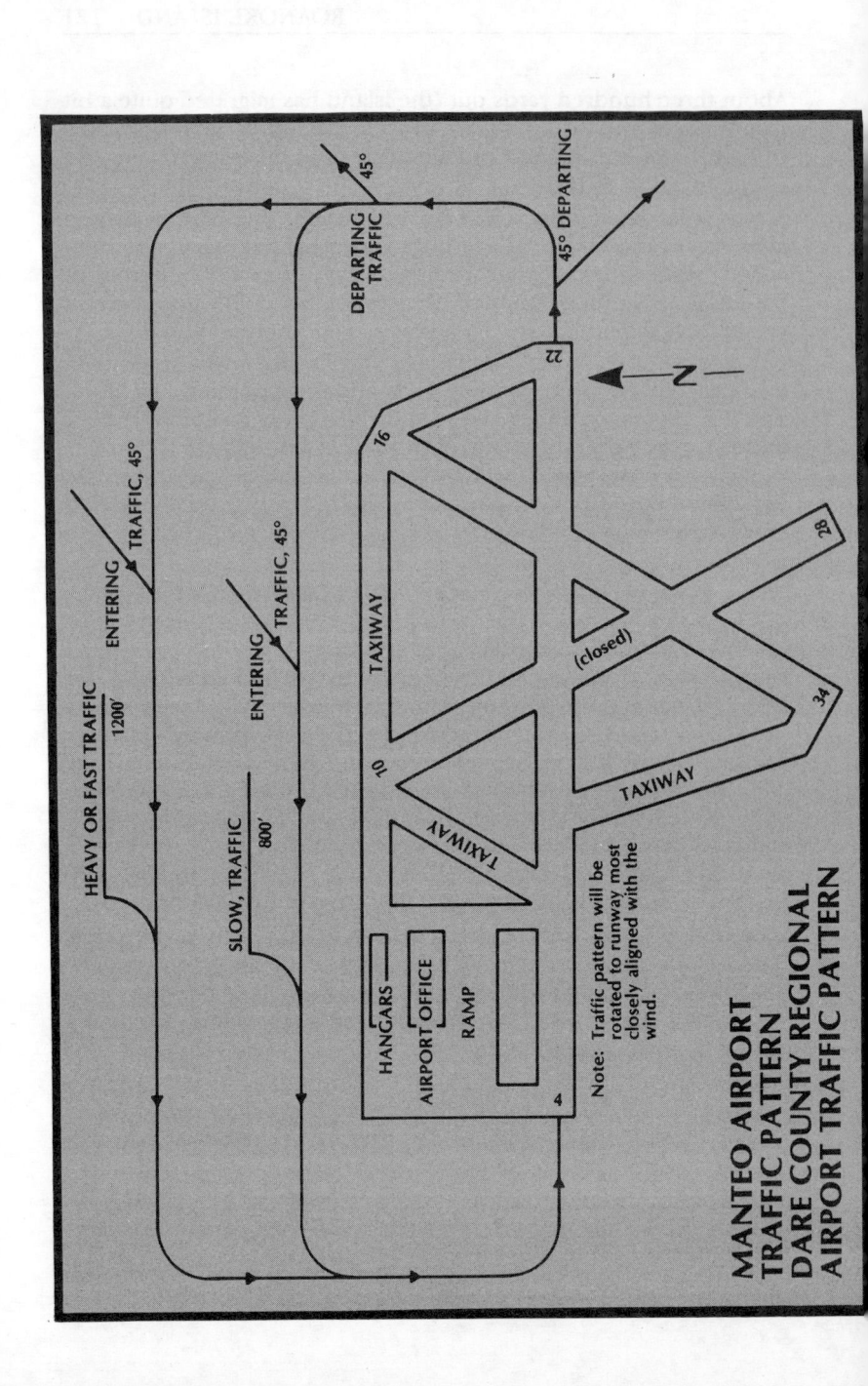

MANTEO AIRPORT
TRAFFIC PATTERN
DARE COUNTY REGIONAL
AIRPORT TRAFFIC PATTERN

Outer Banks Airways has recently inaugurated daily service to Norfolk International Airport from Dare County. The price is $48. It also charters "anywhere." Call (919)441-7677 for reservations and information.

Kitty Hawk Air Tours, with a location here, also provides air tours and aircraft maintenance (473-3014) at a new hangar. Open 8 a.m. - 7 p.m., 7 days a week.

MOTHER VINEYARD

Manteo

'Mother Vineyard Scuppernong, the Original American Wine' is still produced by a company in Petersburg, Virginia. Old-timers in town say the wine once produced in Manteo was far superior, but the Petersburg product did not taste bad when we sampled a couple of bottles. It is a pink wine, quite sweet. If you like white port or Mogen David you will take to scuppernong wine. You can find it in many of the Banks groceries.

All this is a roundabout way of getting to the fact that the oldest grapevine in the U.S. is in Manteo.

That's right: the oldest. You see, when the first settlers arrived here, the Banks were *covered* with wild grapes. Arthur Barlowe wrote to Sir Walter Raleigh in 1584:

"...being where we first landed very sandy and low toward the water side, but so full of grapes as the very beating and surge of the sea overflowed them, of which we found such plenty, as well there as in all places else, both on the sand and on the green soil, on the hills as in the plains, as well on every little shrub, as also climbing toward the tops of high cedars, that I think in all the world the like abundance is not to be found."

The Mother Vine is one of those ancient grapevines, so old that it *may* have been planted even before whites arrived in the New World. Certainly it was already old in the 1750's, as records attest, and scuppernong grape vines do not grow swiftly. Another story is that this vine was transplanted to Roanoke Island by some among the Fort Raleigh settlers. Whichever story is true, whoever planted the Mother Vine, it is ancient -- over three hundred years old, most likely. And still producing fine fat tasty grapes.

In fact, for many years a small winery, owned by the Etheridge family, cultivated the vine on Baum's Point, making the original Mother Vineyard wine until the late 50s.

Despite all its history, the Mother Vine doesn't offer much to the eye, nor is it easy to find. To try, drive north out of Manteo on Route 64. About 3/4 mile past the city limits, turn right on Mother Vineyard road. Go about half a mile, to where the road makes a sharp turn to the right at the bay. The patient old vine crouches beneath a canopy of leaves, twisted and gnarled, ancient and enduring, about three hundred feet on the left past the turn. It's private property -- so please stay on the road.

DARE COUNTY LIBRARY

Manteo   473-2372

Sometimes there's nothing for it but to curl up with a good book.. From a location on Highway 64, about half a mile north of Downtown Manteo, Librarian Amelia Frazer runs a 37,000-volume library with recordings, video tapes, slides, tapes and videos,

meeting facilities, and a local history room that's invaluable for probing more deeply into the lore of the Banks. Hours: Monday, 8:30 a.m. - 7 pm.; Tuesday through Friday, 8:30 a.m. - 5:30 p.m.; Saturday, 10 a.m. - 4 p.m.; closed Sunday.

DARE COUNTY TOURIST BUREAU

Manteo   473-2138

Got a question? The Dare County Tourist Bureau is set up to help, with a large collection of brochures, maps, and the latest data on hand and available to the visitor. They're located at the corner of Virginia Dare Road (Route 64/264) and Budleigh Street, in a low white stucco building. Parking is available in back; the information desk is through the right-hand door, fronting on Budleigh. Open year round Monday through Friday, 8:30 a.m. to 5 p.m., and open Saturdays and holidays as well during the summer season, 10 a.m. to 3 p.m.

In case you want to write ahead for specific information and a detailed and beautiful Vacation Guide, Dare County's mailing address is P.O. Box 399, Manteo, N.C. 27954.

THE ISLAND GALLERY AND CHRISTMAS SHOP

Manteo   473-2838

There is only one word for the Christmas Shop and Island Gallery: *fascinating.* From hundreds of miles away people travel to the Banks for the (nearly) sole purpose of visiting Edward Greene's burgeoning world of fantasy.

Basically, you might say that this establishment is a store...because things are sold here. There, all resemblance to conventional stores ends. There are seven rambling, multilevel buildings in the Shop, but there's not a single counter, display rack, or glass case. Instead there are rooms, room after room, furnished with antique furniture (*not* for sale), and each is filled with wonder.

"We stock a minimum of about 50,000 different items, from 200 companies, 150 artists and craftspeople, and 35 countries," says Greene, formerly an actor in New York City. "And there isn't a thing in the building anybody *needs* to have. So we have to let each product tell us how it wants to be displayed."

The result is mind-boggling...like a child's dream of everything you ever wanted in the world rolled into one. Whole walls are filled with toys, pottery, handcrafts. Whole rooms of porcelain eggs, others filled with baskets, with carvings, with miniatures, with handmade jewelry, with ornaments, with seashells, art, Christmas cards. 125 switches light innumerable atmosphere lights that give everything a magic glow. Imagine, added to all this, thirty-three decorated christmas trees. It sounds like quite a production...and it is. You'll have to see it before you realize what a fantastic place this is. Bring plenty of money or your credit cards.

The Shop and Gallery also contains a Garden Shop (thousands of house plants), an old-fashioned candy store, a card and stationery shop, a basket shop, candles, ice cream, suncatchers, and fun things for kids.

The shop and Gallery is located about half a mile south of Manteo, on the sea (east) side of Route 64/264. Hours: mid-June through mid-October, daily 9:30 a.m. - 9 p.m., Sundays 9:30 a.m. to 6:00 p.m.; mid-October through mid-June, 9:30 a.m. to 6:00 p.m., Sundays 9:30 a.m. to 5:30 p.m. Closed Christmas and New Year's Day.

THE WEEPING RADISH BREWERY

Manteo   473-1157

Did you know that the first beer brewed in America was right here on Roanoke Island? True. History tells us that when Lane's exploratory colony was here in 1585, they made a batch -- to befriend the Indians or maybe to keep their nerves calm while waiting for the next encounter with the "new world" they had come upon(?). In any event, Roanoke Island again is the home of its own brewery at the Weeping Radish. A brewmaster makes both lager and fest beer to be sipped on-site at the restaurant of the same name. But five-liter minikegs are sold to take home.

Curious beer-lovers can actually see the brew being made -- there are daily tours at 11 a.m. until 4 p.m. -- and, afterwards, sit and have a mug or two. We found it to be especially tasty -- richer than the six-pack variety.

Annual SpringFest and OktoberFest events are held at the Weeping Radish, complete with oompah bands and German folk dancers. The festivities can be watched from the comfortable outdoor beer garden.

ANDREW CARTWRIGHT PARK

Manteo

This small state park commemorates the Outer Banks' black community. Born in northeastern North Carolina in 1835, Andrew Cartwright devoted his life to spreading the Gospel among his brethren. After organizing 12 A.M.E. Zion churches on or near Roanoke Island after the Civil War, he founded the first Zion Church in Liberia and worked on in Africa until his death in 1903. Plaques recount the history of the Freedman's Colony on Roanoke Island; the Pea Island Crew; and the African Methodist Episcopal Zion Church. To reach it turn west off Highway 64 at Sir Walter Raleigh Street and go three-tenths of a mile. The park is on the right.

WANCHESE AND MILL LANDING

Wanchese

Don't look for downtown Wanchese -- you won't find any. This quintessential small town is miles of winding country roads, lined with white-clapboard 1920s-style homes, each with a boat in either the front or the back yard. Girls riding bareback on horses clop along the roads, and the people (almost all year 'round residents -- Wanchese is no summer community, like Kitty Hawk or Kill Devil Hills) are North Carolina at its best, honest and hard working and friendly. Small shell, curio, and handicraft shops are open in the summer, and if you're after sand-cast pewter, patchwork tablecloths, rusty old trawler anchors, or handmade shell goods, you can easily spend a day just wandering, looking, and buying.

At the very end of Route 345, you'll find one of the most picturesque, and also most overlooked, parts of the entire Outer Banks -- Mill Landing. Painters, photographers, those who love the sea, and just plain tourists shouldn't miss it.

Mill Landing is a quarter-mile of crowded soundfront that is home port for a small but highly productive fleet of oceangoing fishing trawlers, These sea-battered ships spend most of their lives off Cape

May and Hatteras, fifty miles out at sea, bringing in the seafood that appears in a day or two in restaurants all along the East Coast. Mill Landing is fish companies: Wanchese Fish Co., Etheridge's, Jaws Seafood, Quality Seafood, and Moon Tillet's. In the middle of it all, perched above the booms and nets, is the Fisherman's Wharf Restaurant. Mill Landing is hardly a "touristy" place, but it has its appeal. It's a real work-intensive fishing village and if you want to lay in a stock of fresh fish, shrimp, or scallops, stop at the Wanchese Fish Company, or Ethridge's Retail. Fisherman's Wharf is the tall wooden building with the stairway.

Out beyond the inlet, you'll see the concrete bulkhead built by the State of North Carolina as part of their effort to develop the fishing industry. It was designed to bring the really big companies in to pack fish right here in Wanchese. The current difficulty is the shoaling that Oregon Inlet (under the bridge to Hatteras Island) is experiencing; several trawlers have gone aground there, and many are avoiding it by using other, but less convenient, means of getting to the open sea. Large-scale dredging is necessary, and even this might not work. It has the local trawler operators worried (see "Oregon Inlet"). Meanwhile, though, the visitor can enjoy the photo and painting opportunities. An especially interesting facility is a four-hundred-ton marine railway at Wanchese Shiplift, Inc. It's an interesting sight even if you don't have a hole in your hull! Wanchese Marina (473-3247) hosts trawlers and drop-netters with fuel and a small, homey store. Farther south from Mill Landing, Davis Yachts has been building large fiberglass Sportfishermen since 1984. They turn out over 20 beautiful boats a year. Plant tours are given on 24-hours notice (473-1111).

The residents of Wanchese generally welcome visitors, but there *are* a few common-sense things to keep in mind. The trawlers are working boats, and are *not* enthusiastic about having uninvited visitors aboard. The fish processors and boatyards are also industrial enterprises, as well as presenting special hazards to the unwary, so don't go bumbling around; sketch and photograph as much as you like, but please don't interfere with work.

PIRATE'S COVE

Manteo-Nags Head Causeway Resort　　　　　　　　473-1451
Marina　　　　　　　　　　　　　　　　　　　　473-3906

There have been a lot of changes at Pirate's Cove, and more are on the way.

The marina now has about a hundred wet slips for 15-foot outboards to 75-foot yachts, with plans for more. A quickly-growing number of charter boats run Gulf Stream fishing trips out of here to where the big ones roam; cost is about $700 for six people. Other types of charter, both inshore and sound, can be arranged individually. Nags Head Divers' boat, *Sea Fox,* operates out of here (see the SCUBA diving section for more details), as does Alan Foreman's perennially popular head boat, *Crystal Dawn.* Alan now books cruises from the Ships Store, or you can call 473-5577. June through August he runs two trips a day, plus an enjoyable evening cruise, six days a week; and he takes a break on Sundays. During the off-season he runs one trip a day.

The marina has a new Ships Store, serving almost any nautical need with a full line of marina supplies, groceries and clothes. 1990 is the seventh year for the popular Annual Bill Fish Tournament, run here in mid-August; other fishing contests exercise anglers of red drum, blues, and king mackerel. Tournaments run from May to September. Write P.O. Box 1997, or call (919)473-3906 for details. Rudee's, a restaurant serving fresh seafood and great steamers, is located on the second floor above the Ships Store.

Perhaps the biggest news is Pirate's Cove's growing, residential-marina-resort community. Of the 600-odd acres on the north side of the causeway, 500 are being left as untouched marsh preserves, and the remaining 100 acres turned into 627 residential units over the next three years -- single-family townhomes and condominiums. All will have deep-water dockage. A clubhouse, pool, tennis courts, and boardwalk surrounding the entire development are already in place.

DOWNTOWN
MANTEO

Despite its indirect "Cittie of Ralegh" antecedents, Manteo, as a town, is not all that old. There were only a few houses on Shallowbag Bay, on the eastern coast of the island, when Dare County was formed in 1870 and the town designated as the county seat. ("Manteo" was one of the two Roanoke Indians who accompanied the explorers back to England after the first expedition.) Today, though, after over a century of slow growth, Manteo is the largest town on the Banks, and a year round, comfortable, diversified community.

The downtown area, fronting directly on the bay, has undergone intensive redevelopment in the last few years. "The Waterfront," a pleasingly styled shopping and residential project, and Tranquil House, a 28-room inn built after the style of an inn of the same name that stood nearby early in the century, both projects of Renaissance Development Corporation, are the main attractions of this new look to Manteo. Within the three-story, courtyard design of the Waterfront, twelve specialty shops, 34 condominiums and a first class restaurant are located. With the breezeways and water views and the exceptional landscaping that surrounds the Waterfront, it provides a relaxing, cool alternative to the busier shopping available in the beach area. More information on The Tranquil House can be found in Manteo Accommodations. There are also 53 modern docks with 110 and 220 hook-ups and a comfort station with restrooms, showers, washers and dryers. Sales for the condominiums are handled by Hudgins Real Estate.

Across the street from the Waterfront, in the center of the downtown area, are other shops well worth your visit. Establishments such as Fearing's, the Green Dolphin pub, Manteo Booksellers, the Duchess of Dare Restaurant, the Pioneer Theatre, Tickled Pink, The Natural Selection health food store and almost forty other small-to-medium-sized businesses are packed into a four-square-block area, just like the center of every small town used to be before Henry Ford came up with his infernal carriage. (There's plenty of parking, though, across the street from Manteo Booksellers.)

There's more to do than shop and eat. Around the southeast point of the waterfront stands the town's American Bicentennial Park. Read the inscription under the cross...and shudder at its relevance today. There are picnic benches and comfortable places nearby to sit and enjoy the view.

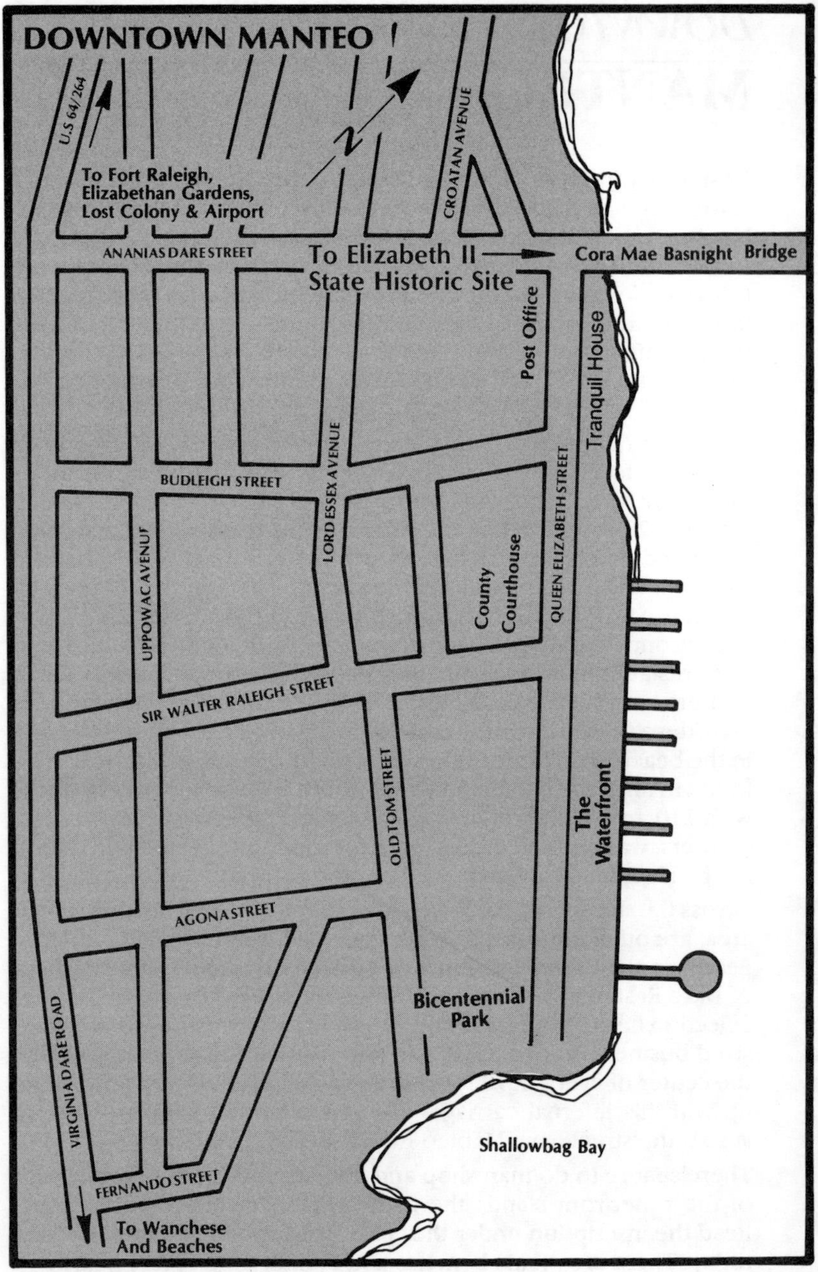

DOWNTOWN MANTEO
U.S 64/264
To Fort Raleigh,
Elizabethan Gardens,
Lost Colony & Airport
N
CROATAN AVENUE
ANANIAS DARE STREET
To Elizabeth II
State Historic Site
Cora Mae Basnight Bridge
Post Office
Tranquil House
BUDLEIGH STREET
LORD ESSEX AVENUE
QUEEN ELIZABETH STREET
UPPOWAC AVENUE
County
Courthouse
SIR WALTER RALEIGH STREET
OLD TOM STREET
The
Waterfront
AGONA STREET
Bicentennial
Park
VIRGINIA DARE ROAD
Shallowbag Bay
FERNANDO STREET
To Wanchese
And Beaches

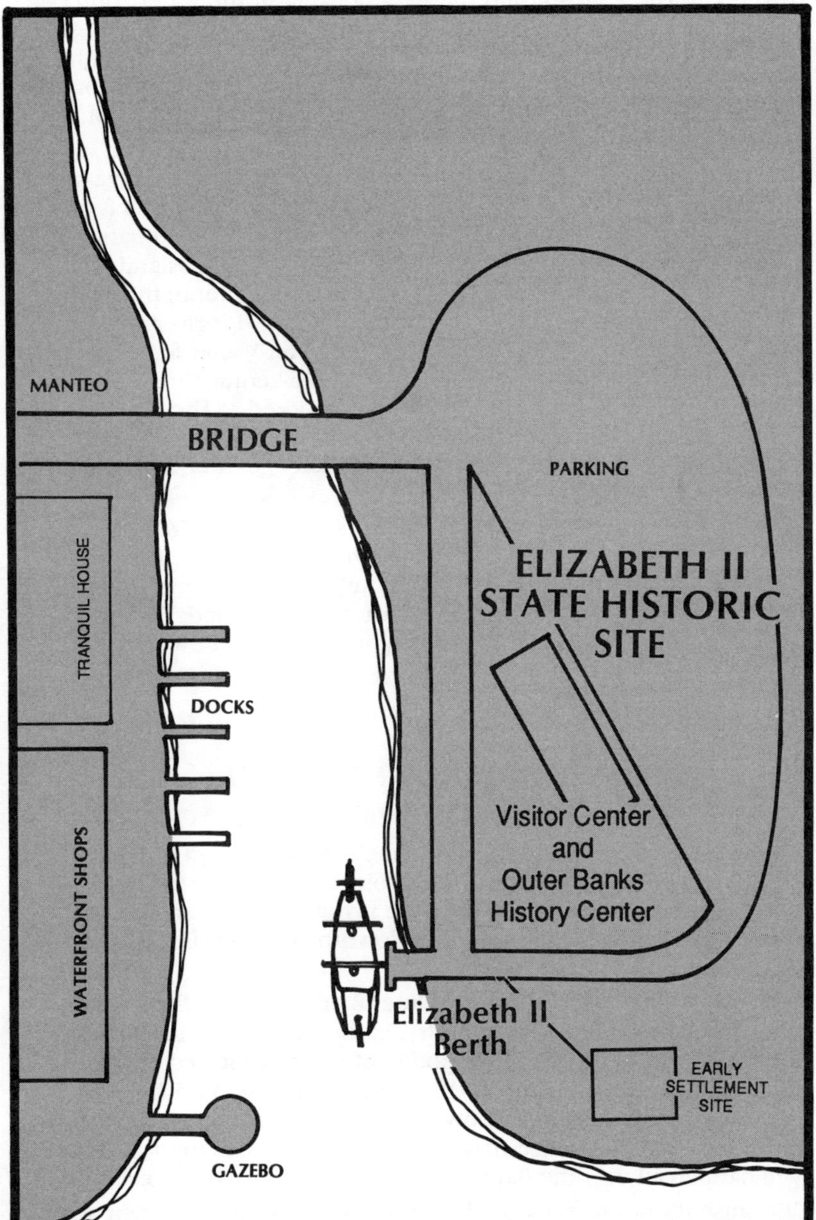
MANTEO
BRIDGE
PARKING
TRANQUIL HOUSE
DOCKS
ELIZABETH II
STATE HISTORIC
SITE
Visitor Center
and
Outer Banks
History Center
WATERFRONT SHOPS
Elizabeth II
Berth
EARLY
SETTLEMENT
SITE
GAZEBO

Turning north, you will find the new docking of the waterfront a pleasant place to stroll, sit on weathered benches, and take pictures. The Four Hundredth anniversary of the Roanoke Voyages brought the *Elizabeth II* to her mooring across Dough's Creek; more about her in a moment. A bit farther north is the municipal parking lot, a public boat ramp, and the Manteo post office.

The relaxed, small-town atmosphere typical of Manteo in the years we have known it picked up quite a lot during Dare County's four-year-long commemoration of the Roanoke voyages (see "Roanoke Island"). During these celebration years visitors to the island, and to the town, found a lot of new construction and a lot of things to do. Several downtown streets were resurfaced with river rock. A boat construction way was built at the end of Sir Walter Street, and the *Elizabeth II*, a full-size reproduction of a 16-century English sailing ship, was launched there in 1983; it is moored at The Elizabeth II State Historic Site (see "Elizabeth II"). Be sure and head across the bridge and take in the Visitor's Center, History Center, and beach there.

If, as most visitors do, you reach the Banks via Route 158, you can find Manteo by continuing south till you reach Whalebone Junction. Turn right there on Route 64/264. Continue across both bridges and the causeway and turn right again at the T at its end. Turn right at either of the town's first two stoplights to go downtown.

We think you'll like Manteo, and make friends there. We certainly have.

PERSPECTIVE: DOWNTOWN IN YEARS TO COME

To gain some perspective on where the downtown area is headed, we talked with Jerry Workman, the project manager for the Renaissance Development Corporation, the privately-held company that owns Waterfront and several other downtown properties. He had this to say.

"The main thing we feel about the Outer Banks is that it's finally been discovered by the rest of the country. In the past four years I've seen a transformation from a hodgepodge of unsophisticated development to major investment. Not all of this will be good. I hope the planning boards can direct growth rather than just oppose or try to stop this economic juggernaut. Because it can't be stopped. This will happen all over the Banks. And this leads us to Manteo.

"Because it's not directly on the ocean, Manteo has a different appeal. I see it as supporting the beach, in that many people who will service it will need a year round place to live. And so Manteo will inherit a great many of the new permanent residents. It now has the nucleus of a small town, but it's never going to be the attraction that Jockey's Ridge will be. And that's why we have recently gone into home building on the island, to provide for these support people.

"In the next few years we'll see the development of downtown, but it'll be more relaxed -- quaint may be an overused word -- but without the hustle and bustle of the resort beach.

"We (Renaissance) are not here for the quick buck or the short haul. We're expecting a long-term, stable type of development. Schools, churches, businesses, professional people who like a small-town atmosphere.

"We've finished the Tranquil House, across from the Waterfront; the old Davis store, now leased to the county school board; and development of the old IGA store into courtrooms and the Clerk of Court's offices. We have a 20-year lease on the town waterfront for the Dough's Creek Marina development. The old Fearing site will be developed into more retail space.

"We have so far generally enjoyed a good relationship with most of the planners. Most people here want to see controlled growth. A lot of the things we've done could have been done cheaper, but we don't want to do chain motel style things. We want to fit into the flavor of downtown Manteo, to retain it ten years from now, and I hope we can."

THE WATERFRONT

Manteo Docks   473-2188

The Waterfront is a 34-unit condominium and marketplace at the head of downtown Manteo overlooking Shallowbag Bay. The four story architectural style is Old World, and its scale complements the small town feel of Manteo. With its festive shops, opening onto a breezy courtyard, it is one of the cornerstones of the revitalized downtown area.

The first level of the development is reserved for private parking. Level two contains some 20,000 square feet of retail space. The third and fourth levels are entirely residential. Residents get to keep their "yachts" at the backdoor docks on the Manteo harbor. A ship's store, shower facilities, and washer and dryers are available for boaters' use. The north and south channels and Shallowbag Bay were newly dredged in 1989.

One of the biggest, and we do mean that literally, additions to the Manteo waterfront is the cruise ship *Viking Sun*. The ship will offer lunch, dinner and sightseeing cruises around the sounds. Call 473-5777 or 1-800-262-7471 for more informaiton.

Visitors can enjoy the public areas of The Waterfront which include a dockside walkway, a restaurant, and a variety of shops, including a men's clothing store, several boutiques, a hair salon, a bakery, and a health food store.

THE ELIZABETH II

Elizabeth II State Historic Site   473-1144

The centerpiece of the quadricentennial, moored in the harbor of downtown Manteo, is one of the most characteristic artifacts of English preindustrial civilization -- a wooden sailing ship.

And a beautiful one. Unexpectedly colorful in bright blue, red, and yellow, her hull of nut-brown, gradually weathering wood, she lifts her foremast, mainmast, and lateen mizzen sharply toward the sky. Her rigging is a hempen web of tackle, so complex as to confuse the eye. Her high-sided hull and sloped stern and foredeck lend her the awkward grace of a newly hatched duckling.

Elizabeth II's story properly begins in 1584, when Thomas Cavendish mortgaged his estates to build the Elizabeth for the second expedition to Roanoke Island. With six other vessels, she took the first colonizing expedition to the New World.

Four hundred years later, galvanized by the approaching quadricentennial of that faraway beginning, private and governmental entities in North Carolina began planning for an ambitious commemorative project: an authentic reproduction of an Elizabethan ship, a living and sailing link to the past.

After thorough research of available plans and histories, the American Quadricentennial Corporation, the organization funding and directing the construction, concluded that there wasn't enough information today to faithfully reconstruct one of Sir Walter's original vessels. But there was, fortunately, some data available for one of the ships in Sir Richard Grenville's 1585 expedition. With this as guidance, William Avery Baker and Stanley Potter, probably America's foremost experts on Elizabethan-era sailing ships, designed the Elizabeth II.

The construction contract was let in 1982 to O. Lie-Nielsen, a shipbuilder in Rockland, Maine, and construction began at a for-the-purpose boatyard on the Manteo waterfront. The completed fifty-foot, twin-decked ship -- all seventy feet of her -- slid smoothly down hand-greased ways into Manteo Harbor in late 1983. She is as authentic as love and research could make her. Built largely by hand, her frames, keel, planking, and decks are fastened with seven thousand trunnels (pegs) of locust wood. Every baulk and spar, every block and lift are as close as achievable to the original, with only two exceptions: a wider upper-deck hatch, for easier visitor access, and a vertical hatch in the afterdeck to make steering easier for the helmsman.

In July, 1984, the official opening of the quadricentennial, Elizabeth II was turned over to the state of North Carolina for berthing and display at a brand-new visitor's center and dock, across a bridge east of downtown Manteo. Currently, she leaves the island in spring and fall for trips to nearby towns, making her the only traveling historic site in the state.

To reach the ship, you can park in downtown Manteo and walk across, or drive over the new arched bridge and park on the island (on the whole, we recommend the latter). Once there, you'll find the Visitor's Center with the new addition of the Outer Banks History Center, picnic area, and a shallow, sandy beach.

The Visitor's Center is built after the style of the classic old Nags Head cottages, with cedar shake roofing and wide porches. Inside, you'll find an exhibit area, a gift shop, auditorium, and restrooms. Behind the Center a raked path leads to the ship and to another summer event, the Early Settlement Site. *Elizabeth II* is to the right and the settlement to the left. The site is an eternally frozen August 17, 1585, with soldier's tents, a general's tent, and living history demonstrations of woodworking, ninepins, and cooking.

Admission is three dollars for adults; $2.00 for senior citizens; $1.50 for students; free for children under 6. Group rates are available; call 473-1144. The price of admission includes the twenty-minute presentation, held every half hour in the auditorium, a tour of the ship, and settlement site. Costumed sailors and soldiers explain how the ships of Elizabethan England were built and sailed (in authentic Elizabethan dialect). Hours of operation: November 1 through March 31, 10 to 4 Tuesday through Sunday; closed Mondays. April 1 through October 31, 10 to 6 daily. (The costume presentation is Tuesday through Saturday in the summer only, from early June through August.) Note: the *last* tickets are sold at 3 p.m. from Nov. 1 through March 31, and at 5 p.m. from April 1 through Oct. 31, to allow time for a complete tour.

A statue of Virginia Dare, first white child born in America, greets visitors to the Elizabethan Gardens in Manteo. DCTB

OUTER BANKS HISTORY CENTER
Ice Plant Island   473-2655

To the right of the Elizabeth II Visitor's Center, a new (1988) clapboard addition contains a 1500-square-foot gallery, library, and research facility. The casual visitor will be most interested in the gallery. It displays a changing collection of Frank Stick paintings, photos from the Aycock Brown Collection, and coastal art. The journalist, genealogist, or history nut will want to meet curator Wynne Dough and explore 5000 square feet of collected Outer Banks literature, the largest collection of coastal North Caroliniana in existence. The building also contains study carrels and a reading room. The gallery is open on the same schedule as the *Elizabeth II*.

THE MANTEO WALKING TOUR

For a leisurely-paced introduction to the town of Manteo, there's no better mutual friend than a walking tour. "The Manteo Walking Tour," available at gift shops and bookstores throughout the Banks, is a chapbook of vintage photos and reminiscences of the town as it was in 1900, 1923, 1938. The pictures and stories are woven into a two-hour walking tour. The mile-and-a-half circuit starts at the foot of the Basnight Bridge, and proceeds around town by way of 34 stops, tales, and photos back to the waterfront. It's a relaxing and serene way to pass an afternoon.

SHOP

ISLAND NAUTICAL

Art • Antiques • Collectibles • Gifts

Outer Banks headquarters for unique, original and authentic nautical items — including work of local artists. Located near the waterfront in historic downtown Manteo, North Carolina.

103 Sir Walter Raleigh St.
Manteo, NC 27954

P.O. Box 1399
919-473-1411

SHALLOWBAGS

At the Waterfront Shops
Manteo, NC 27954
(919) 473-3078

A most distinctive shop for the well dressed woman. Upscale ladies' clothing and a full complement of stylish accessories.

COLLECTIBLES, BASKETS, WREATHS
FINE CUSTOM GIFTS & CANDIES
"We make our own Fudge"

Open Year Round
(919) 473-2737

yvonne's

At the Waterfront
Downtown Manteo

MANTEO

Duchess of Dare Restaurant

106 Budleigh St.
Manteo, NC 27954
(919) 473-2215

"Where Locals Gather"   5 a.m. - 9 p.m. year round
Salad Bar • Homemade Desserts

Manteo Booksellers

105 Sir Walter Raleigh St.
Manteo, NC 27954
(919) 473-1221

Eastern Carolina's most complete bookstore
Open all year. Mail and phone orders welcome.

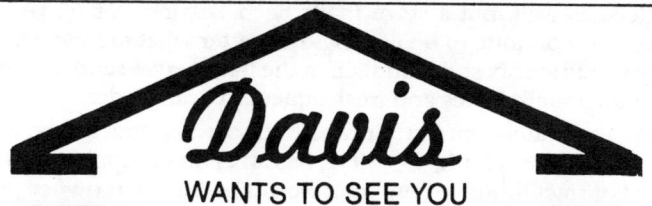

Davis
WANTS TO SEE YOU
"everything to wear"

473-2951
Manteo

441-2604
Kill Devil Hills

ROANOKE ISLAND
SHOPPING

MANTEO

No shopping trip to Roanoke Island would be complete without a stop at **The Island Art Gallery and Christmas Shop**. See the write up under Attractions.

Qwik Shot, 473-5598, at Chesley Mall on Rt. 64/264 is a one-hour photo processing service can be a handy place to know about. Also at Chesley Mall is **Ben Franklin**, 473-2378 (The name was changed to Moncies a few years ago; now it's Ben Franklin, again.) No matter what they call it, it's the same store. They carry a lot of different things, in the spirit of the old five-and-dimes, but this is a different league altogether. Name-brand clothing and accessories for men, women and children are a strong suit.

The **Davis Clothing Store**, 473-2951, carrying "clothes for the whole family" is next door. They've been around for many, many years and have a loyal following. The selection of kid's clothing and shoes is especially good, and they frequently have great sales. They have another shop in Kill Devil Hills carrying formal wear.

A mile or so down the highway is **Second Time Around**, 473-3127, a fundraising shop for Outer Banks Hotline. Clothing, household goods and furniture make up most of its inventory but, as with any secondhand store, they often have unusual items. The nicest thing about this store, staffed entirely by volunteers, is that whatever you spend goes to Hotline, a much-needed community service.

Fearings, 473-5465, on Budleigh Street, has been a downtown Manteo institution for most of its 60 years here although it's taken several turns in terms of what it offered the community. Another change is in the works: The women's clothing and gift items are being phased out, according to Pat Fearing, and she'll be concentrating on the children's market from now on. She wants to change the name to Piglets, as well, but a store that's been Fearings for 60 years will probably continue to be Fearings no matter what the sign says. The **Pig and Phoenix** soda fountain in the back serves sandwiches, old-fashioned milkshakes and fresh-squeezed orangeades.

Near the waterfront on Sir Walter Street are the **Essex Square Shops**. **Tickled Pink**, 473-5951, has an endless supply of gift items and gourmet foods to stuff into the gift baskets that owner Jeannie

Midgett and her staff create. The baskets overflow with colorful tissue and ribbons and, stuffed with whatever goodies you select, can be delivered on the beach or shipped anywhere in the country.

Next door is **Island Nautical**, 473-1411, a fine little browsing store for anyone who loves the sea, opened by Jack and Marilyn Hughes last year.

And next door to Island Nautical is one of the finest bookstores within hundreds of miles, **Manteo Booksellers**, 473-1221. Don't take our word for it: Go see for yourself. Just be sure to allow plenty of time to browse through the three rooms that are packed with books of all description. Steve Brumfield, the manager and buyer, has eclectic taste, to say the least. But the hundreds of people who visit the store every year and leave convinced it's the best bookstore they've ever been in can't all be wrong.

Right down the street are **The Waterfront Shops**, part of a condominium and waterfront renewal project spearheaded by Ray Hollowell and his Renaissance Development Corporation. **Shallowbags**, 473-3078, is a chic women's boutique carrying what could be termed "contemporary classics." Accessories and gifts are also offered. Across the courtyard is **Donetta Donetta**, 473-5323, a beauty salon that overlooks Shallowbag Bay and the *Elizabeth II*. Even if you don't need your hair done (they do women and men), you might consider a facial or manicure just to enjoy the gorgeous view. **Island Trading Co.**, 473-3365, features a smattering of lots of things: antiques, original art, greeting cards and more. Like it's sister store,

Scarborough INN

☆ 10 rooms with antique furnishings

☆ Private Baths

☆ Color TV, refrigerator and telephone

☆ Moderately priced

FOR RESERVATIONS WRITE OR CALL:

P.O. BOX 1310

HIGHWAY 64-264

MANTEO, NC 27954

☆ Separate Annex

☆ Two pots of coffee in your room

(919)473-3979

> **CROCKETT'S SEAFOOD MARKET**
> Specializing in **FRESH SEAFOOD**
>
> 1/4 mi. West of Christmas Shop
> U.S. 64, Manteo
> 473-2912
>
> *CALL AHEAD SO YOUR PURCHASE WILL BE READY*

Island Nautical, it's a good browsing spot. Another browser's store is **Yvonne's**, 473-2737, where you'll find -- among other things -- crystals, collectibles and fudge. For casual women's and men's clothing and accessories, visit **Sidney's**, 473-1988, and **Sidney's Him**, 473-1822. Their selection is so good that hardly anyone leaves without something in one of their signature bags. We'd be remiss if we didn't mention **The Cloth Barn**, 473-2795, on Etheridge Road. Linda and Harry Bridges keep this store packed with fabrics of every description, along with patterns and notions and everything else you need to sew up a storm.

For groceries, **Food-A-Rama** on the highway offers the best all-around selection and you can usually get in and out quickly. If you're shopping for meat or chicken, though, locals swear its best at **S&R** right down the road.

You can find natural foods, bottled water and other healthy things, along with wines, beers, and cheese at The **Natural Selection**, 473-6113, in their new location at The Waterfront.

For bakery goods, try the New York-style **Argyle Bake Shoppe**, 473-1660, just opened this spring. They offer a tempting selection of muffins, cookies, pastries, pies and cakes all baked fresh right in their kitchen on the premises.

There's no need to drive any farther than **Crockett's Seafood Market,** 473-2912, on the Main Highway for the fresh catch-of-the-day. They have all your favorite shellfish, too.

Revco Drug, 473-5056, right by Food-A-Rama, has the biggest selection, but you might enjoy the small town flavor and personal service at **Island Pharmacy**, 473-5801, a family business, just up the street.

WANCHESE

Nick-E, 473-5036, on Old Wharf Road, is the place to go if you like stained glass. Owned by Ellinor and Robert Nick, this classroom, workshop and store, all under one roof, is filled with their art. They make their own patterns and have created several local pieces, featuring the lighthouses and other area scenes. You'll probably be able to watch someone making a leaded or copper-foiled piece in the workshop. If not, the Nicks will be happy to take you on a tour and explain the process -- and the history, if you're interested. In addition to the stained glass pieces the Nicks or their students make, they sell tools and supplies for making stained glass, along with other gift items.

If you head down toward the Seafood Industrial Park, you'll come to **Added Touch**, 473-2972, another local craft shop. It was opened nearly 10 years ago by Maxine Daniels, a friendly local who enjoys telling customers about the crafts she sells. She carries all sorts of things, almost all made locally (Maxine makes quite a bit of the inventory herself). Most of them are useful or decorative crafts, not souvenirs, as such, with a country flavor. The handmade baby clothes at this shop are outstanding.

At one time, almost all travel along the Outer Banks was on sand roads in the woods.

I May Become A Cultivated Man:
NICHOLAS LONGWORTH MEEKINS
A LIFE IN MANTEO

The house is small, neat, one of dozens just like it in the tract in western Manteo. Inside it, wrapped in a vanilla-scented cloud of Captain Black that fills the living room, Nicholas Meekins is sitting back, repacking a curved briar pipe. He is a tall man with a pepper and salt moustache. He's still not entirely gray, but he finds it difficult to get up from his easy chair.

"When I was born? July twentieth, nineteen oh five.

"My father's name was Theodore Meekins. They have a plaque down there right where Pea Island Station was located. It mentions the fact that my father was on patrol that particular night when this *E. S. Newman* run aground. And he sounded the alarm and rushed to the station, and the crew got ready to go out and rescue the passengers.

"Now, I might be a little biased, but a neutral report, if it was given, would say that not only did my father sound the alarm, but -- they have what they called a Lyle gun. They shoot this line across the bow of a ship. And they attach the breeches buoy and bring them ashore. Well, the Lyle gun wouldn't work that night, the powder or something was wet. They had no way of gettin' the line across. But my father -- don't mind my sayin' so -- was the best swimmer in the outfit. He weighed two hundred and thirty-five, forty pounds. I'm not that small but my mother weighed a hundred and twenty. You see why I'm not big.

"But anyway, they had to tie a rope around his body. And he swam out there in that ragin' surf to the ship. And they pulled him aboard so they could get the lines. And they brought the women and children safely across on shore. They didn't lose a single passenger. Now, as a memento for that they gave my father the name plate off'n the side. A board about six seven feet long. *E.S. Newman*. And he had a storage place down in the yard and he had that tacked across there. That was one of the most eventful or historic things that happened on the coast there, at the Pea Island Station.

"That was before I was born. It was eighteen something. I guess it was ten or fifteen years before I was born.

"It was after I was born and grew up to be 'bout eleven years old, my father used to have me to come down with the man who was coming back on liberty, coming back the day before my father was due to come on liberty. I'd go down and spend the night with my father. And once I went on the south patrol with him when he was on duty there. Well, I didn't walk that patrol. They had big horses that used to haul the surfboats around. And so he took me in a buckboard. So he carried a clock with him that they would punch. Your key was down at the end of the patrol. You strike that clock, then at the keeper's station the next morning he could tell exactly when you hit that clock. Well, I went in the Coast Guard myself in World War Two and I was glad to go, for I wanted to follow in the same footsteps he had gone. And I had the same duty up in Long Island. It was a similar patrol to the one he was on when he sighted the *Newman* on shore, in a storm, on that particular night.

"I'd give anything if I had my father's picture. He was, you might say, quite a specimen of a man. One of the tests that some of the men found difficult to do he found easy. He had to dive down in six feet of water and bring up a fifty-pound weight. My father had eight gold stripes on his arm. That was for good conduct and unbroken service.

"My mother's name was White. Her father was Rowan White, her mother was Sarah White. She had about four, five sisters, and three brothers. They all grew up here. But they moved after they were grown. I had a uncle once lived in New Bern the rest of his life, and some of them went up to Hampton, Virginia; but they didn't go too far away.

"I really don't know how my people happened to come here. My father's father was John Meekins. Now a lot of the people who came here, they came from Hyde County, but most from Tyrrell County. Most of the people I knew were from Tyrrell and Washington County. I taught school in Washington County and I met quite a few people who knew people I knew when I was growing up. The short migration was from Hyde and Tyrrell. I think most of those who came to Roanoke Island came when they were freed, after the war. Maybe it was somewhat of a haven. There was a place they used to call Burnside, after General Burnside, in the Civil War. Burnside used to belong mostly to Negroes. And the fellow who owned the best land up there was Ben and Hannah Golden, which was my wife's grandfather.

"I grew up here until I was thirteen. And I was here off and on then. 'Cause I went to high school in Elizabeth City. I was there for about six years. I was here off and on and during the summer. After I finished high school I was here more infrequently, but I never stayed away more than two years at a time.

"The first thing I remember in growing up? At an early age -- I suppose I must have been about seven, eight years old -- when my father, I was the youngest, he took me when he was on vacation once and we went to see my oldest brother and sister, who were living in Phoebus. That was you might say the most eventful trip in that it was the first one I had leavin' the island. They had the steamboat to Elizabeth City, then we'd take the train, the Norfolk & Southern, to Norfolk. First they had a gas boat, the *Hattie Creef*, then they had the steamer *Trenton*. The *Trenton* was the main boat I took going back and forth from Elizabeth City there.

"I went to the Roanoke Academy here in Manteo until I was thirteen. It was a frame two-story building. We had hygiene, history, geography. We had the Riverside Literature and the regular Milne Arithmetic. I haven't thought of that book in years. It wasn't as standardized as it might have been. But I wasn't too far behind, when I went to Elizabeth City. They put you back a grade anyway. It has its advantages and disadvantages. You do a little bit of repeating, but some things stick better going over them a second time.

"We didn't teach the Bible as such in school. The last principal we had here was the Reverend Dickens. He was a minister, but he didn't dwell on anything too religious. Maybe, more, morality. (Laughs.) Growing up here I went to Haven Creek Baptist Church. Our ministers were just way above par. They had been to seminaries and they were well versed in the Scriptures. I tell you frankly -- well, I go to church now and I really find that some of the sermons I heard then were more educational, more revealing, and better prepared than many of the sermons I hear now.

"My mother took me to church. We had the morning service, then we had Sunday School. Then the evening service. So I went to church three times a day on Sunday. I still remember some of the texts that I learned when I was 14, 15 years old. I recall two ministers in particular. Reverend Sharp, from Edenton. And one of the best sermons I ever heard, he gave from the Eighth Psalm. I memorized it afterward:

> Oh Lord our Lord, how excellent is thy name in all the earth! who hast set thy glory above the heavens.

Out of the mouth of babes and sucklings hast thou ordained strength because of thine enemies, that thou mightest still the enemy and the avenger.

When I consider thy heavens, the work of thy fingers, the moon and the stars, which thou hast ordained;

What is man, that thou art mindful of him?

" -- And so on, I won't go on with the rest of it. That was one of the best sermons. But I gave you the wrong man. Reverend Sharp preached a sermon wonderful like that, but this was Reverend Delanie, from Washington County. But we had on our baccalaureate sermon, Reverend John Moore, and that was one of the best I ever heard. And he took his text which I remember from Jeremiah, 48th chapter, 11th verse. "Moab hath been at ease from his youth." I won't quote that. But all the worthwhile sermons -- well, maybe all of them are worthwhile -- but the best, they were in my earliest childhood here.

"The only game I played mostly was we played a little sandlot baseball. We usually had a homemade ball, but once in a while we had a little league baseball. But we only had one, so if you knocked it over in the bushes that stopped the game until you found it. They had a lot up here about where you see the community building out here. There weren't any houses being built up there then. We had almost two acres of playing ground. No, we never played with the white boys while I was here. They played cross town.

"When we had quite a influential speaker here we would reserve seats for part of the white congregation. One of the old gentlemen was quite a close friend of mine. Mister Acie Evans. My aunt used to cook for them. I don't know why he took a liking to me. He ran the Tranquil House downtown. That was the main hotel here then. His son Charlie was the postmaster here for a while. I knew old Charlie and his father very well. In fact Mister Evans thought so much of me he used to have me around in the flower yard as a companion for him. When grown men were gettin' a dollar a day for work, he'd pay me a dollar just for helpin' him set out flowers. Let's see, I was eleven or twelve then.

"In those days a dollar would go quite a distance. When you only had to pay a penny for a postcard and two cent for a stamp letter a dollar would go pretty good. It was like in Depression days. When I first went to New York in '29, down in Delancey Street on the East Side, you could go to a stand and get a kosher, strictly beef hot dog and a mug of root beer for five cent. The hot dog was full dressed with onions and sauerkraut. So you could buy a whole lot for a dollar.

"The first time I tasted liquor? Well, when my father came home from the Coast Guard station on his liberty he might have a bottle of gin. He didn't ever give me any, but I might have sneaked a little bit. Not enough to be noticed, or for it to go to my head. But he would make apple cider. We had a lot of fruit trees. See, my father had two months vacation -- they would come home first of June and stay till the first of August. Unless they had a wreck or a storm, then they had to go back. But during that time my father would have us to farm. We raised everything we need. Chickens, and hogs, and all kind of crops. But he would grind up apples and make a 55-gallon drum of apple cider. Um hum. Now we could drink all that cider we wanted till he put sugar in it. Then he'd put lock and key on it. See, after you put the sugar in it ferments, and it gets as strong as your average liquor. He would save that for his company. He might let you have just a little sampling of it. But it wasn't free like it was before he made it hard. It was very delicious, but it'll slip up on you. You can become intoxicated before you realize it.

"Our farm was down there near where the Hardee's place is -- that takes in part of it. It was all strictly along the highway, over a quarter mile long. Twenty-five acres, fifteen of it cleared. And you had about ten acres of woodland back of you. I would never have let that land been broken up, just in honor of my father. But you know you can't do what you want. You'll always have some members of the family are going to pull off and do things, and they wanted to sell and get rid of it. I don't know what each one got, but I didn't get anything because I was off at school. If I had stayed here and watched things we'd have it now. For whatever it sold for a different one, is worth ten times as much now.

"When I was a kid we would go down there to Mill Landing and meet my father and my uncle when they came back from the Coast Guard, and bring them home. Old man E. R. (Zeke) Daniels' store was there. He was about the wealthiest man in property on the island. They claimed Clary Pugh had more cash money, but old man Zeke had more property. He owned several boats, I think he owned the *Hattie Creef. Pompano* was another boat Uncle Zeke owned. I remember his son Preston well. He used to come by home flyin' on a motorcycle.

"Oh, yeah, they allowed us to go in that store. My aunt and another lady used to cook down there for him. And George Pledger, who used to live in front of us across the highway, he worked with him for just about all his life. Old man Zeke was very liberal, just like old man Acie Evans. I came home some years ago and I met his son Charlie so he said to me, he said, 'Nick, have you been over t'see my father?' I said, 'No, I haven't.' He said, 'Would you go over and see him? He's getting quite feeble. He thought so much of you, I know he'd be glad to see you.' So I went over to see him. He was just a fine old gentleman.

"See, some of the people were just like that. People like I'm tellin' you about, like the Evanses, the Creefs -- one my very best friends was Albert Evans. His father was the blacksmith here. My father used to get him to make all his carts. He always had a nice horse cart so that during bad weather -- we had to walk about a mile and a quarter from my home to the school. But when it was bad weather my brother used to drive us to school.

"My father died on October the thirtieth, nineteen seventeen. He and another man, Kitt Miller, were coming back from Pea Island in Miller's boat. And the engine quit. And the tide carried them out to sea into a storm. They said they could see them from shore for a long time. They were trying to make it back but they couldn't against the current.

"My mother was the finest little black woman I have ever known. After she was widowed she never married. She talked to a lady when my father passed, Miss Ella Dunbar, who was a teacher here, about what to do about putting me and my sister in the right place. We were the two youngest. I was twelve when my father passed, and she was fourteen. I only had one sister and five brothers. All older -- I was the youngest.

"So Miss Ella Dunbar told her the best thing to do was to put my sister and me in the Normal School in Elizabeth City. 'Cause she was getting a small pension from the government because of my father's death, and till my sister and I were eighteen we would draw enough money to go to school. But my mother could not stand to see us go. She found a lovely place for us to board. Mrs. Mary Hargood's. She had a big home then on Southern Avenue extension. I loved her, she treated me like her own son. My mother stayed there a few days with a friend of hers after she dropped me off. But when she got ready to leave it was all she could do to leave me. And she would come over there and get some work around the school, they had a farm there, vegetables and beans. Not that she -- well, she did need the money, but she did it to be near me.

"In fact my first year at State Normal, that was at Elizabeth City, it was interrupted by the flu. We had gone there my sister and I for about two or three months and the school closed down on account of the flu epidemic. They opened up after a few months, but I didn't go back till the following year. I stayed there until twenty-five, 1925, when I finished high school.

"I enlisted in the Coast Guard the 15th of August 1942. And I stayed there exactly thirty-seven months. Here's a copy of my discharge. I was seaman first, then I changed to fireman. I wasn't anxious to go to sea, and I had a better chance to go to shore duty as a fireman. See that there? If you stayed in over three years and didn't come back late or anything you got the Good Conduct medal. Sixty-nine dollars a month. That was big money then.

"I was up in Long Island right after a German sub put those spies ashore there. I was stationed with the fellow, John Cullen, the boy who turned them in. Cullen when he intercepted those spies all he had was a nightstick. And they offered him five hundred dollars as a bribe to let 'em through. Their mission was to blow up the bridge between Newark and New York. They said they was rumrunners. They gave him $480 -- shortchanged him -- and he hightailed it to the station and reported it. Within minutes they had all of Long Island cut off. I don't think they treated Cullen right. They had so many ninety-day wonders. Why in the world didn't they make him a lieutenant? What if he had just put that money in his pocket?

"When I enlisted I was working as a redcap in Penn Station. Before that I had two or three jobs. I worked as a postal clerk. That was during the Depression and I almost starved. I was a temporary sub, I only worked during the summer, and they gave me all the work. What I did was I took the examination for subway conductor and when I got out of the service they offered me either one. I could go back to the railroad or I could go there. So I went back with the railroad.

"I wore these legs out in eighteen years at the railroad. I had a family to take care of and going to school too. I went to school days from nine to three and I had to be at work at the railroad at four thirty. But every dollar counted. Every time I took a passenger to a train, or picked up a passenger, that was an extra dollar. It didn't bother me then -- I could run up and down, didn't even stop to wait for the escalator.

"I'd get sometimes three passengers off the same train, they were waiting on the platform for a redcap. Sometimes you'd make two dollars a night, sometimes twenty or thirty. Some would give you a dime, some would just pay for the tags, for the railroad. The highest I had was several ten-dollar tips. But I tell you the worst job I had was Gene Tunney. He came down the station late, so another fellow, Killer Wiggins and I, we ran down to the train just as hard as we could. And just there in time to put his bags on. You know what he handed us? One dollar! Millionaire! That wasn't even enough to pay the tags. Why couldn't he have accidentally pulled out a twenty?

"I admired Jack Dempsey as much as I disadmired Tunney. When I was in service he was a lieutenant commander. He had charge of us in New York, he used to come around and inspect our work in the sail loft. Very soft-spoken, he never spoke above a low monotone. He may have been a terror in the ring, but personally he was a fine man.

"I stayed with the railroad while I went to Long Island University for three years under the GI Bill. Then I resigned and came home and did another year's work at North Carolina Central; and then I started teaching.

"I taught in Washington County for about fourteen years. The first years I taught at the local high school and the last year I was transferred to the Plymouth high school, and that's where I retired from. The Washington County school was predominantly black. After they integrated I was transferred to Plymouth. But of all the black and white students, of all the thousands I taught during those fifteen years, I didn't have more than three ornery ones. Ninety nine and nine tenths per cent were fine students I could reach. These contrary ones, they just didn't want to do their work. I remember one boy from Creswell I used to get on. He was about to fail, but I gave him a D minus to let him go. When he finished school he came and gave me his school picture. I said, 'James, I appreciate it. I guess you always felt I was being too hard on you.' He said, 'No, Mr. Meekins, I wish you'd been a little bit harder.' I was so surprised you could have knocked me down with a feather.

"I taught English and social studies. I really love literature. I took extra hours in college. For a major I needed forty some hours. I think I had seventy hours in English. I follow most of those New England writers. One of my favorites is Channing. And Longfellow and Emerson, and Theodore Parker. Hawthorne -- I liked most of Hawthorne. But The Scarlet Letter, I liked it and hated it. Hester suffered too much.

"William Ellery Channing was one of my favorites. He was speaking about books. He said, if I can give you this: 'In the best books, great men talk to us, give us their most precious thoughts, and pour their souls into ours. God be thanked for books. They are the voices of the distant and the dead, and make us the heirs of the spiritual life of ages past. Books are the true levelers. They give to all, who will faithfully use them, the society, the spiritual presence, of the best and greatest of our race. No matter how poor I am, no matter that the prosperous of my own time would not enter my obscure dwell-

A monument at Ft. Raleigh National Historic Site tells the story of the Lost Colony.

ing. But if the sacred writers will enter and take up their abode under my roof; if Milton will cross my threshold and sing to me of Paradise; Shakespeare, to open to me the world of imagination, and the workings of the human heart; Franklin, to inject me with his practical wisdom; I shall not pine for want of intellectual companionship. I may become a cultivated man, though excluded from what is termed the best society in the place where I live.' That's one of the best things I got from Channing.

"I tried to be emphatic, or dynamic, in my presentation of literature, and my students still ask me for 'Gunga Din' or 'The Raven' when I see them. I memorized quite a few things. Last year we went to Hatteras High School, it was Negro History Week. And they gave us such a warm welcome and asked us to come back. One of the teachers there sent me a thank you letter and forty students had signed it. I don't want to look for it now. But she said 'After you left, the students talked more about you than they did about the senior prom.' Evidently I made a pretty good impression.

"We recited some things from Negro writers. Like Kelly Miller. He was Dean of Men at Howard University. He wrote a World War One history. And one of the memorable things in it was an open letter he wrote in 1917 to President Woodrow Wilson. The other was Frederick Douglass, his speech that he made in Rochester on the Fourth of July of 1852. Did you ever read that? He said, "Fellow Citizens: Pardon me, and allow me to ask, why am I called upon to speak here today? What have I or those I represent to do with your national independence?. . . To drag a man in fetters into the grand illuminated temple of liberty, and call upon him to join you in joyous anthems were inhuman mockery and sacrilegious irony." He knew his Bible; he knew the lament of a woe-smitten people, when the ancient Israelites said, "By the rivers of Babylon, there sat we down; and we wept when we remembered Zion." He thought it was rather ironic during the Fourth of July, to celebrate liberty while he had four and a half million brothers in slavery. His mistress, the white lady, taught him to read. He ran away to Baltimore and worked on the docks. But he sent back and paid for his freedom! The language that he uses is marvelous. You wonder now, how did he master such language?

"And then Paul Lawrence Dunbar, our first renowned Negro poet; he wrote a lot in dialect. Let me give you one they liked:

The Lord had a job for me, but I had so much to do.
So I said, get somebody else, or wait till I get through.
I don't know how the Lord came out, but He seemed to get along.

But I felt kind of sneaky like, 'cause I knowed I'd done him wrong.
Then one day I needed the Lord, I needed him right away.
But way down in my accusin' heart, I could hear him say,
Son, I've got too much to do; you get somebody else, or wait till I get through.
Now, when the Lord has a job for me, I never try to shirk
I drop just what I have on hand, and does the good Lord's work.
And my affairs can run along, or wait till I get through.
Nobody else can do the job that God's marked out for you.

"I was glad to take those things to Hatteras. And you know, that was the first time. I'd been far as Pea Island, and all these years I'd heard so much talk of Hatteras, but I'd never been down there.

"You know, most of my reading I did before I was eighteen years old. I read night and day. But in after years my eyes bother me. When I got in service I had 20-20 vision. But now, when I have plenty of time, I can't read more than five or ten minutes. The reading that I did before I finished high school kept me through college. So many things I had read then I could draw on. It just came in mighty handy in later years.

"My father, he wasn't a highly educated man, but he was self-educated. He bought books. One of the finest books he bought was by William Ellis, *Billy Sunday: The Man and His Message.* World War History by Kelly Miller. He had all about the Galveston Flood, Spanish-American War, the white slave trade. He read all those during his leisure time in the Coast Guard. He had some wonderful books. I wonder how he selected them. But I guess the salesman would come down to the station. I can't find them now.

"I recall he had a power boat called the *Henrietta*, after my mother. It was the best boat around there. And so we were coming across the Inlet, and he revved up the motor. And I wondered why. And about the time he revved up the motor the boat moved to the side. She had hit the current in the channel. So he caught me by the waistband and told me to look over the washboard of the ship. I looked over there and as far down as you could see the water was clear; but you could see that current cuttin' the sand from the bottom. Now little did he dream that was going to be his doom.

"Little things like that I remember about him and I'm proud. As I said, the October 30th, 1917, was my saddest day. I was at school, and there was a boy, Haywood Wise, he was my buddy since we could remember. Eleven, twelve years old. He was superintendent of the Sunday School here for thirty-five years. He passed a few years ago. Now, when the word came that my father had been blown out to sea, we had been out playin'. It hit me so I got up and went over and sat down by myself. Haywood had stopped playing and sat by me too. He didn't know what to say, but he felt my hurt was his hurt. And after that I got my books and started on that mile home. And he walked half the way with me. In Hutchinson's book, *This Freedom*, he says "In our successes, our hours of triumph, there are a hundred eyes that shine with ours in those. But it's defeats you want her to tell. The lights that are gone out; the springs that spring no more; the secret sordid things that hedge you in, that draw you down; those, to have somebody to tell those to." That's what a real friend means to you.

"I went on home. And my home, for the next week, which had been so quiet and peaceful, was bedlam. My mother for nights walked the floor. Maybe she was hoping against hope; hollering and crying for nights. Aunt Victoria Daniels, Nancy Midgett, the neighbors did all they could to console her. But she didn't want to be consoled.

"I don't know why people do things like that, but a month or so later somebody put a article in the paper that Theodore Meekins and Kitt Miller had been picked up by a German tramp steamer and were making their way home. That gave us some terrible false hopes. It was a hoax. They never did find Kitt Miller, but six months later my father -- what remained of my father -- washed up on the beach down there between Oregon Inlet and Pea Island. And they could only identify him by his underwear and his dental work.

"I came back here September before last. After I retired I stayed in Washington County. I had so many friends there. I hadn't been in a rush to come back. I had feelings for the old homestead, but I had some unpleasant memories too. But my wife wanted to come home. She has three brothers here.

"I might say what ought to be my happiest time was when I wanted a son, and when my son was born -- in fact all my children. I had two boys and three girls. I was mighty joyful about that. And thank God they've never given me any problems or trouble, and they're self-sufficient and independent. And they all went to college.

"My oldest son is in the Coast Guard. When he got out of college he enlisted in the Navy, so I got him to switch. This is his picture when he was commissioned. He flies the helicopters. This is my baby girl; she lives in Durham. My other son is in Minnesota. I have one daughter in Los Angeles and my other daughter is a nurse in New Haven. See, all of them are just as far from me as the ends of the country, but I hear from them every week.

"I have so many nieces and nephews here. Must have a hundred of them. Too many! They come to me, speak t' me, 'Uncle Nick,' and I have to get them to tell me who their mother is.

"I feel somewhat depressed when I think of how I'm unable to reach so many young people. Those kids the other day -- suicides -- sometimes I'm just dumbfounded. As much as I took in psychology I never really learned how to reach somebody. The human mind is so intricate! It seems the more I studied the more nonplussed I became.

"The best approach I know is to show them that, you're not alone. There's others have had greater problems than you. I had something prepared for when I went back to Hatteras. I think it would be about as good as any, come to think about it. Dwight Hillis, in *The Battle Of Principles*, has one part on Abe Lincoln. He gave it in such beautiful language. I'll try to give it to you. He said that when the country was threatened, the very existence of government, that God needed a man like Lincoln. He said, "Lincoln was the man who had walked for fifty years under cloudy skies. He was the most picturesque figure in history. He was the strongest, the gentlest, the saddest, the most pathetic figure in history. God chose him. He passed by the palaces and went to a cabin in the wilderness. And he took this little baby in his arms and called to his side his favorite angel, the Angel of Sorrow. And said to him, 'Take this little child of mine, and make him great.' Said, 'Take from him everything that he loves. As he climbs the hills of adversity, let his footprints be stained with his own blood. Till his face is more marred than any man of his time. Then bring him back to me, and I will have him free four million slaves.' So he said, 'God, and sorrow, made Lincoln great.' If kids could think about the problems that others have had, that they're not alone, their depression would be lifted.

"Well, my worst drug is my beer and my pipe, but I'm addicted to that TV more than anything else. Sometimes I have to crawl around on the floor to get over to it. I can't do a lot of walking, but I get stiff if I sit still too long. Hard to believe I was the captain of the football team, isn't it? I could really move then.

"I have some regrets about things I might have done differently. But you know, I don't have any real fear. Yes, I believe there's an afterlife. I tell you, there has to be. Whether it's beyond purgatory or not. If there is such a thing as Purgatory, then maybe it isn't necessary to have a Judgment, if you can be cleansed before a future life. Too much a belief in one might contradict the other. You might be punished in this world. There seems to be some judgement here. But there has to be some reckoning. "I try to do like, what did William Cullen Bryant say in 'Thanatopsis':

Thou go not, like the quarry-slave at night,
Scourged to his dungeon, but, sustained and soothed
By an unfaltering trust, approach thy grave,
Like one that wraps the drapery of his couch
About him, and lies down to pleasant dreams."

INSIDE
BODIE ISLAND

Just south of Whalebone Junction, just south of the intersection of the Manteo-Nags Head Causeway with U.S. Highway 158, the town of Nags Head -- indeed, all the commercial development of the Banks -- comes to a sudden and complete halt, except for the narrow strip of beach houses along the sea side in South Nags Head. For here is Bodie Island, and the beginning of Cape Hatteras National Seashore.

Bodie (pronounced "body") Island is not an island now, though it was one at various times in recorded history. Hurricanes and storm seas opened and shifting sands closed inlets repeatedly in the area where Whalebone Junction now is. Roanoke Inlet, south of Nags Head, closed last in the early 1800s. Faced with changing landforms, the Bankers have found it simpler to stay with island names even when formerly separate islands have merged. As on the other islands, stock was allowed to roam free on Bodie in the old days; later, with the commercial use of Oregon Inlet, it became important as the location of a lighthouse. The late 1800s saw several gun clubs built on the island to take advantage of the vast marshes and resultant clouds of waterfowl wintering over.

BODIE ISLAND
ATTRACTIONS

COQUINA BEACH
Bodie Island   441-7425

This is one of the best swimming beaches on the whole Outer Banks coast -- and, with the exception of a few picnic shelters, it's as wild as it was a century ago. Coquina is a sandy beach about 5.5 miles south of Whalebone Junction on Highway 12. It has restrooms, bath houses, picnic tables with shade structures, showers, and plenty of

BODIE ISLAND

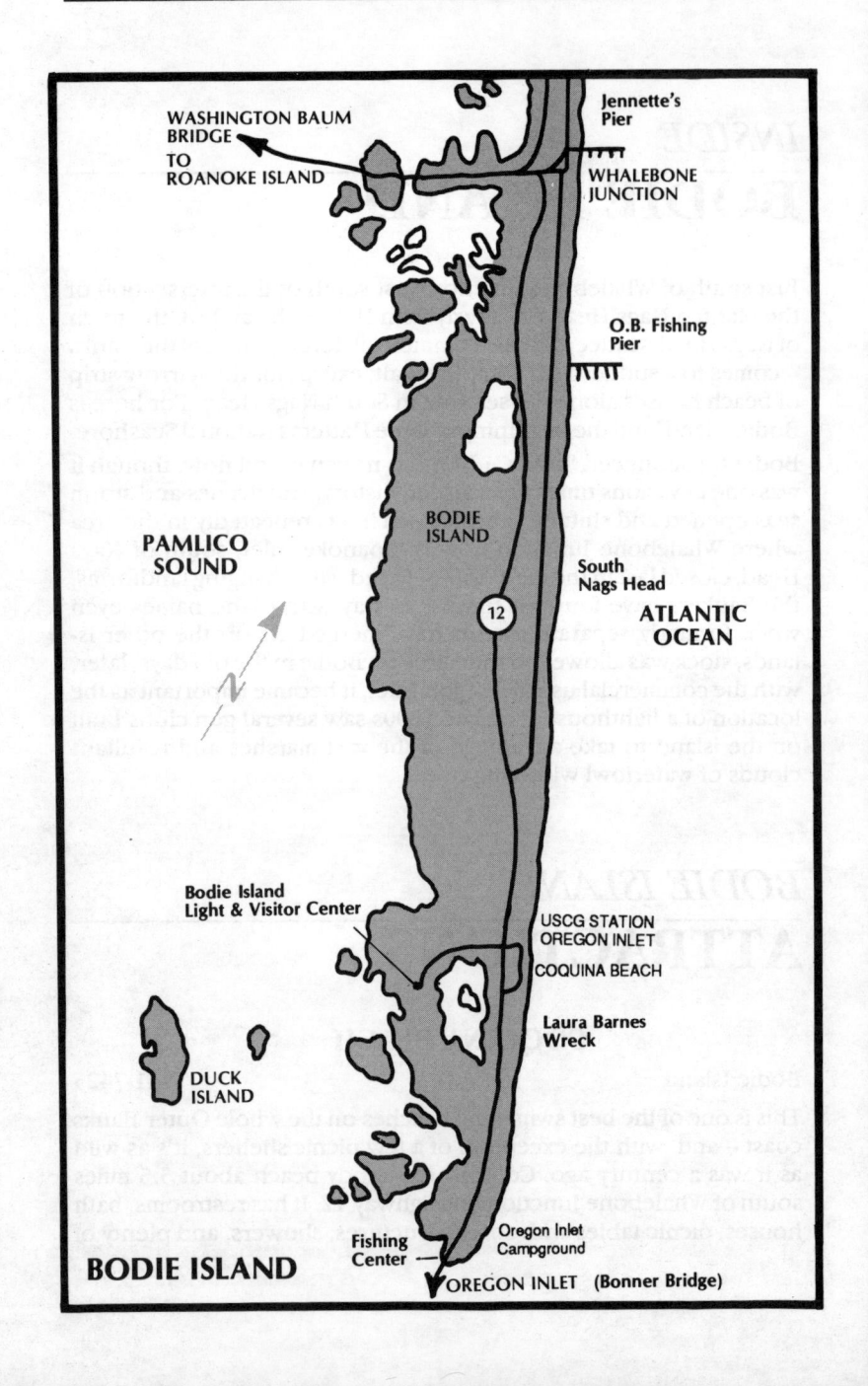

parking. Lifeguards are on duty from mid- June to Labor Day. "Coquinas" are the tiny shells you will find underfoot in the surf, like millions of tiny bronze coins.

From this virtual isolation from the world, the seacoast of Bodie and Hatteras leapt into prominence suddenly in 1942, when war -- in the shape of Nazi U-boats -- came to the East Coast. One of the pivotal battles of World War II was fought here, just a few miles off the beach, often in sight of the islanders; and the turning point of that battle took place just off Bodie Island. The relics lie there still. See "U- 85," beginning on the next page.

After the war, Bodie Island, along with the rest of the Outer Banks, gained new life with the coming of highways and the tourist trade. Fortunately, this stretch of deserted, near-virgin shore was included when the National Seashore was established in 1953, and the wholesale development that has taken place further north will never touch the life-filled marshes and scrublands of Bodie Island.

OREGON INLET COAST GUARD STATION

Coquina Beach   987-2311 or 473-5083

In late 1988 and early 1989, the sea ate most of the former Oregon Inlet Coast Guard station at the northern end of Hatteras Island. The beach movement continues. The Coast Guard shifted their operations to Coquina Beach in November of 1988. The Army Corps of Engineers dredge, *Sweitzer* now moors in Wanchese. The 41- and 44-foot small boats are based out of the Fishing Center.

The two-story white building at the north end of Coquina Beach is thus continuously manned now. As an operating base, Oregon Inlet isn't really set to handle your basic tourist, but they try to be hospitable. Ad hoc tours are available sometimes (depending on workload) from 1 to 4 p.m. weekdays and 8 a.m. to 5 p.m. on weekends. Try not to intrude too much on operations.

Oregon Inlet monitors Channel 16 VHF/FM.

LAURA A. BARNES

Coquina Beach

After a certain length of time has passed, a wrecked ship is gradually transmuted from junk into something romantic and tragic; teredoed wood becomes the fabric of dreams. The *Laura A. Barnes* made that transition in only half a century. Built at Camden, Maine in 1918, she was one of the last coastal schooners built in America. In 1921, under sail from New York to South Carolina in ballast, the 120-foot ship ran into a nor'easter that drove her onto the beach, north of where she now lies (all her crew survived). In 1973 the National Park Service moved her bones to Coquina Beach for safekeeping, and she now lies, high and dry, at the southern end of the parking lot.

BODIE ISLAND LIGHTHOUSE AND VISITORS' CENTER

Bodie Island   441-5711

Bodie Island Light, one of the four famous lighthouses of the Banks, is at the end of a turnoff to the west off Highway 12 some six miles south of Whalebone Junction (opposite Coquina Beach).

The horizontally striped black and white lighthouse is still in operation under Coast Guard auspices. Built in 1872, the present 163-foot brick structure is the third lighthouse to stand at or near Oregon Inlet since it opened in a hurricane in 1846. The first, on the south side of the inlet, developed cracks in the walls due to improper construction and was destroyed. The second was destroyed by the Confederates to confuse Federal shipping. Yes, the present lighthouse *is* rather far inland, but it is on stable ground; and in the nature of the Banks, time has built up the southern end of the island, and the inlet itself has "walked" south.

The Bodie Island Visitors' Center, also built in 1872, was formerly the lighthouse keeper's residence.

Wandering back to the lighthouse (sorry, Coast Guard rules forbid climbing it), you'll notice the broad marshes behind it. A short walk back to them is not out of order if you're interested in life in the marsh. In the marshes you'll find cattails, yaupon, wax myrtle, bayberry, and Eastern baccharis. A short path and wooden platforms or overlooks are provided as vantage points.

The Visitors Center was closed in 1988 for renovations. A reopening date is not yet known. The Whalebone Visitor Center will provide information in lieu of it until the Bodie Center reopens.

OREGON INLET FISHING CENTER

Bodie Island   441-6301

Oregon Inlet is one of the centers of sport fishing activity on the Banks -- especially of deep-sea Gulf Stream fishing. From this National Park Service-leased marina, dozens of charter boats operate, catching thousands of dolphin, wahoo, marlin, sailfish, tuna, and other sport fish every year.

Since they are concessionaires of the Park Service, the thirty- some charter boats that operate from here charge the same prices. You can reserve a full day offshore, including bait, tackle, and ice; full-day trips in the Inlet and the sound; and half-days in the sound (see The Outer Banks Fishing Guide section for what you can expect to catch). You can make reservations at the Booking Desk (the number above) or with the captains themselves...and we recommend you make them well in advance during the summer, for Oregon Inlet is one of the busiest places in the Banks come June.

Don't feel quite up to an 1100-lb. blue marlin? A less demanding sport is head boat fishing, aboard *Miss Oregon Inlet*, a 65-ft. diesel boat out of Oregon Inlet Fishing Center. She carries up to 46 fisherpersons on half-day inlet and sound bottom fishing cruises, catching spot, croakers, gray trout, bluefish, mullet, sea bass, etc., etc. All bait, ice and tackle is included in the price. Schedule: Early spring and late fall, one trip daily, departing at 8:00 a.m. and returning at 12:30. During the season (Memorial to Labor Days) there will be two trips daily, 7:00 a.m. to 11:30 a.m. and 12:00 to 4:30 p.m. at a cost of $20.00 per person. A non-fishing Twilight Cruise Tues, Thurs, Fri, and Sat, at 5:30 p.m., at a cost of $5.00. If you've not fished the salt sea before, a head boat is a rewarding and much less expensive way to start.

Aside from charter and head boats, the Center also supplies a fish-cleaning service, restrooms, and three boat ramps into the sound. The marina restaurant is open from 5 - 9 a.m. for breakfast, and also offers a box lunch service. The tackle shop carries a complete line of surf and deep-sea fishing equipment, as well as basic snacks, drinks, and camping consumables.

Everything at Oregon Inlet is organized around the angler; the fish-cleaning service will take your fish right off the boat to a truck, and there are mounting services to do your lifetime trophy up proud. Don't miss the outdoor display of mounted deep sea game fish, including a World's Record 1,142 lb. Atlantic Blue Marlin caught off the Inlet in 1974.

The Oregon Inlet Fishing Center is nine miles south of Whalebone Junction, west of Highway 12 on the turnoff to the right just before the bridge. This is also a relatively inexpensive place to gas up.

OREGON INLET

Between Hatteras and Bodie Island

Driving south from Nags Head, through Bodie Island, you'll soon find yourself lifted skyward on an immense concrete bridge. From a hundred feet in the air you can see for miles -- to seaward, over Atlantic swells; to soundward, over the vast calm sheet of the Pamlico.

This is Oregon Inlet, the Bank's major avenue for trade and fishing for over a hundred years.

Oregon Inlet opened during a hurricane in 1846, and was named, as was the custom in those days, after the first ship to make it through. Its opening brought shoaling to Ocracoke Inlet, and economic ruin to the once-flourishing town of Portsmouth.

Today it too is shoaling, and its consequences may be just as dramatic.

The Herbert C. Bonner Bridge, built in 1964 to provide access to the southern Banks, may have hastened this process by impeding the free tidal flow through the inlet. (Note, as you pass over it, the mile or more of new land under the bridge supports to the north.) But it is more likely that simple beach migration, the eons-long march of the Banks to the south and west, is the real cause. Whatever the causative factors, the inlet has required nearly round-the-clock dredging for the last few years, and now the silting is overtaking the Corps of Engineers ability to dredge; in fact Oregon has been completely closed for days at a time in recent years. In 1989 erosion at the southern side of the inlet accelerated dramatically, destroying much of the former Coast Guard station and requiring emergency repairs to the bridge.

The controversy over clearing or stabilizing the inlet, or whether it can be stabilized at all, has been going on for some years now. A long rip rap jetty might keep the channel open, at great expense, but it too would have to be dredged, and there is no guarantee that it would work for more than a few years.

The Oregon Inlet jetty project was approved by Congress in 1972, but permits for the rubble structures have never been granted. Since then, over 200 acres of North Point have been lost to the sea. Jetty opponents have argued that jetties would accelerate erosion south of the inlet; they proposed letting nature take its course.

Meanwhile, the boatbuilders and trawling companies of Wanchese, have been hit with skyrocketing insurance rates. Many of them have moved south, to the Morehead City area. It is too soon to write Wanchese off as a fishing port, but there is no doubt that the situation there is serious.

BODIE ISLAND LIGHTHOUSE

The four-day March, 1989 nor'easter and the damage it caused to the bridge supports are spurring renewed effort to get a project started, this time a $20 million revetment and groin.

The potential closing of the inlet also leads to the question: where will the next inlet be? Historically, the closing of an inlet has seemed to portend the opening of a new one somewhere else. All that water in the sounds has to go somewhere. We don't know, and no one can really predict, where an inlet will open. But it can happen pretty quickly, when those winter waves come crashing over the barrier dunes.

U-85

Off Bodie Island

As you stand on Coquina Beach, the sun bright overhead, look straight out to sea. If you could take your car and drive outward for fifteen minutes, you would be over one of the strangest yet least known attractions of the Outer Banks. Only fifteen miles straight out, over a hundred feet beneath the glittering sea, the first Nazi submarine destroyed by Americans in World War II lies motionless in the murky waters of Hatteras.

Almost undamaged, except for rust and the encroaching coral, it lies on its side, bow planes jammed forever on hard dive. Its hatches gape open to the dark interior, where silt swirls slowly between dead gauges and twisted air lines. Its cannon points upward, toward the dim glow that is all that remains of the sun at eighteen fathoms. Its conning tower, flaked with corrosion, lies frozen in a roll to starboard that will last until its steel dissolves in the all-devouring sea.

Here, at 35 55' N, 75 18' W, it is still World War II. Here, and all along the coasts of the Outer Banks, dozens of wrecks lie half buried in the sea bed. It is from here, from the silent hull of a 750-ton Type VIIb U-boat, that we can begin a journey back to the months when the Outer Banks was a battle line, when the German Navy patrolled and ruled our shores.

To Spring, 1942.

Adolf Hitler declared war on the United States on December 11, 1941, four days after Pearl Harbor.

In Europe the war was two and half years old. Deep in the Soviet Union, Nazi and Red forces churned the mud in a precarious balance outside the city of Moscow. In the West the British, in from the first, had come close to strangling in the noose the U-boats had drawn around their island. German submarines had sunk over a thousand ships, over a million tons of material and food; but as 1941 ended, quickly built escorts, ASDIC, and a convoy system were loosening the knot. In his operations room at Kerneval, Occupied France, Admiral Karl Doenitz wondered: where, now, would he find easy sinkings for his thinly stretched submarines?

On the eleventh of December, he knew.

Operation *Paukenschlag* (Drumroll) began on the eighteenth of January, when the Esso tanker *Allen Jackson* exploded a few miles off Diamond Shoals Light.

Within weeks, the entire East Coast was under siege, and it was almost defenseless. Most of our ships had been sent to the Pacific, or to the North Atlantic run, where two of them (*Reuben James* and *Kearny*) were torpedoed even before war officially began. Aircraft? Almost none. To defend the east coast of the United States in spring 1942, there was a total of ten World War I wooden subchasers, three converted yachts, four blimps, and six Army bombers.

When the U-boats arrived, it was slaughter. They struck on the surface, at night, often not even bothering to dive. The stretch of coast off the Banks was their favorite hunting ground. Armed with both deck guns and torpedoes, they would lie in wait at night, silhouette the passing coasters against the glow of lights ashore, and attack unseen by the men aboard. Ship after ship went down in January, February, and March. *Rochester; Ocean Venture; Norvana; Trepca; City of Atlanta; Oakmar; Tiger;* and scores of others. Oil and debris washed up on the beaches, and residents watched the night sky flame as tankers burned just over the horizon.

The "Arsenal of Democracy" was under blockade; and from the protected pens at Lorient and St. Nazaire more raiders, fresh from refit and training, sailed to attack a coast where in three months of war not one German submarine had yet been the target of an effective attack.

One of them was the U-85.

U-85 was a Type VIIb, specially modified for the Atlantic war. A little over seven hundred tons displacement, two hundred and twenty feet long, she was a little larger than a harbor tugboat, or the *Calypso.* She had been built in northern Germany in early 1941, the second year of the war. Her commander was Kapitan-leutnant Eberhard Greger, Class of 1935.

Greger and U-85 spent her first summer working up in the deep fiords of occupied Norway. On August 28 she left Trondheim for her first wartime cruise. On September 10, the wolf tasted blood for the first time. Greger latched on to a Britain-bound convoy. U-85's first five torpedoes ran wild. Throughout that day and the next he ran eastward, staying with the convoy on the surface, just over the horizon. The diesels hammered as U-85 slashed through heavy seas. The convoy's escorts, American destroyers, tried repeatedly to drive her off with gunfire and depth charges. Each time, she submerged and evaded, then came back up and hammered ahead again, rolling viciously, but gradually drawing ahead to position for a new attack.

The next afternoon she reached it, and Greger sent U-85 dashing in on the surface. Boldness was rewarded: at 1642 he made a solid hit on a six-thousand-ton steamer, and, in the next half hour, struck at two more of the heavily laden merchantmen. Then the destroyers closed in for a close depth-charge counterattack. At a little past midnight, September 11, Greger brought her up slowly, and then crept toward home for repairs.

U-85's second war cruise was less dramatic. Battered by heavy weather off Newfoundland, shrouded by fog, she never made contact with her prey, and engine trouble eventually sent her back to St. Nazaire.

For her third war cruise, a new man came aboard. He sounds like a sailor Goebbels would have exulted over; young (26), tall (six feet), blond and well built; but this German must have been different from the Nazi stereotype. For one thing, he kept a diary; and it is thanks to Erich Degenkolb that we know as much as we do about his ship's last cruises.

According to Degenkolb -- we can imagine him wedged into his cramped leather bunk, diary on his stomach, listening to the waves crash against the outside of the hull -- U-85's third war cruise was her most rewarding, both to Doenitz and to her crew.

Operation Drumroll had begun, and U-85 was one of the first reliefs to be thrown into the battle. On the way across she sank a 10,000-ton steamer and took a near miss from a plane off Newfoundland. "Off New York," as Degenkolb wrote in his diary in February, she sank another steamer after a seven-hour surface chase. She chased convoys throughout the month, probably in the Western Atlantic approaches to New York, till her fuel tanks sloshed near-empty, and then set course for home, crossing the Bay of Biscay submerged and arriving in St. Nazaire again on the twenty-third of February.

A month's refit and leave, and it was time to sail again. At 1800 on March 21, 1942, with a brass band on the pier, with a blooded crew, a confident captain, and a well-tried ship, U-85 set out once more for "Amerika."

The drumbeat of the U-boats had grown louder through February and March. No censorship could conceal the fact that ships were being lost. The explosions on the horizon, the oil on the beaches, the boatloads of huddled men being debarked at every seaport told the story too plainly for anyone to deny.

The Navy and Coast Guard, along with civilian authorities, were struggling with this new meaning of the once-remote war. Vice- Admiral Adolphus Andrews, directing the East Coast antisubmarine effort, found that aside from the lack of ships and planes, he had inadequate operational plans and even less clout. He couldn't even get the use of the destroyers and planes already in Norfolk assigned to the Atlantic Fleet.

One of the results of this unfortunate combination of censorship and unpreparedness was, typically, rumor. U-boats were refuelling, people whispered, in isolated inlets along the coast, and they had been seen in Chesapeake Bay itself. Citizens reported odd lights along the shore at night...obvious signals to someone out at sea.

One of the most persistent rumors concerned landings along the Outer Banks. German sailors, it was said, had actually slipped ashore, were mingling with the locals and even seeing movies, as ticket stubs supposedly recovered from sunken U-boats proved. Alas, a good story, but probably untrue. The Germans did land specially trained spies later in the war in Quebec and at Narragansett, Long Island; but according to the Coast Guard, Navy, and FBI, that was it in World War II. No U-boat captain must have had much desire to hazard his craft close inshore, or risk losing a skilled *obermachinist* so that he could report on the latest Errol Flynn epic. All that *can* be proven is that where news does not exist, gossip and invention will swiftly take its place.

And in March and April 1942, reality was bad enough. Eight ships had gone down off North Carolina alone in January; two in February, as the first team of submarines headed back across the Atlantic; and then fourteen in March, as they were relieved. Once the "pipeline" of the eighteen-day cruise out of France was full, there would be eight boats on station all the time.

The Outer Banks were suddenly the focus of world war.

Cape Hatteras was dreaded by every merchant seaman on the East Coast. The "Graveyard of the Atlantic" was earning its name anew in the age of steam, and a new cognomen besides -- "Torpedo Junction." On March 18, for example, the U-boats met an unescorted "convoy" of five tankers, and torpedoed three, plus a Greek freighter that stopped to rescue crewmen from a black sea filled with blazing oil.

This was how it was: in March 1942, three ships were going down every day, one every eight hours. But even worse was the closely guarded secret that the "exchange rate" -- the magic number in antisubmarine warfare -- was zero. Not one U-boat had yet been sunk off America.

It could not continue this way. Either the U-boats would be driven under, or all coastwise shipping would have to stop. America, the Allies, could not afford losses on this scale much longer.

It might not be too much to say, as Churchill later did, that it was the war itself that hung in the balance.

USS *Roper*, DD-147, was a fairly old ship in 1942, as warships go. At a little under 1200 tons, she wasn't all that much larger than U-85.

She had been born in Philadelphia, at William Cramp & Sons, in 1918. *Roper* evacuated refugees from Constantinople in 1919 and then spent a few years in the Pacific before being laid up in San Diego in 1922. Recommissioned in 1930, she spent the slow years of the Depression on reserve maneuvers and patrol duty in Hawaii, Panama, and the Caribbean. In 1937 she was transferred to the Atlantic Fleet.

When war began in Europe, the pace picked up. The old four-piper rolled from Key West to Yucatan, and then north in 1940 to the coast of New England. In early 1942, she ran a convoy to Londonderry, passing the U-85, then on her third war patrol; they may have crossed each other's paths for the first time then, somewhere in the empty spaces of the North Atlantic.

In March, the rigorous glamor of convoy duty ended; she was ordered back to the coast for more patrol. Patrol -- steaming endlessly through fog, storm, calm, night. Her crew carried out innumerable late-night actions: radar contact, a breakneck steam to intercept, the depth-charging that was always futile. Whales? Escaping U-boats? Her crew never knew. Perhaps some day, in a war that everyone knew now would last a long time, they would have their chance to fight. But for now, it was more of the same, everlasting patrol.

Kapitan-leutnant Eberhard Greger sailed U-85 on her fourth sortie on March 21, beginning the long transit submerged. In a few days, though, he was able to bring her up, and dieseled west through seas "as smooth as a table," as Degenkolb, relaxing belowdecks, jotted in his journal. They took some damage from a storm on March 30, but repaired it and continued the cruise.

At this stage of the war, Germany's submariners were confident men -- especially off America.

By early April she was on station, ranging the coast from New York to Washington. On the tenth, Greger took his boat below to sink a steamer with a spread of two torpedoes. But targets were scarce.

He decided to head south, toward the easy pickings off the Outer Banks.

On the night of April 13, as U-85 hammered through calm seas at 16 knots, Degenkolb made his last entry: "American beacons and searchlights visible at night."

Lieutenant-commander Hamilton W. Howe, captain of the *Roper*, was tired. His crew was tired. The ship itself, twenty-four years old, was tired. But they were alert. The old four-piper did not yet have the new gear Allied scientists were racing to produce. But she had enough. A primitive radar and sonar. Depth charges. And plenty of guns -- nice to have, if only a U-boat would play the game for once and surface, instead of skulking away underwater while the horizon crackled with flame from dying ships.

At midnight on the 13th, *Roper* was running southward off Bodie Island. The lighthouse, still operating, was plainly visible to starboard. The night was clear and starry, and at 18 knots the knife bow of the old DD pared phosphorescence from the smooth water. Most of her crew was asleep below.

On the bridge as Officer of the Deck, Ensign Ken Tebo was awake and alert. At six minutes past midnight, the radar suddenly showed a small pip a mile and a half ahead. The ship had been plagued with these small contacts all night. Another small boat, Tebo thought; probably a Coast Guard craft, on the same mission as the destroyer -- patrol. But he felt immediately that there was something strange, something different, about this one.

He ordered an eight degree change of course, to close slowly, and to present the smallest possible target -- just in case. In seconds -- the captain always slept in full uniform at sea -- Howe was on the bridge.

Tebo explained the situation quickly. He still had that strange feeling. *Roper* was overhauling, but too slowly. At 2100 yards range the two men saw the wake of whatever it was up ahead. White, narrow, it glowed in the starlit seas. Howe ordered an increase in speed to 20 knots. It still might be a Coast Guard boat. But Howe made his decision. At the clang of General Quarters, seamen rolled from their bunks and ran to man their guns, the torpedo batteries, the depth charge racks astern, and the K-guns, weapons that threw the drums of explosive far out over the ship's side, widening the carpet of concussion that could crush the hull of any submerged enemy.

Aboard the speeding U-boat, most of the crew was asleep. Degenkolb had thrust his diary into his pocket and turned in. On the darkened conning tower, only a few feet above the sea, an officer and two lookouts stared ahead. They anticipated no trouble. A U-boat had a tiny silhouette, almost impossible to see from a ship's deck at night.

After a time, one of the lookouts turned 'round and tapped the officer on the shoulder. There seemed to be something astern. A target? The submarine's rudders swung, and she began to creep to the right.

Below, her men slept on.

Aboard the *Roper*, now only a few hundred yards astern, Lt. William Vanous, the executive officer, stood panting atop the flying bridge. Commander S.C. Norton was beside him. Below them the two men could hear the pounding of feet on metal as the bridge team manned up. The starlight showed more men on the forecastle, running toward the three-inch guns. Beside them, the searchlight operator was swinging his lamp around, and they heard the clang as BMC Jack Wright charged the No. 1. 50-caliber machine gun.

Vanous strained his eyes ahead. At the end of a white ribbon of wake a black object was slowly drawing into view. Could it really be a submarine? It was awfully small. He noted happily that the men on the bridge below were keeping the ship a trifle to the side of the wake; most U-boats carried torpedo tubes in their pointed sterns as well as in the bow.

Yes, thought the German officer ahead of him, there is something back there. And it was very close. He reached for the alarm toggle, and below him, under the waterline, Degenkolb suddenly awoke.

The two ships were turning. The submarine was slipping to starboard. In a few moments its stern tubes would point directly at its pursuer. Howe ordered the helm hard right, and called into the voice tube, "Illuminate!" Above him, with a sputtering hiss, the searchlight ignited. Vanous coached it out into the darkness, and caught his breath. The beam had swept across the conning tower of a submarine with five men running along the half-submerged deck toward her gun.

Someone shouted to Wright, and with an ear-battering roar the chief began firing. The machine gun tracers swept forward, hung over the black boat, then descended, dancing along the thin-skinned ballast tanks, then reaching up the deck toward the frantically working gun crew. Forward, a second machine gun opened up. The glare of the searchlight wavered, but held. In its weird light men began to fall.

At almost the same moment, crewmen along the destroyer's side pointed and shouted at a sparkling trail in the water: a torpedo!

Inside the hull of the U-85, other men heard the clang of machine gun bullets on metal. They ran for their stations, forty men in a hull no wider than a railway car. The ship shuddered as a torpedo went out astern. Erich Degenkolb swung a locker open and pulled out his yellow escape lung. Could Kapitan Greger submerge and escape? He hoped so, desperately. But from the sounds that came through the steel around him into what the U-boat men called the "iron coffin," it seemed that U-85's luck had finally run out.

On the *Roper's* bridge, Howe had no time for thoughts and no time for feelings. It was a U-boat, and it was *surfaced*. The ship was still shuddering around in her turn. "Open fire!" he shouted.

On the exposed forecastle, in the mounts on deck aft, the three-inchers began to fire. Their target was only 300 yards away now, almost pointblank range. But it seemed smaller. It was submerging. In a moment it would be gone.

The *Roper's* men thought they saw their last round hit just at the base of the conning tower, where it joined the U-boat's pressure hull.

With the sound of a solid hit in their ears, the *Unterseeboot*- men knew their battle was lost. The ballast tanks were already filling, and the machine gun and shell fire must have holed them too. U-85 was on her last dive. There was only one way for her men to live now, and that was to get out of her narrow hull before it slipped forever under the icy sea.

Erich Degenkolb joined the crowd struggling under the ladder. Seconds later he found himself topside. The deck was familiar, but fire was still drumming on the sinking boat. A blinding shaft of light picked out every splinter, every weldment of the hull. He stumbled from the blaze of fire and sound over the side. The water was freezing cold. Gasping, he came up, stuck the mouthpiece of the lung between his teeth, and tried to inflate it. His heavy clothes were dragging him down.

Suddenly the firing stopped. The light went out. He drifted, seemingly alone, for a few minutes, feeling the cold of the sea gnaw into his bare hands, into his face.

Then, all at once, a string of deeper detonations brought his attention up, into the night.

The last thing he saw was the American ship. Immense, black, blazing, it loomed over the sinking shell that had been his home, over the struggling men in the water who had been his friends. And from its sides, in brief bursts of reddish light, he saw the depth charges leap into the night and splash on either side, amid the waving, screaming men.

When the black ship slid under, Howe doused the light. He was suddenly conscious of how conspicuous he was. Lights, shooting...the killers, it was common talk among destroyermen, often operated in pairs.

A few minutes later, the sonar operator reported contact. The destroyer, darkened and silent now, wheeled and headed toward it.

"Prepare for depth charge attack," said Howe.

"Men in the water ahead, captain."

"All stop."

Her screws slowing, *Roper* coasted forward. From the bridge he could see them now. One of them was even shouting up at him... *"Heil Hitler."* But he was thinking. He held course. He knew they were there. But the contact was solid. It might be another sub.

"Fire depth charges," said Howe.

Astern, from the fantail, the launchers exploded. The charges arched out, hit, and sank, and seconds later 3300 pounds of TNT went off in the midst of forty swimming men.

Roper made no more attacks that night, but lingered in the area of the sinking, echo-ranging and with every lookout alert. At about six the sun rose, lighting the scene of recent battle. Oil slicked the low waves; life jackets and motionless bodies drifted in slow eddies as the destroyer nosed back and forth, sniffing for the vanished enemy. At 0850, obtaining a ping on a bottomed object, she made a straight run and dropped four more depth charges. A great gush of air and a little oil came up when the foam subsided astern. At 0957, Howe dropped two more depth charges over the largest bubbles. At last he concluded that it was over. The U-boat was still down there, but she was dead. Coached from aircraft from shore, still watching for that constantly-feared other sub, the *Roper* lowered a boat, and began dragging bodies aboard.

One of them, his face and body swollen and discolored from the depth charging that had killed him, was Erich Degenkolb.

The first U-boat! The news was electrifying. At long last one of them had been destroyed, by an American ship, and in the very area where for four months now the wolves had hunted with impunity. The story was immediately released to the press. But this was not the end. *Roper* continued south on her patrol, but the remains of U-85 were far too valuable to be left undisturbed.

Over the next weeks, divers explored the shattered boat. A hundred feet down, clumsily-suited Navy men clambered over torn metal, pried open hatches, traced fuel and air lines and manifolds, and tried unsuccessfully to raise the hull with compressed air. They were unable to get inside and it was impossible to raise the wreck without a major salvage effort -- not an easy option off Cape Hatteras in April.

In the end, they left her there, possibly with some of her crew still inside the now-silent hull, under the canted conning tower, with its painted device of a wild boar, rampant, with a rose in its mouth. The divers, the ships were needed elsewhere. There were valuable cargoes to be recovered. And from now on, there would be casualties from the other side as well -- U-352, sunk off Morehead City in May; U-576; U-701; dozens of others. And, last of all, U-548, sent down a hundred miles east of the Chesapeake Bay entrances three years later, in April, 1945.

The U-boat threat was anything but over, but on the Atlantic horizon more light was dawning than that of burning tankers. In the months after April, 1942, American strength increased steadily in our home waters. The threat was overcome, this time; the enemy was steadily shoved back, first to the center of the ocean, then to his home waters. Finally, with the loss of France in 1944, he could deploy only the few war-worn boats that could slip out from Germany itself past close blockade into the North Sea.

Lieutenant-commander Hamilton Howe retired as a rear admiral in 1956. He lives in Winston-Salem, North Carolina. Captain Kenneth Tebo retired in 1961, and lives in Falls Church, Virginia. Captain William Tanous died the same year in a naval hospital in Annapolis. Erich Degenkolb, N 11662/41, lies in Hampton, Virginia, in plot #694 of the National Cemetery.

Kapitan-leutnant Eberhard Greger's body was not recovered.

U-85 lies rusting on a white, sandy bottom, fifteen miles east of where Bodie Island light still glitters out over the troubled seas of Hatteras.

Cape Point on Hatteras Island draws anglers almost every day of the year. DCTB

INSIDE
HATTERAS ISLAND

Hatteras Island, in many ways, *is* the Outer Banks. In its over fifty-mile length is wrapped up everything for which the Banks are famous. Solitude. Unspoiled nature. In the Pea Island National Wildlife Refuge, comprising the northern end of the island, you can drive for miles, hearing only the sea and the call of the wild geese, seeing only the dunes.

Farther south, you roll through the very stuff of Banks legend: tiny communities whose whole livelihood came from the sea. From Rodanthe, Waves, and Salvo the Bankers of the Life Saving Service battled storm and surf to save strangers' lives. Today's visitor finds wrecks still on the beaches -- and the best pier fishing on the Banks.

Some forty miles south of Oregon Inlet, the island takes a sharp westward turn, leaving Cape Point jutting out into the Atlantic. Here, at its 'elbow', is Cape Hatteras, feared for centuries by mariners as the Graveyard of the Atlantic. Here the century-old Lighthouse still sends its warning beam seaward, and here surfers and surf fishermen find the acme of their sports.

Inland of the Cape, at the widest part of the Banks, small communities have established themselves, nestled in the depths of a unique maritime forest. Buxton and Frisco offer camping, shopping, and a chance to stock up on gas and food before continuing south.

Hatteras Village, close to the western end of the island at the ferry terminus for Ocracoke, is a mecca for sport fishermen -- and for shoppers.

Most of Hatteras Island is part of the Cape Hatteras National Seashore, and is administered by the National Park Service (Pea Island: U.S. Fish and Wildlife Service). This provides for the preservation of most of the island. A well-kept series of campgrounds (3), swimming beaches (4), and fishing piers (2), as well as the Visitor Center by the Cape Hatteras Lighthouse, provide for the convenience of visitors. These are supplemented by numerous private campgrounds and motels listed in other chapters.

In the early years, the Islanders lived cut off from others, evolving their own microculture, preserving old ways of speech and suspicion of authority. Since 1964, the Oregon Inlet Bridge has largely ended that isolation. Yet traces of it linger, and you will find Hatteras *different* from Kitty Hawk and Nags Head. There are no fast food outlets...no bars...no discos...and only one movie theatre. The Hatteras people are friendly, but...they don't accept outsiders immediately. Their villages, their economy, is geared to the summer visitor trade, but still with reservations, as if this, too, may be a passing thing. Living on shifting sand, isolated all winter, and knowing that a northeaster or hurricane can change everything, even the shape of the land, the Hatteras people learn to trust only themselves, and the eternal sea.

No visitor to the Outer Banks should miss the southern islands, Hatteras and Ocracoke. There you will find, still strong, something increasingly rare in the modern world.

Independence.

RODANTHE, WAVES, AND SALVO

Rodanthe, Waves, and Salvo are small communities of perhaps two or three hundred people each...during the winter. In summer they

---

WE'LL GIVE YOU ...

$45.00

Cash!!

for visiting our outdoor resort and taking our tour.

Must be 25 yrs. old earning $25,000 annually. Must be married and accompanied by spouse, only one tour per vehicle. Coast to Coast members ineligible. This offer extended to first time visitors only.

Simply call or visit our RECEPTION CENTER For an appointment Hwy. 12, Rodanthe, NC (919)441-8162 or 987-2318

The Pea Island Resort

blossom with tackle shops, stores, gift shops, campgrounds and small restaurants, all to tempt and serve the thousands of visitors streaming south on Highway 12. Many visitors stop, and discover these tiny towns...but too many drive by, intent on getting to storied Hatteras Village or Ocracoke.

But if you like fishing, Rodanthe has the Hatteras Island Pier. If you like wrecks, this is where they lie, to be covered and uncovered with each winter's storms. History buffs should stop at the Chicamacomico Lifesaving Station. Windsurfing, jet skiing, and fishing are popular sports here, with ever-growing services along Route 12. And if you're a camper, there are half a dozen places to stay, the biggest concentration of camping sites in the Banks. This is a beautiful area and the real estate boom the Insiders predicted a few years ago is *ongoing now*.

AVON

Avon, the last town on the northern arm of the Island before the run through Park-owned territory to the Cape, is thirty miles south of Oregon Inlet. Once remote, it has become much more accessible since the opening of the Herbert Bonner Bridge, and now sees a growing stream of tourists. It's still primarily a summer community, though, with lots of single-family cottages. One quiet summer evening, looking west over a mirrorlike sound toward the setting sun, we understood why; there was at that moment no more beautiful place on the Banks. The winter population is small but still growing with convenient groceries, shops and campgrounds. Avon is becoming a center for year 'round living and recreation.

In previous editions of the Guide, we predicted real estate development in this area, and it is finally happening. Kinnekeet Shores, Hatteras Colony, and Askins Creek, along with others, are selling major developments in Avon. Kinnekett, the largest, plans 450 single-family dwellings on a 500-acre ocean-to-sound parcel. A 120,000-square-foot shopping village, anchored by Food Lion, opened in 1988.

BUXTON, FRISCO, AND HATTERAS VILLAGE

The southern "arm" of Hatteras Island -- from the "elbow" at the Cape west and south, toward Ocracoke -- is more populated and more habitable than the open land to the north. More of it is privately owned, in contrast to the overwhelming proportion of National Seashore land on the rest of the Island. Higher and more stable geologically, the southern arm is primarily a maritime forest habitat, often thick with live oak and red bay, dogwood and loblolly pine. It offers more shelter from wind and storm, and has borne a small

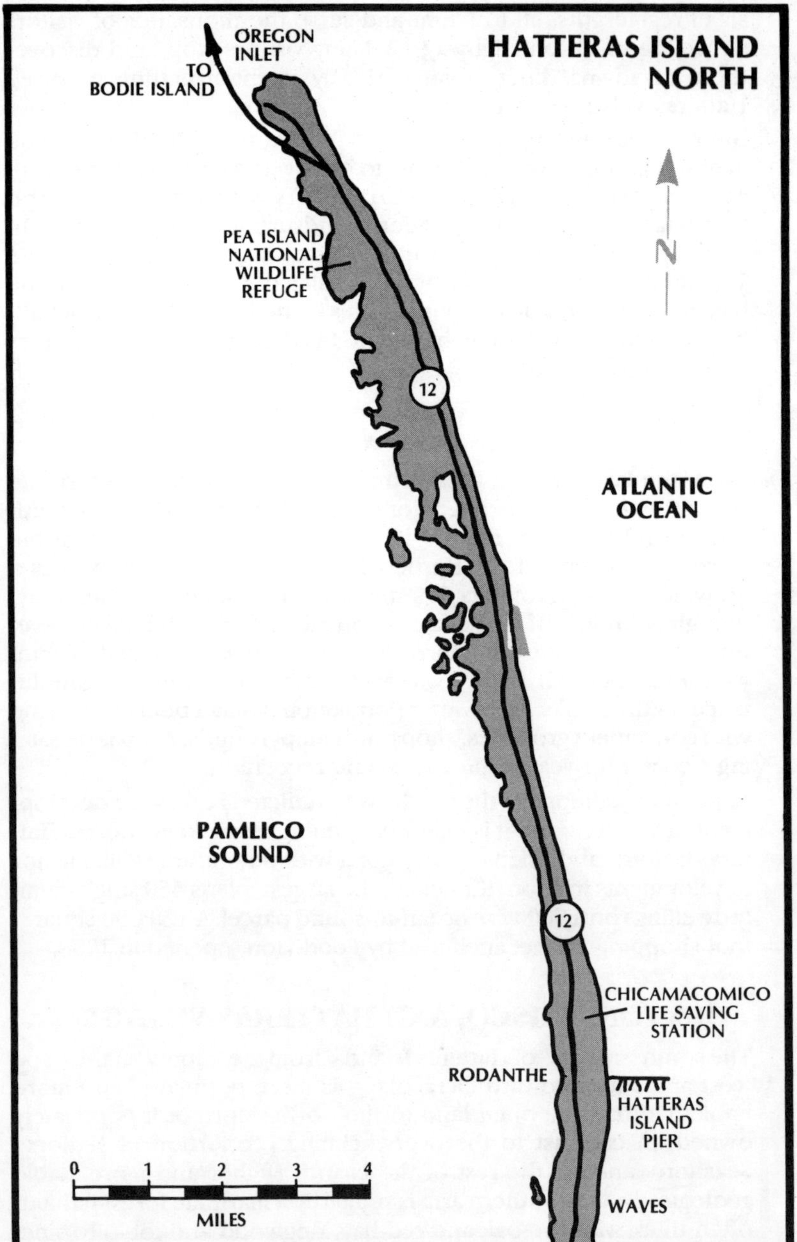

HATTERAS ISLAND NORTH
OREGON INLET
TO BODIE ISLAND
PEA ISLAND NATIONAL WILDLIFE REFUGE
N
12
ATLANTIC OCEAN
PAMLICO SOUND
12
CHICAMACOMICO LIFE SAVING STATION
RODANTHE
HATTERAS ISLAND PIER
0
1
2
3
4
MILES
WAVES

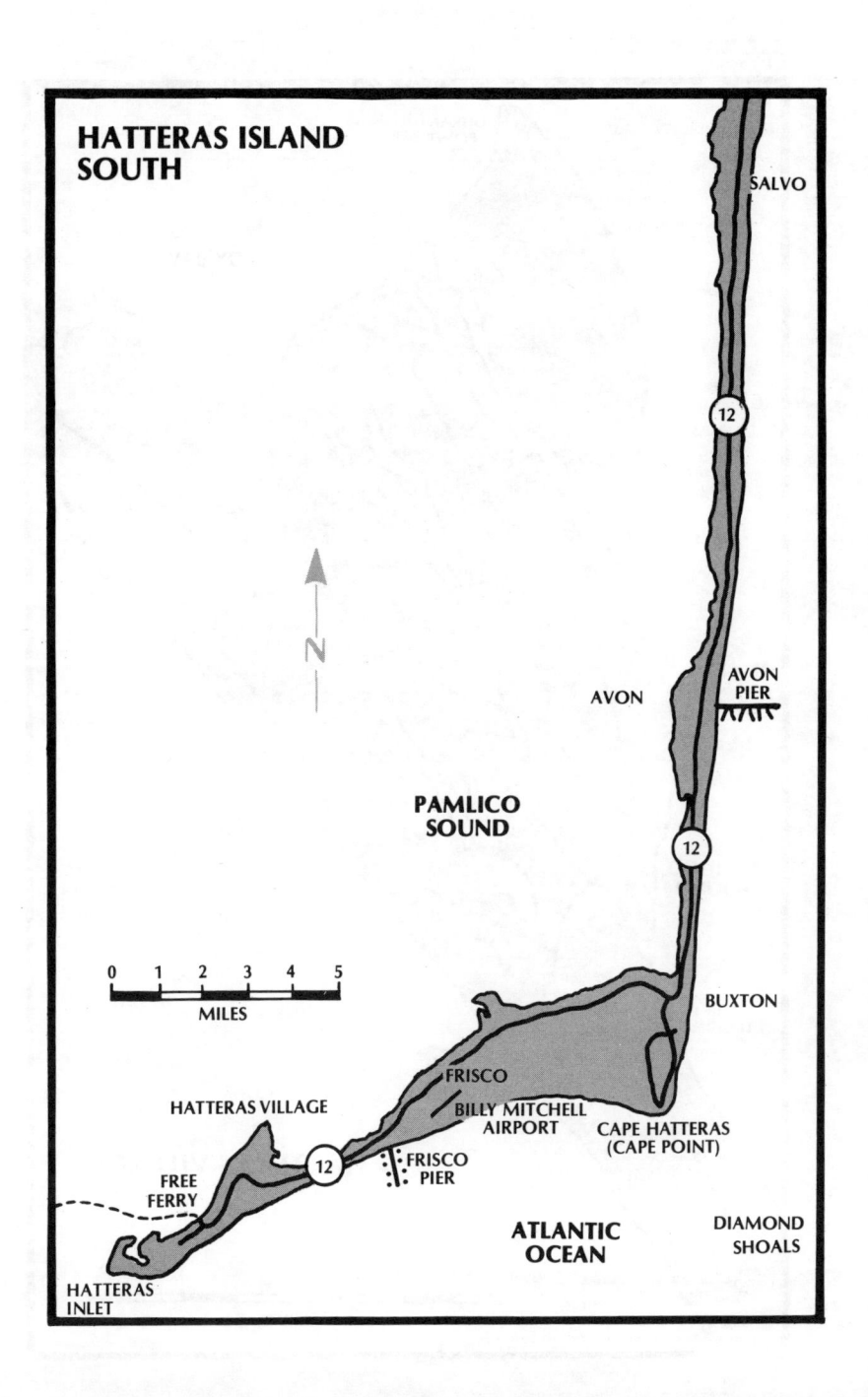

HATTERAS ISLAND SOUTH

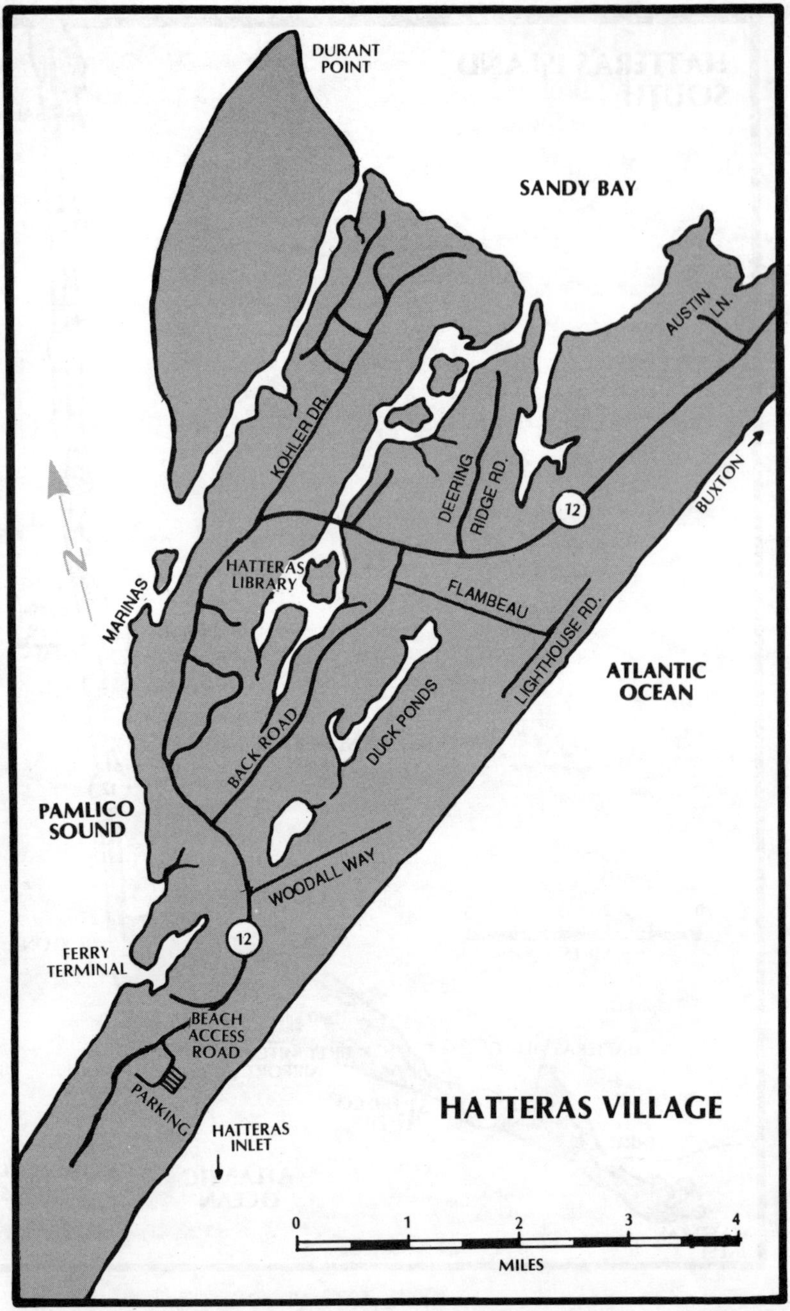
DURANT POINT
SANDY BAY
AUSTIN LN.
KOHLER DR.
DEERING
RIDGE RD.
12
BUXTON
N
HATTERAS LIBRARY
MARINAS
FLAMBEAU
LIGHTHOUSE RD.
ATLANTIC OCEAN
DUCK PONDS
BACK ROAD
PAMLICO SOUND
WOODALL WAY
12
FERRY TERMINAL
BEACH ACCESS ROAD
PARKING
HATTERAS INLET
HATTERAS VILLAGE
0
1
2
3
4
MILES

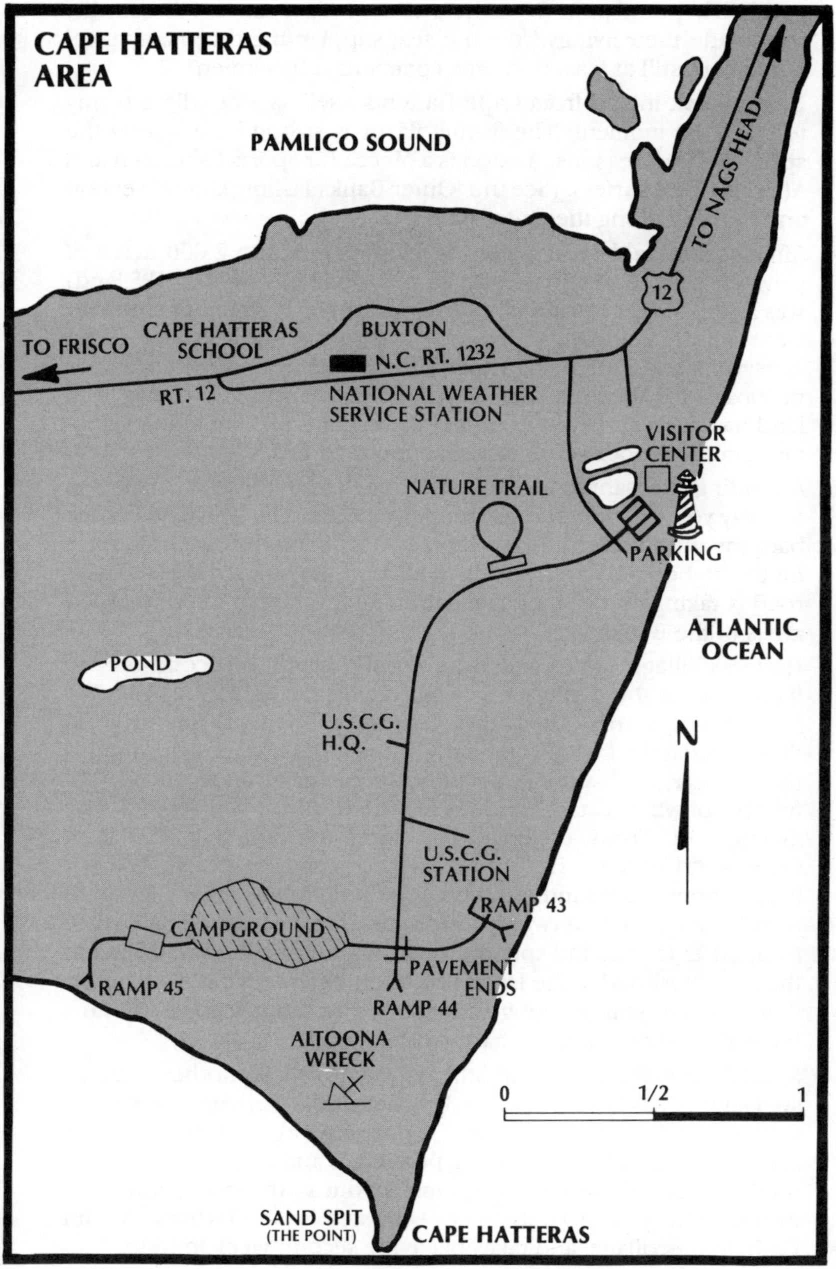

CAPE HATTERAS AREA
PAMLICO SOUND
TO NAGS HEAD
12
TO FRISCO
CAPE HATTERAS SCHOOL
BUXTON
N.C. RT. 1232
RT. 12
NATIONAL WEATHER SERVICE STATION
VISITOR CENTER
NATURE TRAIL
PARKING
ATLANTIC OCEAN
POND
U.S.C.G. H.Q.
N
U.S.C.G. STATION
RAMP 43
CAMPGROUND
PAVEMENT ENDS
RAMP 45
RAMP 44
ALTOONA WRECK
0
1/2
1
SAND SPIT
(THE POINT)
CAPE HATTERAS

and hardy population from the earliest Indian times. Historically, they made their livings from the sea; supplanting this, many local people are still at least part-time commercial fishermen.

Buxton, just inland from Cape Hatteras itself, is a rapidly growing town at the moment. The fishing flavor is strong here during the spring and fall seasons. Buxton is a Mecca for sports fishermen and Atlantic Coast surfers. (See the "Outer Banks Fishing Guide" section and "Surfing Along the Outer Banks").

After considerable discussion development of the 2,000 acres of privately-owned land in Buxton Woods (generally west of NPS land) was approved for low-density development in 1988 under stringent Dare County guidelines. Designed to preserve the maritime forest ecosystem and underlying aquifer, the guidelines rule out previous proposals for the area such as golf courses and sand mining. The land has been surveyed as of this writing and this limited development in the Woods is underway as you read this.

A winding, pleasant road runs west from Buxton towards Frisco. On the way you will pass several campgrounds and many roads leading back into new real estate developments, both on the ocean side and on the higher land overlooking the sound. Previously forested, this road is taking on hte look familiar along the rest of the developed areas of the Banks.

Hatteras Village, at the western tip of the island, is second only to Wanchese as the Banks' center of commercial fishing activity. We have seen upwards of sixty drop-netters (gill netters) run out from there during the late fall and early spring. At the docks, during this time of year, you can see tons of trout coming in under the watchful eyes of wharf cats, gill nets being dried, all the activity of a busy fishing port. Trout, croakers, big blues, and king mackerel from Oden's and Hatteras Harbor are packed in shaved ice, trucked out in five thousand pound lots, and end up in Fulton's Fish Market in New York City within twenty-four hours. Most of these boats come from other towns, and spend the season out of Hatteras, fishing in the neighborhood of the Light. Feel like a different kind of vacation? Sometimes, it you're young and hearty, you can talk yourself into a billet aboard one of these hard working craft.

Sport fishing, for marlin and other big sport fish, is another Hatteras specialty. The Hatteras Marlin Tournament is perhaps the biggest single week in Hatteras Village. Fifty or sixty private boats, carrying some of the East Coast's leading politicians and businesspeople, attend this invitation-only championship, one of the most prestigious in the country. The Tournament is hosted by the Hatteras Marlin Club, in the Village, and takes place the second week in June.

HATTERAS ISLAND
ATTRACTIONS

PEA ISLAND NATIONAL WILDLIFE REFUGE
N. end of Hatteras Island   987-2394

Once you cross Oregon Inlet, leaving the Herbert C. Bonner bridge behind, you're in Pea Island. On your left is the surf, on your right the marsh. And everywhere, everywhere -- are birds.

Pea Island was founded on April 12, 1938, when Congress provided that Pea Island be preserved as a haven for wildlife, specifically as a wintering area for the Greater Snow Goose. Roosevelt's CCC was put to work stabilizing the dunes with bulldozers and sea oats, sand fences were built, dikes were constructed to form ponds, and freshwater marshes and fields planted to provide food for wildfowl. The refuge was seldom visited by tourists until the Oregon Inlet bridge was constructed in 1964. Now Pea Island is one of the most popular spots on the island with naturalists, bird-watchers, and just plain lovers of wildlife.

Both bird watchers and wreck lovers will want to stop at a Rest Area some 4 1/2 miles south of the Bonner Bridge. To the surf side, if you walk over the dunes to your left, you will be able to glimpse the remains of the Federal transport *Oriental*. The black mass is thought to be her steel boiler, all that remains of the ship that went ashore in May, 1862. To the sound side, a short walk leads to an overlook of North Pond and New Field, where special crops are sown each year for the use of the waterfowl that winter over in the milder climate of the Banks. (See "North Pond Trail.")

While there, you may see some of the Refuge's guests. The 5,915 acres of the Refuge are an important wintering ground for whistling swans, snow geese, Canada geese, and 25 species of ducks. Many other interesting species, such as the Savannah (Ipswich) sparrow, migrant warblers, shorebirds, gulls, terns, herons and egrets can be found here during the winter months and the spring and fall migrations. During the summer months several species of herons, egrets, and terns, along with American avocets, willets, black-necked stilts, and a few species of ducks nest at the Refuge. Oceanic species can be expected during most any season but are most common from late summer through fall into late winter. Following storms, many

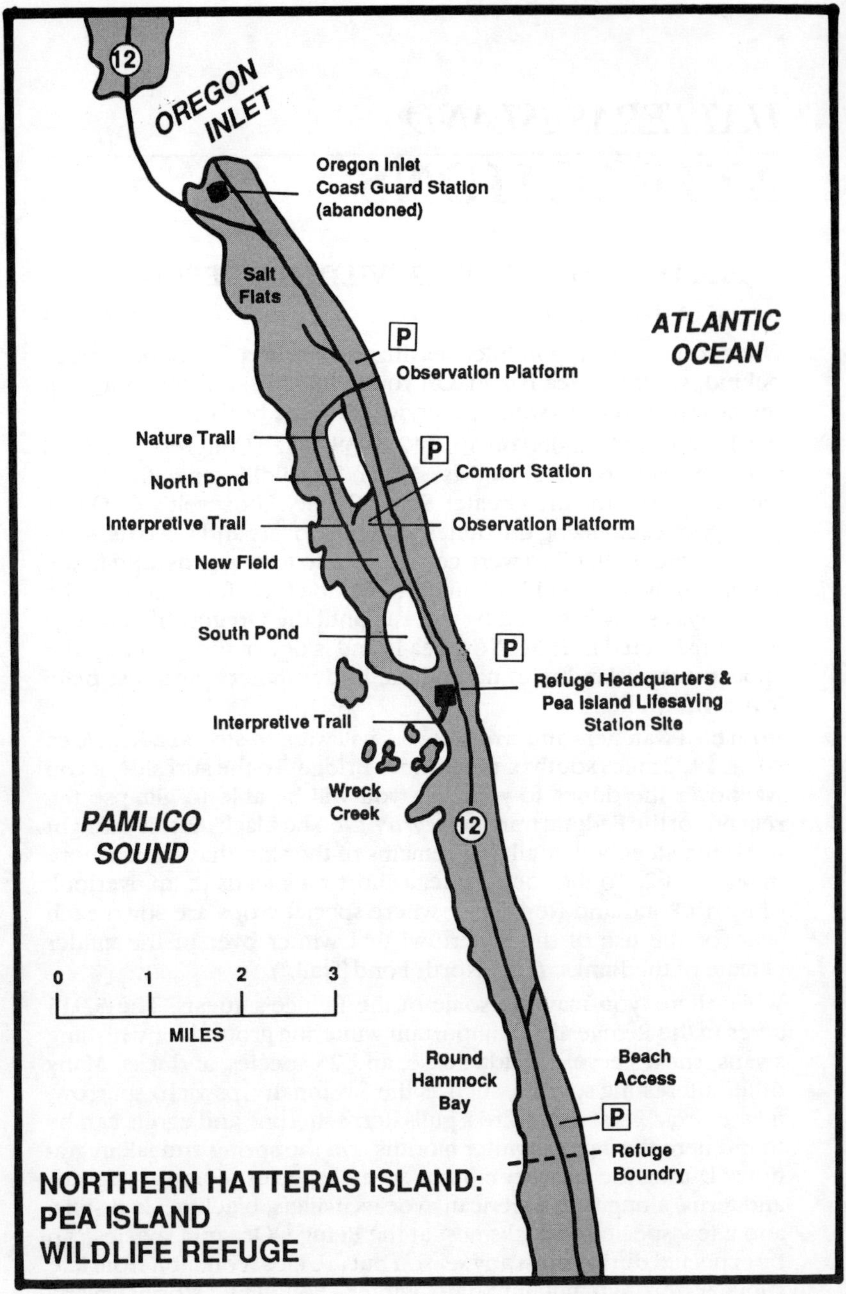

NORTHERN HATTERAS ISLAND:
PEA ISLAND
WILDLIFE REFUGE

species unusual for this area have been observed. In all, over 265 species of bird have been identified repeatedly at the Refuge or over the ocean nearby, with another 50 species of accidental or rare occurrence. Mosquito/bug spray is recommended here March through October. Also see the section on ticks in the back of the book.

Regarding Loggerhead turtles: volunteers patrol Memorial Day to Labor Day looking for nests, relocating them if necessary and guarding hatchlings on their way to the sea. To volunteer, contact the Outdoor Recreation Planner at Alligator River (919)473-1131.

The Refuge is controlled from the Headquarters, some 7 1/2 miles south of Oregon Inlet.

NORTH POND TRAIL

Pea Island

This self-guided nature trail, a favorite with birdwatchers, starts five miles south of Oregon Inlet Bridge, and two and a half miles north of the Pea Island Refuge Headquarters. Parking area and a restroom building mark the beginning of the trail. The trail is roughly a mile long and will take you half an hour to walk briskly to the sound and back.

The trail itself is on top of a dike between two manmade ponds. (It's easily negotiable. Though interrupted by a stepped viewing platform about 200 yards from the road, we judge a wheelchair could negotiate around it, if you have a strong helper.) The ponds and dike were constructed in the 1930s and early '40s by the CCC. Wax myrtles and live oaks stabilize the dike and provide shelter for songbirds. Warblers, yellowthroats, cardinals, and seaside sparrows rest here during their spring and fall migrations.

On either side you'll look out over an intensively managed ecosystem of pond and field. The fields are planted with such bird goodies as rye grass and fescue. In winter you can see hundreds of snow geese and canada geese resting and eating, and cattle egrets in summer. Pheasants, muskrats, and nutria live here year 'round.

The diketop view in ideal for birdwatchers. Bring a tripod-mounted scope of at least 15x, and probably 25x will be better; the ranges are long over the pond. However, this trail isn't just for birdwatchers. It's just a nice break from the near-continual pressure to buy and consume that is now part of the Outer Banks experience. A warning: bring insect spray; check for ticks after leaving.

PEA ISLAND REFUGE HEADQUARTERS
Highway 12   987-2394

On the sound side, 7 1/4 miles south of Oregon Inlet, is the headquarters building. There's a small parking area and a Visitor Contact Station manned by Refuge volunteers (Monday through Friday, April to November, 8-4). Though visitor services there are limited, you may want to stop in. Information is available on bird watching and use of nature trails. Special public programs are offered during the summer months.

We talked with personnel there about what you can and cannot do on the Refuge. You're not allowed to hunt. No camping, no open fires. Dogs must be on a leash. Four wheel drive vehicles are not permitted on the beach. Firearms are not permitted within the confines of the Refuge. Headquarters personnel say that even on the road, driving straight through, shotguns and such must be stowed out of sight. Those hunting farther south on Hatteras are advised not to flaunt their equipment on the Refuge. Beach fishing is permitted. Fishing, crabbing, boating, etc. are allowed on the ocean or soundside, but not in Refuge Ponds.

We might suggest one side trip from the headquarters building. It's only a few hundred feet, but it takes you back a century in time. East of the building, across the highway, you'll find a triptych of plaques. And over the dunes, in the surf or on the beach, you'll find a few remnants of concrete foundation.

Those bare chunks are the remnants of Pea Island Station, the only US Lifesaving Service station to be manned entirely by blacks. How it came to be so, and what they accomplished, is a little-known story that deserves to be told here.

Established with the rest of the stations in 1879, Pea Island was at first, like the others, manned by entirely white crews. Like the others, it had black personnel, but they were confined to such menial tasks as caring for the tough little ponies that dragged the surfboats through the sand.

But this first crew let the Service down. They were dismissed in 1880, one year later, for negligence in the Henderson disaster. The authorities then collected the black personnel from the other stations, placed them under the charge of Richard Etheridge, who was part black and part indian, and set them to their duty.

They fulfilled it magnificently. In dozens of disasters, the Pea Island Crew risked life and health in rescuing the crews and passengers of the vessels that came driving ashore in northeaster and hurricane.

Etheridge became known as one of the best-prepared, most professional, and most daring men in a Service where professionalism and selflessness were a matter of course.

Probably the most famous of their rescues was the *E. S. Newman*. That story is recounted in the dry summary prose of The Annual Report of the Operations of the United States Life Saving Service for the Fiscal Year Ending June 30, 1897:

"Oct. 11 (1896), American Schooner *E. S. Newman*, Pea Island, North Carolina.

"Sails blown away and master obliged to beach her during hurricane two miles below station at 7 P.M. Signal of distress was immediately answered by patrolman's Coston light. Keeper and crew quickly started for the wreck with beach apparatus. The sea was sweeping over the beach and threatened to prevent reaching scene of disaster, but they finally gained a point near the wreck. It was found to be impossible to bury the sand anchor, as the tide was rushing over the entire beach, and they decided to tie a large-sized shot line around two surfmen and send them down through the surf as near the vessel as practicable. These men waded in and succeeded in throwing a line on board with the heaving stick. It was made fast to the master's three-year-old child, who was then hauled off by the surfmen and carried ashore. In like manner his wife and the seven men composing the crew were rescued under great difficulties and with imminent peril to the life-savers. They were all taken to station and furnished with food and clothing, and during next three days the surfmen aided in saving baggage and stores from wreck. On the 14th three of the crew left for Norfolk, and on the 21st the remainder departed for their homes, the vessel having proved a total loss."

BIRDING ON PEA ISLAND

Virginia Valpey, a Refuge volunteer, contributed this advice to the Guide on birding:

Pea Island is a particularly fine birding area, especially during the spring and fall. There is a variety and an abundance of bird life passing through the "Atlantic flyway" over Pea Island, one of several air routes that migrating birds use regularly during their semi-annual trips north and south.

The beginning birder should arm him or herself with a good field guidebook and a pair of decent seven to ten-power binoculars. Among several excellent field guides on the market, the most familiar is Roger Tory Peterson's *A Field Guide to the Birds* (Houghton Mifflin Co., Boston.) This guide and others are available at any good bookstore. (In this area, the National Park Service sells them at the Wright Brothers National Monument in Kill Devil Hills.) The easiest time to spot birds and identify them is spring. In most species, the males are more vividly colored during the mating season than at other times. Also, many "passerines" (perching birds) can be located -- and often identified -- by the particular song sung by the males to mark their territory during nesting season. Pick a warm (not hot), dry day, in the early morning, when birds are feeding. (Woodland birds tend to take a siesta during the hot midday). Dress in drab clothing that doesn't rustle, so that you can hear -- and won't startle -- the birds. Move slowly and quietly, listening and watching for movement in the trees or bushes. When you see movement, without taking your eyes off the spot, raise your binoculars to locate its source.

Some helpful hints for beginners trying to identify birds: first of all, determine the size of the bird. Compare your bird to one you are already familiar with -- a robin or a bluejay, say, or even a pigeon. Note the dominant color, and then note the color of its beak, its throat, breast, wings, back and tail.

Pay close attention to the beak -- shape as well as color. Seed- eating birds such as cardinals or sparrows, for instance, have relatively large, conical-shaped beaks suitable for cracking seeds, while flycatchers, which actually catch insects on the wing and thus have no need for this less aerodynamic appendage, have a slender bill.)

Notice whether the bird has wing bars and, if so, how many. Does the tail have a band across it? A different color under the tail? What shape is it? Finally, pay attention to what the bird is doing. A flycatcher won't scratch around on the ground like a towhee, and you won't find a woodpecker sucking pollen like a hummingbird or probing in shallow water like a dunlin.

Don't be discouraged if you can't identify everything right away. Start a life list to increase your pleasure in birding enormously. You will probably find that even if you are a rank beginner, you can probably list a dozen birds that you already know. Note the date, the species, and the location where you first identified the bird. You'll enjoy looking back over this list many times, and you will find you are eager to add to it. Good birding!

WILDFLOWERS ON HATTERAS ISLAND

Driving south from Oregon Inlet, roadsides afford a mixed wildflower population during most of the year.

Gigantic red drum proliferate in local waters. DCTB

The nearness of the warm Gulf Stream tends to keep temperatures from reaching extremes, and late autumn blooming plants such as the Goldenrods (Solidago) sometimes bloom well into January during a mild winter. Early Cresses (Barbarea) and Chickweeds (Stellaria) begin their flowering in February so there are almost always a few wildflowers on hand.

If you have chosen a late spring visit, roadside plants may include Blue-eyed Grasses (Sisyrinchium). This small, lily-like plant is in the Iris family and is recognizable by its startling bright blue color. It grows in large colonies that create carpets of blue along the highway in wet ditches and other damp places. Avon is a good place to see both this and a tiny, white orchid called Spring Ladies' Tresses (Spiranthes vernalis). Its leaves resemble grass and the flowers are borne pole-style on a single twisted stem.

Groups of Yuccas are also fairly common; they are huge and tough with long, dangerously pointed, fibrous evergreen leaves encircling the thick, trunk-like stem. Fat, cream, bell-shaped flowers bloom in a large cluster that rises above the plant's leafy parts. The hairy, prickly Yellow Thistle (Cirsium horridulum) blooms at this time too. Its hefty size makes it easy to spot, and its large, fluffy looking flower head is palest yellow. A couple of high climbing vines are worth looking for. Yellow Jessamine (Gelsemium sempervirens) has a thick trumpet-shaped flower of brilliant yellow. It blooms in April. Coral Honeysuckle (Lonicera sempervirens) has smaller, narrower flowers of a similar design and is a firey orange-red. Both are evergreen.

Summer brings quantities of Gaillardias (Gaillardia pulchella) or Jo Bells, as they are known locally. Introduced here years ago, these low growing, hardy plants are so salt resistant that you may see them near your oceanfront cottage. Looking a lot like daisies, they are abundant along sandy roadsides and come in mixtures of red and yellow or occasionally solid yellow. Both the Yellow and the White Sweet Clovers (Melilotus officinalis and Melilotus alba) are common -- especially near the villages of Avon and Buxton. Seaside Croton (Croton punctatus), in the same family as the Poinsettias of Christmas fame, bloom near the ferry docks in Hatteras Village as well as quite near beaches. Mowers generally make their appearance by the end of June and from then on, staying ahead of them can be difficult. Everything looks like a short lawn after their passage.

From late summer through early winter, Goldenrods (Solidago), Asters and Bonesets (eupatorium) may all be seen along most roadsides. Bushes with berries become colorful at this time. Yaupon Holly (Ilex vomitoria), from which the old timers made tea, shows red berries beginning in November. Bayberry bushes (Myrica pensylvanica) on the north end of the island bear clusters of silver covored, waxy berries. The foliage smells spicy. Flowering Water Bushes, (Baccharis halimifolia) resemble clouds of white feathers and the Beauty Berry Bushes (Callicarpa americana) produce dense clusters of intensely fuschia berries along their branches. Patches of Hairawn Muhly (Muhlenbergia capillaris), a highly salt resistant grass, looks like purple or pink fog banks on the ocean side of the highway near Salvo.

Cape Hatteras, like much of the rest of the Outer Banks, is home to many other salt resistant wildflowers and weeds. On the widest part of the island near the Cape itself is Buxton Woods, a genuine maritime forest of some three thousand acres. Its dense canopy provides good protection from most salt spray, and a variety of plants flourishes within its borders. The forest covers a series of ridges which are old or relic dunes and low, wet, freshwater valleys called swales. There are also a number of shallow ponds called sedges and a few somewhat deeper ponds.

The best viewing of forest plants is along the Buxton Woods Nature Trail, built and maintained by the National Park Service. The trail is near the Cape Hatteras Lighthouse, but make a right turn instead of the left you would make to enter the lighthouse grounds. There is a clearly visible sign on the right marking the trail's beginning and a parking area with plenty of spaces. Small, well placed plaques provide good information about plants and other items of interest to be found on the looped path. Since its length is only three quarters of a mile, it's a pleasant walk.

A late summer little mint named Blue Curls (Trichostema dichotomum) may be found at the trail's entrance as may Golden Aster or Silkgrass (Chrysopsis graminifolia) with its dusty looking, grass-like leaves. There is Common Bladderwort (Utricularia vulgaris) in the waters of Jennette's Sedge which runs along the edge of the trail's right fork. The thready underwater leaves of this meat eating, freshwater plant have small bladders which entrap tiny water-dwelling animals which the plant then uses as food.

You will doubtless encounter many more plants than have been mentioned. If curiosity is running high, book stores offer some good basic wildflower guides.

Barbara Midgette's soon to be published *Cape Hatteras Wildflowers* contains color photographs and complete descriptions of flowering plants found locally.

CHICAMACOMICO LIFE SAVING STATION
Rodanthe

The buildings, once boarded up, with broken windows, and rusted padlocks, are now restored to their stately beauty, thanks to a group of dedicated citizens who refused to see the historic buildings fade into oblivion. For Chicamacomico was one of the most famous Life Saving Stations on the Outer Banks.

In 1874, Chicamacomico Station was part of a daring new concept in lifesaving. In that year the U.S. Life Saving Service was building a chain of seven stations along the Banks, at the points of greatest danger for oceangoing vessels. (See "The U.S. Life Saving Service" for their story.)

And Chicamacomico Station at Rodanthe, Number 179, was foremost. Under three Keepers -- Captain Little Bannister Midgett III (Ban), Captain John Allan Midgett, Jr., and Captain Levene Westcott Midgett -- it guarded the sea along the northern coast of Hatteras for 70 years. Number 179 and the Midgetts are still legends in the Coast Guard. Since 1876 seven Midgetts have been awarded the Gold Life Saving Award and three the silver; six worked or lived at Chicamacomico.

The Station was active through World War II, until the Coast Guard closed it down in 1954. It languished unused for some years threafter, and many readers will remember its sagging, rotting roof, its boarded-up windows.

Today, like so many previously unappreciated reminders of the Banks' seagoing heritage, it is being restored. The Chicamacomico Historical Association, Inc., a nonprofit organization established for its preservation, has cleaned up the interior, restored the exterior, and has opened displays in the main station building. They've received some federal and state grants, but only on a matching fund basis. So you can help doubly with a check to the Association at P.O. Box 140, Rodanthe, NC 27968. Be a Lifesaver!

During the summer, Chicamacomico is the site of commemorative life saving drills held by the National Park Service. Schedule: every Thursday at 2 p.m., from mid-June to the end of August. Bring your cameras. Admission is free.

THE WRECKS OF NORTHERN HATTERAS

One of our nicest memories is the sunny, still day of late winter when we scrambled over the dunes of northern Hatteras with two friends after a storm. On the bare beach we found a freshly-uncovered wreck. We were able to date it to the mid-nineteenth century by the method of fastening sheathing to ribs. We searched the sand in the still silence and found momentoes: a tiny bottle that might have held opium or perfume, a spar with emaciated iron fittings still attached, a broken teacup, a quaintly shaped whiskey bottle with the rotting remains of a cork. No treasure chest -- not that time.

Yes, literally hundreds of ships have gone ashore on these beaches in four hundred years. And most of them are still here. Wood, buried in sand along the Banks, holds up surprisingly well. The continual wrestle of beach and sea yields them up from time to time. Michael McOwen, who flies a light plane out of Manteo, made out the ribs of an old sailing ship one day in about thirty feet of water off the beach; he snorkled out as soon as it got warm enough and had himself some fine tautog and porkfish. And there are more modern ships as well: in February, 1948, while being towed to Charleston, LST 471 parted her lines and drifted ashore at Rodanthe. Personnel from the then-still-active Chicamacomico Coast Guard Station rescued three of the crew with beach apparatus. Previous visitors will remember that the pilothouse was visible for some years, up till 1985, when a storm tore it apart and sent part of the hull crashing into the fishing pier. The remainder of it is (at least at time of writing) buried by sea and sand. But it willl be back one day, like all the other ghost ships of the Outer Banks.

Anywhere is fine to scramble up over the dunes and begin your search. Wrecks, like gold, are where you find them.

U.S. COAST GUARD FACILITY, BUXTON

Buxton   995-5881

Formerly the Naval facility at Buxton, the grounds and buildings were turned over to the Coast Guard in June of 1982. It's not normally open for visitors, but retired military, dependents, and military personnel may use the few remaining facilities. There's a limited commissary, a small exchange, small mess hall recreational facilities (tennis, basketball, and beach swimming), and a small dispensary. The hours, at all military bases and stations, are subject to change, but don't plan on anything being open after 5 p.m.

THE ALTOONA WRECK

Cape Point

Driving to the end of the Cape Point road, you will see Ramp 44 straight ahead. Don't try to drive over, or even to, this ramp in a regular car. A four-wheel-drive vehicle will make it over the soft sand between the road and the ramp; a two-wheel-drive one will not. We speak from experience, as we tried to and lost...and towing fees in Buxton are, to say the least, uncompetitive. Instead leave your car on the solid ground near the road and walk over the ramp. Walk on over the ramp and continue on the foot trail that veers off at a forty-five degree angle at the base of the dune. At the edge of the seawater pond -- about a 10 minute walk from where you parked your car -- you'll find all that remains of the sea-savaged *Altoona*.

The *Altoona* was a cargo ship, a two-masted, 100'-long schooner out of Boston. She was built in Maine in 1869. In 1878 she left Haiti with a load of dyewood bound for New York. She was driven ashore on the Cape by a storm on October 22, 1878. Her crew of seven was rescued, the deck cargo lost, but the cargo in the hold was salvaged. A few years sufficed for the shifting sands to bury her. She reemerged in 1962 in a storm, and was quickly broken apart by the sea. The bow and part of the hull, still with greenish copper teredo sheathing on it, lie pointing south. A few odd pieces of her ribs and beams lie scattered between her and the Atlantic.

DIAMOND SHOALS LIGHT

Off Cape Point

From the lighthouse, or even from the eastern shore of Cape Point, you may be able to see on a clear night a sudden white flash of light from far out at sea. Time it; if the flashes come every two and half seconds, you are looking at the Diamond Shoals Light, some twelve miles out at sea southeast of the lighthouse, marking the end of the Shoals that have claimed so many ships.

Through the years, there have been numerous attempts to build lighthouses out there, on the shifting sandbars; all have failed. Three lightships have been on station there since 1824. The first was sunk in a gale, in 1827; the second lasted from 1897 until 1918, when it was sunk by the German submarine U-140; and the third remained in service until 1967, when it was replaced with the present steel structure.

How long will it last?

THE MONITOR

Off Cape Hatteras

Every American knows the story of the Monitor from schoolbooks. How, during the Civil War, the Confederates built the first ironclad warship from the hulk of the Union frigate Merrimack, renaming it the Virginia. How, in the early hours of March 8, 1862, the tent-shaped ship steamed out of Norfolk to challenge a Union blockading force of six wooden ships -- and how, by the end of the day, she had sunk two of them and damaged another. Broken the blockade, and written a new chapter in naval history.

The Monitor was an even more daring innovation. Built by John Ericsson, a Swedish-American engineer, the "Cheesebox on a raft" was a low-slung ironclad whose main battery was carried in a futuristic revolving turret. Arriving in Norfolk in the nick of time -- the next day -- the Monitor battled her adversary throughout the ninth, and finally, the fight at a draw, the Virginia retreated back under the guns of Norfolk.

Neither of these first ironclads lived very long. The Virginia was destroyed by retreating Confederates; the Monitor, ordered south, foundered off Cape Hatteras during a New Years' Eve storm in 1862. And there she lay for a hundred and twenty years, unseen by human eye, even her location unknown.

She was rediscovered in 1975, resting quietly upside down, just as she sank, in two hundred feet of water 25 kilometers south-southeast of Cape Hatteras.

Since then, the Monitor has been designated the first National Underwater Marine Sanctuary, and has been the object of repeated dives and evaluations by government agencies and underwater archaeologists. A few small artifacts -- bottles, silverware, that sort of thing -- have been recovered, and in 1983 the ship's distinctive four-bladed anchor was located and raised by a NOAA/East Carolina University expedition.

So far, aside from a collection of artifacts at the Visitor Center, there's nothing to actually see of the Monitor. But someday there might be. NOAA is considering the feasibility of raising the turret, which is relatively complete, and possibly other parts of the ship's hull for preservation and eventual display.

The Hatteras Village Civic Association had attempted to bring a Monitor Maritime Museum to the village, containing relics of the ship and other displays interpreting the long maritime history of the island. Though the powers that be decided the *Monitor* artifacts would go to the Mariners Museum in Hampton, Va., it looks as if the Association and its many allies have finally won through to their goal of a museum. It should be open in 1992. More here as plans develop.

CAPE POINT, CAPE HATTERAS NATIONAL SEASHORE

Buxton

As you continue that leisurely drive south along the length of Hatteras Island, you will come to the sharp elbow in the road that leads into Buxton. To your left, beyond a small cluster of motels, you can hear the surf booming; to the right are the trees of a small forest -- here, on the Banks! As highway 12 curves to the right, signs point to the left, toward the Lighthouse and the Coast Guard Facility. Resist your first impulse to turn, continue about 200 yards past the turn for the Facility, and turn left there to the Cape Point area of the Cape Hatteras National Seashore.

The approach is beautiful in and of itself. It is a winding drive between brush-covered dunes, with the white and black striped Lighthouse looming on your left. There's a nice photograph on your left, about halfway there, where the lighthouse is reflected in the water of a pond.

The Cape Point area contains a number of attractions and recreational opportunities: the Visitor Center, the Lighthouse, a shipwreck, a nature trail, and a campground. Surfing and surf-fishing are permitted year round, and a protected (lifeguarded) beach is available for swimming near the campground (by Ramp 43) in the summer.

HATTERAS ISLAND VISITOR CENTER

Near Hatteras Lighthouse   995-4474

Built in 1854, this two-story frame house was for many years the home of the assistant keepers of the light (the smaller home just to the east was the quarters of the Keeper himself). Today it's a National Park Service Visitor Center, the central one for the island of Hatteras, and extensive historical renovation was completed in 1986 to restore the building to its original condition. The Principal Keepers Quarters has been restored too.

Along with a helpful ranger at the information desk, it now houses a well kept museum devoted to Man and the Sea at Hatteras. The exhibits and displays center around shipping, the Cape at War, Making the Cape Safe, the lighthouses themselves, and the heroism of the Life Saving Service, later to become the Coast Guard. There's information on the rescue of passengers from stranded ships in storms, and a small but well-stocked bookstore carries related books. Last but not least there are clean restrooms.

In addition to its own exhibits, the Center is where you can obtain a schedule for the activities the Park Service conducts on Hatteras Island during the summer, and at a reduced pace in spring and fall. They change each season, of course, but here are samples of what's offered:

SEASHORE ARTS -- What you can create with things you pick up by the sea.

HATTERAS HISTORY -- What it was like at Cape Point a hundred or more years ago.

FISH WITH A RANGER -- Surf-fishing...how to do it. Bring your own bait.

CATCH A SAFE WAVE -- How to surf.

BIRD WALK -- Bird-watching with an expert around the Point.

Most of these programs, as well as others, are conducted weekly. Pick up a schedule at the Center, or call the number above, for exact times and dates.

The Center is open from 9 to 5 daily September through May, and 9 a.m. to 6 p.m. in June, July and August (hours subject to change).

CAPE HATTERAS LIGHTHOUSE

Cape Point

For over a hundred and seventy-five years, mariners rounding stormy, dangerous Cape Hatteras have searched for the glimmer of Cape Hatteras Light to assure them of safety. Sometimes they found it in time; sometimes, as the bare-boned wrecks on the point testify, they didn't.

Hatteras has been a place of danger for ships since the Europeans first began crossing the Atlantic. Its typically turbulent weather is caused by the confluence of two currents: the warm, northward-flowing Gulf Stream, and the southbound, inshore Virginia Coastal Drift. An eight mile finger of shoal water, the Diamond Shoals, and the low, featureless nature of the Banks coastline conspired to lure hundreds of ships to rest in the 'Graveyard of the Atlantic'.

The first lighthouse at Hatteras Point was raised in 1802. When we first began to write about the Outer Banks, not that many years ago, its sandstone ruin was still visible about three hundred yards south of the present lighthouse. A blizzard in March, 1980 finally took it, so utterly that you can now search the beach for a single piece of crumbling sandstone. It was ninety feet high, with a feeble whale oil light, and proved inadequate. Also, as the century progressed, it became evident that erosion would soon overtake it. It was heightened and improved, but as the years went by, erosion weakened it, and by the late 1860s it had to be replaced. The War between the States had left its mark, too; the Confederates, retreating in 1861, took the light's lens with them.

The new lighthouse was built in 1869-70, of 1 1/4 million Philadelphia-baked bricks, at a cost of $150,000. It's built on a crisscross of heavy pine beams, with its foundation eight feet deep in the sand. A granite base sits atop that, and then the brick begins, carrying the lighthouse up to the light at 180 feet, and from there to the very tip of the lightning rod two hundred and eight feet above the foundation. The first light installed was whale oil, with a special Fresnel lens to flash its beam far out to sea. The eye-catching spiral paint job was added to make the lighthouse visible far out at sea during the day, so that ships could determine their position by taking bearings from a known point. When it was completed, the old lighthouse was dynamited. The new lighthouse was in service from 1870 to 1935, when it was abandoned, due to beach erosion. The erosion halted, and in 1950 the lighthouse was reactivated by the Coast Guard. Today its 800,000 candlepower electric light rotates every 7 1/2 seconds, reaching out more than 20 miles to sea.

From the Visitor Center you can walk across to the lighthouse. As you can see, the beach migration that destroyed the first beacon here is seriously threatening the second. The sea seems to hate lighthouses; it either strands them inland, as it did at Bodie Island, or it eats them, as it does lighthouses on the French side of the English Channel -- and as it ate the great Pharos of Alexandria, the first lighthouse ever. Perhaps it is in revenge for the ships these lights have cheated them of...This threat became critical in December of 1980, when the high tide came within fifty feet of the structure's base! There were intense efforts to save it, including sandbagging and the dumping of rubble; but most geologists now agree that the beach built back naturally -- at least for a time.

As a result, though, the National Park Service, the state of North Carolina, and the "Save Our Lighthouse" campaigners (whom we helped) have mounted an intensive effort to thwart the Atlantic Ocean. Various experts proposed options ranging from moving the lighthouse bodily inland to letting it "go gently into that good night." In October of 1986 Congress okayed funds to build a huge seawall or revetment around the structure, at an estimated cost of $5 million. The idea is to stabilize the land the lighthouse sits on and let the ocean rise, or the sand erode, unimpeded around it. Eventually the site will be isolated, an offshore island -- though this will likely take decades. However, action has not yet been taken pending further research. The National Academy of Sciences has recommended that the lighthouse be moved 600 feet inland, and the National Park Service has decided that a move would be the most appropriate and long term solution for saving the structure. Nothing is permanant on the Banks. But one thing is certain: this striking structure is one of the quintessential symbols of Hatteras. Of the men who for centuries have battled its seas, and the women who battled to build their lives and families waiting at home. We hope it's been saved for generations to come.

BUXTON WOODS NATURE TRAIL

Cape Point

The Nature Trail is 3/4 mile long, leading from the road through the wooded dunes, vine jungles, and fresh-water marshes of Buxton Woods. It's one of the best nature trail on the Banks. It is a must...don't miss it.

Beginning on the right side of the road south from the lighthouse to the Point, the trail winds at first among low sand hills, then into the maritime microforest that has gradually established itself on this broadest part of the island. Its natural beauty is enhanced by small plaques, masterfully written, explaining the changing surroundings in terms of the closed, fragile ecosystems of the Banks; the water table, the role of beach grass and sea oats in stabilizing dunes, the beach microforest and its stages of development, and the harshness of the Banks environment of wind, sand, and salt.

There are cottonmouths on this trail, unmistakably fat-bodied rough-scaled snakes in various dull colors (brownish, yellowish, grayish, varying almost to black), though they are rare. Don't stick your hands or feet where you can't see. If you encounter a snake, allow it time to get away; generally it will retreat. The local people advise extra caution when encountering a cottonmouth during chill weather, in spring or fall. During this period, they say, the snakes are less confident of their ability to get away from you, since they're rather sluggish in cool weather, and they're more likely to attack. In mid-summer they will often scurry off quickly. If they stand their ground, though, we advise retreat!

It might also be a good idea to glance over the section on ticks and chiggers in the Directory before starting out.

We don't recommend this trail for handicapped or very small children, but for everyone else, it's a must.

Picnic tables and charcoal grills are located just south of it for lunch.

BILLY MITCHELL AIR FIELD

Frisco

This is a small no-frills landing strip located about a mile south of Highway 12 just west of Frisco. Named after the controversial Army aviator who conducted some of his bombing tests near here in 1921, the strip is 3,000 feet long, 75 feet wide, oriented NE/SW, and asphalt paved.

FRISCO NATIVE AMERICAN MUSEUM

Frisco 995-4440

From the outside this looks like a gift shop, but inside we were rather taken aback to find rooms of Joyce and Carl Bornfriend's personal fifty-year collection of Native American artifacts. Hopi drums, pottery, kachinas, weapons, jewelry -- it's not professionally obtained, catalogued, or displayed, but it's real. Actually this type of hodgepodge of good pieces, curiosa, and outright junk is what all museums were like in the early 1800s (the *Kunstkamera* in Leningrad, for example). Lectures to school groups, etc. can be arranged through a nonprofit educational foundation. Worth a stop on a rainy day. Variable hours off season, summer 10 a.m. to ? p.m. (hours vary at closing, too).

THE "GRAVEYARD OF THE ATLANTIC" MUSEUM

Hatteras Village

We'll jump the gun a little here with advance notice of this planned museum for the Village. Now being designed for a site on National Park Service land near the ferry terminal, the museum's general concept and story line have been approved. We look for it circa 1992.

THE U.S. LIFE SAVING SERVICE

In 1874, the U. S. Life Saving Service was a daring new concept. In that year the Federal Government began building a chain of seven stations along the Banks, at the points of greatest danger for ocean-going vessels. Each station was supervised by a Keeper, and had permanent winter crews of six skilled, strong, and brave surfmen. They quickly proved their worth in an area known to all seamen as the "Graveyard of the Atlantic." Ships had a habit of coming ashore on the Banks in storms; the strong northeast winds and seas that developed during winter storms drove them helpless into shoal waters, where pounding surf soon broke them up. Those who tried

The Chicamacomico Lifesaving Station in Rodanthe is being restored to its former splendor. DCTB

to swim ashore or row in life boats usually perished, battered to death in the icy water by waves and debris, or -- even if they made it ashore safely -- freezing slowly on a deserted coast.

The mission of the Life Saving Service was to rescue those on grounded ships...and a demanding, often suicidal mission it was, too. The surfmen stood watch all along the coast, in the foulest winter weather. Once a wreck was spotted, they had to return to the station, get boats, rescue gear, and the rest of the crew, and then drag everything in heavy carts through the soft sand to where the stricken vessel lay. There they might go out to her by boat, driven not by engines but by strong arms on the oars; might attempt to swim out; might fire a line with a Lyle gun and pull the shipwrecked mariners and passengers to safety one by one by breeches buoy high above the deadly surf. In the wrecks of the *Metropolis* (1878), *A..B. Goodman* (1881), and dozens of others, these hardy men, for the most part native Bankers, distinguished themselves in courage and seamanship.

Some flavor of what they went through is preserved between the faded blue covers of the Annual Reports of the Operations of the U.S. Life-Saving Service. A century old now, their pages fragile as old iron found in the surf, their laborious prose still evokes the terror of gigantic, freezing surf, the incredible heroism of these common men. Here, shortened a bit and paragraphed more closely to modern tastes, but otherwise unchanged, is the story they tell of one day in the Life Saving Service: the disastrous 24th of October, 1889.

"Wreck of the schooner *Henry P. Simmons.*

"October, 1889, was in general a very tempestuous month, but there can be little doubt that the most destructive storm experienced on the Middle Atlantic coast of the United States during the month was that which reached the coasts of Virginia and North Carolina on the afternoon of the 23rd, and raged with great violence and with but slight intermission until the evening of the 27th. The easterly wind blew at times with the violence of a hurricane, and drove the sea into mountainous billows which endangered all craft so unfortunate as to be within its influence. The low beaches of Virginia and North Carolina were literally strewn with wrecks, and the hardy crews of the Sixth District were kept exceedingly busy saving life and property. The storm had come with such suddenness that many coasters were unable to reach a harbor, and this will account for the great number of casualties . . . . In three instances . . . there was lamentable loss of life, the particulars of which are here given.

"The vessels involved were the schooners *Henry P. Simmons, Francis E. Waters,* and *Lizzie S. Haynes*; all three being wrecked within a few miles of each other, the first two in the night of the 23rd and the Haynes on the following day. The case of the Simmons was a particularly harrowing one, as, owing to the long duration of the storm and the great distance from the shore at which she sunk, it was not until the morning of the 28th that anything could be done by the crews of the neighboring stations . . . .

"The *Henry P. Simmons* was a fine, staunch three-masted schooner of about six hundred and fifty tons, hailing from Philadelphia, Pennsylvania. She carried a crew of eight men all told, and was commanded by Robert C. Grace, who owned an interest in her. She had sailed from Charleston, South Carolina, on or about October 17th, on her way to Baltimore, Maryland, deeply laden with a cargo of phosphate rock for use in the manufacture of fertilizers. The place where she sunk is a mile and a half to the northward and eastward of the Wash Woods Station . . . .

"The voyage was without special incident until the afternoon of the 23rd, when the gale set in from the northeast and with it a high and dangerous sea, which caused the vessel to plunge deeply and ship a great deal of water. The sole survivor, Robert Lee Garnett, a colored man, says that the deck was so constantly deluged by the seas that at 8 o'clock, when the fury of the storm made it necessary to take in the already closereefed mainsail, the men were unable to handle it for fear of being washed overboard; and all hands were driven to the rigging for safety. The helm was lashed amidships, and with no one to guide her the schooner was thus practically helpless, and drifted completely at the mercy of the wind and waves. Rain was also falling in torrents, so that it was impossible to see anything around them, and the poor fellows were quite ignorant of their distance from the shore, knowing only that they must be in the vicinity of False Cape, Virginia. The laboring of the vessel had also caused her to spring a leak, and this added to the peril of the situation, for she was liable to sink at any moment.

"In the midst of these dangers the men, by watching their opportunity, would descend to the deck and work the pumps until again driven to the rigging by the seas. At half past 10 o'clock that night the schooner struck with a crash on what is known as Pebble Shoal . . . and there she bilged and quickly filled with water. The top of the cabin was almost immediately swept away, and the vessel settled into the sand until the hull was wholly submerged, leaving nothing but the masts above water. What passed during the remaining hours of that dreadful night is a blank, beyond the statement of Garnett that at 3 o'clock in the morning (24th) the steward, a colored man, unable to hold on any longer, fell into the storm-lashed sea and was lost. This greatly shocked the rest.

"When day dawned the scene from the rigging of the wreck was a wild and terrifying one. The wind still raged and the waves broke into surf as far offshore as the eye could see through the pelting rain and spoon drift, while to the leeward lay the low sand hills, which ever and anon came into sight and were then hidden by the towering billows that madly chased one another shoreward, and were there scattered with thunderous roar into a smother of foam and spray upon the desolate beach.

"The first intimation the Wash Woods crew had of there being a craft in the offing was after midnight, when the incoming patrolman from the north beat reported a faint white light, apparently some distance off. This he had answered with his Coston danger-signal. It should be stated here that the storm tide had risen so high that it swept completely across the low parts of the beach, the water in some localities being over the lower floors of the stations. Under these conditions patrol duty was attended with the greatest difficulty and danger, the men having in places to wade hip-deep and being frequently driven to the knolls for safety.

"The next patrol upon returning at daylight brought news that a vessel had sunk during the night well off shore; the masts at that time showing above water about two-thirds of their length, while the end of the jib boom was just visible between the seas. The vessel lay with her head shoreward. And it was scarcely light when the patrolman passed her, he saw nothing of the crew. Another surfman was at once dispatched up the beach to obtain more definite information, and returned with the report that he could see several men in the rigging. It was impossible to handle the beach apparatus just then, by reason of the condition of the beach, but as soon as the water fell off on the ebb tide the men set out with the long-range gear and after a hard tug reached the scene at about 10 o'clock in the forenoon.

"In the meantime ... the second mate had been swept from the rigging and another man shared a like fate an hour or so later. Thus but five men were in the rigging when the station crew arrived, and shortly afterwards another fell into the sea.

"An attempt to reach the craft with a line thrown from the wreck-gun failed utterly, the shot dropping into the water about half way. It was thus demonstrated that, owing to the great distance, the beach apparatus was practically useless ... the schooner was at least one thousand yards off. Indeed the purpose of the keeper in firing the gun was more to reassure and encourage the poor fellows than from any hope of reaching them with the line. At the same time the surf was so high and dangerous that no human power could have forced a boat through it. The hands of the beachmen were practically tied. They could do nothing but watch and wait for the storm to abate and the sea to run down, and the outlook for this was not promising. Here, on the one hand, was a sunken vessel with her crew in the rigging, looking imploringly to the shore for help, and, on the other, a band of sturdy men skilled in the handling of boats in the surf and equipped with the most approved appliances for the saving of human life from the perils of the sea, but withal powerless to save. Yet this was the exact situation.

"At noon the party on the beach was reenforced by the arrival of the False Cape crew from the north . . . but their coming did no good, since the storm continued with unabated violence all day, and absolutely nothing could be done. With the approach of darkness driftwood fires were lighted and kept blazing all night to encourage the hapless sailors on the wreck. On the following day, (25th) at 8 o'clock, the tide being low, an effort was made with a picked crew to launch the boat, but although the gale had slackened a little, the surf was still tremendously high and the attempt failed. The agony of suspense the poor fellows suffered must have been terrible, as cold, wet, and hungry they clung with the desperation of despair to the dripping shrouds, watching for the relief which could not reach them, waiting for their awful doom. Towards noon one more unfortunate fell exhausted from the rigging and disappeared. This left but three remaining alive. . . "

The beach was vigilantly patrolled that night, an extra force of men being out watching for a lull . . . Three attempts were made (on the 26th) to reach the *Simmons,* but every time the boat was driven back full of water, the wind having changed to the southeast and set in more fiercely than before, with, if possible, a higher sea. Two of the remaining men were washed out of the rigging during the day in plain view of the people on the beach, and the day closed with but one man left on the wreck. The weather on the morning of the 27th was no more favorable, the wind falling in torrents, with a continuance of the southeasterly gale. Towards evening, however, the storm had nearly spent itself, and there was promise of a shift of wind to the westward. This was what the life-savers had been hoping for and it gave them encouragement, though there must necessarily be one more night of horror for the sufferer in the rigging before the sea could run down sufficiently for him to be reached. If he could hold on a few hours longer he would be saved.

"By midnight the wind had canted to the southwest and subsided to a moderate breeze. The sea also fell rapidly, so that at 5 o'clock in the morning of the 28th, before daylight, the surfboat was again moved down to the edge of the water in readiness for a launch. Life belts were then strapped on by the picked crew of oarsmen from the Wash Woods and False Cape crews, including Keeper O'Neal of the last-named station, and with the veteran keeper, Malachi Corbel, at the steering oar, a bold and successful dash was made through the heavy line of breakers at the bar. Once through these the boat was not long in reaching the sunken wreck, which, in the darkness, had to be approached with some caution to avoid entanglement in the cordage hanging from the spars. To the great relief of every man in the boat a faint response came to the keeper's hail, and presently there crept out into view the form of the sole survivor of the dreadful tragedy. He had been ensconced within the sheltering folds of the mizzen gaff-topsail, and this protection, with the aid of a splendid physique, had enabled him to withstand the great hardships to which he had been exposed. He had been without food of any kind for over four days, his only sustenance having been rainwater caught in the sail, and his survival was simply marvelous. Once in the boat no time was lost in transferring him to the shore, where restoratives from the medicine chest were quickly administered, and he was then conducted to the station, comfortably clad in warm garments from the supply box of the Women's National Relief Association, and otherwise cared for.

" . . . Five of the bodies of the drowned seamen were subsequently recovered at various points along the shore, that of the captain being found on November 19th, nearly four weeks after death. All were given decent burial, the body of Captain Grace being afterward claimed and removed by relatives . . . .

"Wreck of the Schooner *Francis E. Waters.*
"Next in order is the wreck of the schooner *Francis E. Waters*, of Baltimore, Maryland, which was capsized and driven on the coast of North Carolina about two and three-quarter miles north of the Nag's Head Station, (Sixth District,) the same night that the *Henry P. Simmons* stranded, October 23, 1889. The entire crew perished. As shown in the preceding account, a furious storm raged all that night. Nothing was known of the disaster on shore until the next morning, when the schooner was discovered bottom up in the breakers. The story is necessarily brief. It appears that the *Francis E. Waters* left Georgetown, South Carolina, with a cargo of lumber and shingles for Philadelphia, Pennsylvania, on or about October

20th, her crew consisting of six men. The much-dreaded Frying Pan and Hatteras Shoals had been safely passed and the prospects seemed good for a quick voyage up the coast when, in the afternoon of the 23rd, the freshening easterly wind and the gathering clouds gave portent of the coming storm. By sundown the wind backed to the northeast and increased to a gale of terrific violence, the night becoming, in nautical phrase 'as dark as a pocket.' This, together with a tempest of driving rain and the blinding spray flying shoreward from the crests of the breakers, produced atmospheric conditions upon the shore absolutely impenetrable to human vision. There was also an extraordinarily high tide, so that after midnight almost the entire expanse of low beach was submerged, compelling the patrolmen for their own safety to take to the higher and remote parts of the shore, thus increasing the distance between themselves and the outer line of the breakers on the bar, where vessels might be expected to fetch up. This distance was fully from one-half to three-quarters of a mile, and in some places probably greater. The patrols of the Nag's Head and Kill Devil Hills Stations, between which the unfortunate craft stranded, met regularly and exchanged checks up to the time stated, but after that the surf and rising tide swept over the beach in greater volume, and cut such deep gullies in the sand that the man who took the north beat from Nag's Head at 3 o'clock in the morning of the 24th was unable to get nearer than within half a mile of the point where he should have met the south patrol from Kill Devil Hills.

"Therefore, after peering as far as was possible through the storm towards the end of his beat, he turned back, reporting upon reaching the station that he had been unable to get through, and that he had seen objects which he took to be lumber or wreckage of some kind floating in the swash of the surf. This it should be remarked is not an unusual occurrence . . . The patrol from the Kill Devil Hills Station, who should have met the patrol from Nag's Head, upon arriving at the halfway place and not finding anyone, pushed on south to ascertain the cause of the man's nonappearance. He had not gone more than a quarter of a mile beyond his own beat when, in the early gray of the morning, for it was now about 6 o'clock, he was startled by the discovery through the rain and mist of a vessel half submerged and bottom up in the breakers out on the bar. His first thought was for the crew, but there was not a soul to be seen on the ill-fated craft, so after satisfying himself on that point, and taking a long and searching look in every direction as far as the weather would permit, he retraced his steps to the station and reported his grim discovery to the keeper. The latter (Keeper Partridge,) at once telephoned the news to Keeper Van Buren Etheridge at Nag's Head; the wreck lying within the latter's patrol limits. Etheridge immediately turned out his men, and as the launching of a boat was out of the question, proceeded with such appliances as he thought might be needed to the locality of the wreck, the party arriving there at about half-past 8 o'clock. It was plainly to be seen that there could be no one on the half-buried hull against and over which the surf was dashing incessantly. A man could not have maintained himself there for a moment. The surfmen were therefore deployed along the beach in quest of bodies, and before long the search resulted in finding one corpse, that of a negro, entangled in a part of the rigging attached to a broken mast which had washed up some distance from the wreck, and been left by the now receding tide. This body was decently interred later in the day, there being no marks upon it which might lead to its identification.

" . . . A second body, that of a white man, was cast ashore nearly two weeks afterwards at a point at least thirty miles to the southward, and recovered by the crew of the Gull Shoal Station. It was identified as the body of R. W. Lecompte, of Cambridge, Maryland, one of the schooner's crew, and relatives came and removed it. . . .

"It is therefore supposed that, losing her canvas or springing a leak and becoming water-logged and unmanageable, she let go her anchors to avoid drifting into the breakers, when, the ground tackle failing to hold her, she fell off into the trough of the sea, rolled over on her beam ends, and in that condition drifted ashore before the gale and sea. This view is supported by the fact that after the subsidence of the gale, and the sea had gone down sufficiently to permit the launching of the surfboat . . . the crew found a quantity of wreckage outside the bar about a quarter of a mile from the shore, and this was attached in some way to the anchors on the bottom. Or it is possible that she capsized under too great a press of sail in the effort to work away from the treacherous sands under her lee. . . . "

"Wreck of the Schooner *Lizzie S. Haynes*.

"The third of the group of three disasters in the Sixth District attended with fatal results during the great October storm was that of the *Lizzie S. Haynes*, a three-masted schooner owned in Bath, Maine, which was wrecked between the Oregon Inlet and Pea Island Stations, on the coast of North Carolina, in the forenoon of October 24, 1889.

"The northeast storm was then raging in all its fury, and there was a frightful sea. Her crew numbered seven men, and of these all but two perished. She was a vessel of four hundred and thirty-seven tons and was bound from Savannah, Georgia, to Baltimore, Maryland, with a cargo of yellow-pine lumber. From the accounts received it appears that she was first sighted by the crew of the Oregon Inlet Station at about half past 8 o'clock, a mile or two distant to the northward and eastward, and could just be dimly made out through the blinding rain, as she plunged and rolled in the turbulent waters under scant canvas and with her head pointed offshore. It was soon evident that she was making no headway, but, on the contrary, was drifting to the leeward toward the land very fast. As she came nearer it was noticed that her crew had taken refuge in the rigging, a sure sign of her helpless condition. Two men could be seen in the fore shrouds, three in the main, and two in the mizzen. Keeper Paine, anticipating difficulty in rescuing them while such a high surf was tumbling in upon the beach, telephoned the news at once to Keeper Etheridge of the next station south (Pea Island), and asked his aid.

"By 9 o'clock, when the schooner was nearly abreast of Oregon Inlet, Paine and his men had set out with the breeches-buoy apparatus to follow her down the shore, but she drifted so rapidly before the gale, and the beach was so deeply flooded in places that it was found impossible to keep up with her. She struck at twenty minutes to 10 o'clock, three hundred yards from the beach, at a point three and three-quarter miles below Oregon Inlet and a little less than two miles north of the Pea Island Station. She was thus within Etheridge's beat. The latter, as requested by Paine, had promptly left his station with a spare shot-line, (a No. 7,) the medicine chest, and a bag of blankets, and being therefore lightly burdened and having the shorter distance to travel, he and his crew reached the scene first. Thinking that the sea would force the schooner along the bar still further south, and nearer to his station, Etheridge dispatched his men back with the horses for his own beach apparatus, while he proceeded on north to meet the Oregon Inlet crew to lend them a hand, and at the same time consult with his brother keeper. The latter arrived abreast of the vessel at 10 o'clock, before the Pea Island crew could return.

"In the meantime a distressing and terrible accident had befallen the hapless people on the schooner, which practically sealed the fate of all but two of their number. It happened about five minutes before the Oregon Inlet crew arrived. The two crews were at this moment hurrying to the scene from opposite directions with their life-saving appliances, when . . . the Oregon Inlet crew, then but a short distance away, were horrified by the sight of all three of the schooner's masts breaking off by the board, leaving nothing standing above the deck but a stump of about twenty feet of the mizzenmast. The masts fell toward the stern and carried all but one of the crew to the deck, that one falling overboard and being immediately swept out of sight.

"This appalling and exciting incident infused fresh energy into the little band of jaded life-savers as they pressed forward, and within five minutes of the time of their arrival the Oregon Inlet crew had thrown a line over the wreck. The line landed near the stump of the mizzenmast. This was not more than ten minutes after the spars fell. The lumber of the deck load was already coming ashore on every sea, and this, with the broken spars, the sails, and the rigging, formed quite an entanglement between the vessel and the beach.

"Only two men could be seen on board, the rest either having been severely injured or killed outright by their fall. These two were the captain and the steward. The latter caught the shot-line as it came near him, and both men began hauling it off in order to get the whip or larger line which would follow, but before they could gather much of it in the shot-line fouled the wreckage, and in the effort to free it it was broken or cut in twain. A second line was quickly fired from the shore as successfully as the first, but the current setting along the beach was so swift and strong, and there were so many other difficulties to contend with, the principal of which was the inability of the two men to haul off the line through the wreckage, that notwithstanding the most persistent effort it was nearly 4 o'clock in the afternoon before the poor fellows on the wreck, weakened and exhausted by exposure, could complete the rigging of the apparatus to the stump of the mast a few feet above the deck.

"When this was at last done the two men turned their attention to the mate, the only other member of the crew remaining alive, and made strenuous exertions to place him in the buoy first. But, injured as he was and suffering also from exposure, he had become delirious and resisted the efforts for his removal to the shore. The captain and steward were unable to manage him either by persuasion or force, and as night was nearly upon them, they reluctantly abandoned him to his fate and resolved to look out for themselves. The captain therefore got into the breeches buoy and was drawn safely to the beach, the steward following him just as darkness closed upon the scene. . . .

"The two rescued men, thoroughly used up, were conducted to the Pea Island Station as quickly as possible and properly cared for. As the tremendous surf on the rising tide had gradually pushed the schooner farther onto the shore, the crews of the two stations . . . returned to the beach and waited for an opportunity to board the wreck, hoping from what the captain had told them to be able yet to save the mate.

Pea Island National Wildlife Refuge is home to thousands of snow geese during the winters months. DCTB

"The opportunity . . . came with the ebb of the tide, which about midnight left her in such a position that the men were enabled to wade out to her. Quickly climbing on board they found two bodies, one the mate's, the other that of a seaman, the rest having been washed away. Both bodied appeared to be dead, but as the mate's was still supple, though cold, it was landed without delay and carried to a house on the beach, where, with restoratives from the medicine chest, all possible means were resorted to for its resuscitation. These efforts were kept up for two hours, until the stiffening muscles gave indubitable proof that life was beyond recall. Thus five of the little band of seven men composing the schooner's crew, who but a few hours before were in the full flower and promise of manhood, became the victims of the storm.

". . . The two bodies recovered from the wreck were provided with decent burial near the life-saving station. The rescued men remained at the station for a week, until able to travel to their homes, and during this period the crews of the two stations were engaged whenever opportunity offered -- for as shown in the account of the loss of the Henry P. Simmons the bad weather lasted for several days -- in recovering such articles as it was possible to save from the wreck.

"The following is the captain's letter:

"Oregon Inlet, North Carolina,

"November 1, 1889.

"Mr. S. I. Kimball,

General Superintendent U.S.Life-Saving Service, Washington, D.C.:

"I desire to express my thanks for the prompt service rendered by the keepers and crews of the Oregon Inlet and Pea Island Life-Saving Stations at the wreck of the schooner *Lizzie S. Haynes* on Pea Island, October 24, 1889, and would state that no default on the part of the life-savers or defect in the working of their gear was responsible for the loss of life that occurred on that day.

"W. A. Sawyer,

"Late Master of Schooner *Lizzie S. Haynes*."

The U.S. Life Saving Service was merged with the older Revenue Cutter Service in 1915 to form the U. S. Coast Guard. Its aircraft, surface craft, and support personnel, from stations at Coquina Beach (Oregon Inlet), Buxton, and Ocracoke, still guard the Banks and their offshore waters today.

HATTERAS ISLAND
RECREATION

HATTERAS ISLAND FISHING PIER
Spur Rd. 1247, E. of Hwy. 12   987-2323

The National Park Service has leased two piers to concessionaires along the fish-rich shores of Hatteras Island. Hatteras Island, in the small village of Rodanthe, is the northernmost. As you drive south on 12 from Oregon Inlet you'll find it on your left, well advertised by signs, as you pass through Rodanthe.

Hatteras Island Pier, also includes a motel and a restaurant. During the open season (April 1 to November 30), Louise Twine, the pier manager, provides bait, tackle, ice, tackle rental, and "all sorts of fishing paraphernalia." The pier is accessible to handicapped. Prices: $5.00 daily. Call Hatteras Island Motel at 987-2345 for weekly and seasonal rates.

Local fisherfolk recommend this pier for large channel bass, and as a matter of fact the (then) world's record of *ninety pounds* was caught here by Elvin Hooper in 1973. It is mounted here for view, and it's quite an inspiration. Plenty of parking.

WATERFALL PARK
Rodanthe   987-2213

This is the first, and so far the only, water slide and go-kart track south of Oregon Inlet. It includes Bumper Boats, Quad Runners, Can Am Races, and Honda Odyssey, Malibu Speed Races, Slic-trac, and 36 holes of mini-golf. You'll find it just south of Spur Road 1247, on Highway 12, sea side. The slide is an impressive structure, both from an engineering and a fun point of view. Four corkscrew turns provide a ride that the more common slides built on hills just can't match.

We liked the go-karts. Five-horse Honda engines propel these miniscule speedsters around the oval track. If you haven't tried go-karts yet, they operate just like a full-sized car, with gas pedal, brakes, and a centrifugal clutch, but everything happens *a lot faster*, especially with several other drivers competing for the road. This fun spot is open from 10 a.m. until 10 p.m. Memorial Day through Labor Day.

CAPE HATTERAS PIER

(Frisco Pier)
Frisco   986-2533

The second National Park Service concession pier on Hatteras, "Frisco," as it's called locally, is about two miles west of the village of Frisco -- and closest to the Gulf Stream. Built in 1960, the wooden pier is 600 feet long. Same species as the other piers, perhaps with more king mackerel. It's lighted, of course, and stocks bait, tackle, ice, and rental rods. There's a snack bar. Rates: basic fee $5.00 per day, $25.00 weekly, $100 for a season pass for an individual, $150 for a family, and $130 for a couple. Open from about April 1 to the end of November with hours being Sunday - Thursday, 6 a.m. to 11 p.m.; Friday and Saturday, 24-hours..

TEACH'S LAIR ISLAND YACHT CLUB

Hatteras Village   986-2532

This is the largest marina in a village full of marinas. Its eighty-six slips accommodate everything from ten feet long up to 42 feet, all with full hookups (no sewage). Services include a boat ramp, a medium-sized tackle shop with a good range of fishing gear, all kinds of bait, and ice; dive boat and skiff rentals; and dry storage for boats and campers. Several charter boats operate from here. They'll take you out in the Gulf Stream for about $600 a day or thereabouts. Finally, there's a campground next door, with full hookup drive-through sites. A lot of services, conveniently located a stone's throw from the Ocracoke ferry terminal.

HATTERAS HARBOR MARINA, INC.

Hatteras village   986-2166

HHM is located on the sound side of Highway 12, about 1 1/2 miles northeast of the Ocracoke ferry landing. There's been a lot of effort and construction going on here in the last few years, and the result is the most modern marina on Hatteras, in our judgment. It's the center of operations for 21 deep-sea charter fishing boats, making it pretty much the home of the Hatteras Village charter fleet. For charter reservations *only* call 1-800-356-6039.

Facilities: 46 slips, accommodating boats up to sixty feet long, with water and 110/220V power at each slip. Exxon petroleum products are also available. The basin was dredged in 1978 to seven feet at mean low water, so if you've got a really big one this is the place to put it. The office complex contains a lounge, restroom with hot showers, washers and dryers, ice, soft drinks, and bait, along with a nice big freezer. The marina store carries fishing supplies, but is primarily a yacht chandler, with a nice selection of marine hardware, instruments, and clothing. Store hours are basically variable, depending on the season and the fishing weather. Guards VHF 16.

HATTERAS LIBRARY

Hatteras Village   986-2385

Librarian Suzanne Kyle administers this 10,000-volume facility across from Burrus's Red and White, in the Civic Building. Hours are 9:30 a.m. until 5 p.m., Monday through Thursday, closed Friady, Saturday, and Sunday. See the former world record marlin mounted in front, too.

HATTERAS INLET (OCRACOKE) FERRY

Hatteras Village

This free state-run ferry service links Hatteras with Ocracoke Island with an enjoyable 40-minute trip. The ferries accommodate cars and even large camping vehicles and are scheduled often enough during the summer so that your wait will not be long. Reservations are not required, as they are for the Cedar Island and Swan Quarter ferries from Ocracoke Village. Yes, Johnny, there are (small) bathrooms on the ferry. The summer schedule is as follows:

SUMMER SCHEDULE

APRIL 15th thru OCT. 31st

Leave HATTERAS	Leave OCRACOKE
5:00 AM	6:00 AM
6:10 AM	7:10 AM
6:50 AM	7:50 AM
7:30 AM	8:30 AM*
8:10 AM *	9:10 AM
8:50 AM	9:50 AM
9:30 AM	10:30 AM
10:10 AM	11:10 AM*
10:50 AM*	11:50 AM
11:30 AM	12:30 PM
12:10 PM	1:10 PM
12:50 PM	1:50 PM*
1:30 PM*	2:30 PM
2:10 PM	3:10 PM
2:50 PM	3:50 PM
3:30 PM	4:30 PM
4:10 PM	5:10 PM*
4:50 PM*	5:50 PM
5:30 PM	6:30 PM
6:10 PM	7:10 PM
7:00 PM	8:00 PM
8:00 PM	9:00 PM
9:00 PM	10:00 PM
10:00 PM	11:00 PM
11:00 PM	

*Priority for commercial vehicles (permit only)

WINTER SCHEDULE NOV. 1st thru APRIL 14th

Leave Hatteras every hour on the hour from 5:00 AM to 5 PM, and at 7:00 PM, 9:00 PM, and 11:00 PM.

Leave Ocracoke every hour on the hour from 6:00 AM to 6:00 PM; 8:00 PM and 10:00 PM.

HATTERAS ISLAND
SHOPPING

Hatteras Island is going through the same kinds of changes Duck experienced a couple years ago. Building and development is everywhere. Stay away a few weeks and the entire look of the community changes. Rodanthe and Avon, especially, have grown and opportunities to shop are keeping up. Unlike the northern beaches, where year 'round shopping has become the rule not the exception, most shops on Hatteras Island close for at least a month or two in the winter and may have irregular hours in all but the peak season.

RODANTHE

Island Convience, 987-2239, has been the one stop shopping spot for several years. Owners Mac and Marilyn Midgett keep a better-than-convenience-store stock of grocery items, souvenirs, tackle and bait year 'round. The store was remodeled for the '89 season and now includes a small deli. While the store does carry a good selection of over-the-counter drugs, you'll need to go to Nags Head or Buxton to get a prescription filled. Island Convenience is also a service station and AAA garage. They do a brisk business towing stuck cars off the beach.

The Sea Chest, 987-2303, a gift and antique store at the Capt. John Allen motel, was opened in 1973 by Myrna Peters. Peters' great uncle (the aforenamed captain) was with the Chicamacomico Lifesaving Service. She's a collector of all sorts of things: the store is packed with decoys, antique dolls, glass and ceramics, as well as toys and souvenirs.

AVON

In Avon, big things started to happen and then fizzled out. **Food Lion** came to town as promised, but the rest of Hatteras Island Plaza became mired in the financial woes of its developers.

```
┌─────────────────────────────────────────────────┐
│     Fresh Meat,              Amoco Gas          │
│  Produce & Groceries      Sentry Hardware       │
│    Beach Supplies          Complete Tackle      │
│                                                 │
│   AVON SHOPPING CENTER                          │
│        Hwy. 12 Avon                             │
│          995-5362                               │
│                                                 │
│  Full hookups      Kinnakeet Campground         │
└─────────────────────────────────────────────────┘
```

Up the road and nicely situated near the sound is a small shopping center that opened last year and seems to be thriving. **Avon Waterside Shops** houses **Windsurfing Hatteras**, 995-4970, that carries sailboard and surfing gear, accessories and clothing and offer lessons and rentals. See the write-up on Fox Water Sports, Hatteras, for more information.

Next door is **Home Port Gifts**, 995-4334, where you'll find the work of more than 50 local crafts people according to Susan Wilkinson, one of the owners. They also carry other gift and decorator items.

Next to Bubba's Barbeque is **Kitty Hawk Sports**. They carry a complete line of windsurfing equipment and they have the best selection of windsurfing t-shirts on the island.

An alternative to Food Lion for groceries is the **Avon Shopping Center**, where, locals say, you'll get the best meat and it can be cut to order. It's the closest thing to an old-timey general store we've seen, carrying bologna to nuts and bolts, and everything in between.

For fresh seafood, try **Carol's Seafood** (formerly Best Seafood), 995-4232, where you'll find fresh fillets, soft shell crabs, and other treats from the sea.

BUXTON

Here, shopping focuses on the area's popularity as a surfing and sailboarding mecca. At **Cape Creek Landing** you'll find **Daydreams**, 995-5548, a clothing store for almost everyone in the family. Some minor remodeling this past winter has made space for more clothes and additional fitting rooms. Owner Carol Dawson has put together a super inventory of women's apparel and accessories -- the jewelry selection is especially nice -- that emphasizes the casual and comfortable, but includes a few tailored lines. She shops for lines not carried by other stores in the area. The men's wear is strictly casual and mostly well-known designer surf lines like Jimmy Z and Instinct. Her children's department has grown significantly and the swimsuit selection for children, as well as men and women, is excellent.

Hatteras Outdoors, 995-5815, adjoins Daydreams, to service the board sports enthusiast with equipment, accessories, rentals and lessons. They advertise that they are the closest sailboard shop to the Canadian Hole. It's true, but in a small community like Buxton, with other board shops within walking distance, we think their friendly service and good selection is a better reason to stop in.

Ormonds, 995-5012, has been the local department store for nearly 45 years. It's another one of those stores that always seems to have something you've been looking for.

DAYDREAMS AND HATTERAS OUTDOORS

✔ Sailboards
✔ Surfboards
✔ Sportswear
✔ Rentals
✔ T-Shirts
✔ Windsurfing Lessons

Rt. 12, P.O. Box 947, Buxton, NC 27920
(919)995-5815 or (919)995-5548

Right next door is **Cape Hatteras Sand-Alls,** 995-5585, where sandals, in a variety of styles and colors, are custom made to fit your foot while you wait.

Buxton Village Books, 995-4240, is more than a bookstore. Owner GeeGee Rosell has figured out several ways to get customers into her small but well-stocked shop. Rent a VCR and movies. Buy greeting cards: some feature illustrations by local artists. Pick up office supplies; send a FAX. Pet Buddy, the bookstore cat (does every bookstore on the Outer Banks have a cat?!). If all this fails to pique your interest, browse through her offering of fiction, nonfiction, children's books and regional literature. Rosell's speciality is stories about the sea.

Ted James has built a reputation among surfers and sailboarders with his Buxton store, **Fox Water Sports,** 995-4102, and custom boards, made here on Hatteras and in Florida. He's also a part-owner in Windsurfing Hatteras in Avon. At either store you can buy booms, sails, harnesses, bases, rigging and all sorts of other sailboard and surfing accessories. Or, you can rent surf, sail or boogie boards. They also carry swimming and beach gear, wet suits and lots of t-shirts.

Also in Buxton, **Natural Art Surf Shop,** 95-5682, is a "surfers' surf shop," say owners Scott and Carol Busbey. Now in its 13th year, it may the only one on the Outer Banks that has resisted the temptation to branch out into other board sports. Scott Busbey makes custom surf boards, does surf board repairs, and dispenses generous advice to beginners. His wife, Carol, makes clothing sold in the shop: shorts, shirts, skirts and dresses, mostly in cotton prints. Her children's shirts and dresses make great gifts. The store also carries beach ready-to-wear, t-shirts, wet suits and bathing suits. They sell and rent other brands of surfboards in addition to their own line, In The Eye.

If fishing interests you, shopping at **Red Drum Tackle Shop** in Buxton, 995-5414, is something you won't want to miss. It's the place to go for up-to-the-minute advice on offshore, inshore and shark fishing. Bob Eakes is the resident specialist on bow and where to surf fish on Hatteras. They carry a complete line of surf and offshore fishing gear, custom rods, bait, ice and tackle. Fish mounting service is also available.

Ollie and Kathy Jarvis opened **Dillon's Corner,** 995-5083, in 1981. Ollie explains that his father-in-law, Bill Dillon, was a well-known fisherman in the area: The store started as a bait and tackle business and it was called Dillon's Corner -- it sits on a corner -- in his honor. The store still sells bait and tackle, as well as custom fishing rods and fishing guide services. They specialize in surf fishing, and while the store itself isn't open all winter, Ollie says the phone rings at his house and he's happy to help a customer any time. Kathy Jarvis has turned part of the store into a gift shop specializing in local crafts.

You can drive up to Avon to the Food Lion for groceries, but Buxton has a convenient and well-stocked -- for its size -- grocery store of its own, **Conners Cape Hatteras Supermarket.** They carry a nice selection of produce, meat and wine.

For baked goods, go to the **Orange Blossom Pastry Shop,** 995-4109. They are famous for Apple Uglies (giant apple fritters), but we think you'll find all their goodies have a homemade tastiness.

The only pharmacy on Hatteras Island is here at the **Beach Medical Center**, one mile south of the Lighthouse: **Beach Pharmacy,** 995- 4450.

FRISCO

Browning Artworks, 995-5538, is a first- rate gallery featuring the work of North Carolina craftspeople. The shop is owned by Linda and Lou Browning and his parents, Dixie and Lee. Dixie is a well-known watercolorist and romance writer (you can pick up copies

N.C. Fine Crafts

The work of over 100 North Carolina craftspeople creates a distinctive selection of fine crafts, perfect for the discriminating gift giver and the experienced collector.

BROWNING ARTWORKS

Highway 12, Frisco, North Carolina 27936
Just a few miles south of Cape Hatteras Lighthouse

of her books at the gallery). A unique selection of porcelains, baskets, stoneware, weavings, decoys and jewelry -- all handmade in North Carolina and of fine enough quality to truly be called art -- make this shady quiet stop on the way to Hatteras Village a true delight. Knowledgeable staff can tell you all about the artists and their work.

The oldest gift shop on Hatteras Island is the **Pirates Chest**, 995-5118, opened in 1953 and now owned by Linda and Jack Monsell. It's a big store -- much larger than it looks from the outside -- offering a huge variety of merchandise: scrimshaw, sea shells (native shells, as well as specimen shells from around the world) and coral, glass sculpture, regional books and crossstitch supplies. A Christmas room features handmade ornaments, most made at the shop. Shell ornaments with nautical themes are their specialty. There's a small room of art, too, featuring work by local artists. An old Hatteras home has been restored right next door and now houses their large

For All Your Beach & Fishing Needs

FRISCO ROD & GUN

Groceries • Gas • Ice
Offshore Tackle • Optics
Custom Rods
Camping Supplies • T-Shirts
Binoculars • Outdoor Clothing
Hunting Accessories

FRISCO SHOPPING CENTER
Hwy. 12 • Frisco, NC
(919) 995-5366

t-shirt selection. And, if that's not enough variety for you, there are always the hermit crabs and everything you need to make a hermit crab happy.

If you thought country crafts was just a fashionable flash-in-the-pan, take a look at the growing number of country craft stores on the Outer Banks. **Take A Gander,** 995-4366, is one of the newer ones. It's one of those roadside shops you'll probably miss the first time by, and have to slam on the brakes and turn around to hit the second time through. We're happy to tell you that, if you like country, you'll find it worth the trouble.

It's the 7th season for **All Decked Out,** 995-4319, a furniture factory owned by Dale Cashman. The business really got its start, he says, when he found a deck chair at the Frisco Pier and replicated it for his own use. Friends began asking for copies of the chair and pretty soon he had a growing business. Dale and his crew build chairs, picnic tables, and other outdoor wood furniture, and ship anywhere in the U.S.

If you enjoy fancy baked goods like napoleons and eclairs... danish that melt in your mouth with buttery sweetness...you'll have to stop at **The Gingerbread House,** 995-5204. Go early, they don't bake in huge quantities and are often out of the best things by afternoon.

Groceries and other necessities -- including fishing bait and tackle which, on Hatteras, falls into the "necessities" category -- can be found at the **Frisco Shopping Center,** 995-5022. Opened in the mid-60s, the shopping center has been owned for the past ten years by Bryan Perry. Shopping center may sound a little grandiose for a

Honey BEAR

Formerly Sea Bear
Under New Ownership

HATTERAS VILLAGE 986-2802

Natural Foods · Vitamins · Beauty Aids
N.C. Weavings, Rugs, & Afghans · Gifts

> **"WE MANUFACTURE THE FINEST, MOST COMFORTABLE OUTDOOR FURNITURE ON THE OUTER BANKS"**
>
> *WE SHIP ANYWHERE VIA U.P.S.*
> *CALL OR WRITE FOR BROCHURE*
> *MAIL OR PHONE YOUR ORDER*
>
> MasterCard   VISA
>
> **P.O. Box 363 Hatteras, NC 27943**
> **Shop on Hwy. 12 • Frisco, NC**
> **(919) 995-4319**

grocery store, gas station and rod & gun shop; but when you realize that it was built -- and named -- over 25 years ago, right after the Oregon Inlet bridge was completed, it begins to make sense.

HATTERAS VILLAGE

The times are a changin' and there's nothing more telling than this: where Fishin' Stuff used to sell fishing reels and offshore tackle, **Summer Stuff**, 986-2111, is now selling designer sandals. Evidently customers had all the fishin' stuff they wanted, but as their billboard says, "You can't get enough Summer Stuff." The store has gone into men's and women's casual clothing in a big way: It's t-shirt selection is one of the largest on the island. The swimsuit choices are good, too. There's still an impressive toy department and nice collection of nautical gifts, prints, books, sunglasses, and more.

Right in the middle of the Village is **Honey Bear Country Store**, 986-2802, (formerly Sea Bear) now owned by Billy and Linda Manieri who moved here last fall. Those who enjoyed the shop in the past when it was owned by the Skakles won't be disappointed; changes have been minimal. It's still the kind of store we love to recommend. It has history to show and tell, occupying the old A. S. Austin General Store building that was built in 1904 by the former owner's grandfather. Like the Skakles, the Manieris are hands-on managers who meet and greet their customers. They carry some packaged natural foods, vitamins, beauty products and pure fruit juices. You'll find bins of bulk snacks: carob and yogurt candies, nuts, dried fruits. You can get hand-dipped ice cream, imported beers, ground-to-order coffees...choose from dozens of deli cheeses. There are a few antiques, some country crafts, colorful woven packs and fanny bags.... They rent bicycles, too. We hope we've whetted your curiosity about this place. It really is a "must" shopping stop.

The **Lee Robinson General Store,** 986-2381, is another spot with a long history. It opened in 1948. The original store was replaced last year by a new building that duplicates as closely as possible the old one, with its wooden floors and wide front porch. It still smells wonderfully woody and new, but has the old-fashioned feel that owners Virgil and Belinda Willis wanted to keep. The store carries what it always has -- a little of everything. It's as general as a general store should be, although we have to mention that the wine selection is exceptionally good. Another specific note: You can pick up the book about Cap'n Ernal Foster (see "A Life in Hatteras earlier in this book) here. Cap'n Ernal is credited with starting the charter

---

WELCOME TO HATTERAS ISLAND

SUMMER STUFF
ISLAND CLOTHING & GIFTS

Swimwear	Shoes/Sandals
Souvenirs	Toys
Sportswear	Kids Clothes
Jewelry	Decoys

"YOU CAN NEVER HAVE ENOUGH SUMMER STUFF"

986-2111   Hatteras Village

Volleyball has become a popular beach sport, with tournaments held throughout the warm months of the year. DCTB

boat fishing business on the Island and you might even see him around the store where he comes to talk with other locals when the fish aren't biting.

Locals say they drive up to Food Lion "to buy the big stuff," but they're unanimous in praising **Burrus' Red & White** for their good meats and produce. Unless you're doing heavy-duty shopping, you'll find this local store has everything you need.

For fresh fish and other things from the sea, a good bet -- in spite of its name -- is **Risky Business Seafood,** 986-2140. You can watch the fish being brought in and processed here. It's not very glamorous, but you can't get much fresher than this.

The only pharmacy is **Beach Pharmacy** in Buxton.

All the elements of a peaceful day are here on the Outer Banks - sand, sun, sea, and sky. DCTB

CAPTAIN ERNAL FOSTER
A LIFE ON HATTERAS

"Yep, I got to get cleaned up some in here one of these days."
Captain Ernal Foster looks slowly around the interior of what he calls his "equipment building." Against the walls are stacked bundles of hand-tied nets. In the roof beams are bamboo poles, rods, old outriggers striped red and white. Covering the plank floor are heaps of bronze propellers, fighting chairs, Pflueger Altapac reels, old cans of Athey and Pettit paint and varnish. "That's my father's sail bag over there, with his needles and palms. And his sea chest, there in the corner. One of these days. Come on, let's talk in the house." The gray house on the sea side of Hatteras Village looks small and commonplace from Highway 12. But inside, its pine panelled walls are covered with mounted marlin, sailfish, swordfish. The furniture is oak, from old ships; Hazel shows you a Singer that washed ashore in the 1890s. Even the bathroom doors came from a vanished schooner.

Foster is not a large man, but at 76 his shoulders still bulge under his loose shirt as he lowers himself into his armchair. The steady eyes are the color of a blue marlin's back. And then the only sound is the soft voice, and faintly from outside the endless crash of the surf.

"I was born and raised on this spot, spent most of my life here. My father, he was raised down here on this hill, but they claim his father was a Yankee. My mother was born and raised here. I grew up one of seven children. Three girls, four boys. I happened to be the oldest boy.

"When I grew up there wasn't much to do round here. We boys entertained ourselves. We had shove-skiffs we made -- wasn't no harbor here then, we kept the boats out in the sound, on stakes, and you went back and forth on a shove-skiff. You didn't row, you had oars and you shoved back and forth. We boys, we sewed some sails out of these burlap bags. Them skiffs didn't have centerboards on them, they was flat-bottom -- and on a northeast wind, we'd race down to the point beach, three or four miles, four or five of us. And then we'd shove back. If it was southwesterly we'd shove down there and race back home. And we had horses to chase and catch, and ride on the beach. And we played cat. How do you play cat?

Take socks, and unravel the yarn and make a ball out of it. You throw the ball at the man, and if you hit him he'd be out. Didn't have no money for baseballs. We boys had teams. When anybody lost there'd be a fight. But we had games like that. I don't know how we could have had a better time.

"Then when we got to our teens boys and girls would get together at their homes, and get some cocoa, try and get some sugar, and we'd have a cook-candy. And some of the boys didn't get invited, when you'd set the candy out to cool they'd come around and steal it. When we did taffy you'd pull it out, a boy and a girl. If it didn't break she'd have candy in both hands and you could kiss her. Then on Fourth of July we'd take our boat and go to Ocracoke, to the dances. I had me a Ocracoke girl. Ever heard of Aycock Brown? He married my girl friend.

"My father started working me when I was a boy. He didn't let me lay around. When I was small, on Saturdays I'd go out with him fishing. In the winter the shad, they had a lot of good roe into them, I'd take and bust them and get a bucket of roe out of them and take it home.

"When I was thirteen I was mess-cooking at the factory for sixty-five men, two dollars a week. That was down in Southport. That's thirty miles below Wilmington, on the mouth of the Cape Fear River. My father was captain of a menhaden boat, and they moved the factory from Portsmouth down to Southport. That was a lot of money. You went to the movies -- silent, they didn't have no talkies then -- Friday nights, ten cent movies, get you a bag of peanuts for a nickel. Only sound in the movie house would be the poppin' of them peanuts. In World War One we moved to Beaufort, fishing that menhaden boat. When the war ended in 1918 I was in school there.

"When I come to be fourteen my father turned the boat over to me. I had a two-cylinder Lathrop in to her. Straight drive, you didn't have clutches then. You had to learn how to handle that switch. You had to know how to judge the wind and the distance comin' in. One time when we were going up the sound when I was sixteen she kicked back and smashed that finger there. So I still got a mark from that engine. I hauled cars across to Ocracoke with that boat. Down the shore side there I got two skiffs and I put 'em side by side and put planks on 'em. Then I'd put the cars on 'em and tow 'em across. Got ten dollars a car. See, boys were working away from home, Philadelphia and them, and they'd come home want to show their car off. Didn't have a road, but just flatten your tire down fourteen or fifteen pounds you could ride in the sand. Catch low water and you could ride the surf line. I've gone from here to Oregon Inlet in an hour. Course you didn't have traffic then.

"I used to have to hunt when I was a teenager. They had a private club there my father took care of. That's an unpleasant job, working for rich people. It was on the Sound, up on the Reef about four miles from here. In about six feet of water. We had blinds up on the reef and we had about 65 geese there in the yard. We were guides. They come down to go hunting, we had to go put the decoys out. We had metal pegs you tied their foot to it. Use about fifteen to eighteen to a battery. Live geese. See, they outlawed that.

"I think the hardest work I ever done was pushing a clam-rake. You only got fifteen cents a hundred for 'em in the thirties. That's hard work, worse'n any. You'd get three and four hundred clams a day. And you get you a can of sardines for a nickel, a coca-cola for a nickel, some crackers, well you had to catch a hundred clams to pay for your lunch. And pound netting for my father, that was hard work. And fishing in the ocean, and we pulled our nets by hand. They don't do that no more. Those nets out in the equipment house my mother and I knotted in the thirties. It all used to be cotton, linen. We used to buy the twine and tie them. We'd make our wooden gages the size we want the net. You don't tie too many yards in a night . . . we used to haul eleven hundred yards of net, get on the stern and pull them in by hand. About the second week of that you'd be gettin' in good shape. That's the way we used to work. But everything's push a button now.

"My father started going to sea when he was fourteen years old. His name was Charlie. He got eight dollars a month. He worked his way up to mate. He was on a three, four-mast schooner, I don't remember the name. He used to sail down to the West Indies, all that way.

"Ain't too much I know about my mother. She was born here in the woods and she never liked to go places. We lived in Beaufort for two years and then we come home. We were coming out of Beaufort Inlet and she told my father, this is my last trip to sea. Over the years she never had any use for the water. I had my first boat and she wouldn't never go to the dock to look at it. It didn't mean a thing to her. She was a Ballance. Her family was mostly fishermen, that was all there was here. They practically owned this beach down below the ferry dock. They just let it go; it wa'n't worth nothing. There was a local man here in the twenties taking it up for taxes and he sold it to some Yankees. And they had a fence across it all the way to the ocean, which was wrong. So I pried into that. A good friend of mine, the governor of North Carolina, said they'd back me in a test case. Some of them got mad at me over that. Then when the Park Service came along in the fifties they was the first to sell, because they know they'd lost their rights. Park Service, best thing that ever happened to this island.

"I started the sport fishing out of here in '38. And the first summer I went it was a hundred dollars for four day trips out to the Gulf Stream. Twenty-five dollars a day was money then.

"What made me get into fishing? I just wanted to. I left home to keep from fishing. I went to New York, went two years in the Coast Guard in rum-running days. Then I worked in a sheet metal shop out in Long Island. It was pretty work, I spent five years putting copper roofs on them big summer homes. Then in '33, after the election, money people just closed up. And you can't live up there without work. So I came home. That depression running me home was the best thing ever happened to me. I lost the boat we had in '35, out on Diamond Shoals, my brother did. So then I built the Albatross in '37.

"I got my lumber. It grows on the swamp, over on our mainland. Other people calls it white cedar, but we call it juniper. Cost me 4 1/2 cents a foot and the framing three cents a foot. I carried it down to Marshallburg and a man there built my boat. When I got her home she cost me eight hundred and five dollars. Without a engine. I want to the bank and borrowed seventy-five dollars, put a shaft in her. And I bought a Buick for fifteen dollars. Man said, drive it home, ain't nothing wrong with it. I said, don't want the car, just want the engine! Local man, Lloyd Styron here, he put her in for me. He said, Pay me when you make it. I borrowed a propeller. I borrowed a steering wheel. I borrowed a gas tank. That's how I started out in the Albatross. A lot of people don't believe a lot of this, but that's just the way it happened.

"It didn't take too long to pay that $75 back. Man at the bank said Ernal, just let that ride. I said no, I want that note! Because it was on my boat.

"So we went along. Later on I got a Chrysler engine, Airflow, straight eight, '34 model. But I got it hot and busted it. Then Burris, who owned the Texaco station, said, Ernal, I'll get you a engine. Six hundred dollars, a Chris Craft. So I went to the bank and borrowed it. This was in thirty-eight. That was some engine. We went along. Money was scarce. We were getting half a cent a pound for croaker, three cent for trout. I got that note paid off in December of 1941. And the second week after I got her paid off I got my notice from the Army.

"Draft! That killed me. I had a row with the girl in the office. I said, I'm thirty-two years old. I'm living, taking care of my father and mother. How can I support them on $21 a month? She said, that's your problem. She give me two weeks to think it over. Lloyd and I was the two oldest, he was thirty-seven, but we was drafted first! There was some paid off, so they wouldn't go. Think so? I know so.

"So I went to Norfolk, got in the Coast Guard. The Hooligan Navy. I knew I would, I'd been fishing for a year with this commander. I went in as a first class petty officer. Eighty-four dollars a month. I married Hazel here in '42. She's one of those Midgetts, they say the first one washed ashore in a whiskey barrel. Her grandfather you might have heard of, he saved a lot of people.

"I never been across the Atlantic. My brothers did, they were in the Navy. I was one of the lucky ones, I was here for four years. Baltimore was the farthest I got away from home.

"I was on a boat -- harbor duty, sabotage, patrolling. We used to patrol the pierheads and Newport News, and the bridgehead. One merchant ship there come in with blood comin' out of the scupper holes. Had a mutiny on it. And when they paid off ships I stood guard. They paid off in cash, men come in one door of the mess hall and out the other. Wouldn't let but one man in at a time. I didn't like being guard -- a gun's something I never had any use for. I got me a shotgun back there I bought in 1929 and I never had any use for it.

"Then for eighteen months I was on a patrol boat out of Morehead when they was sinking of these ships out here. It was bad. I didn't sleep when we were out on patrol -- I was afraid one of those subs would blow us out of the water. This was a old 75-foot chaser they built to chase the rum-runners. We had a one-pounder on the bow and a fifty-caliber machine gun. I could throw a shell about as far as that one-pounder would shoot. We carried four depth charges. You dropped one of those, it was full speed ahead or it would knock the caulking out of your hull and you had to head for the shipyard.

"During the war you couldn't even rest here at night. It would jar you off your bed, almost knock the lights out and shake your windows. The concussion. You'd look out and see two or three ships burning at one time. I've fished over a lot of 'em. My son says oil's still flowing out of one of them.

"And then they took my boat! I get so mad about that I don't like to talk about her. They had here down there in Fort Macon and painted her gray. They used her for a play toy.

"I had a time getting her back. I had a big row in the captain's office. 'You've been paid for that boat,' he said. I said, 'Show me where it's paid for.' I knew it hadn't because when they sent me the papers I put them in the stove and they went up the chimney. So he said, 'Well then we got a boat for nothing.' We had it out but when I was leaving I said, 'Captain, there's bigger men than you are.' He figured I was just a sailor. But I wrote to my congressman. I knew him since I was a boy. And I wrote a lawyer in Washington, DC, which his father was some of my mother's people. And about two weeks I was called back in the office, and the captain invited me to sit down. And he wanted to help me get my boat back then.

"It was in bad shape. Painted gray inside and out, and they had burned the engine and clutch up. But I accepted it as it was. I wanted her back.

"I got back in forty-six. I'd had some lung trouble, spent six months in the hospital. Later on they found a growth in my lung. Took part of it out, some of my ribs. Doctor told me I couldn't work no more in the winter. So I figured then I'd just stick to my charter fishing. Didn't anybody else want to, they'd leave them on the dock to go shrimping. So I turned around, and instead of building a home I built the second boat, in '48. I had a little disability, but they cut that off in '52. So then instead of building a house we built the third boat. Then in '55 we finally had to tear down the old house, and I built this one. And we finally got it so we can live in it.

"Then my son Ernie was getting up in age, and we wanted him to go to school. So we saved. We cut a lot of corners. No automobile, nothing. We could have asked for a handout from the government, but we didn't. My father always told me the government owes you nothing. You got to make your own way. And I never got on that social security till I was sixty-eight, cause I was working. Ernie's a schoolteacher up in Manteo now, and he comes down here summers. After I had the heart trouble I turned the boats over to him.

"But I got into this charter business, and just liked it. It was something different every day. At first we fished wrecks. Then we fished billfish. Out in the blue water you don't know what you're going to catch. It does something to you. When you see the fish come out'n the water walking on their tails. The more you do it the more you get encouraged. And it made you feel good to catch a fish.

"I used to have some nice customers. I've fished governors, ambassadors, senators. Ray Trallenger, from the New York World. Senator Duff. I used to have a bunch of girls, too. One of them got sick on me out catching bluefish. She was redheaded. Blondes, lightheaded people get sick easier than darkheaded. All over I used to have coming in here. Those days it was a week or ten days at a time, man and his wife. If you didn't catch a fish, well, you'd catch one tomorrow. It's not like that anymore. It's groups, five and six, and if they don't catch a boatload of fish they're mad.

"The most beautiful thing I ever saw at sea was a school of marlin. I thought at first it was porpoises. It was in the small tuna season. And they were knocking them in the air, then they'd jump. And there might be ten or fifteen of them in the air at the same time. And the sun was shining, and the water run off their back. A person hasn't seen it can't imagine it. It's blue and changes. And when they went into the air the sun would shine on them, the water running off almost like a blue rainbow. It's the only time I ever seen that.

"We don't have them out there like they used to. Used to be you'd hook two or three at a time. Big marlin. They're being overfished.

"The man who wrote this book about the Albatross Fleet, John Cleveland, he was the first one to release a marlin. He started fishing with me in '58. And he made me release the biggest sailfish ever caught on this coast. I imagine he was ten feet long. They live after they're released, if they're not bleeding. Sometimes I just cut the wire, but if I can sit on the stern and shake the hooks out of 'em. I don't like to kill fish if you're not going to use them.

"These tournaments are just disgusting. A bunch of millionaires had this tournament, up at this club. And they lie, steal, cheat -- it's sad. Instead of having a fun tournament money got involved, and they'll do anything to win. Used to be they'd release them. Then one of those yachts was fishing close to my boat and he lost the fish, a hundred yards back when he jumped off. And he called in that he released a fish! Now they have to bring them in, they stopped trusting each other. But there's all a new group there at that club now. I walk up there at night and I don't know anybody. Some of them there now got a glass in each hand and one in their mouth. To drown their problems. They're not happy people.

"Fishing is going to go up and down. But now there's laws, and limits. That's federal. State don't mess with it. But I don't like that. And now I got to pay tax on my boats, same as commercial fishermen. Another thing I don't like is people selling their fish off my boat. If they don't want to take them home and eat it themselves, I say release it. But there's more people fishing now. Used to be I was out for five, six days and I was the only boat out there.

"I never used charts. Or compass. I never used Loran. I carried a boat to New York with no chart. Every place on the coast is in my mind just like you're on a highway. I know how much time I make and I just go where I want to go. I can't tell anybody the courses, but it just comes to me. My family is all natural born watermen. Now they got depth recorders. Colored depth recorders! They got temperature gauges! I used to use my finger.

"You know, I think if the people today had to live like we had to live they'd see it differently. Young people today, all they think is money. They get sixteen, they got to have them a car! You got to have money to live, but if you get to craving it you can forget living. I never worried to pile up a lot of it. I wouldn't be doing anything different if I was rich. I done what I set out to do and I'm happy.

Mending nets is done the same now as it was 75 years ago.

"I look back over the years and how I had to struggle. And in a way I still ain't got nothing. But I got Hazel, home, children, we got a lot to be thankful for. Two years ago I had a heart problem, they told me I couldn't go to the dock no more. I guess I let little things get to me too much. When the boat broke down, things like that. Had to give up everything! But I haven't. I invited those doctors down in August and took them out fishing.

"I still mess with the boats every day, piddle around. But now I try not to let things bother me. I sit on the dock and whittle. Don't make nothing but a mess. And I wait for my boats and my boys to come back in."

THE ISLAND INN

An Inn with a flavor of yesterday

featuring the island's only
heated swimming pool

(919) 928-4351

P.O. Box 9
Ocracoke, North Carolina 27960

THE ISLAND INN RESTAURANT

"The oldest and finest dining on the island"

P.O. Box 637
Ocracoke, NC

(919) 928-7821

INSIDE
OCRACOKE ISLAND

Ocracoke Island is the most remote inhabited island of the Banks, and Ocracoke is the southernmost town within the limits of the National Park.

It's reached by ferry from Hatteras Village (see previous chapter). The trip across is fast, free, and scenic, following a winding course west of Hatteras Inlet, in the calm waters of the sound. Even when the surf breaks whitely on the bar the ferry hardly rolls. Feeding the gulls that hover over the moving ferry and dive for tidbits is part of the fun of the crossing. They'll actually snatch bread from your hand when the action gets competitive!

Bring binoculars, if you own a pair. To your left as the ferry hums along you can see the distinctive vegetation and wildlife of the Sound side of the banks. Low, sandy islets slip by on either side as the ferry approaches the pier on the northeastern end of Ocracoke Island, and Highway 12 resumes.

Most of the island is still just as uninhabited as you drive down it as it was on a spring day in 1585, when seven English ships appeared off Ocracoke Inlet.

Sir Richard Grenville was in command, a seasoned, experienced soldier. He had about three hundred troops aboard his fleet. His mission, entrusted to him by Sir Walter Raleigh and the Queen, was to establish a permanent English base in the New World. He was to fail at Roanoke Island; but that summer no one yet suspected the fate that awaited those first colonists.

The Banks welcomed him in characteristic fashion, leaving his flagship, *Tiger*, hard aground on the bar. He and Ralph Lane took advantage of the delay to explore north and west in smaller vessels (see 'Ocracoke Pony Pens,' in this chapter -- these hardy ponies may stem from stock lost from the *Tiger*). When the ship was floated and repaired, he headed to Roanoke, leaving the island sleeping and deserted once again.

It's thought that the name 'Woccocon,' which was applied to the island at first, was derived from the neighboring Indian tribe the 'Woccons.' But its precise derivation, like that of so many Outer Banks names, is unclear, as is its subsequent degeneration through

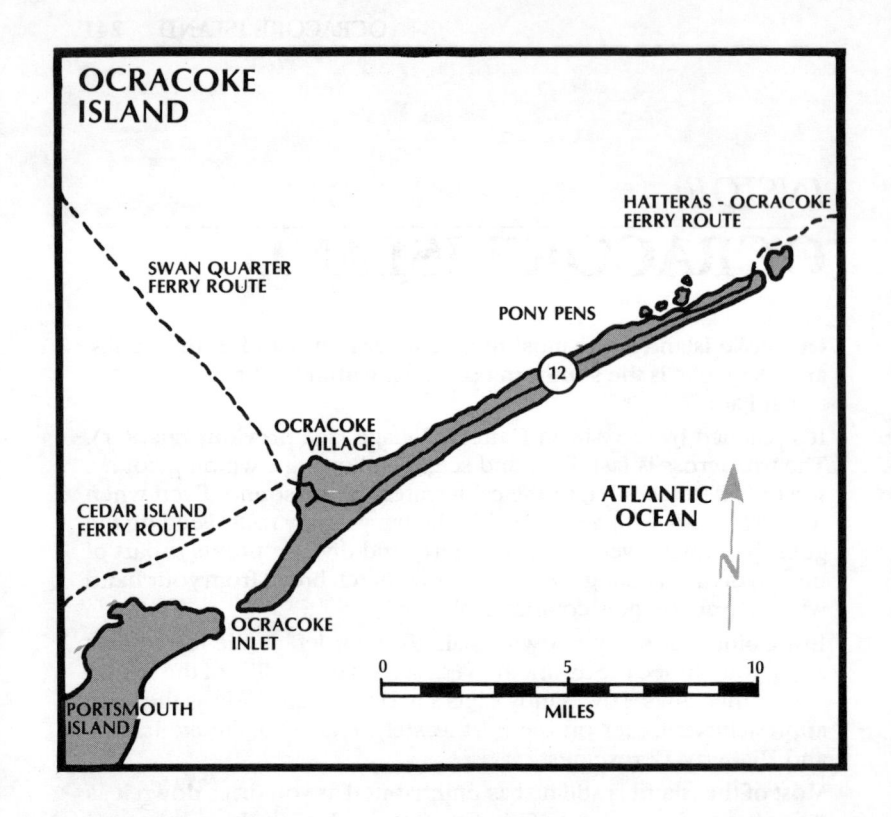

'Wocockock,' 'Occocock,' 'Ocreecock,' and other variations to the present 'Ocracoke.' Spelling held a low priority in those days, a state to which the English tongue seems to be reverting.

Most of the island remained in its wild state, with sheep, cattle, and horses released by the early owners to graze freely. But the gradual increase in colonial trade in the early 18th century saw more and more ships using the Inlet, in those days deeper than it is now (too, ships, were of shallower draft). In 1715 the colony of North Carolina established Ocracoke as a port, setting aside land on the western tip of the island for the homes of pilots (for midwesterners, and other non-seagoing types, a 'pilot' meets incoming ships at sea and guides them safely in. Pilots are generally older men, brine-encrusted, who know the configurations of sand bars and channels from painful experience).

A new problem also arose: pirates. They interfered with the pilots, terrorized the inhabitants of the islands, boarded and robbed ships at sea, murdered crews and passengers, and made themselves generally unwelcome. John Cole, Robert Deal, Anne Bonny, and dozens of others operated along the Caribbean and Southern Atlantic coasts in the early eighteenth century.

But it was the notorious Blackbeard, standing out as the worst of a bad lot, who left his name stamped on the Outer Banks, and, on Ocracoke, one of his lairs. Much of his early career lies somewhere between conjecture and legend. It is thought that he started as an honest English tar named Edward Drummond, born, perhaps, in Bristol.

He may have started, like many pirates, as a privateer -- a sort of seagoing guerrilla. But by 1716 he had turned pirate, calling himself Edward Teach. He had found his metier, and his rise was rapid. He seems to have been a man of organizational ability, for in short order he was in command of a sizeable fleet of ships, and some hundreds of men.

He also understood advertising. An evil reputation is a great thing to a terrorist, for it weakens the other side's morale and leads to quick capitulations. Blackbeard was a master in dressing for success and winning through intimidation. Tall, broad, and with a bushy coal-black beard, he festooned himself with cutlasses, dirks, and loaded pistols. In battle his beard was plaited, with little ribbons to add a festive air. Lighted cannon fuses dangled from under his hat, an affectation of dubious safety with primed flintlocks in his belt, but unquestionably effective in giving him the air of the very devil.

And a devil with political clout. He bought Governor Eden, of North Carolina, and was able to move ashore to Bath with his booty in 1718. Like many men, he became bored with retirement, and before the year was up he was out raiding again part-time. Eden stayed bought and did nothing, so a few citizens went north to ask a favor of Governor Spotswood, of Virginia.

Spotswood sent the Royal Navy. In November of 1718, Lt. Robert Maynard left the James River, heading south in two sloops manned with sailors from British men-o'-war. Maynard must have had confidence in himself; his two small sloops had no cannon, only small arms. The shallow-draft boats were able to penetrate where larger warships could not go, and Maynard was able to track Blackbeard's *Adventure* to Ocracoke Inlet.

Dawn, November 22. Ocracoke Inlet resounded to the boom of pirate guns and the crackle of British musketry fire. The *Adventure* grounded, but her well-laid cannon took heavy toll of the Royal Navy men. Maynard ordered them below, then stood ready on deck as his sloop drifted down on the larger ship.

They met. Teach's men launched a volley of grenades and swarmed aboard. The sailors came up from below to begin a merciless hand to-hand struggle. The pirate chief and the lieutenant faced each other. An exchange of pistol balls wounded the pirate, but in the next moment he had broken the officer's sword with his cutlass. Another sailor sliced the massive buccaneer in the neck, but he fought on...then collapsed. The battle was over. The pirate's head was cut off and hung from the rigging for the trip back, that all might see he was dead. The body was thrown overboard, where, island legend has it, it swam seven times round the ship before sinking. Most of the rest of his crew were taken to Williamsburg and given a fair trial before they were hanged. His treasure? Probably there was none -- he spent what little money the coasting trade yielded. But legends persist....

With the pirates cleaned out, trade flourished. Most of the seaborne commerce of North Carolina, and much of that of Virginia, came through the inlet, and gradually families settled there to service the ships. There were sporadic Spanish incursions and raids in the 1740s and 50s, and at one time they even had a camp on the island. Eventually peace came between England and Spain and they went home.

It was in 1753 that the village became a recognized town, and then there were only about a hundred inhabitants. Most of the island remained in a wild state. The inlet was fortified in 1757. Across the water, the town of Portsmouth was also growing up, and the little port of Beacon Island Roads, as the two towns were commonly called, was doing well when the Revolution arrived. Much of Washington's army was supplied through Ocracoke, and coastal North Carolina trade remained intact although the British patrolled outside, landed troops, and engaged in various futile retaliations.

After the war, the lighthouses were built by the new government, the first in 1798 on Shell Castle Rock, the second (the present one) in 1823. But even as they went up the golden age of Ocracoke was drawing to an end. Hatteras and Oregon inlets opened during a storm in September of 1846, and as these were deepened by outflow, Ocracoke Inlet began to shoal. The fort was abandoned by the Confederates in 1861 and the Government sank several ships loaded with rock in the channel to seal it. Such seagoing traffic as remained to the Banks -- for by now oceangoing ships had grown much larger and deeper -- shifted to Hatteras Inlet. After the war the village declined to a hundred or so inhabitants, who subsisted as fishermen, boatmen, or lifesavers. Many went to sea, and not all of them returned.

It took a war to bring new life. Silver Lake Harbor (formerly Cockle Creek) had been dredged out in 1931, and in 1942 a naval base was established there. As cargo ships burned offshore, as oil and debris and dead bodies drifted ashore, telephones and paved roads were brought to the villagers. The base was closed in 1945, but in the mid-50s the National Seashore and the highway brought a new source of revenue: the tourist.

Today tourism has taken over from fishing as the island's livelihood (though the same road service that has brought visitors also made crabbing commercially feasible). And they do come, more every year, in a two-season economy of tourists in the summer and fishermen in the fall. Regret it or welcome it, the nineteenth century is giving way to the twentieth at last in Ocracoke Village. Electricity came in 1938 and the first paved road in 1951. In the late seventies an ABC store, a doctor and a night spot arrived; in 1985, television, in the form of a 3.5 meter dish and cable; in 1987 the first multistory hotel and the first lakefront condo opened. Gift shops are proliferating and sadly so are signs.

But a walk or a bike ride will show you that Ocracoke hasn't been spoiled yet. There's still no record store, no barber shop, no movies, no crime, not one fast-food joint. Many of the streets are only sandy paths, still unpaved and not likely ever to be. Walking them on a soft summer's night is as close to inner peace as many Americans will ever get. Even some of the paved roads are so narrow and winding that two Caddies will scarce pass abreast.

And still, to the north and east...Ocracoke Island stretches out unpopulated and untamed. The sea roars against the rows of dunes; the road, silent and empty, shimmers amid the beachgrass and yaupon. Toward the Sound the ponies graze warily, and Ocracoke is quiet by the jealous sea.

OCRACOKE
ATTRACTIONS

OCRACOKE PONY PENS

Soundside

'Ponies?' The word conjures up a picture of something small, shaggy, and friendly. None of these adjectives, however, exactly fits the semiwild Ocracoke ponies. They're not really that small, perhaps thirteen or fourteen hands high. They are shaggy, in the winter. But they are definitely not friendly.

History, economics, and even anatomy have been used to try to explain the derivation of these hardy russet-colored animals that, in former days, roamed wild on the length of the island, as well as on Hatteras Island. A popular version goes as follows. In 1585, the vessels carrying the first colonists to Roanoke made their first landing at Ocracoke Inlet, where the flagship, *Tiger*, grounded. Sir Richard Grenville ordered the ship unloaded, and its cargo, which included a brace of horses purchased in the West Indies (then under Spanish rule), was put ashore while the *Tiger* was taken off the shoal. The usual method of getting horses ashore in those days was to let them swim; and it is thought that some escaped, and began their wild existence on the Banks. Other theories say they came from Spanish shipwrecks, or, more prosaically, were introduced by the early Bankers as a ready source of horseflesh. The rugged, wild ponies have been proven of Spanish mustang descent by the number of lumbar vertebrae and number of ribs.

At one time there were more than a thousand of them, roaming free, subsisting on marsh grass. As civilization came to the Banks they were penned and sold off. When the Cape Hatteras National Seashore was established they were taken over by the Park Service. There are now about twenty-five ponies in the herd.

The Pony Pen is located some six miles southwest of the Hatteras-Ocracoke ferry landing, on the sound side. Park Service signs will direct you to a wooden observation platform overlooking the mile-long fenced pasture. Don't count on seeing the ponies, especially in rough weather; they have shelters down near the southwest end that they retreat to. *Don't* cross the fence into the pasture. These are wild ponies, and they can bite and kick.

HAMMOCK HILLS NATURE TRAIL

Opposite Ocracoke Campground

Ocracoke's not all sandy beaches and small town. This 3/4-mile nature trail shows us a cross-section of the island, from dune through maritime forest to salt marsh. Learn how various plants adapted to conditions of salt and stress. A pleasant walk, the trail takes about half an hour to complete. You don't have to be *spry*, but one hill of soft sand will present an obstacle to people with impaired mobility. Bring the camera. See notes for snakes for Buxton Woods Nature Trail.

OCRACOKE VISITOR CENTER

Near Cedar Island and 928-4531
Swan Quarter Ferry Slips

The Ocracoke Island Visitor Center is run by the National Park Service as part of the Cape Hatteras National Seashore. It's in Ocracoke Village, at the very southwest end of Highway 12, on Silver Lake. To reach it from 12, just stay on the highway past the Island Inn until

Sharon Miller Realty

*Sales Rentals
Residential Appraisals*

Sharon Miller
Broker

Free information on request

P.O. Box 264
Ocracoke, NC 27960

Bookings through this office for:

Sportfishing aboard the
RASCAL

Big Channel Bass, Cobia, King Mackerel, Amber Jack, Flounder, Trout, Blues, etc.

Capt. N.E. Miller
C.G. Licensed

1/2 DAY   FULL DAY
INSHORE
OFFSHORE

(919)928-5711
(919)928-5731

you reach the Lake and a T. Turn right and continue around the shore of the lake in a counterclockwise direction till you see the low brown building to your right. Parking is available there.

The Center has an information booth, helpful people, a small book shop, and exhibits. It's also the place to make arrangements for use of the Park Service docks.

It's open seasonally; Memorial Day through Labor Day. That means that things are pretty quiet during the winter, as they are in the rest of the village, but during the warm months the Rangers offer a couple of dozen "Discovery Adventures," all free, presented several times each week (check at the desk for what, where, and when). In the past these have included beach and sound walks, interpretations of the life and times of a pirate, day or night walking tours of the village, bird-watching, history lectures, and quite a few more. Once you've looked around the village for a couple of days you may appreciate the Park Service's thoughtfulness in arranging things for you and the kids to do.

OCRACOKE COAST GUARD STATION

Silver Lake (Business) 928-4731

emergency (SAR line) 928-3711

The southernmost of the chain of Coast Guard stations along the Banks is Ocracoke. Its complement of twenty-one men maintain a 44-foot motor lifeboat and several other, smaller vessels for search and rescue, law enforcement, and servicing aids to navigation. In an average year, they respond to 250 calls for assistance from fishermen and boaters. Visitors may enjoy looking around the station building, built in 1938 to replace an older building on the same site, and strolling down the two piers to see the Coast Guard's pride -- its boats. You're welcome for an accompanied tour from 2 to 4 p.m. Monday through Friday, operations permitting, year round; check in at the communications station on the wide front porch.

OCRACOKE MUSEUM AND VISITOR CENTER

Silver Lake

To the west of the NPS parking lot in Ocracoke, you'll see a two-story white frame building in process of reconstruction. The house was built by David Williams, the first chief of the Ocracoke Coast Guard Station. In 1989 it was moved to its present location on NPS land. The Ocracoke Preservation Society, a group of interested local people, and the Park Service are restoring the building for use as a museum and visitor center. Like the restoration at Chicamacomico, this will benefit both local residents and tourists. The Preservation Society need donations. Write them at P.O. Box 491, Ocracoke, NC 27960.

OCRACOKE CIVIC CLUB

24 hour answering machine   928-6711

You can call during business hours if you have specific questions about Ocracoke, or write: Civic Club Box 456 Ocracoke, NC 27960.

OCRACOKE VILLAGE

West end of Highway 12

The little village of Ocracoke is a world of its own. Reclusive, hidden, romantic...these are words used by those who know her. A haunt of writers, artists, and lovers, this small lost hamlet at the world's end (or at least at the end of the highway, a phrase that has a touch of the mysterious itself) is unlike any of the other towns on the Banks.

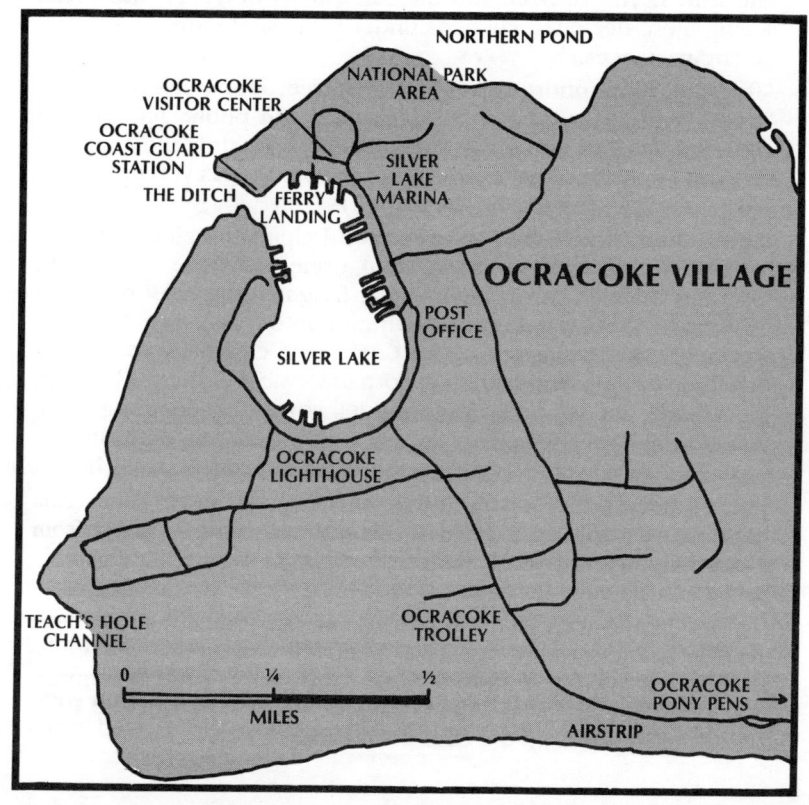

Things have changed since WWII and the coming of paved roads, but not all that much. The map of the village shows you nearly all that's there. The roads are still narrow, the people friendly but a touch reticent, with manners and a speech of their own distinct from mainland North Carolina. We love Ocracoke, and you will too.

For a short walking tour of the village, park in the lot opposite the Visitor's Center. Turn left out of the lot and walk down Route 12, along the shores of the Lake.

The village waterfront, formerly quite sleepy, is beginning to resemble St. Davis's Bermuda. You'll pass many small shops (see "Ocracoke Shopping" for profiles) and some large new hotels: the Anchorage, Harborside, Princess Motel. For the tour, keep walking till, on your right, you see a small brick post office.

Opposite the post office, a sandy, narrow street angles to the left. This is Howard Street, one of the oldest and least changed parts of the village. Note the smallness of the old homes, the cisterns attached to them for collection of rain water, and the detached kitchens. If you've been to Colonial Williamsburg you will recall seeing these detached kitchens under somewhat more monumental circumstances.

After some four hundred yards Howard Street debouches on School Street: tirn left for the Methodist Church and public school. The church is usually open for visitors, but use discretion; there may be services in progress. (Also, please wipe your feet as you go in; the sand doesn't look good on the carpet.)

If you enter, note the cross displayed behind the altar. Thereby hangs a tale, and not so very ancient a one. The cross was carved from a wooden spar from an American freighter, the *Caribsea*, sunk offshore by U-boats in the dark early months of 1942. By the strange workings of circumstance, the *Caribsea's* engineer was James Baugham Gaskill, who had been born in Ocracoke. He was killed in the sinking; and local residents will tell you a further strange fact; that several days later a display case, holding, among other things, Gaskill's mate's license, washed ashore not far from his family home.

There's been a Methodist church on Ocracoke since 1828. This building was built in 1943, with lumber and pews salvaged from older buildings. A "historical sketch" pamphlet is generally available in the vestibule for visitors.

If you'd like to walk to the lighthouse on the tour -- it adds about another half mile -- turn right (west) and follow the road past the Island Inn about five hundred yards. You will see the lighthouse towering on your right. After inspecting it (see 'Ocracoke Inlet Lighthouse') return to the church and school.

The next leg of the tour takes you across the grounds of the public school and out onto the paved road beyond it to the east. Turn left. This was the first paved road on the island, and was constructed by Seabees during WW II. Turn right after a third of a mile (first stop sign). A few minutes' walk along this narrow, tree-shaded road will bring you to the British Cemetery. You have to watch for it; it's on your right, set back a bit from the road, and shaded by live oak and yaupon. The big British flag makes it a bit easier to spot. It's not an impressive site; very small, very understated; entirely appropriate. The *Bedfordshire* was a trawler, one of a small fleet of twenty-four antisubmarine vessels that Churchill loaned to the United States in April 1942 to help us against the U-boats. She was a small ship, only 170 feet long, displacing 900 tons and armed with a single 4-inch deck gun, but full of fight. She had no chance; she was torpedoed off Cape Lookout during the night of 11 May by U-558. Six bodies washed ashore. Four were interred here by the Navy and Coast Guard, and the little cemetery is maintained by the USCG.

To return to the Visitor Center, walk west till you reach the lakeshore, then turn right.

OCRACOKE LIGHTHOUSE

SW corner of Ocracoke Village

This, the southernmost of the four famous lighthouses of the Banks, is also the oldest and the shortest. It's the second oldest operational lighthouse in the United States as well. Yes, it's still "flashing" away, -- one long flash from a half hour before sunset to a half hour after sunrise -- still warning mariners away from the ever-changing shoals offshore.

When it was built, in 1823, this was a busy port. The present lighthouse replaced a still older one, the Shell Castle Rock lighthouse, which had been built in 1798 but which was rather left behind when the inlet moved south.

The Ocracoke Inlet Lighthouse houses a 360-degree non- rotating light with a range of 14 miles. Focal plane height is 65', overall height of the structure is about 75'. The brick walls are five feet thick at the base. That pretty, textured white surface is mortar, hand-spread over the bricks. The two-story white house you will find nearby was originally meant for the lighthouse keeper. It underwent extensive reconstruction in the late 1980s, to Historic Preservation standards, and now serves as quarters for Ocracoke's Ranger and the maintenance supervisor. The light itself is operated by the Coast Guard and cannot be entered.

The gleaming white lighthouse in Ocracoke serves as a landmark on land as well as sea. DCTB

To reach the light, turn left off Route 12 at the Island Inn, and go about 800 yards. A white picketed turnoff on the right allows you to park your auto and walk the last few yards to the base of the structure.

SILVER LAKE MARINA

At Visitor's Center   928-4531

Silver Lake is the Park Service-run marina in Ocracoke, and is the only large one there. It is run differently from a commercial marina in that there are no dockage fees and no reservations. The marina has no slips, only four hundred feet of frontage on Silver Lake with tie-up facilities. Water is available, and so are power hookups ($1/night). The basin has been dredged to eighteen feet.

Basically, the way to get a slip is to arrive at the right time. If there's one open just pull in and tie up. There's a fourteen- day limit in the summertime. Actually, the rangers tell us that it's possible to get a slip there even in the summer, although it gets crowded on weekends.

If the marina should be full when you arrive, don't panic. Just anchor out in the lake, staying out of the channel way and out of the way of ferry operations.

O'NEAL'S DOCKSIDE

Behind the Community Store   928-1111

O'Neal's is your friendly hunting and fishing center, owned by Charlie O'Neal. This is where you book your offshore fishing charters on the *Miss Kathleen, Seawalker, Bluefin,* and *Outlaw,* and where you can charter trips to Portsmouth Island. They also sell a full line of supplies, boat gear, and fuel.

OCRACOKE TROLLEY

Trolley Stop, Highway 12   928-4041

It's one thing to see Ocracoke Island through your own eyes, and another thing altogether to see it through the eyes of a local, someone who knows every nook and cranny of the island. The Trolley runs three times a day during the week and twice on the weekends and takes you past some of Ocracoke's history you'd never know was there on your own.

The narrated tour includes the Coast Guard Station, the WW II Naval Base, several Sam Jones homes, the British Cemetery and Howard Grave Yard, a WW II Mine Control Tower, the Civil War headquarters for the Union Forces, and lots more.

Reservations are required for buses or groups numbering over 25, but for others, just show up at the Trolley Stop (you can grab a quick bite there too while you're waiting). Tours leave at 10:30 a.m., 2:30 p.m., and 5:00 p.m. Mondays through Saturdays. (No tours on Sundays.)

OCRACOKE FISHING CENTER
Silver Lake   928-6661

New in 1989 and part of the Anchorage Inn operation, these five 200-foot piers and new building act as a center for charter boat operations to the sound and close inshore. There's a minimum six-foot depth alongside. Docking ($.60/foot/day) includes showers, pool, telephones, and other extras. Gas and diesel are available and the boat ramp is two dollars. There are marine supplies and a small tackle shop. Open March 1 to November 30.

CARRIAGE RIDES
Anchorage Inn   928-1101

W. R. Bell and Cookie will provide tours of Ocracoke in a reproduction Victorian vis-a-vis (passengers face each other) carriage. The usual ride takes an hour or more and visits most local points of interest. Expect it to start from the Inn at 4, 5:30, 7, and 8:30, Memorial through Labor Day. Fare is $10.00 per person. Call 928-1581 to arrange a carriage for weddings or other special occasions.

OCRACOKE
SHOPPING

Ocracoke shopping hasn't caught up with the rest of the Outer Banks, yet...and thank goodness it hasn't! There's been no influx of souvenir shops or chain stores. Almost every shop is owned and managed by year 'round residents who specialize in local arts and crafts. That's not to say you can't get a t-shirt that advertises where you've been (Ocracoke has dozens of t-shirt designs; every store has a different selection) or a coffee mug that pictures a grinning fish; but, all in all, you'll find Ocracoke shopping more low key. Most stores are not open all year, and you may find that hours are loosely kept.

On the highway before you reach the Village, you'll find the **Ocracoke Variety Store**, 928-4911, and you'll probably find one of the owners, Cecil -- better known as "Hutch" -- or Julia Hutcherson, too. This is really more of a one-stop shopping spot, with groceries and other staples, beach wear, magazines, camping supplies, wine and beer. And, if you want an Ocracoke t-shirt, don't make any decisions until you've seen the Hutcherson's selection. Even if you don't want to shop, you can stop to take a look at current menus for all the Ocracoke eateries. They're right by the front door of this all-year store.

Next door to the Variety Store is the **Ocracoke Art Co-op**, 928-1451. It's not always easy to find the Co-op open because they're dependent on members to take turns "minding the store." Unfor-

OCRACOKE ISLAND REALTY

Residential & Commercial Property Sales

Rentals

Property Management

B.J. Arn-Oelschlegel
BROKER

Established 1982

REALTOR®

FREE SALES FLYER ON REQUEST
P.O. BOX 238-G • OCRACOKE, NORTH CAROLINA 27960
(919) 928-6261 or (919) 928-7411

tunately for us, they all have other stores to mind, too! It's worth pursuing if the local art scene interests you. Artists are frequently invited to show their work or give demonstrations, so it seems that there is always something new to see.

Down the road, before you get to the Village, is the **Whittler's Bench**, 928-7201. In years past, they occupied a small space behind the hardware store; now they've built more spacious quarters to display their handmade baskets, decoys, quilts and pottery.

Right on the main street in the village is **Merchant Mariner**, 928-6141, one of those stores that goes in a lot of different directions. They carry Ocracoke gifts and greeting cards, a nice selection of clothing for infants and children -- including swim wear.

Directly behind the Merchant Mariner is **The Old Post Office Shop and B.W.'s Surf Shop**, 928-6141. The old part of the building was actually used as the Ocracoke Post Office from 1954 until 1967. The old combination mail boxes are still in place and used to hold merchandise. The store has undergone some changes since last season and is primarily a boutique-style clothing store now, carrying casual and beach clothing and accessories for men and women.

The Community Store, 928-3321, also on the main street right on the harbor, is a place locals shop all year. It's a country-style, general store with bare wood floors and a potbellied stove. A bulletin board on the front porch offers a wealth of community information. David and Sherril Senseney own this store, along with **The Gathering Place**, 928-3321 (same as Community Store), just across the parking lot on the Harbor. The Gathering Place is a turn-of-the-century building, formerly a residence on the Island, moved to its present location and restored. They carry local crafts and artwork, as well as country antique "collectibles" like old phonograph records, shoes and kitchenware. One of the upstairs rooms is a gallery for New Bern artist Franz Van Baars.

Stop in at **Kathy's Gifts & Clothing**, 928-6461, to see a striking selection of t-shirts and jewelry. Her collection of women's ready-to-wear is the best on the island.

One of the friendliest places to shop on Ocracoke is **Harborside Gifts**, 928-3111. Owned by the same family for 25 years, this shop has also undergone major changes since last season, and is now much more of a clothing store than it had been in the past, carrying a nice selection of active wear and t-shirts. They still carry a good selection of gifts that don't scream "tourist." Look for the model train set that runs overhead throughout most of the store.

Phillip and Julia Howard have run **Village Craftsmen**, 928-5541, for twenty years. It's located on Howard Street -- an unpaved lane, actually -- a pleasant walk from the main street of the village. (Having done this several times myself, I feel compelled to warn you: It won't be pleasant if you haven't used a mosquito repellant.) The Howard family has played a prominent role in Ocracoke history: Eight generations ago, William Howard owned the entire island and, Phillip suspects, is the same man who was listed as Blackbeard's quartermaster. The store has the feel of an old general store and carries mostly North Carolina crafts, including the work of several local artisans. Phillip, himself, is an artist and prints of his work are sold in the shop. His ink drawings on driftwood are a popular item, but often out-of-stock. You'll also find books of regional interest, tapes of Irish harp and other soothing music.

Mickey Baker and Carmie Prete opened **Island Ragpicker**, 928-7571, several years ago to sell beautiful, handmade rugs. This pleasant shop now sells other quality crafts, including local work, in addition to the woven rugs that started their business. Their selection of handmade brooms and woven baskets is unusual. Finely crafted wood items are also out of the ordinary, as are the cards and jewelry. There's a book room, too. It's an excellent spot for browsing, located near Silver Lake, on the highway, with plenty of parking -- at least by Ocracoke standards -- at the front door. This is also the Ocracoke headquarters for **LegaSea**, an environmental group united to oppose offshore drilling on the Outer Banks -- a cause worthy of your support. Ask Mickey and Carmie for details, and, if you feel like it, make a donation to the cause.

You'll be better off to shop for your groceries on Hatteras and bring them with you to Ocracoke, but you can find the basics at either the Community Store or Ocracoke Variety. Try **Nat's Fresh Seafood**, across from the British Cemetary, for local catches. They also carry smoked and salted fish.

There is no pharmacy on the island, so get prescriptions filled before you go to Ocracoke.

Ocracoke Harbor retains its age-old charm. NC Dept. of Natural and Economic Resources

ELIZABETH ANN O'NEAL HOWARD
A LIFE ON OCRACOKE

The bridge of time can be crossed in one direction only. But we can, by listening to those who have crossed it before us, find out much about the journey. And about how things were, back then.

The house is small and white behind its picket fence and its two live oaks. The lane is so small it has no name. "But we call it Curiosity Lane," says Elizabeth Howard, laughing like a mischievous thirteen-year-old. "Because everybody who lives here is so curious. Come on in! Let's sit in the living room. I talk better from my chair."

"I was born in nineteen ten, in what we call the Trent Woods. It was beautiful up there. I wish I could take you up and show you. There wasn't a many of houses; we all lived in that one little neighborhood; there were three houses, and then one farther down, and then that was all. It's up on the Bay. I better not say what the name of that bay used to be...when I was born there were six of us, me and my two brothers and my father and mother, and then there were my cousins.

"My daddy when he was young, he went to sea. He was born up in Trent too. There was forty-seven acres and there was my grandmother, my uncle and aunt, and my father and mother. And my uncle and my father each had three children, so there were six of us. My mother had four children, but my oldest brother died. He saw a duck, and he shot the duck, and he went in to get it. And it was freezing cold, and he caught pneumonia and died four years before I was born. Doctor MacIntyre gave him medicine but it didn't pull him through.

"I can go back in my family to seventeen hundred and fifty-nine. William Howard came and bought the island in 1759. And with him came John Williams, who was a pilot. And he witnessed the deeds. Then two months later John Williams came back and bought half of the island from William Howard. I married a Howard; but I'm an O'Neal. And my mother was a Williams. So I am about...fifth generation from John Williams.

"The O'Neal that I came from, I can't go back farther than 1774 on the O'Neal side. That's when Elizabeth Jackson married John O'Neal. And they had ten children. And I came from Christopher O'Neal, who was the youngest boy.

"My grandfather Horatio Williams was an old sea captain. My mother and her sister sailed to New York City on his vessel, the *Paragon*. And he gave them money and told them to go ashore and buy whatever they wanted. My mother's sister bought a bedroom suit, and my mother bought cashmere and embroidery and ribbons and things. For her trousseau. There were three men on the vessel, and he sent them ashore to look after them. But they all three got drunk and she and her sister had to get back to the boat the best way they could.

"When I was two and a half years old, my father bought the house that's around the corner. And they moved down here to the creek side of the island. Then later my father bought the store on the Lake. My daddy was then in the Lifesaving Service, so my double-cousin and my brother operated the store. So I've lived in this neighborhood seventy-three and a half years.

"When I was a little girl we played bob-jacks, little things made out of metal and you throw the jack up and catch them. We didn't use a ball. And we played what we called hop scotch, and croquet, and dolls. I had a lot of books with paper dolls in them; and we also cut the pictures out of the catalog and played with them.

"We had what you call a Hot Blast -- a big stove that would hold wood and coal. In our living room we had a two-burner stove that looked like a piece of furniture. Kerosene. And then the kind you carry around in your hand, we had those in the bedrooms. And a fireplace in the living room, but I never used that when I was young, and now I'm old I still don't. In the kitchen we had a big iron stove with a reservoir to keep the water hot. That burned wood.

"In the summer my mother would cook on the oil stove to keep the kitchen from getting hot. In the winter she would use the wood stove. For breakfast we would have ham and eggs, or hot rolls homemade; or you could have oatmeal; or grits; or fish if you liked. I never liked fish for breakfast, I didn't like the smell. We had our main meal, what we called dinner and is now called lunch, in the middle of the day. Because when you don't have 'lectric, dark especially in the wintertime comes early. That's an old kerosene lamp there that belonged to my mother. For dinner we had chicken, it could be baked or stewed; we had lamb, my daddy had sheep on the Banks. We had oysters, fish, crab, clams, wild duck, hog meat. The hogs lived in pens in people's yards. My father had cattle down below and every week he would kill a heifer and sell it in the store. He had a refrigerator in the store that would hold sixteen cakes of ice, and twice a week he would get ice and have a man cut the meat up and he would sell it. The sheep lived on the banks, from where the pony pen is now to the town. They just roamed free. My daddy's branding iron was a diamond shape. My daddy would buy the stock and the feed and my uncle would do the work.

"Our water came from cisterns. And some people had rain barrels. A cistern catches rain water from the roof. And a lot of people had wells and lift pumps. Well, honey, you had to bathe in a wash tub or a wash basin. I played in the dirt and I took a bath every day. You were never put to bed dirty, I can tell you that. The cleanest people on earth are right here on this island. And that still goes in our family.

"I saw my first airplane in 1916, 1917. I was six or seven. It was at a funeral, it was a family connection. People were standing around out in the yard and heard the roaring of the plane. And everybody fell on the ground. They were frightened, they didn't know what the plane was there for. It was World War One. Wouldn't you have been frightened?

"I don't know how old I was when I first went off the island. I took the mail boat. It was a bugeye. It took nine hours. It went out every day, except in the hurricane of '44. I got seasick. When I was a little girl I never wanted to travel around. Later on I wanted to but I never did. And now it's just too hard. I don't really want to any more.

"I could go anywhere I wanted on the island when I was a little girl. But I couldn't wear pants, my daddy wouldn't let me. I wear them now, but he never saw me in pants. I had pretty dresses. My mother had three boys, so she knew how to make boy clothes, but she wasn't too good at making girl clothes; so my aunts, my blood kin and my aunt by marriage, made all my dresses. I had three or four silk dresses, Sunday dresses, and maybe seven or eight cotton I wore the rest of the week. The Sunday dresses I would wear all day. And I remember the minister's son lived right across from us, and this little boy and I were playing, and we got in to some briars and I tore my silk dress. And my mother didn't spank me. She never spanked me for tearing my dresses. She only spanked me when I talked back to her.

"I wasn't allowed to go barefoot either. My daddy wouldn't let me go barefooted because we had horses in the yard. He was afraid of lockjaw. I wore Mary Janes, with straps, patent leather. But when my father wasn't home I used to go across the street with the parson's children and take my shoes off and play in the sand.

"At Christmas we would have a tree and Santa Claus would come. And everybody would go to the church, to the exercise on Christmas Eve. The Methodist church, that's all we had then. There would be a tree there too, and it's traditional that everybody who goes gets a bag of candy and peanuts, raisins, apple, orange in that bag. All of my life that happened, and I don't know how many years before. And on Christmas Eve night all the children had recitations, and we would put on a pageant. I can't remember anything I recited, but I remember one little boy, I can always remember the things I don't need to -- he had a recitation that went, "Who's old Santy, I don't know/Great long whiskers hangin' down so." That little boy's name was Thomas Gilbert Jackson. He is still living here.

"You gave presents, you gave every member of your family presents. I remember when I believed in Santa Claus, that is I didn't know but what there wasn't a Santa Claus, I remember my cousin taking me to the other side of the Lake, to John McWilliam's store. She got a little toy cooking stove, and little frying pan, little pot, and then she bought a little clothesline and pins, and a big ball. Maybe I was a little stupid, but I didn't think anything about it. Oh, and a little tea set, and a little piano. And we left and I never thought about it and my mother hid everything for Christmas. But I searched, and I found it and I was in trouble. To this day I can never put anything back in a drawer the way I found it. But the next year the other children told me there wa'n't any Santa Claus. I don't know how I thought he got here -- probably on the mail boat.

"What did we do in the winter? Some people quilted; I don't but I have some beautiful ones that were given to me. Do you know what a Chautauqua is? The Chautauqua came twice a year. And there were dances for the adults maybe every weekend, and in the summer every night. At the dance hall. One was down near the docks and the other was at the Pamlico Inn. And then there was one at the Odd Fellows' Lodge. When I grew up I danced at all of them. And people had parties in their homes. Dinner parties, and parties for the children. And candy-pulling, where you make candy and pull it and put it on a plate and let it get hard. And people would put on shows, they still do. Of course we had radios. But no one on the island knew how to fix them. So we just bought new ones when they wouldn't work any more.

"I grew up fast. All through my childhood I was taller than most children my age...when I was ten years old my father left the store in the neighborhood and moved down to the waterfront. My first cousin went with us and my mama sent me down there too. I had chores to do; I had to empty the Pepsi container, where they'd throw their empty bottles, and I had to take the trash out, sweep the front porch, and I had to take the oranges that were going bad out of the orange box, and the apples, and the grape box, had to throw away all the things you couldn't sell. The name of the store was Big Ike's. His name was Ike. It was on the waterfront. When I was a little girl the big boats couldn't get into the creek. The sailing vessels had to anchor out in the sound and you'd have to send a man out in his skiff and get my daddy's goods off the boat and bring it to my daddy's pier. You could pole out with a big oar.

"I was about twelve years old when a man from Hatteras came over here selling Model T Fords and my daddy bought one. And you know what he paid for it? Five hundred dollars. And Dallas Williams and David Williams bought one from the same man. Then later Captain Bill Gaskill bought a great big truck. He had the Pamlico Inn, that was where they took boarders -- tourists. Tourists came here before I was ever born. This picture was taken in 1915 when I was five years old...this hotel had a hundred rooms. And I remember we were looking at that truck and somebody said, 'Captain Bill, is that a Ford?' And he said, 'It's all I can a-ford.'

"The cars could take you to the beach, but frankly you pushed more than you rode. If we left the island, going to Hatteras, we rode the high-water mark. We'd have to leave the car down at the inlet and took the Coast Guard boat across. On the other side we'd visit among our relatives and come back the same way we went.

"During the depression there wasn't any money here. People who were in the Coast Guard, or the lighthouse, it didn't hurt them. But it hurt our family. It knocked the props from under my father. Because if you have a business and nobody has any money you can't sell anything, and if you do it just goes on the books...but even at that, nobody here went hungry. You couldn't here, you had fish, crabs, oysters were plentiful. That's what they'd give you at the store. Everybody had gardens.

"I finished the eighth grade here, then I went to school in North Carolina. Most children did that. I was fifteen when I went away to school. It was a private school which I thought was the army -- you got up by the bugle and you went to bed with the bugle. It isn't there any more.

"After high school I wanted the bright lights and glitter, and the five and ten cent store. I had a job offered to me in Raleigh, to work with a doctor. I wrote to my mother telling her that and she wrote telling me to come home, my father needed me. So I came home. And I worked in my daddy's store. And after that I worked for Robert S. Wahab at what used to be the Wahab Hotel. They had the hotel, a skating rink, a movie theatre, and the dance hall, the Spanish Casino.

"That's another thing, why people came to Ocracoke and lived during the summer. Malaria, on the mainland. And you wouldn't get it on Ocracoke; these salt water mosquitoes don't carry malaria. All the little houses along the sound side were the people who came here during the summer to get away from the malaria.

"I married a Howard, Robert Wahab Howard. Did we grow up together...yes and no; I was three years older than he was and he grew up to me. That's a picture of him over there in his Navy uniform. He was a good-looking man, and he was smart. He was only in for the duration of the war but he made permanent chief. He could have stayed in. I wanted him to, but one day he took me aside and said, 'I got something to say and I want you to listen. If I stay in we won't have much time together. I want a home and a family, and I want to be home with my family. So don't tell me any more you want me to stay in the Navy.' I always thought he could have gotten the pension...but he died when he was only sixty. I thought then, he must have known. We were married in 1942. August the seventeenth.

"My daughter was born in the house around the corner from me. She wasn't supposed to be. I was supposed to be in Washington N.C., Little Washington the Tarheels call it. But she came early when I was getting dressed to get on the mail boat. I was making coffee when I felt the first pains. They brought a bed downstairs and that's where they put me. They had a registered nurse here and a practical nurse, Lola Williams, and they delivered my daughter. Lola stayed with me for ten days. And I remember my father said to my mother, 'Helen, that child will talk sooner than any child ever talked.' And my mother said, 'Why do you say that?' And my father said, 'Because she's been in that room with Lola and Elizabeth for ten days and they haven't shut up once.'

"In World War Two things changed. You could go down to the naval base, if you had family in the Navy, and you could buy anything you wanted -- a gold watch or anything. They had entertainment, USO shows. I never saw a ship actually get torpedoed; but we could hear it, boom boom booom. And you could step up on my daddy's porch and see the blaze. In that respect it was scary here. Everything was blacked out. The lighthouse had a blind on it. I asked my daddy one night, 'Papa, if the Germans take Ocracoke what will we do?' He said, 'Well honey I don't know what you'll do, but I think I'll kill m'self.' And my sister-in-law's a full-fledged German.

"Now things are changing here like everywhere. I don't think people here are as friendly as they used to be when I was growing up. People used to share their food. And we still do in this neighborhood, and I'm sure in the other neighborhoods too. But not everybody's like that. They can't afford to be. One thing, we don't have too many original families here any more. That's the Williamses, the O'Neals, the Garrishes, the Howards, and the Gaskills. And the Scarboroughs and the Spencers. They're all originally Ocracokers. Well, I won't say all the children are originals because their fathers or mothers may have come from some other place. I'm actually all Ocracoke.

O'Neal and Williams and Tolson and Jackson. English and they say the Williamses are Welsh. Isn't it different where you live, where your grandmother lived, than it is now? I don't want to say things that will offend anybody, but when I grew up Ocracoke had the best class of people.

"The nicest thing about it still is that people here have more freedom. You don't live in fear here as much as in the cities. When my little girl was little she could run anywhere on the island, and in fact we'd let her take people around. Nothing has ever hurt me so I've never been afraid of things.

"My granddaughters now, for instance, they're nineteen and twenty-one. And they come and stay with me every summer. They wear pants. So that's changed. But I remember something my daddy said to my mother once, when I was fifteen and my cousin and I wanted to go to Hatteras for a dance, the Woodmen of the World opening, and stay overnight with our relatives. My mother said I shouldn't go, that her mother would never have allowed her to. But my father said, 'Let them go. Time changes. And people have to change with it.' I always remembered that because like it or not I think he was right.

The stately "cottages" near the 13 milepost in Nags Head are reminiscent of years gone by. DCTB

OUTER BANKS
RESTAURANTS

The food service traditions of the Outer Banks center around seafoods which are caught in local waters by the resident fishing fleet. The "fish-of-the-day" might be Bluefish, Speckled Trout, Croaker, Spanish Mackerel, Bluefin Tuna, or even Dolphin depending on the seasonal catch. Flounder, the flat fish with delicate taste, is plentiful and is featured in every seafood establishment. Filets fried whole in a light batter to a golden crispness, broiled with a lemon butter topping, or served fried with a crabmeat stuffing, are the favored preparations. This species provides the most popular entrees on the beach.

Crabmeat entrees are also a staple on Outer Banks menus. The Blue crab's backfin meat is highly prized for flavor and recipe versatility. She-Crab Soup, praised by President George Washington in 1791, is a complex cream based soup with a hint of sherry. Not every chef tempts this gourmet's delight, so try it, if available. Don't confuse it with plain Crab Soup, a tomato broth based soup with vegetables and bits of crab. Crabmeat also appears in cocktail appetizers, or stuffed into mushrooms, but it is the entree list that gives it star billing. Crab Cake are almost universally offered. (Ask for them broiled instead of fried for a purer crab taste).

Soft shell crabs are more readily available since the advent of methods to "hold" the shell changing crustaceans and improved freezing methods. While we think fresh ones are best, if you've never tried a soft shell, you're in for a real Outer Banks treat anytime.

Sauteed Crabmeat and Crab Imperial will also be seen. And with the popularity of pasta dishes, don't be surprised to find a Crabmeat Alfredo offered as the evening special.

True crab lovers, however, may yearn for the family restaurant where the butcher paper is spread across the table and a few dozen steamed crabs are piled in the center for picking. Alas, about the only way you can dig into a pile of steaming crabs these days (short of steaming them yourself) is to get carry-out from one of the seafood stores or attend one of the many "crab feasts" that are held throughout the season. Don't be afraid to try steamed crabs if you are a novice. There will always be someone nearby who'll be happy to share their secrets for extracting the sweet crabmeat from its shell.

The legendary bivalve, the oyster is next in the culinary list of Outer Banks restaurant treats. Under soups and appetizers, you will see them served as Oyster Stew (with or without milk), and on the half shell. Select oysters are usually served fried.

The clam is usually served on the Outer Banks in Clam Chowder, or French Fried Clam Strips, or in Clam Fritters. The ocean clams harvested here abouts are too large and tough for eating on the half shell. You will see Cherrystone Clams on the half shell, steamed Hard Shell Clams, and Clams Casino in some places.

Scallops, however, are another matter. Beautiful scallops are brought to port almost everyday, and native cooks generally prepare them fried, sauteed in butter, or broiled. More imaginative chefs will create a Coquille St. Jacques, Scallops en Brochette, or even a Scallop Creole. If you enjoy eating scallops, the Outer Banks is one of the best places we know to sample this meaty textured seafruit.

The final star on the seafood menu is the Shrimp. It appears in cocktail appetizers, in deep fried baskets, or steamed with spicy condiments. It is also welcomed in Shrimp Creole, on a Seafood Kabob, or simply sauteed or broiled. Several restaurants offer the spicy Scampi.

The alternative to making an individual pick from this seafood bounty is to have it all on a combination platter. And that's what most people do, at least on their first restaurant night out.

OUTER BANKS STYLED CLAM CHOWDER

Every seafaring area takes its clam chowder seriously. Chowders come in three basic varieties. Manhattan Clam Chowder has a tomato base and may be on the spicy side with hints of Tabasco, thyme, basil, and oregano. New England Clam Chowder is generally considered to have a milk base and has salt pork, onion, and always potatoes added. The Outer Banks variety (call it Hatteras style, Wanchese style or whatever) uses neither tomato or milk, but prefers to feature the clams in their own broth or liquor. Other ingredients may include diced potatoes, chopped onions, celery, parsley and the chef's choice of spices which enhance the clam flavor. Chowder will sour very easily if it is not handled properly, especially if made in big batches. Chowder chefs agree that the cover on a pot of chowder should never be left on while it is cooling because the condensation will spoil it. A chowder should never go into the refrigerator until it has completely cooled to room temperature. Any skin that forms on the top of a cooled chowder should be carefully skimmed off. A chowder always tastes better on the second, or even third day, if it doesn't ferment first! Chowder is not easy to make and even harder to keep. It is little wonder that chowder chefs are so sensitive, and proud of their vulnerable creations.

It is very possible that no two Outer Banks clam chowders are the same. Perhaps they are not even the same at the same restaurant from one day to the next. It is the challenge and delight of the would-be chowder gourmet to sample the field and declare his own preferences.

HUSHPUPPIES

Nearly every seafood restaurant on the Outer Banks serves up a basket of hushpuppies with its entrees. Hushpuppies are a traditional Southern deep fried corn meal bread. The corn meal, flour, baking powder, salt, sugar, egg, and milk batter is dropped by the spoonful into deep hot fat and allowed to fry until it is golden brown.

Some Southern areas add finely chopped onion to their mix and like to fry the hushpuppy in the same oil used to fry the fish. But the quintessential Outer Banks hushpuppy cook eschews the onion and the fishy hint to his creations in favor of a sweet, almost cake-like quality that is achieved by increasing the flour and sugar ratio and frying in oils reserved just for hushpuppies.

Hushpuppies can vary in diameter. Some cooks believe that the size of the round crispy breads is the secret to their texture and taste. Others guard their batter recipes in the conviction that they have discovered the perfect hushpuppy formula. Many restaurants on the Banks have loyal followers who are convinced that their hushpuppies are the best.

To tell the truth, few restaurants make hushpuppies from scratch anymore. There are excellent commercial mixes which get "doctored" so that the cook can claim it as his own. The quantitative and qualitative difference may actually be very small.

By legend, and this is perhaps a true one, hushpuppies got their name as southern cooks prepared the evening meal. Hungry hunting dogs would hang around the kitchen and bark for their share of the meal being prepared. The harried cooks, trying to get a meal completed for a waiting family, attempted to appease and quiet the dogs with bits of corn bread batter dropped into the hot frying fat. The little fried dough balls were thrown out the kitchen door with the admonishment, "hush puppy".

PLANNING & PRICING

For many years almost all seafoods served on the Banks were deep fried. Today, the broiler and grill is just as popular, and there is a trend toward even further preparation diversity as chefs trained in other traditions come to cook on the Outer Banks.

The establishment of liquor by the drink on the main resort strip (Kitty Hawk, Kill Devil Hills, Nags Head) in 1981 heralded a remarkable surge in new restaurant construction, renovation of established places, and rethinking all along the beach. The bar and lounge business has contributed to upgrading restaurant menus, decor, and service wherever it has been allowed. Beer, wine and brown bagging are available on Roanoke, Hatteras and Ocracoke Islands and in Corolla. (See Service Directory-Liquor Laws for more information.)

The restaurant competition on the Outer Banks is keen. The prime vacation months account for a large percentage of a restaurateur's income, so the good business person cannot afford to be outmaneuvered by menu pricing. Competitive enterprise seems to be working here to the consumer's benefit.

We see a basic uniformity of entree pricing for the most popular items. For example, a flounder filet stuffed with crab meat presented in restaurants of equal ambiance and kitchen quality will cost about the same price.

For our readers convenience we have established four categories as a guide to menu prices. The costs are based on dinner for two persons which includes appetizers, entrees, two vegetables or side dishes, desserts, and coffee. Specials and other factors can lower the basic check total just as cocktails, wine, and flaming tableside desserts can increase it. For restaurants that don't serve dinner, the guideline is based on relative expense.

Restaurateurs with pocket calculators can easily challenge our best intentions in offering these guidelines. Personal choices and menu changes will prove us wrong in some cases. But we hope you'll bear in mind that these are only meant to be guides and adopt our dining-out attitude: Enjoy your favorite offerings on the menu and be prepared to pay the bill.

Here are the guidelines that are reflected in the restaurant profiles to follow:

A basic meal for two under $25	$
A check for two of $26 to $40.	$$
A check for two of $41 to $55.	$$$
Over $55 for two.	$$$$

These guides do not reflect the 5% NC sales tax or the gratuity which should be at least 15% for good service.

Some restaurants offer discounts and specials for early evening dining in order to encourage their patrons to avoid the peak dining hours. It is no secret that in-season, and on shoulder season weekends, the waiting lines at popular restaurants are long. Few restaurants will accept reservations except for large parties.

We list a season of operation for each restaurant. But please note:While we make every effort to get accurate information, in a competitive, active market like the Outer Banks, even the best- laid plans can get scrapped mid-season. If you're visiting off- season, it's best to call ahead before you make dinner plans.

The restaurants profiled in this guide are arranged by mile marker, north to south, Corolla to Ocracoke. Each location is keyed to a detailed strip map for your further convenience.

SOUTHERN SHORES, DUCK, SANDERLING, COROLLA
RESTAURANTS

THE SANDERLING RESTAURANT

Sanderling, north of Duck   261-3021

$$$$ MC, VISA, AMEX

Housed in the Historic Landmark, Caffeys Inlet Station, one of the many life saving stations that dotted the coastland during the early part of this century, the restaurant carries through a comfortable yet very classy nautical theme in its five main rooms. The main dining room is in the Boat Room, the area in which the lifesaving boats were originally stored. Several very large glass doors give the room a bright, airy feel and provide nice views too. The Captain's Galley, a window-lined addition to the back of the building, provides an oceanfront view. Upstairs is the Life Saving Lounge, a full service bar. An oceanfront deck right off the Lounge, was enclosed this year. It will be used for private parties and overflow dining on busy nights.

Sand castles are a perennial favorite by the shores of the Atlantic Ocean. DCTB

The new room offers a spectacular view of the ocean. Hickory grilled appetizers and entrees with a southern twist are the specialties of their limited but well rounded menu. Several new items were added for the 1990 season. The Sunday buffet is especially nice, with a chef on hand to prepare your omelets and Belgian waffles to order. Open year round for breakfast, lunch and dinner. A 15% service charge (an enforced gratuity) is added to all bills. Children's portions available at dinner. Reservations are accepted.

BLUE POINT OYSTER BAR & GRILLE

The Waterfront Shops, Duck   261-8090

$$-$$$ MC, VISA

The decor and dinner service -- colorful reproductions of the classic 40s Fiestaware -- will take you back in time, but the food is strictly 90s cuisine, with the emphasis on healthy and fresh ingredients. You get three dining options at this waterside bistro: a table on the enclosed porch, a table inside, or an old-fashioned stool at the large counter.

The dinner menu changes daily and has a true gourmet touch. It won't delight the diehard steak-and-potatoes diner. But The Blue Point is sure to please the person who enjoys new blendings of flavors and textures, and fresh ingredients not overcooked or masked by heavy sauces. A shrimp appetizer is accompanied by black beans and pink grapefruit butter; corn chowder is seasoned with dill; grilled tuna is served with jalapeno-mango salsa; it's different, but it's good.

Since they opened in 1989, The Blue Point has become a real favorite with locals and word-of-mouth travels fast. Come early or expect a crowd. Open for lunch and dinner all year. Closed on Mondays except during summer.

DUCK DELI

Rt. 12, Duck   261-DELI

$ No credit cards

This is the new (in '89) Duck Deli: new owners, new decor, new menu. We're not sure why they didn't give it a new name, too (it's no longer a "deli" in the real sense of the word), but no matter. It's still good eating. Cream cheese and sprouts are out and we're talking barbecue. Hickory smoked buffalo wings (spicy chicken wings served with a blue cheese dip), ribs and North Carolina pork BBQ (a vinegar-based sauce, not the sweet, tomato sauce popular in the north), baked beans and cole slaw seem to be what everyone orders, but the turkey and cheese on whole wheat was fresh and filling. Open most of the year.

ELIZABETH'S CAFE & WINERY

Scarborough Faire, Duck   261-6145
$$-$$$ MC, VISA, AMEX

If you were a Capt'n Franks fan, you may be upset to find this new cafe in its place (you can still go to Kitty Hawk for one of the Captain's junk yard dogs). Elizabeth's is as different from Capt'n Franks as night is from day. But if you enjoy good food, you'll get over your disappointment. The space has been remodeled: lace panels cover the windows, shelves of books line the walls, a fireplace at one end of the dining room adds a warm touch. Table settings at lunch are casual; for dinner they bring out the tablecloths and china. Weather permitting, lunch and evening appetizers are also served on the boardwalk in front of the restaurant. The lunch menu offers sandwiches and salads accompanied with freshly baked breads and their own dressings. The tuna waldorf salad is excellent. The dinner menu is limited but interesting, with most entrees centering on fresh seafood.

Both menus change continually to reflect what fresh ingredients are available. Elizabeth is a real person; she's been on the Outer Banks restaurant scene for several years as manager of Sweetwater's. She plans to be open for lunch and dinner all year, except for a week at Christmas. Dinner reservations are advised.

FAST EDDIE'S

The Marketplace, Southern Shores   261-8585
$ No credit cards

Excellent hamburgers are the stars here. The meat is ground fresh by their butcher and cooked to order. Oyster boats and fresh tuna salad sandwiches are good, too. Save room for dessert from their bakery or ice cream shop. The sweets are all made on the premises. Open all year for lunch and dinner.

KITTY HAWK
RESTAURANTS

SPORTSMAN'S RESTAURANT

Rt. 158, MP 4   261-4600
$ MC, VISA

Formerly owned by well-known Outer Banks restaurateur Al Van Curren, Sportsman's is one of those popular mass feeding stations where function supercedes flash. Prices are excellent, with huge portions and all-you-can-eat specials being the primary appeal. The food is dependably good--not great, not unusual--and fast, efficient service keep locals and visitors alike coming back year after year. When the restaurant was bought by Lacy McNeill and his partners, they didn't tamper with success. Breakfast starts early year 'round and the restuarant stays open for lunch and dinner. Full bar service is available.

KEEPER'S GALLEY

Rt. 158, MP 4-1/2   261-4000
$$ MC, VISA, AMEX

This is R.V. Owen's newest venture on the Outer Banks restaurant scene. If you've been in the area before, you were probably familiar with his popular RV's restaurants right down the street and at Whalebone Junction in Nags Head. R.V. and his partners split, with the Whalebone Junction restaurant staying with R.V., and the Kitty Hawk location going to the partners who've kept the basic format but renamed the business Frisco & Co. Keeper's Galley is less of a bar and more of a restaurant than his old location.

The lifesaving station theme is carried throughout the architecture and decor, and the resulting ambience is cozy, casual and comfortable. Lunch and dinner are nearly identical to the old -- and dependably good -- RV's fare. A personal favorite is the Nachos Grandes (more than a meal!). Breakfast is the real stand out, however. It's the most varied breakfast menu we've seen on the beach, offering local dishes like seafood stew and crabcakes with eggs. Keeper's Galley is open for all three meals, all year.

JOHN'S DRIVE IN

Beach Road, MP 4-1/2   261-2916
$ No credit cards

John's has been a north beach summertime favorite for years. This author knows people who'll drive from Roanoke Island just for one of John's fresh fish sandwiches. Locals watch for his opening in late April like a pelican watches for fish. The menu offers subs and sandwiches with a variety of side orders; but it's the fresh fish sandwiches and platters that have made his reputation. There is also a very large selection of ice cream treats (soft serve), running the gamut from milkshakes and malts to specialty sundaes.

Parking is limited at this popular hangout and anytime near mealtime the few picnic tables are likely to be full. Service is reasonably fast, though, and it's inexpensive. If you're looking for "fast food," John's Drive-In is a good local alternative.

CAPT'N FRANKS

Rt. 158, MP 4   261-9923
$ No credit cards

The Hess family has been serving hot dogs to the Outer Banks since 1974. The lunchtime crowd is thick all year long, and you wouldn't have to look far to find someone who'd fight you for a Captain's Junk Yard Dog (that's a hot dog with chili, cheese, onion, the works). In addition to hot dogs, they offer an assortment of other sandwiches. During the summer only, Capt'n Franks is open for dinner, with steamed shrimp, fried clam platters, tossed salads and other easy-to-cook, easy-to-eat items. Capt'n Franks is open all year.

KITTY HAWK PIZZA

Rt. 158, MP 4   261-3933
$ No credit cards

Established in 1984, this restaurant is another place that has built a loyal following among locals and vacationers alike.

The pizza is excellent: They go to great pains to see that their crust (only one kind) is just right; the sauce is tangy and memorable, but not overpowering (my husband swears it's the only pizza in the world that doesn't give him indigestion); real cheese and fresh toppings finish it off. But they may actually be better known for their Greek salads and spinach pies. And, yes, they have a selection of all-American sandwiches and such, too.

The restaurant has been remodeled and expanded. If you've been put off by the crowds before -- and on a summer weekend, it can be very crowded -- you'll be happy to know that an additional dining room has alleviated that problem. The new room sports etched glass doors and a wall mural; not your ordinary pizza parlor touches, to be sure. We think you'll find it a comfortable, pleasant restaurant, especially when you're in the mood for Mediterranean cooking.

TRADEWINDS

Rt. 158, MP 4-1/2   261-3052
$$ MC, VISA, AMEX

Tired of the same old thing? Think that if you see another bluefish, fried or otherwise, you'll turn green at the gills? If it's one of those days, Chinese may hit the spot. Tradewinds is the place to go. They offer a varied menu, featuring Mandarin style dishes, far spicier than the mild Cantonese versions of the Chung King empire. Kung Pao Shrimp with its crunchy vegetables and hot peppers is a personal favorite. The Fried Rice and Low Meins (like Chow Mein, only served over a pasta-like soft noodle) are always good. You can eat in or take out. Service is fast and pleasant. Tradewinds has full bar service and is open for lunch and dinner year 'round.

Kitty Hawk Pizza

The Wright Choice

4½ m.p.
Kitty Hawk

carry out
261-3933

pizza
gyros
salad bar

KILL DEVIL HILLS
RESTAURANTS

STACK 'EM HIGH

Rt. 158, MP 4 1/2 261-8221
Rt. 158, MP 9 441-7064
$-$$ No credit cards

The official name of this breakfast spot is Stack 'Em High, Pancakes and So Forth. The first Kill Devil Hills location was opened in 1981 by Kiki and Perry Kiousis. They added a second location in 1987 across from Kitty Hawk Plaza. Service begins early, as patrons move along a cafeteria-like line to pick up juices, fruits, beverages, and utensils. Food orders are given, a number placed on your tray, and the hot food delivered to your table. Blueberry and Banana Pan-

---

stack 'em high

PANCAKES & SO FORTH

Waffles, blintzes, omelettes, eggs to order, and more

Serving 6 a.m. to 1 p.m. daily
AT TWO LOCATIONS:

US 158 at MP 9 1/2	US 158 at MP 4 1/2
in Kill Devil Hills	in Kitty Hawk
441-7064	261-8221

cakes are the specialty: short stacks of three, and high stacks of five. Short stacks can also be ordered in other varieties such as buttermilk, strawberry, pecan, apple, etc. Bagels, blueberry muffins (baked in their kitchen), English muffins, danish, and cereals are also available, as are the traditional eggs and bacon and sausage. Stack 'Em High serves breakfast all hours they are open and also offers a limited lunch menu. They close in the early afternoon. Both locations are open from early spring through late fall.

FINELY RON'S

Rt. 158, MP 5-1/2   441-1664

$$$ MC, VISA, AMEX

Opened three seasons ago, this attractive restaurant in Seagate North Shopping Center is owned and managed by Ron and Jean Davidson. They have nearly 20 years of experience in fine restaurants and Ron is a graduate of The Culinary Institute of New York.

Menu offerings are a little out-of-the-ordinary, but center around the usual Outer Banks fish and seafood. Sunday night features a lobster special. Soups are unusually good: we highly recommend

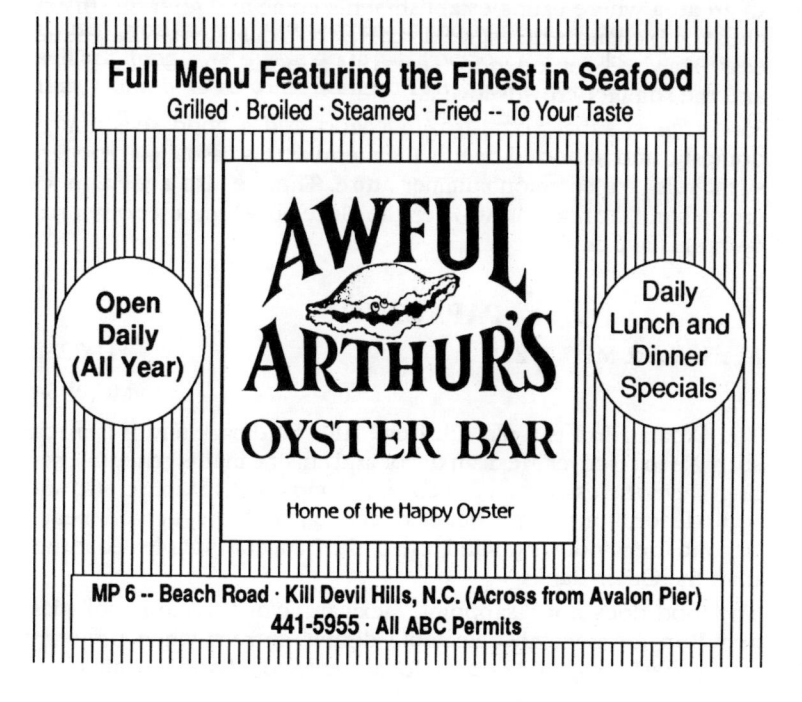

Full Menu Featuring the Finest in Seafood
Grilled · Broiled · Steamed · Fried -- To Your Taste

AWFUL ARTHUR'S OYSTER BAR

Open Daily (All Year)

Daily Lunch and Dinner Specials

Home of the Happy Oyster

MP 6 -- Beach Road · Kill Devil Hills, N.C. (Across from Avalon Pier)
441-5955 · All ABC Permits

the Sweet Red Pepper Bisque, a creamy, well seasoned recipe that made the most of a vegetable normally used to accent other flavors. Finely Ron's is open for dinner all year. They offer a children's menu.

AWFUL ARTHUR'S

Beach Road, MP 6   441-5955

$$ MC, VISA, AMEX

This is a very popular watering hole with locals. It's casual with a long, long bar and picnic style tables. And its probably the best place on the beach to pig out on oysters or steamed shrimp by the basketful. If you feel like hanging out with the working crowd, knocking back a few tall, cool ones, and enjoying some good, fresh seafood -- by the way, they do have more on the menu than just steamed shrimp and oysters -- this is the place to go. Open all year.

NEWBY'S

Rt. 158, MP 6   441-7277

$ No credit cards

In an area where eating establishments come and go faster than a ghost crab changes holes, we'd say Newby's qualifies as a huge success. They've been open for years, it's a locals' favorite for lunch, and the summer crowds love it.

Sandwiches, subs, pizza, frozen yogurt and a good selection of domestic and imported beer is the menu at this casual place where swim suits are common summer attire. They've also added an ice cream bar. Late night hours keep the place busy long after other restaurants have closed.

PAPAGAYO

Beach Road, MP 7 1/2   441-7232

$$ MC, VISA

The Croatan Inn is a old Kill Devil Hills landmark and it is a real surprise to discover Mexican decor and cuisine in this venerable setting. Nevertheless, the basket covered lamps, festive table cloths and wall decorations, pine beamed ceiling, and the lighted beach beyond the windows remind one of the Baja coast of Mexico rather than the Outer Banks.

The food does not disappoint. Mexican favorites like Enchiladas, and Burritos become delectable dinner entrees when prepared using fresh vegetables and local seafood. Tortilla Chips and

Open Late 7 Days a Week

Newby's Restaurant

Subs   Pizza   Bagels
Pocket Sandwiches
Deli Sandwiches
Breyers Ice Cream
Columbo Frozen Yogurt
and NEW!!
Ice Cream Bar

For Quick Take Out — 441-7277
MP 6, 158 Bypass, Kill Devil Hills

Nearly famous since 1972

Guacamole are made fresh daily. There are both hot and mild Mexican specialty dishes, plus traditional Outer Banks seafood and Cajun-style blackened fish. The coffee selection and desserts (Key Lime Pie, Bunuelo Relleno, and Sopaipillas) also show flair. This is a fun place with a lot of color. The original Papagayo is in Chapel Hill, and the experience shows in the operation of the location here. Papagayo's on the beach is open from mid-spring through Thanksgiving for dinner. The bar, La Cantina, stays open late and often features live entertainment. See write-up under Night Spots.

PORT O'CALL

Beach Road, MP 8   441-7484

$$$ MC, VISA, AMEX

For 25 years the Port O' Call has been a Banks favorite, and since the mid 1970s Frank Gajar's skilled management has set the pace for sophisticated dining in the area. The Mobil Travel Guide rates Port O' Call at three stars.

The large, ornate Victorian dining room is a nice change of pace from the typical Outer Banks restaurant. Hanging painted glass lamps festooned with prisms and heavy draperies pulled back to expose lacy sheers brings to mind dining rooms in fine turn-of-the-century hotels.

A gallery of paintings, jewelry, glass, and brass artifacts can be browsed before or after dinner or you might choose to stop in the Gaslight Saloon, where Victorian love seats and railed mezzanine, complete with a velvet-draped box, recreate another era. (See write-up under Night Spots).

The Port O' Call menu reflects a continental cuisine influence with entrees like Bouillabaisse and Veal and Scallops Romano. But whether you like your seafood dressed up or plain under the grill, you're sure to find something to please your palate on their extensive menu. You can choose a fresh fruit compote to accompany your meal rather than a salad, which is a nice option. Dinner is served with your choice potato or rice and a fresh vegetable. A children's menu is available.

They are open for dinner only, except on Sunday when they put on a Buffet that has to be seen and tasted to do it justice. If you would enjoy an all-you-can-eat meal that offers as much quality as quantity, this is a meal you must try. There's nothing to match it on the Banks. Port O' Call is open from before Easter through November.

THAI ROOM

Beach Road, MP 8 1/2   441-1180
$$ MC, VISA, AMEX

The Thai Room opened a few seasons ago and word has spread among locals that this is the place to go for good oriental cooking. You'll notice we didn't say Chinese: the cooking is Thai. Although the ingredients and names of dishes may sound somewhat familiar, you'll find the flavor out of the ordinary. There are a few traditional Chinese dishes on the menu so that those less daring in your party won't be disappointed. But if you're willing to try something different, you have a real taste treat in store.

Start off with a fresh Thai egg roll, a concoction of sprouts, bean curd, sausage and cucumber steamed in a soft pancake. If you enjoy soup, try Shrimp and Lemon Grass -- delicate and spicy -- or the Thai Room Soup made with chicken and coconut milk and spiced to really excite your taste buds. For your main entree, the Thai Beef Curry or the spicy Thai Noodles with shrimp, bean sprouts, dry bean curd and peanuts are both highly recommended.

We should warn you that Thai spices are hot. Your waiter will ask what degree of spiciness you want: mild, medium, or hot. Medium will make even the most dedicated jalepeno pepper eater break out in a sweat. We can't even imagine what hot is like!

While the food makes the restaurant out of the ordinary, the decor does its best to convince you that you've found an American-Chinese storefront restaurant, complete with tropical fish tank. The owners and an assortment of relatives are on the premises, providing excellent service. They're more than willing to describe dishes and make suggestions.

It's easy to end up with far more food that you need. But don't worry. They cheerfully package up all the remainders and give you a fresh carton of rice to go with them.

The Thai Room is open most of the year for lunch and dinner. Carry out and full bar service is available.

MEX-ECONO

Beach Road, MP 8 1/2   441-8226
$ No credit cards

If you like a place that has a lot of character, and if you like imaginative cooking, then Mex-Econo is a place you should try. It won't be for everyone (most people would say it's not a place to bring children) but if it suits you, you'll go back time after time.

Renovations have improved the looks of the place, inside and out. You'll probably be too busy staring at the elaborate door pulley system to notice, but the entryway floor has been tiled (possibly by the cook after a hard nights' work). In spite of the improvements, it's still the same old crazy place and the walls in the dining room are still covered with the same crazy stuff. If you're easily offended, you might prefer to not look. The music can be loud, but there are tables far enough away from the speakers to allow fairly normal conversation.

Now, if we haven't scared you off, we will tantalize you with reports of food that is truly remarkable. The menu offers the standard tacos and burritos, but the standouts are the specials. Sometimes they serve a Fried Bluefish and Marinated Cabbage Burrito served with Red Sauce and Sour Cream. It's served on a paper plate, but presented as attractively as anything you'd get in a three-star restaurant, carefully sauced and garnished with chopped green onions. The taste is out of this world. Another special (they change weekly) that sounds gross but tastes heavenly is Sauteed Eggplant and Smoked Oyster Taco with Scallions and Pumpkin Guacamole. You might find "color scheme" meals -- red food, green food...this is no ordinary place, as we said.

The owners and chefs at this unusual eating establishment have been in the restaurant business on the Outer Banks for several years. Chris Campbell and Miguel Geissinger worked together at the Port o'Call years ago and did time at several top Outer Banks restaurants before joining forces at Mex-Econo. As the name suggests, it is economical. They're also one of the few places that keep their kitchen open until very late. They have a very long list of imported and domestic beers, perhaps one of the best selections in the area (see write-up under Night Spots).

Mex-Econo is open most of the year but winter hours are irregular. They offer take-out service, so if you don't think you can handle the atmosphere, you could, at least, enjoy a very good, inexpensive meal.

ETHERIDGE SEAFOOD RESTAURANT

Rt. 158, MP 9   441-2645
$$ MC, VISA

The Etheridge family name has been associated with good, fresh seafood on the Banks for just about as long as there have been people coming here. In 1986, to everyone's good fortune, they opened a restaurant to show off some of that seafood their fishing fleet brings in. The main dining room is unusual -- it's round -- with semi-private corners labeled "Stamtisch" (German for meeting place), where locals preside over coffee and gossip. The attractive decor is nautical and casual.

The menu is traditional Outer Banks fare, with fresh seafood given star billing. Their crabcakes are delicately seasoned, full of sweet crabmeat. Their children's menu includes non-seafood meals for finicky eaters.

Open for lunch and dinner seven days a week April through December.

CHARDO'S

Rt. 158, MP 9   441-0276

$$$ MC, VISA, AMEX

When two people who eat dinner together almost every night of the year can linger over dinner for nearly three hours and say it was one of the most memorable dinners they've ever had..well, it has to be more than the good company.

Etheridge SEAFOOD RESTAURANT

Capt. Will

LUNCH 11-3 ▪ DINNER 4:30-UNTIL
7 DAYS A WEEK
Milepost 9-1/2 Croatan Hwy.
Kill Devil Hills, NC • 441-2645

The decor is elegant, the waiters and waitresses formally dressed and obviously well-trained in the art of serving. While not personally an opera buff, we found the Italian opera selections, played along with light classical music, a perfect complement..

The menu offers a variety of seafood and meats with northern Italian twists: Steak Pizzaiola, a filet mignon covered with a light basil and tomato sauce, topped with mozarella cheese; or, Seafood Medley, oysters and scallops served on a bed of linguine with fresh vegetables and a marvelously rich and tasty cream sauce. The salads which precede dinner are almost an antipasto with large chunks of vegetables and slices of salami attractively arranged and topped with a choice of dressings that include an excellent house Italian.

The wine list is a good one, though it overlooks several excellent Italian choices in favor of the standard Outer Banks' selections of California wines. Children can be served half portions of any menu item at half price. Chardo's accepts reservations.

MILLER'S SEAFOOD & STEAK HOUSE

Beach Road, MP 9   441-7674
$$ MC, VISA, Choice, AMEX

Eddie and Lou Miller and their family own this and three other Outer Banks restaurants: Miller's Waterfront, Daniels' and Fast Eddie's. They position themselves for the family trade and their nightly specials and all-you-can-eat dinners score big with folks on a budget.

The broiled, fried, and sauteed seafood selections are always fresh and plentiful. Among the beef selections are two cuts of Prime Rib and Filet Mignon, a Beef Kabob, and a Surf & Turf Combination.

This restaurant is in a handy location if you're staying at any of the motels in the 8-10 milepost area. It's a good spot to grab breakfast. They offer just about anything you could want and its preparation is a cut above many of the other breakfast mills on the beach. Miller's is open March through November. They have full bar service and a moderately-priced children's menu.

OSPREY ISLAND GRILLE

Rt. 158, MP 10   441-6894
$ MC, VISA

This restaurant, opened two years ago by Chuck Voigt, formerly the manager of Papagayo, has become a locals favorite for lunch and inexpensive family dinners. The menu is small but well-rounded, leaning toward the Italian border with pasta dishes, but giving Taco Bell a run for its money with frequent Mexican specials. Cajun cooking makes an appearance, too. Portions are generous and the quality of the food is surprisingly good for the low price. Daily specials are always tasty bargains. Full bar service. Open all year.

EBBTIDE FAMILY RESTAURANT

Beach Road, MP 10   441-8557

$ MC, VISA

The Ebbtide is starting serves breakfast, lunch and dinner, a departure from past years when they were mainly a breakfast spot. A very popular one, too, we should add, with even locals willing to wait in line for one of their large breakfast platters.

The interior of this small restaurant was totally remodeled for last season. The result is an open and modern look: it almost feels like the dining room of a private, contemporary home.

Menus for all three meals offer wide variety, at some of the lowest prices for sit-down service on the beach. There's nothing fancy here, but if you enjoy homestyle cooking, friendly service and pleasant surroundings, you'll be hard-pressed to find better on the beach.

NAGS HEAD NORTH
RESTAURANTS

SWEETWATERS

Rt. 158, MP 10   441-3020

$$ MC, VISA, AMEX

A mixture of polished wood, brass, stained glass and plants helps to create the inviting atmosphere of this year 'round restaurant/lounge in Nags Head. The mood here is casual and fun.

Lunch at Sweetwaters features gourmet burgers, large deli sandwiches, good salads and daily specials like Quiche. Dinner offers fresh seafood and steak and well as some lighter entree items. The full-service bar features every drink you can think of (and probably a few you can't). Open all year. A children's menu is available.

KELLY'S

Rt. 158, MP 10 1/2 441-4116
$$$ MC, VISA, AMEX

Anyone who has spent much time on the Outer Banks probably will recognize the name Mike Kelly. He's well-known in these parts for his expertise in the food business.

It's almost impossible to eat at Kelly's without being greeted by Mike. And you'll see him throughout the evening going from table to table, chatting with guests, clearing dishes, serving coffee...his reputation as a hands-on owner is well deserved.

As you enter the building, you're greeted by an attractive combination of wood, brass, greenery and stained glass. A notable twist to the decor is the extensive use of mounted fish and wildlife throughout the restaurant. One particularly large feathered bird hovering near the open staircase causes many a surprised comment. Dinner is served either in one of several rooms, upstairs or downstairs. The dining area was enlarged for the '88 season, making it possible to accommodate a larger private party while remaining open to the public (but it didn't make a noticeable difference in the waiting line on Saturday nights!). A large bi-level lounge, also recently enlarged, is a popular singles gathering spot (see write-up under Night Spots).

Kelly's offers plenty of well-prepared seafood dishes as well as chicken, beef and pasta. It seems that everyone is offering pasta right now but, for what's it's worth, Kelly's was one of the first on the beach to make it a house specialty. A raw bar has a selection of steamed or raw shellfish, depending on what's in season. Dinner is accompanied by fresh breads, baked in Kelly's kitchen. The sweet potato rolls are wonderful. I'd say they were better than dessert, but desserts at Kelly's are in a class by themselves: sinfully rich and always good. A children's menu is available.

This is one of those places where waiting for a table is expected in-season unless you go early. Once you're seated, we think you'll find the good service and excellent food make the wait well worth it. Kelly's is open all year for dinner only.

Kelly's, the Outer Banks' favorite gathering place, features items such as fresh caught gulf stream fish, North Carolina seafood, and Iowa beef.

2316 South Croatan Hwy, MP 10 1/2 Bypass
Nags Head · 919-441-4116 · Open Year Round
Dinner 5 pm 'til 10 pm
Tavern open 4:30 pm 'til 2 am

Enjoy the beautiful sunset on the Sound as you dine on beef, poultry and North Carolina Seafood at Penguin Isle.

6708 South Croatan Hwy, MP 16 Bypass,
Nags Head · 919-441-2637 · Open Year Round · Dinner 5:30 pm 'til 10 pm
Gazebo Deck open 5:30 pm 'til 2 am

SOUNDSIDE GRILL & BAR

QUAGMIRE'S SHELLFISH BAR & RESTAURANT
MP 11, Beach Road   441-RAWW
$ MC, VISA

Will Thorpe and John Kirchmier opened Quagmire's last winter in the building that had housed the very popular Gandolf's restaurant until a fire closed it down a couple years ago. If you'll excuse the pun, it's still a hot spot: within weeks, Quagmire's was the talk of the Outer Banks and the crowds haven't died down yet. The inexpensive menu features Caribbean specialties like Jamaican jerk beef and fried plantains. Crawdads are available, in season. You can get steamed vegetable platters, shrimp by the pound, oysters by the dozen. And on Wednesdays nights, you can get sushi. Go early if you want one of just a few tables. Food is also served at the large bar and on the porch, weather permitting. Open all year.

CHEF'S CORNER
Rt. 158, MP 11 1/2   441-6042
$ MC, VISA

This is a great little deli and bakery, now in its fourth year, owned by Craig and Donna Hartman. Fresh vegetable, pasta and fruit salads, seafood and chicken salad, all made in their kitchen...sliced-to-order meats and cheeses...fresh bread and rolls straight from their ovens...and always a mouthwatering assortment of their own desserts. It's the perfect place to stop for lunch or a light dinner. Take it with you or, weather permitting, eat at one of their outdoor tables. The Chef's Corner is open all year.

THE WHARF
Beach Road, MP 12 1/2   441-7457
$

If you've driven down the Beach road at dinner time, you've seen the line at The Wharf. They offer menu service, but the line is there for just one thing: the all-you-can-eat seafood buffet. The line usually forms by 6:30, but it moves along quickly. They take your name and the number of people in your party and fill tables as they become available. It seems that parties of one or two often get seated without much of a wait. Once you're inside, you'll probably be surprised at how efficient the service is.

The atmosphere is definitely beach basic, and it's not the place to go for a romantic, relaxed dinner. This is a place to visit when eating -- and eating a lot -- is your prime objective. You won't be disappointed.

The list of what they offer is too long to itemize here, but the selection is varied enough to tempt anyone. Alaskan crab legs and the steamed shrimp seem to be what many head for first, but if you don't try the seafood gumbo or the barbecued pork chops, you've missed out on some tasty fare. There's a good selection of salads and vegetables along with several other entree items. We've never made it to the dessert table, but they appeared to be your standard whipped-topping plus cake or pudding selection.

Open Easter through October.

DAIRY MART

Beach Road, MP 13   441-6730

$ no credit cards

The Dairy Mart has been around since the 1960s. For the past 15 years, It's been owned and operated by the Ron and Carol Rodriguez. It's an old fashioned drive-in, with the best ice cream (soft serve) concoctions on the beach. Their sandwiches, fries and onion rings are made to order -- and they're all mighty good. A Dairy Mart "Big Daddy Burger" is a real treat.

During the summer months there's almost always a crowd but you'll be pleased to find that service is reasonably fast and friendly (better than the fast food giants in "french fry alley," we'd wager). Picnic tables with umbrellas are out front for those who want to eat there. The Dairy Mart is open from May to October and closed every Wednesday.

WINDMILL POINT

Rt. 158, MP 16 1/2   441-1535

$$$$ MC, VISA, AMEX

Windmill Point is right on the sound. The view, along with all the artifacts and memorabilia from the S.S. *United States*, makes you feel as though you're aboard a fine cruise ship. Most of the furniture came out of the old luxury liner's dining salon. Upstairs, in the lounge area, several interesting artifacts stand out. Most prominent is the kidney-shaped bar, from the promenade
deck of the ship.

Chef Cary Vanischak has returned for another season to work his magic on local seafood. Entrees like Dolphin Mediterranean offer a new taste for the Outer Banks diner. His Curried Scallop Bisque has a wonderful mix of spice that complements, rather than masks, the scallop. The breads and desserts are all made in Windmill Point's kitchen and van Ischak even grows his owns herbs. Open for dinner only, most of the year.

PENGUIN ISLE SOUNDSIDE GRILLE

Rt. 158, MP 16   441-2637

$$$$ MC, VISA, AMEX

This restaurant is owned by Mike Kelly and Doug Tutwiler. Kelly, already well-known for his restaurant up the beach, says he takes a back seat at this eatery.

Both the lounge and dining room have panoramic views of the sound. I was eating dinner there one evening last spring, watching a windsurfer skim over the water at sunset, with the marsh grasses waving golden in the brisk wind, and it truly was one of the prettiest sights I'd seen in a long time.

Beautiful sunsets make nice memories but they don't do very well as dinner entrees. Not to worry. You won't go hungry. The menu is decidedly different from Kelly's; it's more novelle cuisine with a definite New Orleans influence, featuring Outer Banks seafood. Several offerings make use of the mesquite grill. Chicken Blackbeard is our personal favorite: a boneless chicken breast, grilled and served over spicey black beans, accented with pink grapefruit. But everything we have tried has been excellent.

What about the name Penguin Isle? Penguins are hardly a native bird. According to Mike Kelly, there are two small islands in the sound, immediately to the west of the restaurant, one called Big Penguin Island and one called Little Penguin Island (there's a third, larger island known as Nags Head Island). Mike talked with area oldtimers about the origin of the name. The stories are cleverly retold on the menu. Penguin Isle is open most of the year for dinner only.

THE DUNES

Rt. 158, MP 16 1/2   441-9953

$ No credit cards

The three large rooms at the Dunes seat lots of people so don't be put off by a full parking lot. It doesn't necessarily mean a long wait. Breakfast starts early and the menu offers just about anything you could want. There's a daily special and heaping servings of fresh fruits are available. "Heaping servings" describes most of their portions with the combination platters served on huge rectangular platters. The emphasis is definitely on quantity; but quality hasn't been forgotten. They've started an all-you-can-eat breakfast buffet this season on weekends and holidays; it may become a daily feature.

Rufus and Roxie Pritchard, the Dunes' owners, personally oversee the operation, and with the help of one of the most pleasant staffs on the beach, they provide service that is both fast and friendly.

Breakfast is served until noon when they close until dinner. The evening menu features local seafood, all breaded and cooked to order, and a good selection of meats. The popcorn shrimp are very good. All-you-can-eat specials are popular, but we think you'll find the regular dinners are more than enough for all but the biggest of appetites. A well-stocked all-you-can-eat salad bar comes with dinner. Children's menu available, too.

The Dunes is open for breakfast and dinner from March through November.

OWENS'

Beach Road, MP 17   441-7309

$$$$ MC, VISA, AMEX

Established in 1946, and at the same location for over 30 years, Owens' has been the most consistent quality restaurant in Outer Banks history. Many patrons return year after year, and have seen succeeding generations of Owens family members take their turns as host.

Part of the restaurant is the old Nags Head Life Saving Station and the place is filled with artifacts from the days when men manned its lifeboats to rescue sailors from the sea.

When you come to Owens', expect to wait, unless you arrive before 6. The Station Keepers Lounge is such a pleasant place to pass the time, that you won't mind. A large staircase leads to the full-service bar furnished in polished light woods, brass, and Tiffany styled glass (see write-up under Night Spots).

The Owens' reputation is built on seafood. Their broiled or fried Seafood Platter has set the standard for this entree up and down the Beach. House specialties are Coconut Shrimp, huge shrimp lightly coated in shredded coconut and served with a sweet-sour sauce, and Crabmeat Remick, lump crabmeat in a special sauce topped with cheese and served in a true scallop shell. The Lobster Bisque is expensive but worth every penny: the bisque is perfectly done and brimming with lobster chunks. A mesquite grill, added a couple of seasons ago, has proved popular, but we think there are other things they do much better. If you're not in the mood for seafood, their Steak and Prime Rib are excellent, as is the Chicken Cordon Bleu. A children's menu is available.

Portions are more than generous, but if you can, save room for one of their desserts. They offer a selection of ice cream desserts and pies guaranteed to make your mouth water, even if you're already full!

Owens' service is another standard that other beach restaurants strive to match. Staff turnover is low from season to season and it shows. From the hostess down to the bussing staff, you'll get courteous, efficient and totally professional service. Owens' is open from April until after Thanksgiving for dinner only.

SAM & OMIE'S

Beach Road at Whalebone Junction 441-7366

$$ VISA, MC

Sam & Omie's has been a Nags Head institution for over 30 years. Although the originators of this weather-beaten retreat have been long gone, no one would dare change the name. Two sisters, Judy and Jakey Waits, have carried on the Sam & Omie's tradition for over 16 years.

Fishermen and other locals still consider Sam & Omie's their place to hang out for breakfast, lunch, dinner and in between. It's no surprise that the restaurant motto is "Everyone should believe in something. I believe I'll go fishing."

At the center of the large, wooden floored, L-shaped room is a full service bar. You can sit there, or at one of the dozen or so booths and tables that are packed in to accommodate their growing business. For those who come to dine, numerous windows looking out toward the beach, light pine walls covered with colorful photography, and fresh flowers on the tables compensate for a pool table in the back, and large screen tv in the middle of the dining area.

Sam & Omie's is saved from being just a neighborhood bar by virtue of the food. The food here is good. Fresh ingredients with an emphasis on seafood and vegetables provide a wide variety of salads, sandwiches and full meals priced below fancier nearby places. Open almost all year.

R.V.'S

Nags Head-Manteo Causeway   441-4963

$-$$ MC, VISA, AMEX

R.V. Owens, of the Owens Restaurant family, is the host and owner of this very popular restaurant and his newest eatery, Keeper's Galley in Kitty Hawk. R.V.'s is a sound-side watering hole built high on stilts. The style of R.V.'s is contemporary. Food service can be at the long bar, or in two raised areas with tables. Better, we think, is to ask for a table on the enclosed porch where you have a great view of the sound.

A large gazebo for beverage and raw bar service was added last season at the edge of the sound, and proved popular with the locals and singles who pack into RV's on the weekends.

The menu is large. Some of our favorites are the Seafood Pasta Salad, Crabcake or Oyster Sandwiches, Potato Skins, and Nachos (big enough to feed TWO hungry people). Regulars order one of the three or four daily specials; they're always tasty and priced right. Open from before Easter through mid-November for lunch and dinner. The lounge stays open late.

THE SHIP'S WHEEL

Nags Head-Manteo Causeway   441-2906

$$ MC, VISA

This restaurant is owned and operated by the Van Curen family. Al, the father, "invented" the 99-cent breakfast and the all-you-can-eat entree concept on the Outer Banks. He started Miller's, The Dunes and Sportsman's and, once they were established, sold them. A couple of years ago, Al bought the Ship's Wheel and sons Keith and Michael left other established careers to join him in the family business.

The atmosphere is nautical and casual. The sign out front says "Fishermen Welcome," and they mean it. The food isn't fancy, but portions are generous and it's well prepared. There's a good selection of seafood and meats, as well as all-you-can-eat specials. Dinner includes the huge salad bar (52 items at last count), which can easily be a meal in itself.

Children or senior citizens portions available. Open for breakfast and dinner seven days a week, March through November.

OASIS RESTAURANT & LOUNGE

Nags Head-Manteo Causeway   441-7721

$$ MC, VISA

The Oasis was built in the 1940s, which qualifies it as one of the oldest restaurants on the beach. Bought from the original owner by Violet Kellam in 1950, it became the home of the "barefoot girls," comely waitresses whose portraits now fill the lobby, and known for it's lace cornbread. The family sold the restaurant in 1980 and it's name was changed to The Dock. Last year Violet's grandchildren -- Mike, Mark and Kellam France -- bought the place back, really spruced it up, and renamed it the Oasis.

They've brought back their specialty, lace cornbread, a family secret for years -- it is more like a crunchy hush puppy than cornbread -- but the barefoot girls are just a memory. This is a pleasant place with a great view, where a full dinner and drinks won't cost you an arm and a leg. Open April through November.

ROANOKE ISLAND
RESTAURANTS

RUDEE'S RESTAURANT & RAW BAR

Nags Head-Manteo Causeway at Pirate's Cove   473-6200

$$ MC, VISA, AMEX

If you're from the Tidewater area, you may be familiar with Rudee's on the Inlet. Rudee's on the Outer Banks is much the same. Located on the second floor (there's an elevator), the dining room and bar overlook Pirate's Cove marina and the sound. While the dining room offers romantic views, this isn't a restaurant for intimate dining. It's a place to come and enjoy the camaraderie of the sportsfishing crowd and other people who enjoy being on the water. You can ar-

Rudee's
Restaurant & Raw Bar

Enjoy our new deck overlooking the marina and sound.

Mon. Nite Shrimp Special 1 lb. Steamed Shrimp ...Only $6.95

♦ Fresh local seafood
♦ Thick juicy steaks
♦ Famous raw bar
♦ Daily lunch special
♦ Sunday brunch
  11am - 2pm

Rudee's on the Cove
Pirate's Cove Yacht Club
Nags Head - Manteo Causeway
Manteo, N.C. (919)473-6200

Open Daily 11am - 2am

Rudee's on the Inlet
Inlet Station Marina
227 Mediterranean Avenue
Va. Beach, Va. (804)425-1777

The Manteo waterfront is a busy place in the summer. DCTB

rive by boat, if you wish. The restaurant has slips for your use. The menu offers a variety of shellfish from the raw bar, sandwiches, salads and entrees. Seafood, of course, is the house specialty. French fried sweet potatoes are an interesting option to accompany your meal.

Open for lunch and dinner with a Brunch on Sundays.

DUCHESS OF DARE

Budleigh Street, Downtown Manteo 473-2215

$$ MC, VISA

The Duchess of Dare is Manteo's most enduring restaurant, and its position at the heart of the Island's civic, business and municipal center makes it a popular year 'round meeting place. If you want to eat what the locals eat, and hear their native tongue, this is one place to have the experience. Neighbors get special service here, but visitors are also welcomed. There are three dining areas with booths, and also counter service.

The products from Doris Walker's kitchen (son Tom is now the head honcho, but you'll still see Doris around) focus on local seafoods. You can count on excellent sweet dough hush puppies, too. Look for daily specials, and sample one of the homemade fruit pies. You also can't miss if you come for the regular Sunday brunch -- great salads, seafood and other meats, vegetables and more. The Duchess opens very early to serve breakfast to the fishing and boating crowd and stays open through the dinner hour all year. Menu and price wise, this is a good choice for family dining.

THE SHIP'S GALLEY

Downtown Manteo, on the waterfront 473-3333

$ No credit cards

Richard Brown owns and operates this cheery and convenient sandwich shop overlooking the sound and the *Elizabeth II*. It has become a Manteo "thing" at lunch when, it seems, every local within easy distance descends on the place between noon and 2 p.m. They come for good reason. Richard serves up the best selection of made-to-order sandwiches on the Island. His fresh tuna salad and all the grilled sandwiches are especially good. Soups, chili, salad plates and ice cream are also available.

The Ship's Galley is open for lunch all year. During the busier months it opens early for breakfast with scrambled egg and bacon sandwiches, bagels with cream cheese and other light snacks.

CLARA'S SEAFOOD GRILL

Downtown Manteo, in The Waterfront · 473-1727

$$-$$$ · MC, VISA, AMEX

A meal at Clara's means a spectacular view of Shallowbag Bay. You can watch the boats coming into the marina and brown pelicans diving for fish; or marvel at the *Elizabeth II,* moored just across the harbor. The view is complemented by a comfortable ambience that's casual, yet sophisitcated. The menu is extensive. Appetizers, full meals and lighter fare are available at both lunch and dinner.

In addition to seafood served dozens of ways and a nice selection of chicken and beef dishes, vegetarian entrees are available. The shrimp toast appetizer -- a melt-in- your-mouth toast point slathered with shrimp paste, deep fried and sprinkled with sesame seeds -- is "shrimply" delicious and a Clara's specialty. Clara's Chicken Melt with its tangy guacamole dressing makes a good lunch, although the fresh tuna salad is always tempting. For dinner, try one of the daily specials or the seafood kabobs. Should you care to have a bottle of wine with dinner, you'll find the wine list more than adequate. Clara's also stocks a good selection of imported beers.

Clara's Seafood Grill is owned by the Owens' family, who also own Owens' Restaurant, considered by many to be the premier dining spot on the Outer Banks. They've built their reputation by being hands-on managers; their service is impeccable, the food preparation remarkable. Clara's is no exception. Those familiar with Owens' will find Clara's more casual, less expensive, but just as satisfying. Clara's is open March through Christmas.

THE NATURAL SELECTION

Downtown Manteo, in the Waterfront · 473-6113

$

You might not expect to find a health food restaurant in Manteo, but it's here! Actually, this is a health food store that fixes sandwiches, salads, and vegetarian dishes daily to please the lunch crowd. While they don't have a big selection, if you tend towards the no-meat persuasion, you'll be thrilled to find this place. They also carry plenty of health food grocery items if you want to fix it yourself.

THE WEEPING RADISH

Manteo 473-1157

$$-$$$ Most major credit cards

This re-creation of a Bavarian inn offers a real alternative in dining on the Outer Banks. It has several unique things going for it, not the least of which is its European ambience.

The restaurant takes its name from the radish served in Bavaria as an accompaniment to beer. The radish is cut in a spiral, sprinkled with salt and packed back together. The salt draws out the moisture in the radish and gives it the appearance of weeping.

The menu is German (and we mean *authentic*, since the chef is German), offering Weiner Schnitzel, Bratwurst and other specialties; but there are always choices for the diner who would prefer something more familiar. Our personal favorite is the Sauerbraten, a German-style pot roast, topped with delicious gravy that just hints of ginger and red wine. Homemade spaetzle (noodles) and cooked red cabbage make great side dishes. And, you really ought to try the Weeping Radish Beer, made right there at the working brewery (see write-up under Attractions). Even if beer isn't your beverage of choice, the flavor of a fresh Bavarian lager is so different from your standard PBR, you may be pleasantly surprised.

There's an outdoor beer garden with a "fast food" window serving sandwiches, salads, sausage platters, beverages, desserts and ice cream. The Weeping Radish is open for lunch and dinner most of the year.

DARRELL'S

Manteo 473-5366

$-$$ MC, VISA

Darrell's has been around for over 30 years. First as an ice cream stand and for the past fifteen years or so as a lunch and dinner favorite for locals and tourists-in-the-know.

Owned and operated by the Daniels family, this is a restaurant that offers good, down-home, Outer Banks cooking -- nothing fancy, but consistently good food and more than adequate portions. Their fried oyster (generally offered on Friday evenings) and popcorn shrimp specials are excellent.

The special-of-the-day will usually be offered at both lunch and dinner. Even taking into consideration that the lunch portions are somewhat smaller and the selection of accompaniments more limited, the lunch special is priced to be a real bargain. Because it is a favorite lunch spot for locals, you might want to avoid the 12 to 1 hour when they are the busiest.

Darrell's closes around Christmas and reopens in the spring.

QUEEN ANNE'S REVENGE

Wanchese   473-5466

$$$-$$$$ MC, VISA

Two friends with a mutual interest in food, Donald Beach and Wayne Gray, conceived this restaurant in 1976. With family support, amid the doubting eyes of onlookers, they built a quality establishment far off the resort path on a dead end road in the woods of Wanchese.

Despite the location, the caliber of both the food and the service have attracted patrons...in droves. During summer, either get there when they open or be prepared to wait.

Is it worth the wait? We think it is. Dinners start with a cheese crock and crackers, a large and attractive garden salad -- try one of the house dressings -- and an unusual selection of appetizers.

North Carolina Crayfish Cocktail, prepared cajun style, and Bouillabaisse are both great openers, though my personal favorite is the Black Bean Soup (it's interesting to note that Wayne added the Black Bean Soup to the menu three years ago; this year, everybody's serving black beans). By this time, if you're not careful, you just might be full. But the best is yet to come. The menu has an emphasis on seafood but includes a generous selection of steaks. A 32 oz. Chateaubriand for two, carved at the table and accompanied with sauteed fresh vegetables, is not common Outer Banks fare. Among the seafood offerings, the Crab Slough Select Oysters are always good. They are always fresh and from local beds, so they are served only when the oysters are in season. The Wanchese Seafood Platter and Blackbeard's Raving are huge platters of seafood which seem to inspire happy moans and groans whenever served. A children's menu is available. The desserts are all homemade. The servings are usually more than generous. We'd suggest splitting an order.

Wanchese has no liquor by the drink, but Queen Anne's offers a nice selection of wines and beers to accompany your meal. They'll also serve setups if you'd like to brown bag it. This restaurant continues to be one of the top dining experiences on the Outer Banks and worthy of the pleasant detour to the quiet woods of Wanchese. They are open for dinner only all year -- seven days a week during the season and on a more limited schedule off-season.

FISHERMAN'S WHARF

Wanchese   473-5205
$$ MC, VISA

Fisherman's Wharf is near the end of Highway 345 at Mill Landing, overlooking -- in the middle of, actually -- a working commercial fishing port. The dining room is located above a wharf where fish are unloaded from the trawler fleet and you can view the water traffic and vistas over the sound in air conditioned comfort while enjoying an excellent lunch or dinner.

The Daniels' family -- an old Wanchese fishing family -- are your hosts, April through October. In the spring and fall, you'll find a lot of locals enjoying a Fisherman's Wharf lunch before the summer crowds arrive.

The lunch selection is large including meals like popcorn shrimp plates that could easily be dinner, with the cole slaw, hushpuppies and other accompaniments. Dinners includes the salad bar. Save room, if you can, for dessert. Their homemade Chocolate and Coconut Pies are recommended. A children's menu is available.

HATTERAS ISLAND
RESTAURANTS

EMILY'S SOUNDSIDE RESTAURANT

Waves   987-2383
$$ Most major credit cards

Since 1972, Jim and Emily Landrum have been serving traditional Hatteras Island cuisine at the Soundside. It's an attractive restaurant located near the Chicamacomico Lifesaving Station with a reputation for wonderful dinners.

The dining room is attractive; most seats have a view of the water. During the summer, there is seating upstairs which provides an exceptional view. It would be worth waiting to get a table upstairs at sunset.

Dinner sounds great, with fresh crabmeat and seafood dishes, steamed or raw shellfish, handcut steaks and fried chicken, made-from-scratch soups, salads and homemade pies. Beer and wine are served.

But, let us tell you about breakfast. Creamy omelettes that melt in your mouth, stuffed with fresh ingredients, lightly sauteed. (These are omelettes prepared the way the French intended.) The chunks of crispy potatoes, delicately seasoned, are not the least bit greasy. And the biscuits are light and flaky...our resident Southern cooking expert, who tends to judge all biscuits against his own, even said they were good.

A breakfast buffet is served every Saturday and Sunday throughout the summer and occasionally during the off-season when traffic warrants. The Soundside is open for breakfast, lunch and dinner mid-March through most of December.

Emily & Jim's Original SOUNDSIDE RESTAURANT
Since 1972

Located on Highway 12, Waves Village on Hatteras Island. Casual sunset dining. Outer Banks Seafood - Daily Fresh Fish Specials. Steamed Shrimp, Soft Crabs, Lobster and Legs. Genuine Hickory Cooked Barbecue. Baby Pork Back Ribs. Prime Rib, Pasta, Chicken and Celebrated Steaks. Chowder and Gumbo. Real Homemade Pies. Childrens Specials. Lunch Specials. Seafood Salads and Sandwiches. Sunday Lunch Buffet. Breakfast Soundside. Holiday Breakfast Buffets. Emily's Famous Biscuits. Banquets to Barbecues. Private Dining. Major Credit Cards. ABC License.

Jim & Emily Landrum
(919) 987-2383

Box 128
Rodanthe, NC 27968

Closed Mondays

THE FROGGY DOG

Avon 995-4106

$-$$ MC, VISA

This is one of our favorite places to eat on Hatteras. The restaurant is always comfortable: in the summer, its wood and greenery offer a cool break from the sun; in winter, it has a cozy feel. Major work was done over the winter, doubling the seating space. Even with all the extra space, the restaurant is still packed on busy weekends.

Breakfast here means getting to listen to locals discuss fishing and what the state ought to do about the roads. The food is good, portions are hearty and the biscuits are homemade. For lunch, the offerings center around sandwiches and salads. Their hamburgers are probably the best on the island and they have great onion rings, freshly cut and dipped in a light batter to order.

You can have the chef -- who is also the owner -- fry, broil or saute fresh seafood for your dinner. Several meat entrees are offered as alternatives to fish and shrimp.

The Froggy Dog is open all year, seven days a week. Children's and senior citizen's portions are available.

DIAMOND SHOALS RESTAURANT

Hwy. 12, Buxton 995-5217

$$ MC, VISA

If you're staying in Buxton, the Diamond Shoals is probably within walking distance. It's the kind of place people come back to year after year because they know what to expect.

The menus for both meals offers a large variety of consistently good, typical Outer Banks fare. Breakfast platters are large. All-you-can-eat dinners featuring -- you guessed it -- fresh seafood are a specialty.

The service here is dependably fast and efficient. There may be a little chit-chat with fishermen who frequent the place regularly but, for the most part, these waitresses are seasoned professionals who get right down to business. Your coffee cup will never be empty, she'll remember that you wanted ketchup, and you'll get your check when you're ready go. Open for breakfast and dinner all year.

JOE'S STARVIN' SHARK

Buxton   995-4146
$ No credit cards

Joe's 1/3 lb. "made fresh daily" burgers are a hit with the young beach crwod, as well as local fishermen and construction workers. The made-to-order burgers and a good selection of other subs and platters are all reasonably priced. Pizza is available in the evening. You can eat in or take it out. Open for lunch and dinner. Beer is served.

THE PILOT HOUSE

Buxton   995-5664
$$$ MC, VISA

The original Pilot House burned to the ground in 1986. It was rebuilt in the same location and reopened for business in the spring of 1987. Situated right on the sound, and designed to make the most of it, the view is exceptional. The upstairs lounge has a view of both sound and ocean and is worth the climb up two flights of stairs.

The light blue and white decor is simple and, while not elegant by city standards, polished. It is not a restaurant meant for intimate dining, however. The one large, open room, while affording an excellent view, tends to be noisy.

The menu has changed again, going back to the thing that built their reputation in the first place: seafood. They prepare and serve seafood in just about any form -- and combination -- you could want. The fish-of-the-day is always a fresh catch. Soups are all made in their kitchens from scratch. The Seafood Bisque is loaded with fresh crab and shrimp. It's creamy without being rich enough to ruin the appetite.

The Pilot House is open from the week before Easter until late fall, seven days a week, for dinner only.

BILLY'S FISH HOUSE RESTAURANT

Hwy. 12, Buxton   995-5151
$$ MC, VISA

Billy and Chalaron May turned this former fish house into a restaurant a few years back and it's built a fierce following since. Billy's is place you either love or hate. Evidence of its fish house past is everywhere; from the painted, concrete floors that slant for water run-off, to its location on Buxton Harbor, a small, working inlet that is not so much picturesque as typical fishing village waterfront. Most of the picnic-style tables have a view and, in good weather, you can eat right out on the dock.

Lunch and dinner both are served on foam plates with plastic table service and paper napkins. Before you get upset about paying full dinner prices for food served on plastic, you might want to know that Billy can't get a permit for a septic system that would allow him to wash all those dishes he'd have if he used china and silver. (Come on, be a good sport. It will make a great story back home.)

Whether you do or don't love Billy's will be decided on those factors because everyone agrees that the fish is above reproach. Billy personally selects the seafood and he has a reputation for being very, very picky.

You can order dinners at lunchtime or you can choose from a variety of sandwiches and seafood salads. We would recommend the fried fish sandwich, of course. Seafood is king on the dinner menu: fried, broiled and steamed. There are a few choices for the diner who's not in the mood for fish. House wines and variety of beers are served.

Billy's is open for lunch and dinner from Easter until after Thanksgiving.

FRISCO SANDWICH SHOP

Frisco   995-5535
$ MC, VISA

For a dozen or more years, this small, family-run restaurant has enjoyed a good reputation. Originally just a small roadside drive-in, they built a new building a few years back and the small dining room stays packed during mealtimes in-season.

For lunch and dinner, owner Stan Lawrence and his staff make their own deli-style salads and offer a variety of breads for hot and cold sandwiches. There are crabcakes and fried chicken, along with other specials. You can get ice cream cones, sundaes and shakes. They also serve beer and wine.

The Frisco Sandwich Shop is open for breakfast, lunch and dinner seven days a week during the summer. Closed on Sundays the rest of the year.

BUBBA'S BAR-B-Q

Frisco   995-5421
Avon   995-4385
$ MC, VISA, Choice

Larry Schauer (Bubba) and his wife (Mrs. Bubba) are former West Virginians who left their farm for the seaside. Bubba's Bar-B-Q is an extension of something they do best: cook. This is the original Bubba's; they opened a second location in Avon in 1988.

Bubba's barbecue is the real thing. You can see the ribs, chicken and pork shoulders cooking on the grill over a hickory-wood pit fire. Ribs come by the slab, on a sandwich, or with a plate of homemade cole slaw, cornbread and french fries. The pork barbecue comes sliced, chopped on a bun or on a plate. The chicken comes in quarters a la carte or with homemade side dishes on a plate.

Mrs. Bubba cooks several different pies everyday, and they are tried and proven winners. She does Paul Prudhomme's (K-Paul's of New Orleans) Sweet Potato-Pecan Pie, Feeling's (also New Orleans) Peanutbutter Pie, and her own heavenly Coconut Custard among others.

It's hard not to overeat. When jazz great Maynard Ferguson performed in Hatteras last year, he told the audience he couldn't hit the high notes because he'd eaten at Bubba's earlier in the day. The comment drew a knowing laugh from the locals.

Bubba's Bar-B-Q

RIBS · CHICKEN · SLICED PORK · TURKEY BEEF

All cooked on an open pit with hickory wood

Call the Hog Line — 995-5421 in Frisco

or 995-4385 in Avon

oink!

Everything is for take out, or you can enjoy your meal at one of the inside (air conditioned) picnic tables. Bubba's in Frisco will now be open all year. The Avon location closes during the winter.

GARY'S RESTAURANT

Hatteras Village   986-2349

$ No credit cards

Opened in 1985 as a fast-food style restaurant, Gary's made big changes in 1989. The dining area was expanded, waitress service added, and they now serve beer and wine.

It's a pleasant eating spot, with a comfortable country decor. Early in the morning -- and we do mean early, they open most of the year around 5:30 -- it's a great place to have a cup of coffee and one of their freshly made breakfast biscuits. They have a full breakfast menu, including a variety of pancakes, too. Lunch and dinner offer a couple dozen sandwich choices, a salad bar and several fresh seafood plates.

Open all year.

THE CHANNEL BASS

Hatteras Village   986-2250

$$ MC, VISA, AMEX

This restaurant beside the inlet bridge is a Harrison family affair that's approaching its 25th season. You can meet Brenda and Debbie -- the daughters -- during the dinner hour, April through November. One runs the kitchen while the other manages the dining room. All the fishing trophies on the foyer walls belong to Shelby Harrison, the mama!

The fare, of course, features fresh Hatteras seafood with broiled or fried Platters, Broiled Scallops and Crab Imperial being popular choices. For variety, see what The Channel Bass can do with barbecue Beef Short Ribs, char-broiled steaks, and a new Steamed Seafood Platter.

Some of the fish you're served will have been caught aboard the Miss Channel Bass. The boat landed the largest Blue Marlin caught in 1980 (591 lbs.) and has a citation for a world record Red Drum. It's little wonder that sport fishermen hang out here. The restaurant has a children's menu and wine and beer are available.

Piers, boats, and decoys - all the symbols of waterside living are captured on Silver Lake, Ocracoke's harbor. DCTB

OCRACOKE
RESTAURANTS

THE BACK PORCH

Ocracoke 928-6401
$$$ MC, VISA

John and Debbie Wells, who own and manage this excellent restaurant, have been on the Ocracoke restaurant scene for several years. They renovated this older, rustic building when it opened a few seasons ago, and it continues to be a pleasant spot to linger over dinner.

The screened "back porch" is our favorite location, weather permitting, where the tree-filled yard and quiet nieghborhood surrounding the restaurant add a special ambience.

Debbie is in charge of the food. The emphasis is on fresh, with all the sauces and dressings, breads and desserts made in their kitchen. She tries to buy all ingredients in as raw a state as possible. Breading and most of the meat cutting is done to order. They even grind their own coffee.

```
BACK PORCH

SCREENED PORCH DINING
ORIGINAL DISHES with a PERSONAL TOUCH
5:30 - 10:00PM

Ocracoke Island, NC
(919) 928-6401
```

You'll find that with the exception of the Crab Beignet, nothing on the menu at The Back Porch is fried. (They will fry items on request, however.) Speaking of the Crab Beignet, it is offered as an appetizer and we caution you that it can easily serve three people in that capacity. The serving is large and deliciously rich. You might find the Smoked Bluefish, which is excellent, a far better choice to whet your appetite.

The menu is new for 1990 and just as inventive as ever (but includes many of the old favorites). They continue to prove that you can enjoy traditional Outer Banks seafood without having the same old thing: Gratine' of Scallops Florentine, for example. The menu shows a distinct New American influence, with addition of things like pan-fried chick pea cake appetizer, topped with tahini sauce and garnished with a tomato salsa. The cuban black bean and monterey jack cheese casserole entree was excellent.

A substantial wine list and selection of imported beers complement the menu.

CAP'T. BEN'S

Ocracoke   928-4741

$$-$$$ MC, VISA, AMEX

Ben Mugford has been in the restaurant business in Ocracoke for over 15 years. He's been at this location on the edge of town since 1978. It's a quiet restaurant, tastefully decorated with nautical antiques, and well-appointed table settings. It may, in fact, be the fanciest dining-out spot on the island. Be that as it may, this is a resort island and you can still "come as you are" and bring the kids, too.

Ben himself is the chef. His special crab balls and crab stuffed mushrooms are worth trying. Over the years he has added gourmet entrees, but we suspect he will continue to be most noted for his Prime Rib, cut to order at the restaurant, and his fresh seafood combo dinners, which would satisfy the cravings of any landlubber. Ben has been around long enough to have his own source for local seafood and you can be assured that the Catch of the Day is always fresh. Dinners come with both soup and salad, a rare thing on the Outer Banks, and another reason you won't leave here hungry. You'll find the wine list offers a good selection that nicely complements the menu.

Lunch, which is served most of the afternoon, centers on sandwiches and light meals.

Cap't. Ben's is open April through November, 7 days a week and there is a children's menu for dinner.

ISLAND INN RESTAURANT

Ocracoke 928-7821

$$ MC, VISA

The atmosphere of this dining room at the Island Inn captures the flavor of a bygone era of country inns with the red terra cotta tile floor, rough hewn columns supporting the ceiling, french blue tables and chairs and homey decorating touches.

Chester Lynn, an Ocracoke native and 16 year employee of the restaurant, took over the management two years ago and he immediately began working to restore the reputation of the food which had been excellent until just a few years ago. Chester went back to some of the original recipes from the kitchen and he says he's trying to stick to good southern cooking, using as many fresh and local ingredients as possible.

Oyster omlettes at breakfast are one of their specialties that you won't find elsewhere. They're also famous for their crabcakes and hush puppies. Seafood and fish items are all lightly breaded to order and their Catch of the Day special may be the best buy on the island.

The Island Inn Restaurant is open for breakfast and dinner, March through November. Children's and senior citizen portions are available atdinner.

PONY ISLAND RESTAURANT

Ocracoke 928-5701

$-$$ MC, VISA

The Pony Island Restaurant has long been a favorite with vacationers and locals alike on Ocracoke. Located right beside the Pony Island Motel off the main highway coming into the village, the restaurant offers lots of special dishes in a casual atmosphere.

They're known for their steamed shrimp and homemade desserts, but there are plenty of other good menu items. Seafood in just about every combination possible, either fried or broiled, as well as hand cut rib eyes are offered. There is a children's menu.

Another claim to fame for the Pony Island Restaurant is their nightly specials. Believe it or not, you can actually get Chinese food there on one of the special nights...a real popular thing with locals who welcome a diversion from all that fresh seafood! You can also bring them your own catch -- cleaned -- and they'll cook it for you.

PONY ISLAND RESTAURANT

- **Nightly Specials**
- **"Bring Your Own" Fish Dinners**
- **Famous Homemade Desserts**
- **Steamed Shrimp Specialty**
- **Children's Plate**
- **Beer and Wine**
- **Breakfast and Dinner Served Daily**

Located next to Pony Island Motel.
Breakfast served from 6:30 a.m.-11 a.m.
Dinner served from 5 p.m.-9 p.m.
Call 928-5701.

THE PELICAN

Ocracoke Village   928-7431

$$ MC, VISA

The Pelican opened in 1980 and, in spite of several management changes in the last few years, it has built a reputation as a good place to eat. Located in a hundred-year-old cottage right in the heart of the village, The Pelican offers a wonderful vantage point for observing village activity on its large porch. There are also two smaller dining rooms that have a homey feel to them, but we'd wait for a table on the porch. Linen cloths and fresh flowers on the tables add a touch of class.

The menu offers standard fare for lunch and dinner and, as with all the island restaurants, centers on fresh seafood. The crabcakes are especially good.

With the constant management changes, it's hard to know what season the restaurant will keep. This past year they closed in mid-fall and re-opened in May.

CAFE ATLANTIC

Ocracoke   928-4861

$$ MC, VISA

This attractive restaurant, owned and managed by Bob and Ruth Toth, opened March, 1989 and it's been getting rave reviews ever since. The two-story building with its pickled wood interior and large expanses of glass affords good views of the surrounding dunes and marsh. Hand colored photographs by Ann Ehringhaus hang on every wall, giving the light, airy rooms a gallery feel.

The Toths aren't Ocracoke natives, but they have lived on the island since the mid '70s. Opening the restaurant, says Bob, is something they always wanted to do. They make all their soups, sauces and dressings from scratch. Ruth makes all the desserts.

The lunch menu offers soups, salads and sandwiches. The black bean soup was nice and spicey; cole slaw was in a vinegar dressing, tangy and crisp. Chicken salad, accented with just the right touch of grapes and pecans to be interesting without overpowering the chicken, comes in an edible flour tortilla shell. The reuben sandwich was generous to a fault and grilled without being greasy.

Dinner centers on seafood. They offer fried fresh fish, but all the other menu items are grilled or sauteed. One of the most popular entrees is the grilled seafood platter which includes a full portion of fresh fish, a kabob of shellfish and vegetables, clams casino and a soft shell crab.

Cafe Atlantic is open most of the year for lunch and dinner. They have carry-out service and a good selection of wines and beers.

OUTER BANKS
NIGHT SPOTS

The sun and surf are the main draws on the Outer Banks. Nightlife and live entertainment don't even figure into the top ten reasons people come to our fair islands. After a day on the beach -- or sightseeing and shopping -- and a satisfying evening meal, most of our resort visitors never see the clock hit midnight.

For those who do want to dance and mingle late into the wee hours, there are a few obliging spots. While the entertainment scene has improved since the legalization of liquor-by-the-drink several years ago, quite frankly, it's still not too exciting.

That's not to say you won't find big crowds at some of the favorite watering holes on a Friday or Saturday night. And it doesn't mean there is some variety in the possibilities for a late-night rendezvous.

But compared to the growth and change in almost every other facet of Outer Banks' life, this one has remained remarkably stagnant. Most of the following night spots have usually offered entertainment on a regular basis in the past and stayed open late until the last legal drink can be served, generally until 2 a.m. We list them because they cater to the late night crowd. There are many other restaurants in the area that may schedule one or two musicians for quiet entertainment during the evening hours. Check the local newspapers to get the update scoop on who's performing where.

KITTY HAWK
NIGHT SPOTS

AWFUL ARTHUR'S
Beach Road, MP 6   441-5955

This raw bar and lounge is a popular place to hang out after the dinner hour. They feature occasional live music . . . and dancing every Monday night during the summer.

FRISCO & CO.

Hwy. 158, MP 4   261-7833

This popular bar attracts the young, professional crowd after work and they stay until late. Because of its size, location and ambience, it's the center of nightlife at the north end of the beach. Live entertainment every Thursday night all year long.

KILL DEVIL HILLS
NIGHT SPOTS

DRINKWATER LOUNGE

At the Sea Ranch, Beach Road, MP 7   441-7126

The live entertainment Tuesday through Saturday nights in this showy lounge caters to a somewhat older crowd than most of the beach lounges listed here. Dance to easy listening music from the 50s through today. The Drinkwater Lounge is open all year.

PAPAGAYO'S CANTINA

Beach Road, MP 7 1/2   441-7232

This popular Mexican restaurant also sports one of the most popular night spots on the beach. The bar is located above the restaurant and the atmosphere is casual and friendly. The somewhat tropical feeling of the restaurant is carried on here and, as might be expected, Margaritas are a favored drink.

Live entertainment is a fairly regular thing in season and usually on weekends off season, usually in the form of guitar or piano. The mood is lively, the crowd usually mid-20s on up. Open March through late fall.

MEX-ECONO

Beach Road, MP 9   441-8226

Just about any time of the year you can find locals hanging out here, enjoying good conversation and the excellent selection of beer. You'll find another group playing pool...and enjoying the beer. And on weekends, you'll find a big crowd enjoying live entertainment... and the beer.

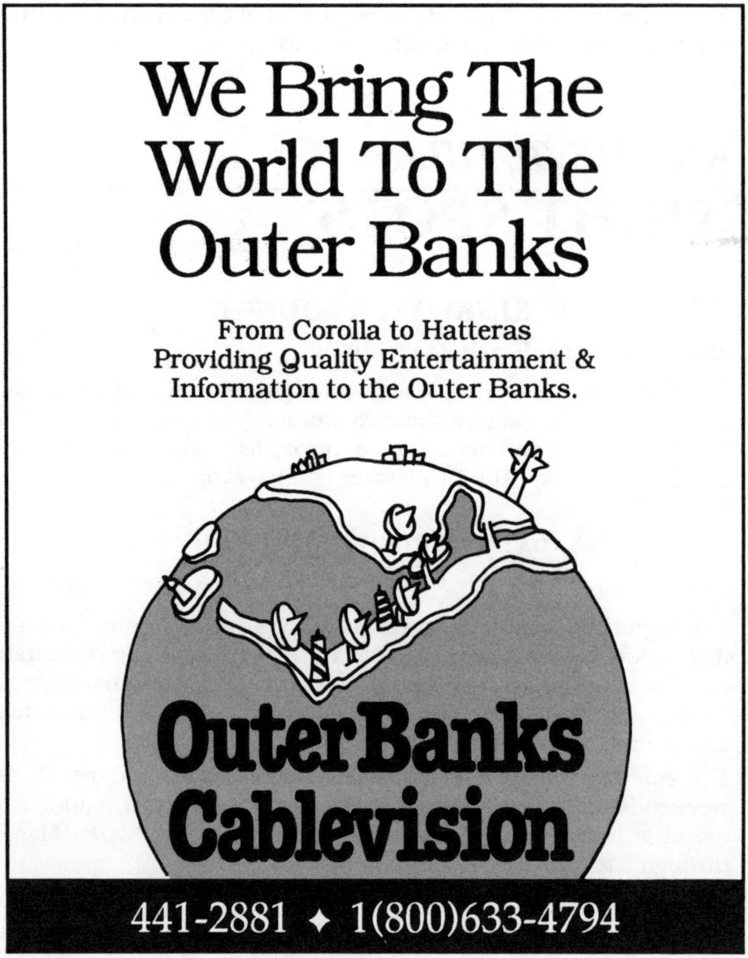
We Bring The World To The Outer Banks
From Corolla to Hatteras
Providing Quality Entertainment &
Information to the Outer Banks.
Outer Banks Cablevision
441-2881 ✦ 1(800)633-4794

The entertainment is good, but totally unpredictable. One week it might be a North Carolina folk singer, the next you might find the most raucous punk group this side of Liverpool. One thing that's for sure: you won't find a group that plays Kelly's or the Holiday Inn. Open all year.

PORT O'CALL GASLIGHT SALOON
Beach Road, MP 8 1/2   441-7484

The 150-seat Gaslight Saloon is a popular addition to the highly rated Port O'Call Restaurant. In decor and concept, it is one of the most elaborate watering holes for a hundred miles. The decor is Victorian with dark wood panels and gaslight effects throughout an open, two-story structure. The long mahogany bar looks as if it came out of a British mens' club. The antique accent furnishings contribute to the theme. There's a real dance floor, too.

The Gaslight Saloon is open March through November, with live entertainment Thursday through Saturday nights in season, weekends off season.

MADELINE'S
At the Holiday Inn
Beach Road, MP 9 1/2   441-6333

From Monday through Saturday beginning at 9 p.m., Madeline's gives those with plenty of energy today's top 40 music for listening and dancing. They book live bands whenever possible throughout the year. On the nights when there isn't live entertainment, you'll find a DJ and music videos to keep the action going.

This lounge location in the Holiday Inn has always been popular with the summer working crowd of young adults. It's a big hit with the local singles set, too. Seats are filled early on weekends, in season and out. The music plays late here all year long. There may be a cover charge -- it depends on the entertainment and season.

NAGS HEAD NORTH
NIGHT SPOTS

THE COMEDY CLUB
At the Carolinian, Beach Road, MP 10 1/2   441-7171

You might be used to seeing these live comedy shows in big cities, but did you know there was one on the Banks, too? This is one fun, and certainly funny, place. Six nights a week, Monday through Saturday, in season, professional comedians from the national circuit entertain the crowds. Reservations recommended.

KELLY'S
Rt. 158, MP 10 1/2   441-4116

Kelly's is a popular night spot with locals as well as vacationers. Live entertainment is offered all year. Groups like the Neurocktics, C. C. Ryder, The Rare and Phil Chestnut are regulars and pack the people in. Even though the lounge was enlarged before the 1988 season started, expect a big crowd.

ATLANTIS
Beach Road, MP 11 1/2   441-6435

The Atlantis is back and from all reports, it's been spruced up, and it's better than ever if you enjoy dancing to a different drummer. Live bands are scheduled almost nightly in season. You'll find up and coming rock 'n roll groups, reggae and other alternative music groups. The music selection is similar to Mex-Econo's, only not quite so kinky.

PENGUIN ISLE
Rt. 158, MP 16   441-2637

With the addition of the large, enclosed gazebo-type lounge at this popular restaurant, night life has become a part of the scene here. Local and out of town bands play for crowds who appreciate the good acoustics created by the domed ceiling. The panoramic view adds to the pleasing atmosphere. It's generally an older (late 20s on up) group that gathers here.

NAGS HEAD SOUTH
NIGHT SPOTS

STATION KEEPERS LOUNGE
At Owens' Restaurant, Beach Road, MP 16 1/2   441-7309

The second floor of the Life Saving Station structure which marks the entrance to Owens' Restaurant is the home of the Station Keepers Lounge. Patrons ascend a free-standing, two-level polished natural wood staircase to a contemporary room of gleaming light wood panels, brass rails and Tiffany-styled fixtures.

The bar specializes in frozen drinks, with fruit daiquiris being the popular summertime request. Piano entertainment on weekends in season.

HATTERAS ISLAND
NIGHT SPOTS

KINNAKEET TAVERN
Avon   995-5959

This popular place is a local's hangout. They're open from 5 p.m. until 2 a.m. during the season, with a DJ on Wednesday, Friday, and Saturday nights. They also serve steamed seafood, subs, and pizza until midnight. A big screen TV, pool tables, darts, basketball, and video keep the beer and wine drinkers lively.

OCRACOKE
NIGHT SPOTS

3/4 TIME DANCE HALL & SALOON
Hwy. 12   928-1221

Ocracoke has one of the best "get down and boogie" night spots on the whole Outer Banks. 3/4 Time, a real dance hall in the tradition of yesterday is located in the warehouse-like building near the edge of town. And it looks like a place for an old fashioned barn dance, though barn dancing isn't really what goes on here. But what does go on is fun and plenty of it...with some dancing on the side. There is a huge platform for bands and their amplifiers to set up. Groups come from the mainland for weekends, and a local band fills out the schedule. The tempo can be Blues or Country, but it's generally rock and roll. Bottle beer, sodas, (no mixed drinks here, either) and light snacks are available at the back bar.

OTHER FUN NIGHT TIME ACTIVITIES

In addition to the bar scene, there are more family-oriented entertainments to be enjoyed after the sun goes down on the Outer Banks. Many, like miniature golf courses and movie theaters, are listed and described in the Recreation sections of the book (by area). "The Lost Colony," the outdoor drama that was one of Andy Griffith's stepping stones to fame, plays only at night during thee summer season. See the write-up under Roanoke Island Attractions. A few other summertime possibilities are offered here:

DOWDY'S AMUSEMENT PARK
Rt. 158, MP 11, Nags Head

Dowdy's is one of those places where you can go pay to whirl yourself into dizzy oblivion. If you're an adult, you don't want to go after dinner. Children, on the other hand, seem immune to the physical side-effects of the Octopus, Scrambler, Tilt-A-Whirl and other nauseous rides. Dowdy's offers a nice family atmosphere and has rides for children of all ages. Open evenings only, mid- Spring through Labor Day.

CRYSTAL DAWN EVENING CRUISE
From Pirate's Cove Marina, Manteo-Nags Head Causeway 473-5577

The popular headboat, Crystal Dawn, takes a two-hour scenic cruise in the sound around Roanoke Island three or four evenings a week in season. Off season (but not during the winter months) the boat goes out on Friday evenings only. It's a nice, inexpensive way to get out on the water.

ELIZABETHAN DINNER THEATER
At the Elizabethan Inn, Hwy. 64, Manteo   473-2101

This delightful entertainment began last summer and it's well worth the price of admission. A 16th century tavern is re- created, complete with straw on the floor, and the troupe of characters -- the innkeeper, his wife, wenches and servants -- lead you through a meal and evening's entertainment in Elizabethan style.

They have tried to be as authentic as possible and it's not only interesting, but educational as well. Forks weren't in use in England at that time, so forks aren't part of the table setting. The actor/servers speak in Elizabethan brogue and express wonderment at modern dress, customs and vocabulary.

The food is plentiful enough to be filling, but strange enough that you can't count on wanting to eat much of it. Our suggestion is not to go too hungry.

After dinner, you'll be serenaded by the innkeeper (who plays a lute and other period instruments) and invited to join in the fun.

It's a hearty -- and sometimes bawdy, depending on whether there are children in the audience -- and thoroughly entertaining evening of merriment for adults and older children.

One note: The setting is a tavern, but there are no alcoholic beverages served. No ale or wine, which many expect, since these drinks would have been commonplace in a 16th century tavern.

The Elizabethan Gardens near Manteo are designed to reflect English gardens as they were around the time of Sir Walter Raleigh's American expeditions to the New World. DCTB

OUTER BANKS
RENTALS

There are well over 100 hotels and motels on the Outer Banks from Kitty Hawk to Ocracoke. Within these properties there are close to 5,000 motel units, of which nearly one-half are efficiencies with some facilities for cooking. Some of the accommodations qualify for the appellation "apartment," because they are fully equipped for housekeeping. There are also more than 5,000 vacation cottages rented out by the week. And, there are over 2,500 campsites available.

The numbers sound staggering, but when, on a peak season day, nearly 150,000 visitors come to the Outer Banks, the most desirable accommodations are as hard to come by as hen's teeth.

The competition for available rentals can be keen. Do not expect to arrive on the Outer Banks in-season, or on a holiday weekend off-season, for that matter, and find the accommodation of your choice unless you have a prior confirmed reservation.

If you make your in-season reservations between January and mid-March, you can generally get the accommodations you want. After mid-March and into April, you will probably be able to come close. By May, the true bargains and the oceanfront properties will be booked solid.

VACATION COTTAGES

If you're planning to stay on the Outer Banks for a week or more, you should consider renting a vacation cottage. The term "cottage" is a misnomer more often than not: while there of hundreds of "economy class" properties, a growing majority of these rental houses and condominiums are large and luxuriously furnished, offering everything from swimming pools and private hot tubs to VCRs and video games, accommodating family groups of 6, 8 and even 12 people.

It would be difficult, if not impossible, to describe the average cottage, its furnishings and cost. Suffice it to say there is something to fit every vacation budget, every family size. Location, age and condition, and size all play a part in the cost. A 5 bedroom/3 bath new oceanfront home in Corolla, with state-of-the-art kitchen and home entertainment center, wet bar and dune top hot tub may rent for $1200 a week during July. At the same time, you could rent an older 3 bedroom/1 bath cottage in between the highways in Kill Devil Hills for $350 a week.

Some people like the convenience and thrift of not having to eat every meal out. Others enjoy relaxing in a home-like atmosphere. For family groups and friends vacationing together, a large cottage may offer a chance to be together more or the opportunity to share the expense.

For longer stays, a cottage may be more economical, whether you eat out or not.

RENTING A COTTAGE

Almost without exception, cottages rent by the week only, with leases usually running from Sunday-to-Sunday or Saturday-to-Saturday. Most rentals are handled through local real estate companies or property management firms, who publish annual brochures listing a description of each available property (usually including a photo and sometimes a floor plan). There are dozens of companies offering this service. You can get an accommodations directory from the Dare County Tourist Bureau (919/473-27551) in Manteo or at the Aycock Brown Welcome Center in Kitty Hawk. This directory will list just about every rental company on the beach. You can then write or call the individual firms to obtain a copy of their current rental brochures.

To get you started, we've listed a few of our favorite companies below. This is by no means a complete listing, nor should the omission of a company's name imply any more than the fact that we just couldn't list them all.

Atlantic Realty, 261-2154 (1-800-334-8401 out-of-state), Rt. 158, MP 2 1/2,(Mailing Address: 4729 N. Croatan Hwy.) Kitty Hawk, NC 27949. Properties from Whalehead to South Nags Head.

Britt Real Estate, 261-3566 (1-800-334-6315 out-of-state), Rt. 12, just north of Duck (Mailing Address: SR Box 272, Kitty Hawk, NC 27949). Properties in Duck and north to Corolla.

SURF or SOUND

**RENTALS ● SALES
PROPERTY MANAGEMENT**

CAPE HATTERAS

Oceanfront and Soundside Cottages all within walking distance of the Atlantic Ocean.

**WRITE OR CALL
FOR A FREE BROCHURE**

SURF OR SOUND, LTD.
P.O. Box 100-IG, Avon, N.C. 27915
919-995-5801

1-800-237-1138

328 OUTER BANKS RENTALS

Cove Realty, 441-6391 (1-800-635-7007 out-of-state), 105 E. Dunn (between the highways at MP 13 1/2), Nags Head, NC 27959. Properties in Old Nags Head Cove, Nags Head, South Nags Head, Village at Nags Head.

Hudgins Rentals, 261-8861 (1-800-334-4749 out-of-state), Rt. 158, MP 2 1/2 (Mailing Address: P.O. Box 720), Kitty Hawk, NC 27949. Properties from Duck to Nags Head.

Kitty Hawk Rentals, 441-7166 (1-800-635-1559 out-of-state), Rt. 158, MP 6 (Mailing Address: P.O. Box 69), Kill Devil Hills, NC 27948 and Hwy. 12, Duck. Properties from Corolla to South Nags Head.

Midgett Realty, 986-2841 (1-800-527-2903 in and out-of-state), Hwy. 12, Hatteras, NC 27943. Properties from Nags Head to Hatteras Village.

Sharon Miller Realty, 928-5711 or 928-5731, Ocracoke, NC 27960. Ocracoke island properties.

Ocracoke Island Realty, 928-6261 or 928-7411, Ocracoke, NC 27960. Ocracoke Island properties.

Outer Banks, Ltd., 441-5000, Rt. 158, MP 10, Nags Head, 27959. Properties from Duck to South Nags Head.

Outer Beaches Realty, 995-5252, Hwy. 12, Avon, NC 27915. Properties from Rodanthe to Hatteras Village.

Riggs Realty, 453-3111 (1-800-654-5224 out of state), Box 1047, Corolla, NC 27927. Currituck beaches properties in Corolla and vicinity.

Salvo Real Estate, 987-2343, Hwy. 12, Salvo, NC 27972. Properties in Rodanthe, Salvo, and Waves.

Southern Shores Realty, 261-2000 (1-800-334-1000 out-of-state, 1-800-682-2002, in state), Hwy. 12 just north of Rt. 158 stoplight, Southern Shores (Mailing Address: P.O. Box 150, Kitty Hawk, NC 27949). Properties in Southern Shores and Duck.

Sun Realty, 441-7033 (1-800-346-9593), Rt. 158, MP 9 (Mailing Address; P.O. Box 1630), Kill Devil Hills, NC 27948. Properties from Corolla to Avon.

Surf or Sound Realty, 995-5801 (1-800-237-1138 in and out-of-state), Hwy. 12, Avon, NC 27915. Properties on Hatteras Island.

The Young People, 441-5544 (1-800-334-6436 out-of-state), Beach Road, MP 6 (Mailing Address:P.O. Box 285), Kill Devil Hills, NC 27948. Properties from Corolla to South Nags Head.

Twiddy and Company, 261-2897, Hwy. 12, Duck (Mailing Address: SR Box 232-C, Kitty Hawk, NC 27949). Properties from Southern Shores to Carova.

Village Realty, 441-8533 (1-800-548-9688), Milepost 15 on Rt. 158, P.O. Box 1807, Nags Head, NC 27959. Village at Nags Head properties.

Williams Realty, 995-5211, Rt. 12 (Mailing address: Box 279), Avon, NC 27915. Properties in Avon.

RENT IT

We offer the most complete selection of beach supplies and vacation needs.

BABY EQUIPMENT	BEACH	COTTAGE
Full crib	Large Umbrellas	Color TV/VCR
Play Pen	Assorted Beach Chairs	Camcorder
High Chair	Boogie Boards	A/C Units
Strollers (sand)	Surf Boards	Coffee Maker
Car Seat	Fishing Rods/Tackle	Grills
Gerry Carrier	Volley Ball	Linen
Walkers	Beach Cruiser Bikes	Roll-Aways/Cots

LIFESAVER RENT–ALLS

MP 9 · Beach Road
Kill Devil Hills · (919)441-6048

CALL FOR RESERVATIONS
1-800-635-2764

MP 1 · Bypass · Kitty Hawk
Three Winks S/C · 261-1344

THE RATE SEASONS

As with motels on the Outer Banks, rates usually change with the season: In-season (generally, mid-June through Labor Day) being the most expensive; the winter months being the least. Most rental companies have mid-, pre- or post- season rates as well, although just when these reduced rate seasons begin and end varies from company to company.

Mid season rates will run between 20-30% less than in-season. Off-season can be as much as 50% less than in-season.

PETS

Some rental cottages allow pets. If they, do there is usually an additional deposit and an extra charge spraying the property after you vacate. Each rental company has their own policy that will be spelled out in their rental brochure.

OCCUPANCY

Each rental cottage has a maximum occupancy designated by the rental company. Your lease will state that if you exceed the number of persons specified it is grounds for not honoring your reservation -- or eviction -- with no return of advance rents paid. It's important that you make your reservation for the proper number of persons, including children.

Many rental companies follow the "families only" policy. They won't be asking you to produce marriage certificates or prove your group is related, but this means that they will generally refuse rental to obvious groups of students or young people. Don't think this is something you can ignore or get away with by sending a more mature member of your group to check in. The Outer Banks is still a "small town" and neighbors keep an eye on surrounding properties. You can be evicted for misrepresenting your group. It's better to be up-front about it. Most companies will have some properties that can be rented to "non-family" groups.

ADVANCE RENTS

In past times, this money was called a deposit. Today, due to legal mumbo-jumbo, it is called advance rent. The transaction is still the same. In order to have a confirmed reservation, you will be asked to pay one-half of the lease amount within a few days of making the reservation.

With few exceptions, this money does not go into an escrow account. That's one reason why it's not called a deposit anymore. Rather, it is forwarded to the cottage owner to provide a cash flow for paying the monthly expenses of the property. (As many as 90% of new properties sold as second homes are put into rental programs to help pay for the investment.) When you sign the lease agreement, you give the rental company permission to pay the owner in advance.

Most rental companies will accept personal checks for the advance rent, provided it's received a month before the occupancy date.

Some companies require that the balance due (50% of lease amount, plus taxes and security deposit) be paid 30 days prior to occupancy. In this case, they usually will accept a personal check. If the final payment is made at check-in it must be in the form of a certified or travelers' check or cash. Make sure you are prepared to pay this way.

CANCELLATIONS

Cottage reservations aren't as flexible as those for a motel and that's one of the drawbacks. Each rental company has their own policy but, generally, the rules is this: If the cottage can be re-rented, you will get your deposit back -- usually minus a cancellation fee; if the property isn't rented, you forfeited whatever money you've paid. Cancellation fees run from $20 to $150 or as much (or little) as 20% of the lease amount.

SECURITY DEPOSITS

Some cottage rentals require a security deposit. The average deposit is around $100. Sometimes the deposit can be paid at check in by personal check. The check will be held until you've checked out, and then returned to you if no damages or losses are assessed. More often, you will be required to pay the deposit as part of your final rent and a refund will be made within 30 days after you vacate the premises.

Whether you pay a security deposit or not, your lease will state that you are responsible for any damages to the property during your stay.

MINIMUM STAYS

Off-season it may be possible to rent a cottage for less than a week. In-season you will find it harder to do this: the one-week minimum is fairly standard with most rental companies. If renting a cottage

THOUSANDS DIE EACH YEAR...

YOU CAN MAKE THE DIFFERENCE!

Many animals are abandoned annually in Dare County... left to wander in search of a home... food... water.

The sad fact is that most of them don't find homes. They die as a result of starvation, injury, abuse or neglect.

We're working to change this. And you can make a difference.

PLEASE HELP US HELP THEM!

Send your tax-deductible contributions to:

**Outer Banks S.P.C.A.
P.O. Box 3006
Kill Devil Hills, NC 27948**

appeals to you but you can't stay the entire week, do a little arithmetic before you discard the idea. In some cases, it's as economical to rent a cottage for a week as to stay in a motel for 4 or 5 nights.

A few cottages require a two-week minimum in-season.

COTTAGE LOCATION

If a cottage is oceanfront, that means there is no structure or road between it and the ocean, and that its property line abuts the beach easement. An oceanfront cottage will usually have an oceanview, although it doesn't hurt to ask and make sure.

The term "oceanside" means the cottage is on the oceanside of the main highway or road. There will usually be one or more other buildings between you and the beach. There may even be another small road.

Cottages listed as "between the highways" are in the area from Kitty Hawk south through South Nags Head. They will be between the new five-lane Rt. 158 and the Beach Road. Some may be as far as four blocks from the ocean, others just a stone's throw away.

Soundside or westside generally means west of Route 158. In an area like Old Nags Head Cove, for example, a house can be soundside and still just a couple blocks from the ocean.

Soundfront property will actually have frontage on the water.

WHAT'S FURNISHED

A rental cottage will have furniture and appliances, dishes and cooking utensils. Many have TVs, but not all, and only some will have cable hook-ups. There may be beach chairs and umbrellas, hammocks--even bicycles--whatever the owner has chosen to make available. Rental brochures usually list major furnishings and extras, and rental agents are often familiar enough with the property to know what's there.

What you will have to bring 99% of the time is bed sheets and towels. Most rental companies provide linen service, if you prefer. Bring your own clocks and radios, too.

MAIL & PHONE SERVICE

Most rental companies accept mail and phone messages for their renters, but you'll have to go to the office pick them up. Emergency messages should be directed through the county sheriff's office.

Make sure you leave information about your rental agent, as well as the rental cottage, with those who may need to get in touch with you.

Most older cottages don't have telephones; many of the new ones do. With phone systems becoming more flexible and calling cards in wide-spread use, we think this will be a continuing trend. Some may mourn the demand for "reaching out" and letting our "fingers do the walking," but others will find it a welcome convenience. In any case, the cost for any long distance calls placed from a cottage phone are the repsonsibility of the renter.

THE MOTEL MARKET

There are, categorically speaking, few resort hotels on the Outer Banks, at least in the terms we think of Miami Beach, Atlantic City A.C. (After Casinos) or the Caribbean resort islands. Less than five properties offer room service, and in only a couple are bellhops or formally dressed restaurant captains to be seen.

There are a few old style inns remaining in operation, a few new inns patterned after the old ones, a few large motel properties with good restaurants and live entertainment nightly on premises, and a few (except on Ocracoke, where there are several) bed & breakfast houses, but the majority of the properties are more or less on par with the well-known motel chains. Indeed, we have several of those chains now represented on the beach. The rooms have wall-to-wall carpet, color coordinated contemporary decor, tile shower/tub combinations, air conditioning, color TV and, perhaps, a balcony. Unless otherwise noted in the profiles, you can expect these standards in the properties we review.

One exception on the Outer Banks is the room telephone. Many motels do not have phones in the room, especially the older ones. If this is one of your requirements, be sure to ask about room phones at the time of reservation.

Of course there are older properties on the beach which do not have national motel chain standards. Most of these motels were built in the 1950s. Many have been modernized, but still show their age. Fishermen and families on a budget love these properties because they lend themselves to an informal, perhaps unshaven, vacation lifestyle that doesn't worry about sand on the shag carpet. These motels can still be comfortable and inviting. In fact, their porches and rocking chairs seem to promote old- fashioned interaction among their guests. It seems easier to meet people somehow at these unpretentious spots. These properties almost always fall in our economy rate class.

With the huge number of motels now available, deciding whether or not to include a facility becomes increasingly difficult. On Roanoke and Ocracoke Islands, for example, each and every motel we visited offered a good value in its price category. We've tried to include a cross-section: different rate categories, different locations, different types of accommodations. And, let's face it, this is a book based, to some extent, on our personal observations and experiences. We hope the book will introduce you to some new and enjoyable possibilities. But please don't feel that these are the only good choices: there were far too many to include them all.

RATE GUIDELINES

Accommodations come in four basic categories: Economy, Moderate, Deluxe, and Luxury. The terms are specific more to room rates than they are to a definitive standard. Motels charging the same basic rates are not necessarily equal. There can be a great deal of qualitative difference between properties in each category. Factors such as location, age, up-keep, amenities, service, and even owner attitude come into play when you look beyond the numbers.

For your convenience, each motel property has been placed within a rate category. The rate range is based on the double occupancy of a standard room with two double beds in the prime season. The rate does not include the 8% state and local sales tax which is added to all bills.

Here are the definitions of the categories by rate:

$25 to $52	$
$53 to $75	$$
$76 to $95	$$$
$100 and up	$$$$

Most motels here have -- and base rates on -- more than one room category. They may have "oceanview" rooms and rooms with a view of the parking lot. There may be standard rooms and efficiencies. Rates may vary depending upon which floor your room is on. Go over the options with your reservations clerk. Look for tips on the preferred rooms in the profiles.

Motel profiles are arranged by mile posts, north to south, Sanderling to Ocracoke, along the Outer Banks. See the map reference for its relative location to restaurants and attractions.

THE RATE SEASONS

Most properties adjust their rates on the basis of three or four "seasons." Whenever we use the terms "in season," "prime season," or "peak season" we are essentially speaking about the period between mid-June and Labor Day. Most properties get their top rate for the Memorial Day weekend, but may not demand it after those dates until the third or fourth week in June.

Knowing the rating periods of the property you want is important if you are cost conscious. If a week or two difference in dates means a 30% saving, it is worth knowing.

The secondary seasons are in the spring and fall months, called the "mid season" or "shoulder season." Rates for these periods are usually the same. Spring dates can start as early as April and run through mid-June. Fall dates usually begin after Labor Day and may run into October. Rates during the mid season run 20% to 30% less than the prime rate.

The off season rates are usually in force during the months of November, December, January, February, and March , although some seasonal properties may call their rates "off season" from opening through Memorial Day weekend, and from late September until Closing. Off season rates are generally 40% to 50% less than prime.

PETS

The North Carolina state law prohibits pets in motel and hotel sleeping rooms. In some instances, cottage courts or motels with apartment units may be permitted to allow pets.

EXTRA PERSONS

There is no uniform standard concerning what constitutes an extra person. Children free in the parents' room could be under 18, under 12, under 6, or under 3 years of age. If you have children, be sure to ask about the specific policy at reservation time.

Extra adults, on the other hand, may not be permitted at all. Large parties that exceed the bed capacity of the room are discouraged in almost every motel. Ask.

Where there are charges for extra persons (be they child or adult) they will probably add from $2 to $12 per person to the daily room rate.

DEPOSITS

All hotels and motels require deposits to confirm vacation reservations. Policies vary, but average 25% to 33% of the total or one night's rate, whichever is greater. To cancel a reservation and get your deposit returned, some properties require only a couple days' weeks notice but many require 30 days. Some charge a cancellation fee. Be sure you understand the cancellation policy when you make a reservation. Deposits are usually due within three to seven days after making the reservation.

CHECK-IN, CHECK-OUT TIMES

In/Out Times

Although there is no complete uniformity on check-in and check-out times, most properties use the 3 p.m. check-in, 11 a.m. check-out policy. During the season, do not expect to get into a reserved room prior to the posted check-in time. House staffs are hard pressed to keep pace with room turnovers, and owners and managers do not like to issue a room key until the unit has been prepared and inspected. For the same reasons, check-out times should be strictly observed. To encourage on-time checkouts, many properties have provided post check-out dressing facilities for those who want a final morning by the ocean or pool.

PAYING THE BILL

Many hotels and motels want the balance of the room reservation paid on arrival. Personal checks are seldom honored except for advance deposits. If the property does not accept credit cards, you had best be prepared to pay by travelers' or certified check. (Don't forget the taxes totaling 8% of your bill.) Make sure that you are clear about the payment policy. No need starting off your holiday with an unnecessary hassle. We do not encourage the carrying of large amounts of cash, not out of any specific fear, but just as a principle of traveler's common sense.

MINIMUM STAYS

To protect their prime times from one-nighters, many hotel and motel properties have established minimum stays for advance reservations. Holiday weekends, for example, may require a three day minimum stay in order to get a reservation. During the summer, some properties may require a seven day minimum, although the tremendous growth of rental cottages has made it prudent for most motels to cater to guests staying shorter periods of time.

Unless dire circumstances exist, do not expect a refund for failure to honor the reserved minimum.

COTS AND CRIBS

Here is another nonstandard policy on the beach. Infants are usually free, especially if you bring your own crib and linens. Some properties provide the crib free. Others provide the cribs at fees of up to $5 per night. Cots, when available (which isn't very often), usually add another $10 to your daily room bill. If you have a baby, and some small ones who have to sleep by themselves, ask about cots and cribs at the time when you are considering reservations. A sleeping bag might be a better solution.

PARKING

All motel and hotel properties on the Outer Banks provide free parking for at least one vehicle per guest room. If you have an oversized vehicle, and we're not talking about vintage Cadillacs, ask your hotel about parking prior to arrival. Your hotel or motel can also advise you about transient docking for your boat, and ramp and parking areas for your boat trailer.

OFF SEASON PACKAGES

More and more Outer Banks properties are staying open all year. The advantages to the owner include keeping the house staff together, and generating revenue in additional off season months. And to this end, many offer reduced-rate package deals. Properties with restaurants may throw in meals at a discount, too. It's a good opportunity to stay at a more expensive motel than you might usually afford.

WEEKLY RATES

There is no way to average weekly motel rates and give a meaningful guideline. Many Outer Banks properties -- especially the older ones -- offer discounts for a week's rental, often equal to one night free. Ask.

OCEANFRONT, OCEANVIEW

Any property that uses the term oceanfront must have rooms which have frontage on the ocean beach. The rooms may or may not have balconies, but they will afford direct access to the beach. Not all rooms of an oceanfront property have the oceanfront view. Many properties advertise an ocean view. We take this term to mean that at least some of the rooms have a view of the ocean. For example, a building constructed on an angle to the ocean, but separated from the actual beach by another building, could still provide an ocean-view from its ocean facing rooms, especially ones above the second story.

Our caveat is to approach the above terms with some reserve. Ask for a description of the view at reservation time. Be sure that you and the reservations clerk are talking the same language.

PERSONAL CHECK CASHING

Unless you have established prior credit, or have a local Outer Banks bank account, the general rule is that you will be unable to cash a personal check. Area banks do give cash advances on VISA and MasterCard accounts. Several have ATMs that are part of regional networks like Relay, where you can use your own bank card to make a cash withdrawal.

GOLF AND TENNIS PRIVILEGES

Any property on the Outer Banks can advertise these two amenities because the local golf courses and the indoor tennis center welcome visiting players. Some properties may have free passes and discount greens fee arrangements for their guests, but if you want to play, your only real problem is finding a playing partner.

GUARDED BEACHES

The Lifeguard Service on the major resort beaches is a private business which profits from the rental of beach chairs and umbrellas. Lifeguard stands are thus located in front of the larger motel properties and at public beach accesses with adequate parking to ensure a crowd. The areas between the lifeguard stands are patrolled by a four wheel drive vehicle equipped for rescue.

Members of the Lifeguard Service are especially trained in ocean rescue and are equipped with surfboards and life rings. Some motels employ their own private lifeguards.

Comfort Inn

SPARKLING NEW THIS SUMMER!

Oceanfront in Kill Devil Hills

120 Oceanfront rooms located in Kill Devil Hills, near the Wright Brothers Memorial at Mile Post 8.

Amenities include HBO, in room coffee, some rooms with refrigerators and microwave ovens, game room, pool, beach access with lifeguards. Excellent shopping and dining nearby.

For Seasonal Rates and Reservations call: 1-800-228-5150 or 919-480-2600

401 N. Virginia Dare Trail
P.O. Box 3427
Kill Devil Hills,
NC 27948

THE BEST VALUE!! 98 beautiful rooms located within walking distance to the beach in Kitty Hawk. All the amenities including HBO, restaurant on premises, swimming pool, and beach access. Excellent shopping and dining nearby.

For Seasonal Rates and Reservations call:
1-800-325-2525 or 919-261-4888

DAYS INN

AMERICA'S WAKING UP TO US.

4½ Mile Post, Hwy. 158 By-pass • Kitty Hawk, NC 27949

SOUTHERN SHORES, DUCK, SANDERLING, AND COROLLA
ACCOMMODATIONS

THE SANDERLING INN
Rt. 12, north of Duck   261-4111
$$$$ MC, VISA, AMEX

When you want to get away for a luxurious, all-your-needs-taken-care-of vacation, this is the place. Opened in the summer of 1985, Sanderling Inn offers prestigious accommodations in an area of the beach that knows no commercialization. The Inn is architecturally pleasing, built in a true old Nags Head style with cedar shakes, dormers and plenty of porches for beach gazing.

Special touches like lounging robes, baskets filled with Evelyn Crabtree toiletries and a welcome basket of fruit and wine provided when you check are indicative of the level of service the Inn offers. During the peak season, wine and hors d' oeuvres are offered each afternoon to guests, compliments of the management.

A library on the second floor Grand Gallery offers a large selection of games, current newspapers, magazines and books. A book of original size Audubon prints that a collector -- or anyone else in the know -- would surely covet fills one corner. All this quiet entertainment is surrounded by a room full of English country antiques, furniture and decorative pieces made by hand especially for the Inn, antique plates depicting Audubon scenes, and a porcelain collection valued in the six figures.

Downstairs in the Audubon Room, you see impressive nautical antiques, sculptures, and an attractive collection of porcelain fish. There's a comfortable lounging room with a bar and fireplace.

The entrance way is enhanced by a cathedral ceiling from which hangs a brass chandelier that was handcrafted for the Inn in Louisiana.

Sanderling Inn offers 28 suites, all tastefully decorated, with well-equipped kitchens and privacy porches. Natural wood wainscotting in the rooms as well as throughout the Inn carry on the old Nags Head elegance. Four loft suites are available featuring living areas, kitchens, privacy porches, and half baths downstairs with upstairs bedrooms, dressing areas and full baths. All rooms provide exceptional sound or ocean views, with the corner rooms giving views of each.

A conference center right next door to the inn has three meeting rooms and a Presidential Suite on the top floor. This suite can be booked by any guest when not reserved for corporate use. Its outstanding features are the size -- "enormous and super-deluxe," according to Paige Beshens, an Inn employee -- the private Jacuzzi bath and two decks, one overlooking the sound, one the ocean.

A third building, "Sanderling Inn North," has rooms similar to the Inn, but without the kitchen facilities. The lounge in this building looks out over a landscaped garden and small waterfall.

All rooms have phones and remote control color TV, but there is no cable on this part of the beach so programming is limited. The Inn more than makes up to its video-loving guests by furnishing each room with a VCR. Video tapes may be checked out at the front desk. Room service is available.

Recreational facilities include an outdoor spa pool, a hot tub and jogging trails. Right across the street is the Sanderling Racquet and Swim Club with an outdoor swimming pool and tennis courts (lighted for night play). The Inn is situated on the border of the Pine Island Sanctuary, an Audubon Society property, which means there are miles and miles of totally undeveloped beach to walk.

The management at the Sanderling Inn goes to any length to make sure their guests receive the attention they would expect to receive

---

Buccaneer Motel and Apartments

3512 Virginia Dare Trail
Kitty Hawk, NC 27949

· Large, Comfortable Rooms
· Outdoor Pool and Sun Deck
· Childrens' Playground
· Basketball, Volleyball and Horseshoes
· Refrigerators in all Motel Rooms
· Full Kitchens and all Housekeeping Facilities in Efficiency Apartments
· Much, much more

For Reservations, call:
919-261-2030

'A FAMILY TRADITION ON THE OUTER BANKS'

at a first-class inn. It has become one of "The" places to stay on the Outer Banks for those who can afford to be pampered. They are open all year.

KITTY HAWK
ACCOMMODATIONS

DAYS INN

Rt. 158, MP 4 1/2   261-4888
$$ 800-325-2525

Most major credit cards

The Days Inn is situated between the highways, but only a short walk from the guarded Kitty Hawk beach. It's an attractive brick, two story motel that offers convenient accommodations at a very reasonable price, especially for families, since all children under 17 stay free. Shopping, restaurants and movie theaters are nearby.

All rooms have phones, color cable TV with HBO, and air conditioning, of course. A full-service restaurant, The Keeper's Galley (see write-up under Restaurants) is on the premises. Queen size beds are available and there is a good sized outdoor pool with a sunbathing area. The pool is enclosed in winter so it can be used year 'round. The Days Inn is open all year. Shopping, movie theaters and other attractions are nearby.

BUCCANEER MOTEL

Beach Road, MP 5 1/4   261-2030
$$ MasterCard, VISA

The Buccaneer has been on the Banks for 36 years. Present owners and managers, Keith and Joy Byers, have been here over five years. Their pride in the property is obvious: fresh paint, colorful flowers and a neat, well-cared for appearance is reinforced by their friendly management style.

Rooms are very well maintained and nicely decorated. They have facilities for the handicapped, and a four-bedroom efficiency that can accommodate up to 10 people. As with many of the older properties, there are no phones in the rooms; but there is a pay phone on the premises. All rooms have color cable tv and refrigerators.

While the Buccaneer is across the highway from the beach, there are no other buildings between it and the water, only a small dune and you're at the water's edge. A dune top deck and private beach access make enjoying the ocean almost as easy as if it were oceanfront. Other things you'll enjoy about this gem of a motel are a children's playground, charcoal grills and a fish cleaning station. Keith Byers says that at least 65% of his business each year is repeat business. It's easy to see why. Open March - November.

KILL DEVIL HILLS
ACCOMMODATIONS

Please Note: The beach has been battered by nor'easter storms over the last few years. Severe beach erosion in some places has done irreparable damage. The motels in this area were hit especially hard. Some, like The Mariner, who lost part of their swimming pool, among other things, to the waves, have already repaired the damage and, literally, replaced the beach. Others have had a harder time undoing what nature did. You might want to ask about the condition of the beach -- if that is important to you -- before making reservations in this area.

TAN-A-RAMA

Rt. 158, MP 6 441-7315

$$ MC, VISA, AMEX

Thirty-three of the units in this 35-unit oceanfront property are spacious efficiencies with fully equipped kitchens; seven of these are 2-bedroom apartments. All feature carpeting, wood paneling, color cable TV, a lounging area, and air conditioning. Twenty-three of the one- and two-bedroom units are directly on the ocean.

There is an ocean front deck from which the patrons can watch the fishing at the nearby Avalon Pier. The large raised pool is located across the highway.

The outside of this family-owned motel is kept looking nice while regularly replaced drapes, upholstery, bedspreads and daily maid service keep the inside fresh.

The Tan-a-Rama is open from mid-March through the first of November. Restaurants and shopping are nearby.

THE MARINER

Beach Road, MP 7   441-2021
$$ MC, VISA, AMEX

The Mariner is a large oceanfront property with a definite resort flavor. The two-story and three-story main buildings form an "L" which shields the parking lot, large pool, walled patio, and recreation area from the highway.

The standard rooms are spacious and well-maintained. All rooms have color cable TV, phones and refrigerators. Two-bedroom apartments in the oceanfront building were refurbished for the 1990 season.

In 1987, the Mariner opened a new building of two- and three-bedroom efficiency apartments across the highway. These rent by the week during July and August. The units are big, nicely furnished and they interconnect, offering flexible living arrangements are large families or groups.

The recreation area has facilities for volleyball, shuffleboard and badminton, in addition to the large oceanfront pool. There are beachside showers. The motel is across the street from the only indoor tennis facility on the Outer Banks. The Mariner is open from mid-February through the end of November.

HOWARD JOHNSON'S

Beach Road, MP 7-1/2   441-0411
$$ 800-338-7761
   Major credit cards

This motel has continued to be an attractive addition to the beach accommodations scene since it opened in 1988. It's part of the chain known for its bright orange roofs, 24-hour restaurants and ice cream. Alas, there's no going into this HoJo's to order a banana split at 2 a.m.; it's a Howard Johnson's sans restaurant. But you probably won't mind because your room is actually a mini-efficiency, equipped with microwave, refrigerator and eating utensils. All rooms have color cable tv with HBO. King beds are available, as well as non-smoking rooms. There's a heated outdoor pool.

The year 'round motel is not oceanfront, but it's real, real close. Shopping and restaurants are nearby.

THE CHART HOUSE

Beach Road, MP 7   441-7418

$ MC, VISA

David and Kristin Clark live in the large brick colonial oceanfront house, and host guests in the 18-unit two-story motel, built in 1966, that sets perpendicular to the beach.

All the rooms, whether they're efficiencies or regular rooms, are huge. The furnishings are nothing to write home about, but for the price they're more than adequate...and clean. Color tv and refrigerators in the rooms. Efficiencies have small, fully equipped kitchens.

There are also a few small rooms available in the oceanfront house that have direct access to the beach. The Chart House has a small pool and patio, not visible from the highway, and a dune-top deck. There is also a playground for children.

The Chart House is open March through November.

CAVALIER

Beach Road, MP 8   441-5584

$-$$ MC, VISA

The three single level wings of this red brick and white columned motel border a large courtyard with two pools, volleyball court, children's play area, and shuffleboard courts.

Parking is at the door of each unit, and the covered Colonial styled porch has furniture for guest relaxation. There is also a roof top observation deck atop the oceanfront units.

Accommodations here are varied. There are units with only shower facilities, pool side rooms with tub and shower, oceanfront rooms with full baths and picture windows, and oceanfront units with kitchenettes. Oceanfront rooms are raised above the parking lot and open onto a broad cement patio facing the surf. All rooms have refrigerators, microwave ovens, color cable tv and phones.

Hot, sunny days and cool, clear ocean waters draw visitors to Dare County beaches. DCTB

This very attractive, well-kept and locally-owned motel is open year round. They also rent several cottages. The highly rated Port O'Call Restaurant is opposite, and the Wright Memorial Monument is nearby.

YE OLDE CHEROKEE INN

Beach Road, MP 8   441-6127
$$ MC, VISA, AMEX

Ye Olde Cherokee Inn was built after the war as a hunting and fishing lodge and was given its name by the original owner. Phyllis and Robert Combs bought the house 12 years ago and discovered it was licensed for motel services. They began renting out rooms. Seven years ago they seriously entered the bed & breakfast business.

The exterior of the house is bright pink: a color Phyllis says she spent a great deal of time choosing, and a color the painter she hired nearly refused to paint. To say that you can't miss it would be an understatement. You get so wrapped up in the color that it's easy to overlook the broad, comfortable porch where guests take their morning coffee or read on a shady afternoon. The Inn is situated right across the road from a public beach access.

The inside of Ye Olde Cherokee Inn is anything but pink. The aged cypress paneling and broad, open rail staircase have preserved the masculine feel that was undoubtedly part of the original design.

There are six rooms on the second floor, each decorated differently, but homey and easy. All have private baths, color tvs and vanities.

The Combs' private quarters are on the first floor, along with a small library that is comfortably furnished with game tables and books and provides a good place for guests to get together. A continental breakfast is served each morning.

The Inn is an excellent choice for singles or couples who enjoy the ambience and personal service of a bed & breakfast house. Open from mid-April through September.

COMFORT INN

Beach Road, MP 8   480-2600
                                                               800-228-5150
$$$-$$$$ All major credit cards

The Comfort Inn is still the newest motel on the beach, opening for the summer season in 1989. The building is oceanfront, running perpendicular to the beach. Rooms are standard motel style rooms.

Some have refrigerators and microwaves. All rooms come equipped with a small coffee pot. The motel has a dune-top pool, a coin-operated laundry and a hospitality room for small meetings.
Open all year.

WILBUR & ORVILLE WRIGHT MOTOR LODGE - DAYS INN

Beach Road, MP 8 1/2   441-7211

800-325-2525

$$ Most major credit cards

The inviting lobby of the oceanfront Wilbur & Orville is like an old mountain lodge. It's a place where guests come together for a cup of coffee and to read the newspapers. Oriental rugs protect the polished hardwood floors and a large fireplace takes the chill off fall mornings. There's an interesting display of old memorabilia dating back to the Lodge's beginning in 1948.

Rooms in the original lodge building are small but were renovated for the 1989 season. Other sections of the building are newer and were all refurbished last season. Their suites -- or efficiencies -- are roomy and nicely decorated, but have no closets and very little storage space except in the kitchen.

Balconies sport old fashioned deck furniture and afford a view of a truly expansive beach. One motel employee suggests the shipwreck just to the north of the building must be protecting the beach. It must be: This is the nicest, broadest section of beach in the main motel strip. The Wilbur & Orville has a large pool and sundeck and a BBQ pit which guests may use.

Closed December and January.

OCEAN REEF - BEST WESTERN

Beach Road, MP 8 1/2   441-1611

1-800-528-1234

$$$$ Most major credit cards

If you're into luxurious surroundings, Ocean Reef is the place for you. Every room is an oceanfront suite in this attractive complex that opened during the 1986 season.

One-bedroom suites are beautifully appointed and include color cable TV and phones. The fully furnished galley-style kitchen has a small refrigerator, range and oven. Tiled floors and generous counter and cabinet space in kitchen and bath help give units the feel of a luxury apartment.

Every unit on the upper floors has a private balcony overlooking the beach. Some of the first floor units open onto the oceanfront pool courtyard, others have private patios. There's a penthouse suite with a private jacuzzi and roof-top deck. The pool is heated and there is a whirlpool nearby in the courtyard. Inside you'll find a workout room with the latest exercise equipment and a sauna. In season, an on-premises deli provides bar service as well as food.

Ocean Reef is a year 'round. While it earns a place in our highest rate category, for the quality and spaciousness of the accommodation, it's actually a very good bargain.

SEE SEA MOTEL

Beach Road, MP 9   441-7321

$-$$ MC, VISA, AMEX

The See Sea was built by John Peterson in the early 60s. Since 1983, it has been owned and managed by Bob and Berni Becker, an energetic young couple from New York. The motel was built in stages, the most recent being a two-story addition by the Beckers, but it is all so well-maintained that age is not a factor. There are accommodations to meet just about any need: regular rooms, efficiencies and a three bedroom/2 bath cottage right in the middle of the complex that can sleep up to 12. During the peak season, all but the regular rooms have a minimum stay requirement.

All rooms have color cable tv, air conditioning and heat. The larger units have microwaves. There's a nice pool and sun deck, and a picnic area with a gas grill for guests to use. A public beach access is right across the street.

Open from April through October and located almost in the heart of the Kill Devil Hills restaurant and shopping district, the See Sea is one of the best values on the northern Banks.

ECONO LODGE

Rt. 158, MP 9   441-2503
$$ 1-800-446-6900

All major credit cards

Built in 1985, the Econo Lodge brought its familiar theme of "spending a night not a fortune" to the Outer Banks' vacationers. It's one of the few motels not located on the Beach Road, but that's one of the things that makes it so affordable. Even so, you're less than 2 blocks from the ocean.

This lodge contains 40 rooms, all with either king size beds or two "extra length" double beds, color cable tv with HBO, phones, air conditioning, and full size tubs/showers. An enclosed, heated pool is provided for year 'round enjoyment.

The motel also offers an "Econo Traveler's Club" for frequent travelers: stay six nights and the seventh is free. There's a coin operated laundry and free coffee is always available in the lobby.

RAMADA INN

Beach Road, MP 9 1/2   441-2151
$$$$ 1-800-2RAMADA

All major credit cards

The opening of the oceanfront Ramada Inn in 1985, gave the Outer Banks a full-service hotel/convention center that has become increasingly popular for tour groups and small conventions. All of this speaks well for the service and accommodations, but if you're wanting a quiet getaway, you might make sure the Noisemakers of America aren't having a sales convention during your stay.

The five story, year 'round hotel contains 172 rooms of which 89 have ocean views. All rooms have a balcony or patio, color cable TV with pay-per-view in-room movies, a small refrigerator and microwave, air conditioning, and phones. And, unlike almost all other accommodations on the Banks, at the Ramada, room service and luggage assistance are available.

The enclosed, all-weather swimming pool is off the second floor at dune top level, surrounded by a large sundeck. When the weather permits, there is volleyball on the beach. There is also a heated whirlpool and an oceanfront gazebo. Food and beverage service is available at the Gazebo Deck Bar by the pool during the warm weather months.

Meeting and convention facilities are housed in a three story commercial tower, complete with grand ballroom on the third floor overlooking the ocean and several meeting suites.

Peppercorns is their good hotel restaurant, serving breakfast and dinner year 'round and providing lunch service on the deck during the summer.

TANYA'S OCEAN HOUSE

Beach Road, MP 10   441-2900
$$ MC, VISA, AMEX

This oceanfront motel was probably once the most talked about place on the beach. Locals have all heard about it now, and without its flamboyant former owner, Tanya Young, the talk has died down. It is still, however, a most unusual place.

"Just for the fun of it," Young and a designer friend created a theme room at the motel. It was such a hit that she went on to create new themes in most of the other rooms, although there are a few "themeless" rooms left for those who prefer to set their own stage. There's the Currituck Barn Room, Jonathan Seagull's Nest, Carolina Party Room... no two rooms are alike.

Each room has a small refrigerator and color cable tv with HBO. Many have waterbeds. This may be a place better suited for a one-night visit than a weeks' stay. Rooms are small and most show their age, though kept very clean.

The motel is U-shaped with a two-story wing running along the beach. This wing is built into the dune; the second-floor units open on to the beach. These rooms have windows front and back which make them far more pleasant than those on the first floor which have only a small window overlooking the parking lot. There is a swimming pool.

Open mid-March through October.

EBBTIDE

Beach Road, MP 10   441-4913
$ VISA, MC

This is an older property, owned by a local couple, Stephen and Pilar Smith, that has a lot going for it. Its low, open layout and perky blue striped awnings give it a nice, small-town resort feeling. There is a variety of accommodations, as with most of the older motels.

While the motel itself is across the street from the beach, they have a private beach access and also rent a few oceanfront apartments. Some rooms have showers only so you might want to ask, if a tub is important to you. All rooms are air conditioned and have color cable tv with HBO. Larger units have microwave ovens and refrigerators. Six new units opened last season. There's a pool, a large hot tub, basketball hoop and horseshoe pit.

The Ebbtide Restaurant, on the property, serves breakfast, lunch and dinner. They have a wine & beer license and run a small convenience store, too.

The motel is open March through November.

JOHN YANCEY MOTOR HOTEL

Beach Road, MP 10   441-7141
$$$-$$$$ 800-367-5941

Most major credit cards

The John Yancey is a bright, cheery motor hotel, affiliated with Quality Inns, and located directly on the water's edge. Recreation

THE EBB TIDE

Family Motel and Restaurant

Mile Post 10½ on the Beach Road

Single and Double Rooms • HBO
Refrigerators and Microwaves
Beach Front Cottages
Swimming Pool and Jacuzzi
Restaurant Serving:
Breakfast, Lunch and Dinner

(919) 441-4913

VISA and MasterCard Accepted

is their strong suit. In addition to 320 feet of sandy beach -- guarded during the summer months by the Beach Service -- for sunning, frolicking and surf fishing, there is a large pool, playground, and shuffleboard courts.

There are standard rooms, efficiencies and family units, all with color cable tv and pay-per-view in-room movies and small refrigerators.

For the 1990 season, the main motel building was totally remodeled (this included nearly all their efficiencies and many of the standard rooms). We're not talking just new bedspreads here. They stripped the rooms down, replaced the plumbing, lighting -- everything -- so that these rooms are really like new. There are now three extra-special, super deluxe rooms that have their own private hot tubs.

Children under 12 stay free. Rollaway beds and cribs can be rented to accommodate extra children.

The John Yancey is open all year.

NAGS HEAD NORTH
ACCOMMODATIONS

BEACON MOTOR LODGE
Beach Road, MP 11   441-5501

$$ Most major credit cards

The Beacon is a large 48-unit property with many accommodation options for their family-oriented clientele. The three wings of the motor lodge contain large one room efficiencies, two and three room apartments, and motel-type rooms with various sleeping arrangements. Some rooms have a tile shower, no tub. All are equipped with a small refrigerator and phones. The oceanfront rooms open onto a large walled beachfront terrace which is lit at night. There are areas with furniture on the terrace where all guests may take in the breezy view of the ocean.

A center courtyard and recreation area is cleverly screened from the highway. Amenities include a landscaped and lighted patio with charcoal grills, large raised pool, two children's pools, playground, electronic game room, and coin-operated laundromat.

Beacon Motor Lodge is open Easter through October.

OCEAN VERANDA

Beach Road, MP 11					441-5858

$-$$						MC, VISA, AMEX

The large two-story rectangular building of the Ocean Veranda sets perpendicular to the ocean with wide galleries running the full length of both sides. Comfortable outdoor furniture on the porches is a nice guest convenience. On the highway end of the building there is an attractive raised pool and deck. Two poolside gazebos can be retreats from the sun or evening conversation nooks.

Rooms here are large and well maintained. They have 2 double beds, AC, a small refrigerator, and color cable tv. Efficiencies have complete kitchens, 2 double beds, and can connect with regular rooms to accommodate large families. Free morning coffee is served in the motel office.

Ocean Veranda is open March through November. The location is in the heart of the resort area and has direct access to the beach. There are picnic tables near the beach, and an observation deck on the dunes for guest use.

NAGS HEAD INN

Beach Road, MP 14					441-0454
							1-800-327-8881

$$$$						MC, VISA, AMEX

The stylish, contemporary white stucco exterior with blue accents of Nags Head's newest motel contrasts sharply with the old-style cottage that has dominated this section of the beach for years. Aside from that, it's an attractive building that features covered parking on the ground floor. Tastefully decorated rooms start on the second floor of this five-story midrise, giving all guests either an ocean or sound view. Each room has a small refrigerator and color cable tv with HBO. There's a heated all-weather pool and spa on a second floor deck that's open all year.

The Inn is open all year.

NAGS HEAD SOUTH
ACCOMMODATIONS

SILVER SANDS MOTEL
Beach Road, MP 14   441-7354

$-$$ MC, VISA

The Silver Sands is one of the few Nags Head motels not located on the ocean side of the highway, but there is public beach access right across the street.

Over the past two years, the small motel has undergone a major facelift. It looks nice from the outside, and the inside won't disappoint. Rooms have color cable TV with HBO, refrigerators and air conditioning. Pine paneling is complemented with bright blue and white spreads and curtains. There are 10 rooms in a newer, two-story building where the second floor rooms have private balconies and an oceanview.

Sixteen units are in an adjacent single-story red brick building which faces the swimming pool. The rooms in this building have showers only.

The motel is open from Easter until first of December.

SURF SIDE MOTEL
Beach Road, MP 16   441-2105

$$$ 800-552-SURF

The Surf Side Motel is a very attractive, newer motel located right on the oceanfront. It's one of the nicest accommodations on the beach, and far from being the most expensive. In the 5-story main building, 60 rooms are large and beautifully furnished. All feature private balconies with views of the ocean (some even have sound views too), phones, color cable tv, and air conditioning. Some rooms -- like the honeymoon suites, which also feature king-size beds and private Jacuzzis -- have refrigerators.

A new 3-story, 16 unit building was completed last year that houses an indoor pool, oceanfront rooms and efficiencies. These new rooms also have either ocean or sound views, and HBO comes with the cable in this building.

Surf Side Motel

Oceanfront

- Efficiencies
- Indoor and Outdoor Pools
- Private Balconies

Charter Boat Available
"The Surf Side"
at Oregon Inlet Fishing Center

On the ocean at Milepost 16

1-800-552-SURF

P.O. Box 400
Nags Head, NC 27959
(919)441-2105

Each morning, complimentary coffee and donuts are served in the lobby and a wine and cheese social hour is held every afternoon for guests.

In addition to the new indoor pool, the Surf Side also has a large outdoor pool on the south side, that offers views of both the ocean and sound from its deck. The beach is guarded by the beach lifeguard service during the summer.

Surf Side is open all year.

BLUE HERON MOTEL

Beach Road, MP 16   441-7447

$$ MC, VISA

The Blue Heron has been owned by the Gladden family since 1969. Wilma Gladden and her son, Jim, live on the premises and are active in the day-to-day management of the property.

This reasonably priced, oceanfront motel with its indoor year 'round swimming pool is one of the best kept secrets on the Outer Banks. It's surprizing how many locals don't know about it. Based on what we've seen and heard, it's a secret worth sharing. We think you'll find it to be an excellent value.

Rooms and efficiencies are comfortable and clean. All have individually controlled air conditioning and heat, refrigerators and coffee pots, color cable tv, and shower/tub combinations. Efficiencies have fully-equipped kitchens.

Open all year.

ISLANDER MOTEL

Beach Road, MP 16   441-6229

$$$ MC, VISA, AMEX

Ed Thompson has made the Islander one of the more attractive and unusual small properties on the resort strip. Although the buildings date from 1973, the extensive landscaping, attentive maintenance, and a regular room refurbishing program have kept this motel from showing its age.

The two 3-story square buildings were constructed so as to meet at the apex of a respective corner. The unusual configuration gives every room a view and creates a number of semi-private patios which have been enhanced by landscaping, and furniture. The rooms on the second and third levels have glass enclosed balconies with large sliding windows.

Rooms here are large with space for a seating area. The coordinated decors and room accessories show good taste. A refrigerator is provided in all rooms. Kitchenettes are available in first floor accommodations. Most units have two double beds, some offer queen size.

An attractive dune-top pool has been added on the south side of the complex. A ramp at the rear of the property leads over the dunes to the ocean beach. The location is convenient to all the restaurants and attractions of South Nags Head.

The Islander is open April through October.

SEA FOAM MOTEL

Beach Road, MP 16   441-7320

$$ MC, VISA, AMEX

Jackie O'Neal is justifiably proud that her 29 motel-type guest rooms, 18 efficiencies, and two cottages attract so many repeat visitors each season. The well-kept red brick, white railing and aqua blue trimmed Sea Foam has single and bi-level units with oceanfront and poolside views. Parking is around the center courtyard where a large raised pool, sundeck, children's playground, and shuffleboard are available for recreation.

There is a gazebo on the beach where guests can meet to enjoy the sea breezes. A lot of work was done over the winter: all the tastefully furnished, air conditioned rooms now have color cable tv with HBO, refrigerators and phones. Five rooms were totally refurbished with king-size beds. Microwaves were added to the efficiencies. And the two cottages were completely renovated. Oceanfront rooms have picture windows, and all units have balconies or porches equipped with outdoor furniture.

The location is within walking distance of several good restaurants, and the Nags Head Fishing Pier. Open March through November.

OWENS' MOTEL

Beach Road, MP 16   441-6361

$$ MC, VISA, AMEX

The Owens' family has been in the same location for over 40 seasons and was one of the first motels on the beach. It is adjacent to the excellent Owens' Restaurant (see write-up under Restaurants), and near Jennette's Pier in an older, and somewhat congested, part of the Nags Head beach strip. The congestion is a relative thing: If you're accustomed to beach resorts along the Maryland shore, for example, this will seem like you're out in the country. There are a lot of shops and services nearby.

The Owens' have earned an excellent reputation for service and value. If you're looking for a reliable, family-oriented, no- frills beachfront motel, this would be a good choice.

A three-story oceanfront addition was added to the strip of single level oceanside motel units in 1981. An additional ten motel units are located on the westside of the beach highway. These rooms were remodeled for the '89 season. An oceanfront pavillion and rocking chairs on an open platform are available for guest enjoyment.

This is a good no-frills motelAll the oceanfront accommodations are efficiencies with large, private balconies. Each room has two double beds, tile bath and shower, and electric kitchen.

The motel swimming pool on the west side. All units have color cable TV and air conditioning. Open April through October.

SEA OATEL

Beach Road, MP 16 1/2　　　　　　　　　　　441-7191

$$$　　　　　　　　　　　Most major credit cards

This year 'round Quality Inn has a prime location near good restaurants, recreational activities, and it is also convenient to the historical attractions on Roanoke Island.

Its 111 units are divided between a three-story low-rise (with elevator), a two-story similar pink brick structure, a few drive-up one-story rooms adjacent to the pool and patio, and an across-the-street annex. The rooms in the main buildings (62 in all) have balconies on the oceanfront.

The Sea Oatel has 400 feet of ocean frontage, and there is a sheltered cabana on the beach which can be romantic for sun rises, or just a place to sit out of the sun with a cool drink to enjoy the view.

This is a well-kept property. The lobby and rooms are kept fresh and appealing with consistent painting and refurnishing. Room decors conform to high Quality Inn standards and all have AC, phones and color cable tv with HBO. There's a coin-operated laundry and a restaurant on the premises. Snack and ice facilities are plentiful, and there is even a"Hospitality Room" with TV, phone and card table. The front desk is open 24 hours and complimentary coffee is served in the mornings.

Open all year.

ROANOKE ISLAND
ACCOMMODATIONS

ELIZABETHAN INN
Rt. 64, Manteo   473-2101
$$-$$$ Most major credit cards

With the addition of their Nautics Hall fitness center, the Elizabethan Inn joined the league of big city hotels in terms of amenities, and our guess is that many vacationers will opt to stay here in Manteo, rather than on the beach, because of the excellent sports facilities. If you're coming to the Outer Banks off-season, it could be an especially smart choice.

They offer a variety of rooms and prices. The least expensive rooms are in an older part of the motel right off the highway. These rooms are clean and have color cable tv, refrigerators and phones, but they are small and have not been refurbished in some time.

Adjacent to these older rooms is the two-story Center Court, the newest building which also houses Nautics Hall and the restaurant.

Behind the Center Court building is the Elizabethan Manor, designed to resemble a 16th century Tudor Inn. The shaded pine wood setting and the off highway privacy has a romantic feel. These units overlook the outdoor pool and an attractive picnic and garden area. All these rooms have phones, color cable tv with free HBO, and refrigerators.

All guests can use the Nautics Hall facilties which include an indoor, competition-size, heated pool, a Nautilus workout room, aerobics equipment, whirlpool and sauna. For a small fee, you can also use the racquetball court or suntanning room.

The Elizabethan Inn is open all year.

SCARBOROUGH INN
Hwy. 64, Manteo   473-3979
$ Most major credit cards

Sally Scarborough had a dream for at least 15 years. Born in downtown Manteo, she carried the image of a country inn that she encountered in her childhood. It was not until her husband, Phil, a Wanchese native and Coast Guard officer, retired that she was able to hope that her dream might become a reality.

Today Scarborough Inn is a reality on Highway 64 across from The Christmas Shop. Architecturally, it is a period piece from a bygone era. It is a two story reproduction of a turn-of-the-century inn, designed by architect John Wilson, IV. Sally, an accomplished furniture refinisher, has filled each of the guest rooms with collectibles and antiques.

Most of the items have a story that includes some Outer Banks history, and when Sally shows you to your room, she most likely will tell you about it. Bathroom doors, for example, were saved from a decaying island church. Most of the bed frames are antiques, and one once framed the birth bed of her mother. Some of the chests, chairs and dressing tables date from the 1800s and are in beautiful condition. Old Singer Sewing Machine cabinets have been pressed into service as tv stands. On the porches you'll find Carolina rockers for outdoor relaxing.

There are rooms and suites, including four units -- remodeled for the 1990 season, with all the bedrooms now off the street side for more privacy -- in a building next door. All the rooms at the Scarborough Inn are comfortably large and have phones, color cable tv (the suites have remote control TV), air conditioning, private baths, a small refrigerator and a coffee pot. Some of the rooms have a wet bar. Sally will stock your refrigerator on request. Complimentary morning coffee and donuts are served in the parlor.

Scarborough Inn

FOR RESERVATIONS WRITE OR CALL:

P.O. BOX 1310

HIGHWAY 64-264

MANTEO, NC 27954

(919) 473-3979

☆ 10 rooms with antique furnishings

☆ Private Baths

☆ Color TV, refrigerator and telephone

☆ Moderately priced

☆ Separate Annex

☆ Two pots of coffee in your room

All in all the Scarborough Inn is a charming accommodation that the discriminating traveler will appreciate. The room rates are very reasonable, especially considering the care and attention the owners give in making sure your visit is a pleasant one.

DUKE OF DARE MOTOR LODGE

Manteo   473-2175

$ MC, VISA

The Duke of Dare is located on the main highway just a few blocks from the Manteo waterfront. Shopping and laundromats are right next door, on the other side of a small pine woods. This is basic accommodations, nothing fancy. But the brick, bi-level, L-shaped motor lodge, trimmed in sky blue and yellow, is clean and has all the standard modern motel features, including phones and color cable tv. Some rooms have queen size beds.

If you're looking for inexpensive family accommodations, the Creef family, who have owned and managed the motel for over 20 years, will make you feel welcome.

Open all year.

TRANQUIL HOUSE INN

Manteo   473-1404

    800-458-7069

$$$ Most major credit cards

Tranquil House Inn is a lovely 28-room bed and breakfast inn is located on Shallowbag Bay in downtown Manteo. It's named after a famous home that stood in, roughly, this location from 1860 until sometime after 1951.

Hospitality and gracious surroundings are the rule here. You'll find fresh flowers and a bottle of wine awaiting your arrival.

Each wallpapered room is large, with a sitting area and private bath. No two rooms are alike, but each is furnished comfortably. Many have canopied or four-poster beds. All have color cable tv with HBO and a phone. A complimentary continental breakfast is served and guests can arrange to have meals brought to their rooms from nearby downtown restaurants. During the summer, evening babysitting will be provided if you'd like an evening out without the children.

Long porches overlooking the bay and *Elizabeth II* sailing ship provide a most comfortable place to relax. "Downtown" in Manteo means the opportunity to observe the locals... browse through some really special shops... borrow one of the Inn's bicycles and pedal through the Mother Vineyard area of the island... go to the movies at a wonderful old theater right down the street that still sells candy and sodas for a quarter. You can take the "Manteo Walking Tour" and get acquainted with the architecture and history of the town. Or, you can sit on the docks and watch brown pelicans dive for a mid-day snack. When you run out of other ways to relax, you can always visit the Inn's library and curl up with a good book.

If you like to travel by boat, Tranquil House Inn is a perfect destination. The marina is right at the back door and the Inn can arrange a rental car or provide transportation for you.

Tranquil House is open all year.

HATTERAS ISLAND
ACCOMMODATIONS

CAPE HATTERAS MOTEL

Buxton   995-5611

$$$-$$$$ MC, VISA, AMEX

Cape Hatteras Motel been here for over thirty years, although many of its units are new. Owners Carol and Dave Dawson have managed to keep some of the motel's old appeal and its old customers -- the families and fishermen who come primarily for the beach -- while branching out and attracting a whole new crowd -- the windsurfers who come to sail on the sound at the popular Canadian Hole, right up the road.

Modern efficiencies overlooking a lighted tennis court and the Pamlico Sound are on the west side of the highway. On the ocean, new townhouses and apartment units have been added in the last year. Older, standard motel rooms and two-story, two-bedroom duplex cottages are on the east side of the oceanfront property.

A standard room has a refrigerator and a coffee pot. Some of the new efficiencies have king sized beds, although the furnishings are spartan and made for indestructibility rather than comfort. We suspect that the outdoor enthusiasts who choose this recreation-oriented motel don't even mind; in fact, they may welcome not having to worry about ruining the sofa.

In addition to the tennis court, there is a swimming pool, heated Jacuzzi and a kiddie pool. Guest conveniences like beach umbrellas, lighted fish cleaning stations and rentals of tennis racquets and balls have helped establish this motel's popularity. Restaurants and shopping are nearby. In season you'll need to make your reservations well in advance.

The Dawsons also own a sailboard and surfing store adjacent to the motel where guests can rent equipment or arrange for lessons.

The motel is open all year.

HATTERAS ISLAND MOTEL

Rodanthe   987-2345
1-800-331-6541 (out of state)
1-800-682-2289 (in state)
$$ MC, VISA, AMEX

This 25-acre vacation complex on the oceanfront includes 32 motel-type rooms and efficiencies in a large double decked oceanside

---

cape hatteras motel buxton, nc

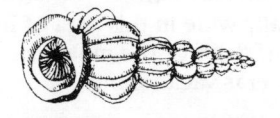

on the ocean
lighted tennis courts
swimming pool with spa
fully equipped cooking units
cable tv
AAA

PO Box 399, Buxton, NC 27920   (919)995-5611

building (plus a few single level oceanfront units), and 35 two-, three-, and four-bedroom cottages arranged in two clusters on the property. All units have color cable tv and are comfortably furnished.

The big attraction here is the Hatteras Island Fishing Pier at the head of the resort property. There is also a large swimming pool and children's pool with slide, patio, and restaurant in the complex.

For the 1990 season, the motel will be open at least from April through December, possibly longer.

OUTER BANKS MOTEL

Buxton 995-5601

$-$$ MC, VISA, AMEX

Carol Dillon maintains a very nice older motel property right next door to the Cape Hatteras Motel. She says that ninety percent of her guests come back year after year, and it's easy to see why.

Rooms are pine paneled, carpeted, and show extra care in decor. Baths are tiled. There are efficiency units, and two- and three-bedroom cottages and beachfront houses. The cottages and houses are restricted to weekly rentals in-season. All the units have air conditioning and color cable tv with HBO. Screened porches make for pleasant siestas in the evening.

A raised pool with hot tub and a coin operated laundry are also available for guest use. There are a lot of extras here. A fish cleaning station is provided as well as a guest freezer for storage. Three rowboats on a southside creek across the highway are also available free of charge to guests for crabbing and fishing.

The beach is especially wide in this area of Buxton, and it's one of the best areas for surf fishing. The motel is open year round. It's a good choice for Hatteras vacationing.

LIGHTHOUSE VIEW

Buxton 995-5680

1-800-225-7651

$$ MC, VISA

The Hooper family operates this growing motel and cottage property that has been serving Hatteras vacationers for over 35 years. There are interesting two-bedroom, two-bath round-shaped beachfront

Lighthouse View

OCEANFRONT
CABLE TV
POOL, SPA

MOTEL
COTTAGES
VILLAS

P.O. BOX 39 BUXTON, NC 27920 (919) 995-5680
1-800-225-7651

cottages in addition to standard motel rooms, one- and two-bedroom efficiencies and new oceanfront villas. Seven rooms have king-sized beds.

There are so many different choices that we can't describe them all. You can count on Lighthouse View to have whatever living arrangements you might need. Older rooms and efficiencies have all been comfortably refurbished and maintained. The round duplex cottages, which rent by the week only, are somewhat newer, roomy and also in very good condition.

The newest building, the Villas, opened two years ago are more like upscale studio apartments. They offer well-designed and nicely decorated living space with full kitchens -- including dishwashers!

All the units have color cable tv and air conditioning. There's an oceanfront pool and Jacuzzi. The location is convenient for fishermen and windsurfers.

Open from all year.

FALCON

Buxton 995-5968
$ MC, VISA

We've looked at many motels and, in our opinion, The Falcon has offered the best, inexpensive accommodations on the Outer Banks for several years. The motel was sold to Hatteras resident Doug Meekins this year, and he says he plans to continue courting the quiet, family-oriented guests that come back year after year.

The motel houses 35 units in a neat, sand-colored, brick building that stretches from the highway to a small creek on the sound. The wide paved drive provides parking at your door. The motel is centrally located, within easy walking distance to several restaurants and shopping and less than a mile from the beach.

Falcon Motel

35 MODERN UNITS
"1/2 Mile from Cape Hatteras Lighthouse"
CABLE COLOR TV - AIR CONDITIONED
SWIMMING POOL - EFFICIENCY APTS.
SPACIOUS ROOMS
QUIET FRIENDLY ATMOSPHERE

P.O. Box 633
BUXTON, NC 27920

AAA

Phone 995-5968
or 1-800-635-6911

Rooms are wood paneled and reflect a functional, yet comfortable, approach to decor. Some have refrigerators. There are also one and two bedroom apartments that rent weekly during the season. All have color cable tv. The thing that is remarkable about these rooms is that, while they're not new, they look and feel really clean, like they've been taken care of with a lot of pride. Meekins plans to refurbish the rooms over the winter; new furniture and a lighter, more modern decor are in store. A swimming pool and a boat ramp are the added amenities.

The Falcon has traditionally been open March through mid-December. Meekins is thinking about staying open all year, starting with the 1990 season.

TOWER CIRCLE MOTEL

Buxton   995-5353

$ No credit cards

A real fisherman's hideaway in the fall and spring, and family retreat in the summer, this well-maintained motel run by Jack and Mary Gray is near the Hatteras Lighthouse. Turn off Highway 12 onto Old Lighthouse Road and look for all the guests sitting on the porch swapping fish stories.

In the nineteen years the Grays have owned this motel, they've built a good following. You'll find that most of the guests have stayed with them before. This is an older property with juniper panelling in the rooms and modest furnishings, including color cable tv and heat/ac, give the place a homey atmosphere. There are thirteen motel rooms and 17 efficiencies.

Tower Circle is open April through November. It's located just a short walk over the dune line from the beach and some of the best surf fishing around. Stores and restaurants are a short drive away.

CAPE PINES MOTEL

Buxton   995-5666

$ MC, VISA

Steve and Hazen Totton, who moved here from Downers Grove, Illinois, after vacationing in Buxton for nearly 30 years, bought this property before the 1988 season. It had been sliding into a state of disrepair for several years but this energetic couple -- along with their daughter and son-in-law, who they convinced to manage the place for them -- has turned the motel around.

It's very inviting and another good value. Red brick efficiency units trimmed in white surround a pool area and lawn where you'll find picnic tables and charcoal grills. Standard rooms are in a separate building next to the efficiencies. A colorful profusion of flowers brightens the entire property.

The motel offers rooms, some with refrigerators, and fully-equipped efficiencies. Microwaves can be rented through the office. Most of the accommodations here have been upgraded. The efficiencies, which were totally refurbished for the '89 season, are thoroughly modern, light and attractive. Standard rooms are being decorated to minimize the dark panelling and furniture. All units have air conditioning and color cable tv.

In addition to the pool, there's a pay phone on the premises and a fish cleaning table. The Cape Hatteras Supermarket is right across the street and other stores, restaurants and a laundromat are nearby.

CAPE PINES MOTEL

Post Office Box 279
BUXTON, NORTH CAROLINA 27920
919-995-5666

- **Lighted Swimming Pool — Cable TV — A/C Rooms and Efficiency Apartments.**
- **Barbecues — Picnic Tables — Refrigerators and Microwaves available for rent.**

With this Ad - Stay one week (7 nights) for the price of 5 nights
With Guaranteed Reservations Only
Offer Expires 12-31-90

DURANT MOTEL

Hatteras   986-2244
$$ MC, VISA

Durant Motel is located on the site of the old Durant Lifesaving Station. One of the buildings, in fact, was part of the station and has been refurbished as a large guest house. The other buildings, housing small apartments, are also old Hatteras landmarks.

The motel is actually a condominium, with each apartment individually owned and furnished. Needless to say, they're all different, but if the five units we inspected are typical, you'll find the furnishings contemporary and comfortable. Most feature living/kitchen "great rooms" with separate bedrooms and baths.

Capt. Lloyd Styron, a retired Coast Guard man, whose father, grandfather and uncle all worked at Durant Station, took us through the old two-story Lifesaving building this past spring. It's been modernized enough to be comfortable without disturbing its true character. The large boat room with its polished wood floor, still has the hooks in the ceiling that once held the life car. Capt. Lloyd related how he'd played many a hand of cards in this room. Upstairs, he pointed out the room where his uncle had slept while serving at Durant. You can still climb into the lookout at the top of the stairs.

The old station now has three inter-connecting apartments that can be rented individually or together.

All guests at Durant Motel have use of the outdoor pool. The beach is just over the dunes. Restaurants and limited shopping is nearby.

The motel is open from Easter through November.

GENERAL MITCHELL MOTEL

Hatteras   986-2444
$ MC, VISA

The General Mitchell was named for "Billy" Mitchell, the young U.S. Air Service colonel who directed the sinking of two retired battle ships off Hatteras to prove the potential of air power. The 30 year old motel is typical of Hatteras accommodations which place function over style. It does have an outdoor pool and Jacuzzi -- two concessions to today's accommodations market. But the General Mitchell is primarily a lodging for those who want to enjoy the exceptional fishing, hunting and beaches the area has to offer.

Fishermen are catered to here, with a lighted fish cleaning table and freezer storage for surf catches. You can call ahead and get a fishing report, too.

Two two-story buildings offer rooms and efficiencies that accommodate from two to four persons. They are clean and well kept, with air conditioning and color cable tv.

The General Mitchell is open year 'round. Restaurants are close by.

ATLANTIC VIEW MOTEL

Hatteras 986-2323

$ MC, VISA, AMEX

Two brothers, Ray and Hal Gray, built the Atlantic View twelve years ago. The office for this California-style block building is on the highway, but the motel itself isn't visible from the road. It sits several hundred feet down a drive, screened by trees, on a large, grassy tract. Sandy footpaths lead off to the beach which is a three or four minute walk away. This is one of only a few motels on Hatteras Island that aren't right on the main road. The park-like setting makes it especially nice for families with small children. There's a nice pool, too, with a slide that the kids love, and a kiddie pool. (One caution about the pool: when we were there last fall, the exposed aggregate around the pool was very rough. Wear shoes.)

The rooms are showing their age, but they are clean and comfortable. The Gray brothers cater to small families (no room can have over 4 people, although some rooms interconnect to accommodate larger groups). For a quiet, family vacation on a tight budget, this motel is a good choice.

One word about the name. The motel rooms do not have an "Atlantic view." There was an old hotel nearby called the Atlantic View which the brothers owned when they built this motel. Originally both properties operated under that name. The old hotel, built over sixty years ago, before the government built the dunes, did indeed have a view of the Atlantic. The hotel is gone, but the name lives on.

HATTERAS MARLIN MOTEL

Hatteras 986-2141

$-$$ MC, VISA

The Midgett family, a name well-known in Hatteras Lifesaving Station lore, operates this motel in the center of activity at Hatteras Village. The location is within sight of the harbor fishing fleet and village restaurants and shops.

There are 40 units in three buildings including standard motel rooms and one- and two-bedroom efficiencies. Two new two-bedroom apartments have been built where older guest cottages used to be, near the back of the property.

The older buildings are close to the highway and face the parking lot shared by the Midgett's gas station and convenience store.

The newest building is at the back of the property and can't be seen from the highway. It is situated along the canal, surrounded by grassy open areas that are often filled with ducks preening in the sun. Ask if one of these rooms is available.

Rooms in all three buildings are furnished alike. While the location of the newer building is more desirable, we think, it's nearly impossible to tell the difference in the rooms themselves because they have been so well maintained. All have color cable tv and air conditioning. There's a pool and sundeck.

Hatteras Marlin is open all year.

Riding the Hatteras-Ocracoke ferries is a special part of a trip to Ocracoke. DCTB

THE ANCHORAGE INN

Beautiful Rooms with A View of the Harbor and Village • Boat dock and ramp • Efficiencies • Pool • Free Continental breakfast • Room phone and free movies

P.O. Box 130 • Ocracoke, NC 27960 •
(919) 928-1581

Princess Waterfront Motel

**Beautiful Rooms with A View of the Harbor and Village
Boat Dock and Ramp · Efficiencies · Pool ·
Free Continental Breakfast · Room phone and free movies**

P.O. Box 157 · Ocracoke, NC 27960
(919) 928-6461

OCRACOKE
ACCOMMODATIONS

ANCHORAGE INN

Ocracoke $\qquad$ 928-1101

$$$ $\qquad$ MC, VISA

Built as a three story motel on the harbor in 1982, the Anchorage kept growing... up. Two more floors were added in 1985, providing a top floor penthouse for owners Scott and Kathy Cottrell. The fourth floor was opened for the 1989 season. It's a no-smoking floor and all the rooms on this floor have king-sized beds. An elevator -- the only one of the island, we think -- services all four floors.

This is a very attractive brick and concrete structure, although its presence among the older buildings in this little village was unsettling at first. As other modern buildings go up around the harbor, it doesn't look quite so out of place.

All rooms at the Inn have a view across Silver Lake. From the third and fourth floors, especially, the view of the village and harbor is beautiful.

PONY ISLAND MOTEL

Ocracoke $\qquad$ 928-4411

$-$$ $\qquad$ MC, VISA

David and Jen Esham host guests at this long-established motel on the island. It is located just off the main highway at the edge of the village, but close enough to easily walk to the harbor. Rooms are clean and simple, but nicely furnished. The property includes a large lawn area with picnic tables, an outdoor pool and plenty of room for family recreation. The motel even has bicycles for rent.

Efficiencies and cottages are available in addition to the standard motel rooms. Open March through November, Pony Island offers color cable tv with Showtime.

The Pony Island Inn restaurant is right next door.

EDWARDS MOTEL

Ocracoke 928-4801

$ MC, VISA

The Edwards Motel, off the beaten path, is one of the oldest motels on the island. It's owned by Ruth and David Sams, who bought it from Ruth's sister, Mary, and her husband Bernie Edwards. Between them, the family has owned it for nearly 25 years.

It's not really a motel, in the traditional sense of the word. It reminds us more of an old fashioned summer resort, with its 13 units spread out over an acre or two. There's a cluster of cottages in one spot, surrounded by pines and opening onto a grassy yard with lawn chairs and picnic tables. These units have screened porches; some are efficiencies; others are like a house, with living rooms, bedrooms and full kitchens. Across the way, there's a building with a few rooms and efficiencies that open onto a veranda. The office is in a house, surrounded by a nice yard and colorful flower beds.

This is one of those places that doesn't offer anything fancy, but has dependable, inexpensive accommodations especially suited to families on a budget.

Open Easter weekend through the end of November.

PRINCESS WATERFRONT MOTEL

Ocracoke 928-6461

$$$

MC, VISA

This motel offers second floor efficiency apartment units only (they're situated over retail space). They were opened in 1988 by Scott and Kathy Cottrell, who also own the Anchorage Inn less than a block down the street. While the building does sit on the edge of Silver Lake, it runs perpendicular to the waterfront so you don't have a full-face view of the harbor from your window.

Each unit is one large room, with a full kitchen, attractive modern furnishings, phone and remote-control color cable tv with Showtime. Occupancy in all the units is limited to two adults and no children. There's a private dock and guests have pool privileges at the Anchorage Inn pool.

If you want more space than a standard motel room provides, and the kitchen is appealing, these are an affordable alternative to other Island accommodations.

OSCAR'S HOUSE

Ocracoke								928-1311
$-$$									MC, VISA

This delightful bed and breakfast guest house is run by Ann Ehringhaus, a local fine art photographer and author of *Ocracoke Portrait* published in 1988.

Built in 1940 by the Ocracoke lighthouse keeper, Oscar's House was actually first occupied by the World War II Naval Commander for the Ocracoke Naval Base. Oscar, for whom the house is named, lived here and worked for years on the island as a fisherman and hunting guide. Many stories have survived Oscar: he loved a good time. And we think you'll have a good time at Oscar's House, too.

There are three air-conditioned rooms -- plus a loft which can be rented with the upstairs bedroom -- in this cozy home located on the highway. No smoking is allowed in the bedrooms, which feature the original beaded board walls and some very nice decorating touches. The large open kitchen with it's big table is available to guests, as well as use of the refrigerator. The stove is off-limits, however.

A large deck area opens on to a small, private yard where you'll find a bike rack and an outdoor shower and dressing room. There's outdoor dining room, too, walled in with the painted sets from Ocracoke School's production of "The Sound of Music," an eccentric but engaging touch that's sure to add atmosphere to meals eaten alfresco.

The harbor and village are within walking distance. Ann serves a full -- not continental -- breakfast to guests. She's happy to accommodate special preferences including vegetarian and macrobiotic diets.

Oscar's House is open, usually, from April to October.

BOYETTE HOUSE

Ocracoke								928-4261
$-$$									MC, VISA

This attractive motel, opened in 1981, is named for a pioneer in Ocracoke hospitality who began to host guests as early as 1941. The 12 unit, two story natural wood structure has wide upper and lower decks in front of the rooms where you'll find rocking chairs for reading and relaxing. A nice sun deck at the back of the building is perfect for sunbathing.

THE Boyette House
A Tradition in INNKEEPING

Ocracoke Island
Ocracoke, North Carolina

919-928-4261
Lanie Boyette Wynn

All the conveniences of a modern motel...
Attractive comfortable rooms
Color television
Tub and shower
Coffee Bar

...the friendly, informal atmosphere of an old inn.
Porches with rocking chairs
Spacious lobby
Library
Sundeck

The Boyette House provides the atmosphere of a bed and breakfast house but is actually a modern, comfortable motel. Each room has a private bath, two double beds, and color cable tv with Showtime. The lobby is set up like a comfortable sitting room and bookshelves offer a selection of reading material for guests to borrow.

The Boyette House is open all year and within walking distance of Silver Lake and most restaurants on the island. They will pick you up at the boat docks or the airport, too, free of charge.

ISLAND INN

Ocracoke 928-4351
$$ MC, VISA

Built as an Odd Fellows Lodge in 1901, the Island Inn has briefly served as a school, a private residence, and Naval officers quarters. It was restored by former owners Foy Shaw and Larry Williams to the point of being recognized in *Country Inns of the Old South*, and *Country Inns, Lodges, and Historic Hotels of the South*. The Inn was purchased just before the 1990 season by two couples, Bob and Cee Touhey and Buffy and Ann Warner, who have recently moved to the island after years of vacationing here. Their goal, at this point, says Cee, is to upgrade the furnishings and give the Inn a facelift; no major changes are planned.

The Inn provides a variety of accommodations to suit many tastes. There are one-of-a-kind rooms on the second floor of the old main building which also houses the Island Inn Restaurant. All have been refurbished and each is like a guest room in a private home. Antiques, quilts and other homey touches make them very liveable. There are three suites with sitting rooms, also. On the third floor is the Crow's Nest, a private hideaway, with king-sized beds and cypress cathedral ceilings.

Children aren't allowed to stay in the old Inn, but they're welcome in the Stanley Wahab wing, named for the man who established the Inn at this location in the 1940s. It's a 19 unit double decked structure of modern motel rooms, including two honeymoon rooms with king-sized beds and bay windows affording romantic sunset views. You'll find rockers on the porchs and a heated swimming pool which they keep open as long as weather permits. The Inn also rents a two bedroom cottage on the grounds.

The new owners are planning to keep the Inn open all year.

PIRATES QUAY

Ocracoke   928-1921

$$$$ MC, VISA

Jo Everhart manages this extraordinary hotel that sits directly on Silver Lake across from the Coast Guard Station. It opened in 1987 and may be the most luxurious accommodation available on a nightly basis anywhere on the Outer Banks.

The hotel is made up of six individually-owned suites, each with living room, dining room, full kitchen, one- or two-bedrooms and a bath-and-a-half. Units on the top floor have cathedral ceilings. Two decks off each suite, a waterfront gazebo and docking facilities make the most of the harborfront location.

Each accommodates up to four adults and one or two children and has a jacuzzi bath, color cable tv with Showtime and central air conditioning. All are beautifully furnished and kitchens are completely stocked with all the dishes and cookware and gadgets you need, although each unit is completely different, based on the taste of the owner. The suites accommodate up to four adults and one or two children. There is a laundry on the premises.

SILVER LAKE MOTEL

Ocracoke   928-5721

$$ MC, VISA, AMEX

The Wrobleski family built that two-story, 20-room motel on the Ocracoke Harbor in 1983. They moved a house, cleared the site(carefully saving as many trees as possible), constructed the wooden double decked structure, paneled the rooms in California redwoods, and even built the upholstered redwood furniture and lamp tables. A new building, housing 12 suites and rooms that can be rented in various combinations, is still under construction was we go to press. It was scheduled to be completed for the 1989 season; some of the rooms are finished and can be rented now.

The older motel rooms have wallpapered bathrooms, louvered shutters, pine flooring and braided rugs that give them a pleasant, rustic character. All have color cable tv with Showtime and air conditioning.

There is a second floor guest lounge which serves beer, wine and soft drinks in the evenings. Its open air deck has an unobstructed view of the harbor. The building is on pilings so while it's technically just two stories to the top floor, you'll have three flights of stairs to climb.

The new units are a far cry from the rustic appeal of the original motel. Although the wood floors and use of wallpaper has been continued, the furnishings are much more elegant and substantial. Units

---

Silver Lake Motel

Nestled in a Grove of Oaks Overlooking Silver Lake
Enjoy the Spectacular View From Our Lounge

The Silver Lake Motel is a family operation.
"We Do Truly Care"

For Reservations call:
(919) 928-5721

P.O. Box 303
Ocracoke, NC 27960

have wet bars and full kitchens, remote control television, and private balconies. The end suites will each have their own private, 8-seat Jacuzzi situated so you can relax in the tub and look out over Silver Lake.

The Wrobleskis can provide a deep water dock for those guests wishing to arrive by boat.

The Silver Lake Motel offers family hospitality and attractive accommodations all year.

BLUFF SHOAL MOTEL

Ocracoke 928-4301
$$ MC, VISA

The seven units of this red brick property face the tree shaded main street in the village. The harbor, post office, community store, and many of the village's shops are practically right next door. The Pelican Restaurant is right across the street. The Bluff Shoal has a raised porch with comfortable wooden furniture for watching the island traffic go by. It's nothing fancy, but Mike and Kay Riddick take pride in keeping this motel well maintained and clean. It has everything you need to be comfortable, including color cable tv with Showtime and a small refrigerator in each room. All the units were refurbished for the 1990 season. They've been brightened up with light pickled panelling, new carpets and drapes. You can now get connecting rooms, too.

The property is open all year.

HARBORSIDE

Ocracoke 928-3111
$$ MC, VISA, AMEX

This bi-level motel sits right across from the Silver Lake Harbor on the main street of Ocracoke Village. It's close to the Swan Quarter and Cedar Island ferry docks and well situated for shopping and exploring the village on foot.

Harborside has been owned by the same family for over 20 years and their attractive accomodations and friendly service have earned them a mention in our book every year since we began publishing eleven years ago.

18 knotty cypress panelled rooms are well-maintained, with regular renovations that keep them fresh and comfortable. Four efficiencies are available. All rooms have color cable tv, and guests can use the

waterfront sun deck, docks and boat ramp right across the street. The motel office is also across the street, in the Harborside Gift Shop.

Harborside is open from Easter through mid-November.

SHIPS TIMBERS

Ocracoke 928-4061

$ MC, VISA

Ships Timbers is located in the center of the Village, down a gravel lane off the main road. The owner is Erik Mattsson, who describes himself as a "summer native."

Ship's Timbers rents three air conditioned rooms with a shared bath-and-a-half on a nightly basis. Weekly rentals are available. The 75 year-old house is on the National Register of Historic Places. It was built with lumber from the *Ida Lawrence*, a ship that washed ashore on Ocracoke Beach in 1902.

Mattsson has a special interest in water sports and caters to guests who enjoy kayaking, sailing and windsurfing. Many guests, though, are families who enjoy the convenient location and hospitable surroundings.

There is a large porch and yard which guests are welcome to use. Mattsson likes to serve a light, healthy breakfast -- fresh fruit, cheese, croissants -- but admits that when guests stay more than a couple days he'll whip up a batch of french toast or pancakes.

The house is open from March through December.

BERKLEY CENTER

Ocracoke 928-5911

$$ No credit cards

The Berkley Center is a beautifully landscaped, three-acre estate on the Ocracoke Harbor, directly adjacent to the Park Service and state ferry dock areas. The buildings date from the late 1950s, but the architecture and the cedar siding make them seem older. The size of the Manor House, with its broad rectangular tower, has led passersby to mistake it for a lifesaving station.

The Manor House contains guest rooms, the dining room, a first floor bar and lounge, and a tower card room and bar with exceptional views of the island and harbor. Additional rooms are rented in the Ranch House. These are large rooms, with nice touches like real closets and double sinks in the bathroom. All the rooms have what could be called the L. L. Bean look...simple, well-made and functional furnishings, with a classic look that was fashionable fifty years ago, is still today, and probably will continue to be.

Your room charge includes a good continental breakfast, usually consisting of fresh breads, real butter and preserves and hot coffee. It's a good chance for guests to mingle.

Ruth and Wesley ("Colonel") Egan, Sr. operate this relaxed and distinctive property. They pride themselves on helping guests enjoy the Island and can arrange for fishing boats and equipment, vehicles for marsh or beach exploration and hunting or fishing guides. It is open mid-March through mid-November.

BERKLEY CENTER COUNTRY INN
On The Ocracoke Harbor

"Casual elegance in an Outer Banks island estate setting"

- A/C and Heat
- Fishing trips arranged
- Group Meeting Rooms

Complimentary Continental Breakfast
Convenient to Restaurants & Shops

**Call or write for reservations
Box 220, Ocracoke, NC 27960
(919) 928-5911**

Ruth and Wes Egan, Owners

Even at the height of the season, a visitor can enjoy the solitude of a sunrise over the Atlantic Ocean. DCTB

OUTER BANKS
CAMPGROUNDS

Despite flourishing popularity, the 1989 season saw the closing of several Outer Banks campgrounds north of Oregon Inlet, most notably in the Colington and Duck areas. The skyrocketing value of land in Dare county dictates that the 90s will be the decade of increased luxury as opposed to simplicity in beach accommodations. It is sad to watch so many campgrounds closing; nevertheless, for those of us who like to get a little sand under our toenails, there are still some attractive choices.

Commercial campgrounds on the Banks currently run from around $9.00 to $16.00 a night, depending primarily on amenities provided. The NPS grounds, those on a first come first served basis, run from $10.00 to $12.00 a night. One note of caution: be sure to make reservations in advance. Demand far exceeds supply. If you're arriving without advance reservations in summer, we urge you to call ahead to find your spot as soon as you read these words. Good Luck.

NORTH OF OREGON INLET
CAMPGROUNDS

COLINGTON PARK CAMPGROUND
Colington   441-6128

This is a large campground on Colington Island and is very suitable for short-term visitors. Unlike most Beach sites Colington is wooded, making it more pleasant in summer. There are 50 sites, all with water and power, and picnic tables, along with hot showers, toilets, laundry, grocery, recreation room. Open all year.

OREGON INLET CAMPGROUND (NPS)
Bodie Island

The northernmost of the four National Park Service campgrounds on the Outer Banks, Oregon Inlet offers 120 delightfully primitive, flat, sandy, windswept, unshaded sites in the lee of the dunes at the south end of Bodie Island (to your left just before you start over the Oregon Inlet Bridge). There are no utility connections, but water, cold showers, toilets, picnic tables, and charcoal grills are available.

All the NPS campgrounds in the Banks operate under the same policy and charge the same fees, except for Ocracoke, which is on the Ticketron reservation system. See "Ocracoke" for an explanation. Oregon Inlet, like all Park Service campgrounds, is open from mid-spring to mid-fall, first come, first served.

The Park Service recommends that persons camping on their grounds bring shading materials, mosquito netting, and long tent stakes (for the sandy ground). Fee is $10.00 per night

During the summer season, you may call 441-6644 for information on any of the NPS campgrounds.

HATTERAS CAMPGROUNDS

Hatteras Island is the camping kingdom of the Outer Banks. There are literally dozens of campgrounds, many large, more of them small. Taken all together, they offer one of the finest areas for the tenter or the trailer camper to be found along the entire east coast of the United States.

The campgrounds covered here do not constitute a complete list of those operating on the island. As in all our listings in this book, we've tried to be selective, picking out for you the best places, and balancing this by looking for those that are different from the rest, offering distinctive camping experiences, locales, or services.

On Hatteras, for example, you'll find two basic kinds of campgrounds, surfside and sound side. The surfside campgrounds are located on the flat sand that is characteristic of most of Hatteras. There is usually little shade, plenty of wind and sun, and lots of sand. As we've noted elsewhere, for these you'll want to have sunscreen and long pegs to hold the tent down. The second kind is the sound side campground. These are located, for the most part, in the small forests of pine and live oak that line the sounds at the widest parts of Hatteras. They offer firmer ground, more shade, less wind; but, although the county is doing its best to control mosquitoes, they haunt the sound side woods in warm weather, especially in wet areas and after spells of rain (mosquitoes breed in freshwater pools). Also, in the wooded locations, you might want to read the section on ticks and chiggers in the Directory.

Whichever campground you choose, whether you camp in tent or trailer or even a mobile home, you'll find the kind of place you need on Hatteras. It's got variety, beauty, and closeness to nature -- and isn't that what camping is all about?

PEA ISLAND RESORT
Rodanthe   987-2318

Pea Island isn't like the other campgrounds in that it's not really open to the public. You have to join to be able to use the facilities, but once that is accomplished, you have access to a myriad of recreational facilities as well as membership in other campgrounds and vacation spots all over the world. It shares some methods with time sharing in its marketing approach and the "exchange program" idea, but it's a totally separate operation.

This Rodanthe operation offers a heated indoor pool and Olympic-size outdoor pool, lighted tennis courts, miniature golf, basketball and shuffleboard courts, fresh water fishing ponds, a clubhouse where regular activities are planned by the full-time recreational director, a fishing dock and boat ramp, jogging trails, and more. The only thing you have to bring is your RV.

Drop in at the information center to get information on the resort.

CAPE HATTERAS KOA
Rodanthe   987-2307

Joan Berry, a friendly person, manages one of the largest campgrounds on the Banks. It's just south of Spur Road 1247, about 14 miles south of the Oregon Inlet Bridge (Bonner Bridge). Hatteras KOA used to be two campgrounds, the Cape Hatteras KOA and the KOA Holiday Campground, just south of it. The southern part is still geared to overnight camping, with 269 sites with water and power, and 41 also with sewer connections. An excellent service here is trailer storage: you can leave it here year 'round if you wish. The northern one ("the original," as Joan calls it) has 180 sites, of which 120 are rented on a yearly basis. There are lots of amenities at KOA: dump station, laundry, three pools, Jacuzzi, playground, game room, restaurant, sailboard rentals, Kamping Kabins, a well-stocked store, and a full time recreation director in the summer. Of course the sea is just over the dunes, and there's saltwater fishing and swimming. There's soundside swimming too, great for smaller kids. Open March 15 to December 1.

NORTH BEACH CAMPGROUND

Rodanthe   987-2378

North Beach is right in Rodanthe and right on the ocean. What more can one ask from a campground? 110 sites, most with water and power. There's also hot showers, toilets, laundry, and a grocery. Just over the dunes are fishing and swimming. Open March till December. North Beach is just south of Chicamacomico Lifesaving Station, so if you're there during the summer, slip over and watch the Beach Apparatus Drill the Park Service puts on.

OCEAN WAVES CAMPGROUND

Waves   987-2556

Clyde and Carolyn Bullock started Ocean Waves in 1985. This seaside camping place has 68 spaces, 64 with full hookups. Laundromat with hot water, game room, ocean fishing and swimming, and a pool too. Open March 15 through November 31. Seaside Route 12 in Waves.

CAPE WOODS CAMPER PARK

Buxton   995-5850

Located on the southern side of the Buxton "back road," Cape Woods is a good example of the sound side forest-type of camping. Over a hundred sites are laid out with wooded strips between, and many of the sites have shade. There are plenty of poplars, pine, and live oak. Another nice thing about Cape Woods is the two small freshwater lakes between which it lies; they're complete with bass and brim. Most of the sites have water, power, and picnic tables, and, of course, hot showers and flush toilets are available. Cape Woods is open year round for self-contained camping; open March 1 through Dec. 15 for tent camping, with prices depending on services.

STOWE - A - WAY
(Formerly Bill and Barb's)
Buxton   995-5970

This is one of the smaller campgrounds on Hatteras; because of its location in the Cape microforest, there are even some trees --and in summer you'll appreciate their shade. About 20 campsites, all with city water and electricity and some with full hookups. Bathhouse with hot showers, flush toilets, and a picnic table at every site. The sign is easy to miss, so keep alert as you round the turn on Highway 12 on the outskirts of Buxton and head west on 1232. It'll be about four hundred yards on your left. Open year round.

CAPE POINT CAMPGROUND (NPS)
Cape Hatteras

Cape Point is the biggest of the Park Service's campgrounds on the Banks, and one of the wildest and nicest, too. Like the rest, there are no utility connections, but there are toilets, cold water showers, drinking water, charcoal grills, and picnic tables. Everything else you supply yourself. The 203 site campground is located just behind the dune line on the southwest face of the point, near Ramp 44, and is on flat, sandy ground. While checking it out we bogged down in what looked like firm sand, so take advantage of our mistakes and stay on the hard surfaced road unless you have four wheel drive and oversized tires. Bring mosquito netting, awnings for shade, and long tent stakes for the sand, And bathing suits -- it's a short walk to the ocean, and if you surf, the campground is located two miles away from the best surfing spot on the Atlantic coast. Cape Point, like most of the other NPS grounds, is open from mid-spring to mid-fall on a first come, first served basis. Fee: $10.00 per night.

FRISCO WOODS CAMPGROUND, INC.
Frisco   995-5208

We found Frisco Woods to be a standout campground. Ward and Betty Barnett, Hatteras natives, have developed its 14-acre sound side, part-forest, part-marsh location with care for nature and an eye for beauty. Frisco has 200 sites, many with full hookup, electricity and water. There are tables and hot showers, but otherwise the furnishings are spartan. The reason is that Frisco caters to the naturally-oriented tent camper, rather than to the trailer crowd. The sites are all either in or beside virgin woods of pine, holly trees, and wild grapes. A naturalist's area on the Pamlico overlooks a wetland marsh habitat, and there's good crabbing and sound fishing. If you like semi wild, basic camping, this is the place. It's also very popular with windsurfers. Open about March to December 1.

FRISCO CAMPGROUND (NPS)

Frisco

Frisco is another National Park Service-run campground. On the southern side of the island, it's about four miles west of Buxton on Highway 12, then a left turn at the sign and drive to the beach. Frisco is open Memorial Day to Labor Day, with 136 no-utilities sites. The location is well away from other activities and this is one of the more isolated campgrounds, so if you like it wild, Frisco's for you. 14 days limit of stay; fees $10.00 per night, payable at the entrance. This campground operates on a first come, first served basis all season. There are toilets, cold water outdoor showers, drinking water, charcoal grills, and picnic tables.

KINNAKEET CAMPGROUND

Avon   995-5211

Located on the sound side off Highway 12, the campground has 35 full hook up sites. This campground is geared towards trailers and mobile homes. Kinnakeet does not take tents at this time. Each site has a picnic table, access to hot showers, toilets and electricity. A dump site and running hot and cold water are also available. Reservations are definitely recommended here. Call and ask for Charles to reserve your site.

HATTERAS SANDS CAMPING RESORT

Hatteras   986-2422

This is one of the largest, and best maintained, campgrounds on the Banks. Located very close to the ferry slips in Hatteras village, Hatteras Sands offers 105 sites with water and electricity. Sewage connections are available at some site. Throughout the resort there are meticulously clean bath houses. Some pull through sites also are available.

An Olympic-size pool is the feature here, though there is also a nice gift shop and game room. A canal that runs through the resort provides for fun fishing and crabbing. The campground is also within easy walking distance to Hatteras village and its shops and restaurants.

The northernmost lighthouse on the Outer Banks, the Currituck Beach Light, flashes its warning many miles out to sea. DCTB

The campground is open from March 1 until December 1. Discounts of 5% are given during off seasons.

OCRACOKE
CAMPGROUNDS

TEETER'S CAMPGROUND
Ocracoke   928-3511

MC, VISA

Teeter's has been here awhile. It's located right in town just a short walk from the harbor. (Turn east at Harborside.) That's probably its biggest advantage. Some campers may appreciate the green grass and trees, too; something the other two campgrounds don't have at all.

Teeter's is open year 'round for self-contained units. The restrooms are closed as soon as the weather turns cold enough to freeze. There are hot showers, water and electric hookups. A few of the 25 sites have sewage hookups. Charcoal grills will be furnished upon request.

BEACHCOMBER
Ocracoke   928-4031

MC, VISA, Choice

This is the newest campground on Ocracoke. It's less than a mile from Silver Lake across from 3/4 Time. A fairly complete convenience store is right there, as well as a gas station which sells diesel and kerosene fuels as well. The nearest beach access is 7/10th of a mile and then you have a hefty walk across a rather wide dune line to reach the water.

The Beachcomber has 31 campsites, electricity is available and there are fully equipped bathrooms and hot showers. The campground is open early April through late October, depending on weather. May through August reservations are advised.

OCRACOKE CAMPGROUND (NPS)
Highway 12, east of town

Operated by the National Park Service, Ocracoke Campground has 136 campsites just over the dunes from the ocean. No utilities, but there are cold showers, a dumping station, drinking water, charcoal grills, and flush toilets.

Ocracoke is the sole NPS campground on the Ticketron reservation system. From Memorial Day weekend to Labor Day, you must either:
1) write Ticketron, Dept. R, 401 Hackensack Ave., Hackensack, NJ 07601;

2) go by the Ticketron office nearest you to make reservations. (No phone reservations). Charge, then, is $12.00 per night;

3) or, if you have VISA or MasterCard, make reservations by calling (900) 370-5566.

There's a limit of stay of 14 days. As in other camping sites along the Beach proper, we suggest bringing awnings for shade, netting against mosquitoes, and longer than usual tent stakes for use in sandy soil with high winds from the sea. The campgrounds themselves are sandy and bare but rather pretty, and are only three miles from all the conveniences of Ocracoke Village. The beach is fine here but there is a guarded beach a mile and a half to the west. Other than that, there's nothing around but beautiful emptiness.

INSIDE

OUTER BANKS REAL ESTATE

After vacationing on the Outer Banks, many people dream of having their own place at the beach. Those not so romantic at heart may simply recognize a good investment when they see it. Whatever the motivation, thousands of people each year are buying into the good life that these barrier islands provide.

Since our book is aimed at visitors to our area, we're only going to talk about owning vacation property. Those properties make up close to 90% of all real estate transactions in Dare County. It's big business and, if you do your homework, it can be very profitable.

TIMESHARING

Timesharing falls under the jurisdiction of the North Carolina Real Estate Commission, so its sale is considered real estate and time share developments on the Outer Banks are all deeded transactions, to the best of our knowledge; you actually receive a deed to 1/52 of the unit property for each week you purchase. But the importance of this transaction is not the value of 1/52 of a two bedroom "villa" (it is negligible); it's that the deed grants you that property and the right to use it in perpetuity. You can give it away, will to your heirs, do with it whatever you can do with real property. Time share can be sold undeeded, which is selling only a right-to-use that reverts back to the developer in the end. It would be always wise to ask if the property you're inspecting is deeded timesharing.

With timesharing, what you are buying is the right to use a specific piece of real estate for a week per share. These weeks are either fixed at the time of sale or they change yearly on a calendar rotation.

The disadvantages of being locked into a time and place have been partly offset by RCI (Resort Condominiums, Inc.), a time share bank and other services like it. Members trade their units to get different time slots, different locations.

As resort vacations go, timesharing is very affordable. If you can qualify for a MasterCharge card, you can probably qualify to have your time share purchase financed. But be aware that finance charges will also be more in line with credit cards than mortgages.

Most time share developments on the Outer Banks are multi-family buildings centered around a broad package of amenities. Swimming pools, tennis courts, playgrounds, and supervised activities are just some of the most common offerings. Time share units come fully furnished, with all maintenance and upkeep covered by a monthly association fee.

But is it really an investment? It is a commodity. You can sell your time share unit if there's a buyer for it. You might get more than you paid for it but, then again, you might get less. The chances that your time share unit will have appreciated in value are significantly less than with real property. Time share doesn't offer the tax advantages of buying property nor is it acceptable as collateral in most lending situations. While there are exceptions, of course, generally speaking, time share ownership is not financial portfolio material.

However, if your main objective is to provide yourself, your family, with a guaranteed vacation spot each year -- if you like the location and the amenities package -- if you can't afford conventional property ownership -- or if you're intrigued by the possibilities of trading your time share unit for vacations in Tahiti or Maui -- you can look at timesharing as vacation insurance.

All the time share resorts on the Outer Banks have used basically the same sales techniques. You're given $50 cash or a free dinner for two or a bass boat -- something of value -- in return for taking a 90 minute tour. While they may not be pushy, these tours are masterpieces of manipulation. Believe us, if the tour didn't sell time share units, they wouldn't use it. Many a couple has gone on a tour "just for the money" and walked out the proud and happy owners of two time share weeks in February.

If you get swept away by the possibilities of timesharing, then decide you really didn't want to buy, you have five days to regain control of your pocketbook. The North Carolina Time Share Act, passed in the mid 80s, protects you in other ways, as well, and this means that, most likely, your time share sales rep is going to play things pretty straight with you. He or she is a licensed real estate salesperson who can lose their license, and thereby their livelihood, if they don't. And most the salespeople we know are genuinely excited about their properties and enjoy representing them.

By the way, you will get the $50 or whatever was offered for taking the tour, whether you buy or not, and generally with a smile and thank you.

BARRIER ISLAND STATION
Hwy. 12
Duck, NC 27949   261-3525

Barrier Island, one of the largest time share resorts on the Outer Banks, occupies a most desirable tract of ocean-to-sound property just on the north side of Duck. They have a year 'round activities director to keep things hopping around the pools (one indoor), tennis courts, and other recreational facilities. A shuttle bus in the summer carries guests around the property making stops at their soundside sailing center and the beach. A restaurant and lounge are part of the complex.

SEA SCAPE BEACH AND GOLF VILLAS
Rt. 158, MP 2
Kitty Hawk, NC 27949   261-3881

Spacious two-bedroom, two-bath villas have use of the community's golf course, tennis courts, two swimming pools, indoor rec facility, weight room, year 'round activity director, game room, banquet facility, and shuttle bus to the beach.

OUTER BANKS BEACH CLUB
Beach Rd., MP 9
Kill Devil Hills, NC 27948   441-7036

This was the first time share resort on the Outer Banks and the oceanfront three-story round buildings have become a landmark, of sorts, on the beach. It was started in 1980 with a prime location, right in the middle of the Kill Devil Hills motel and restaurant strip. One or three bedroom units share one indoor and two outdoor swimming pools, whirlpools, tennis courts, playground, and other amenities. A recreation director plans games and activities for guests of all ages.

DUNES SOUTH BEACH AND RACQUET CLUB
Beach Rd., MP 18
Nags Head, NC 27959　　　　　　　　　　　441-4090

Two- and three-bedroom townhouses feature a fireplace, washer and dryer, Jacuzzi, and hot tub. Outside you'll find a tennis court, outdoor pool, putting green, and playground.

CAPE HATTERAS BEACH CLUB
Buxton, NC 27920　　　　　　　　　　(800) 334-8308
　　　　　　　　　　　　　　　　　　　　995-4115

An oceanside development with a swimming pool. The main attractions at this location are nature's amenities: the beach, windsurfing at the nearby Canadian Hole, and some of the best fishing on the East Coast. When we called to check out the facilities, we were told that golf was included. With careful questioning, we ascertained they were referring to golf courses in the Kitty Hawk area -- a good hour or more away. The lesson is to be specific, whether you're talking to a time share resort or any other accommodation broker. In an isolated area like the Outer Banks "nearby" can mean a hundred miles!

CO-OWNERSHIP

This concept is just a step away from timesharing. With co-ownership, you are sharing the ownership of an actual building with a number of other parties. The most common co-ownership set-up is ten owners, each getting five weeks occupancy, with two weeks left over for maintenance and repairs. The five weeks are usually split up between prime and off-seasons and holiday weekends. Sometimes the weeks are set, staying the same from year to year. Sometimes they rotate.

A co-ownership community is typically a dozen or more very large, luxury homes that share some added amenities like a pool or tennis court. Co-ownership can be offered with just a single house or townhomes, too. As with timesharing, the property comes fully furnished and all upkeep and maintenance are provided and paid for through an owners' association fee.

Co-ownership can offer some of the tax benefits of vacation home ownership (on a much smaller scale, of course, since the dollar amounts involved are less), depending on whether you occupy the property for the five weeks or rent it out.

Appreciation on co-ownership property will not be as great as a comparable privately-owned home, but several co-ownership projects on the Outer Banks have been profitable investments in the past, partly due to prime oceanfront locations and amenities not available at the time in conventional communities. According to area realtors, most Outer Banks co-ownership property owners are able to recover their initial investment when selling their share.

While not nearly as inexpensive as timesharing, co-ownership is still a more affordable way to own a piece of the Outer Banks, in the short-term, at least. It has better investment potential than time share, although most real estate people would, rightly, caution you to not think of it in investment terms. And, most co-ownership properties are far larger and more luxurious (in fact, most are single family residences) than the usual time share apartment or townhouse. It won't give you as many amenities as a time share resort or a sense of "belonging" to some organized group, things that can be important factors in an enjoyable vacation.

If you keep in mind that co-ownership -- like timesharing -- is primarily a vacation not a property, then, says Woody West of Brindley & Brindley, the real estate firm handling Northpoint co- ownership, "as property prices go up, you've got yourself a pretty good deal."

A few of the larger co-ownership developments are listed below. Sales for co-ownership communities are generally handled by the developer initially and then passed off to local real estate companies. The developers use many of the same tactics to attract potential buyers that time share does -- cash, gifts or a free mini-vacation on the property.

PORT TRINITIE

Hwy. 12
Duck, NC 27949   261-3922

Located just two miles north of Duck, Port Trinitie has been offering co-ownership multi and single family units for several years. The property runs ocean to sound, with two pools, a boat dock, and tennis court. Just a little over a year ago, the developer opened up a couple of dozen lots for individually-owned single family residences.

NORTHPOINT

Hwy. 12
Duck, NC 27949

This is a well-built co-ownership development, with both ocean and sound front houses, with an enclosed year 'round pool, tennis and basketball courts, and a long soundside pier for fishing, crabbing, and docking small boats. The community also has individually-owned single family residences.

SHIPS WATCH

Hwy. 12   261-2231
Duck, NC 27949   800-334-1295

Ships Watch, a mile north of Duck, is an ocean-to-sound development of more than 50 luxury homes, each built on large lots, and lavishly furnished. Looked on as one of the most successful developments of its kind, Ships Watch owners have benefited from developer-financing which, according to area real estate agents, has increased the value of the development. The community has a large outdoor pool, tennis courts, jogging trails, and a sound side pier.

RESIDENTIAL RESORT COMMUNITIES

The developments listed here are representative of the kinds of resort communities you'll find on the Outer Banks. The older ones started primarily as communities of vacation homes and have evolved into year 'round neighborhoods (although still including a large number of seasonal cottages). Some offer sound and ocean access; all -- except those north of Corolla and on Ocracoke Island -- offer amenity packages that keep the resale values and vacation rentals of the homes high. Chuck Smith, owner of Cove Realty which handles both rentals and sales of property in Old Nags Head Cove, calls developments like the Cove "the best of three worlds. You have the pool... the sound access and beach... and the ocean, very close. It's very family oriented and makes a great vacation."

CAROVA BEACH

Corolla, NC 27927 For more information, call Riggs Realty

919-453-3111

There are several platted subdivisions north of Corolla, reachable only by four-wheel drive. According to Billy Griggs, a real estate salesman and 4th generation native of Corolla, "People like the remote beauty. They buy in this area because it's the last [outside of preservation areas] largely undeveloped area on the Outer Banks... Carova Beach is a typical community for this part of the beach."

While the road doesn't come this far north -- and, as of this writing, it is not legally possible to build the road across the government-owned preservation lands between Corolla and Carova Beach -- the development does have electricity and telephone service, as well as mail delivery.

The subdivision has lots with direct sound access, canalfront lots, interior lots and some oceanfront property. Other than water and beach access, there are no amenities.

THE VILLAGES AT OCEAN HILL

Hwy. 12 For more information, call the Ocean Hill Sales Office

Corolla, NC 27927 919-453-8866

This new 156-acre, single family development is located at the end of Highway 12. If you're going to go further north along the beach, you'll need a four-wheel drive.

You can still get in on the "ground floor," so to speak, since this community is still in the early phases of development. Plans for recreational facilities include tennis courts, sailing center, indoor and outdoor swimming pools, an 8-acre lake, and clubhouse.

COROLLA LIGHT

Hwy. 12 For more information, call Brindley & Brindley Realty

Corolla, NC 27927 919-453-3133

This was the first of the new wave of planned communities. Started in 1985, it has been enormously successful in spite -- or maybe because -- of its secluded location in Corolla. When Corolla Light first opened, there was virtually nothing in the area except for a few homes, a small grocery store and the post office. Now there are shops, restaurants, and service-oriented businesses. There are tennis courts, swimming pools, an oceanfront recreation center with an indoor pool, private restaurant and lounge, jogging and bike paths, a soundside marina, a driving range and putt-putt golf and more.

The development offers single family homes, townhomes and villas; oceanfront, soundfront and in between. Many of the neighborhoods have been completely sold out, although some of the lots have been put back on the market. The community is still under development.

MONTEREY SHORES

Hwy. 12   For more information, call Bob DeGabrielle & Associates
Corolla, NC 27927   919-453-3600

Monterey Shores, located just south of Corolla, was launched in 1988 and its immediate success is added proof that the area north of Duck is, indeed, hot stuff. Single family homes are designed around a southwestern motif of arched verandas and tile roofs that is echoed in the clubhouse and other common buildings.

SANDERLING

Hwy. 12   For more information, call Sanderling Sales Center
North of Duck, NC 27949   919-261-2181

This community has been setting the standard for quality development on the Outer Banks for years now. Strict building codes and excellent land planning have kept it very exclusive and quiet. Amenities include a pool and health club, tennis courts, nature trails and a private beach. The Sanderling Inn and Restaurant are at the north edge of the community, and the Pine Island indoor racquet club is just a short drive away.

SCHOONER RIDGE

Hwy. 12   For more information, call Britt Real Estate
Duck, NC 27949   261-3566

One of the last oceanfront communities in Duck -- Schooner Ridge -- is still being built. A representative for Britt Real Estate, the company handling new sales in this development, says, "There is no other tract of land available for this kind of luxury development so close to all the shops and services."

Bike paths wind through this single family development where all the amenities are already in place: an oceanfront outdoor pool with whirlpool; an indoor pool, exercise room and racquetball court at the clubhouse; and tennis courts.

SOUTHERN SHORES

Rt. 158 For more information, call Kitty Hawk Land Co.
Kitty Hawk, NC 27949   919-261-2131

This oldest planned development on the Outer Banks, and the largest, was started in the early 1940s. Since 1979 it has been incorporated as a village (but it's mailing address is still Kitty Hawk), administering its own strict building codes which have kept the community remarkably uncluttered despite its expansive growth.

This community of single family and town homes has a country club with golf course, pool, private ocean beach accesses and boat marinas. Some sections of Southern Shores are fully developed, others are still in the works. The Marketplace shopping center is within its boundaries, and all the shops and attractions of Duck and Kitty Hawk are just minutes away.

COLINGTON HARBOUR

Colington Road For more information, call Colington Harbour Asso.
Kill Devil Hills, NC 27948   919-441-5886

Colington Harbour is one of the oldest planned communities in the area. Construction began in 1967 on Colington Island (west of Kill Devil Hills) and by 1974 every lot had been sold, although some lots are back on the market now. It is a "private" community (which means security guards check the coming and going of all vehicles at a single entrance road), with navigable canals, a clubhouse and pool, tennis court, boat ramp and rental slips, and a soundfront beach and picnic area.

BAY CLIFF

Off Colington Road For more information, call Hudgins Real Estate
Kill Devil Hills, NC 27948   919-261-4646

Bay Cliff is a new development also on Colington Island. Only single family homes will be built here and ownership takes a new twist for the Outer Banks: the developer has divided the land into homesites and common areas. The total area of the homesite can be developed by the owner (because the community has central sewage, no drain

Sales · Rentals · Property Management · Construction

Britt REAL ESTATE

S.R. Box 272 • DUCK • Kitty Hawk, NC 27949

If you love the Outer Banks and want to vacation here, or buy a second home or investment property, we think you'll appreciate all of our services.

To learn more about us, just give us a call and we'll send you any or all of the following:

· Free 1990 vacation rental brochure

· Free subscription to *Britt Directions*, a quarterly newsletter related to real estate investments

· Information about the Britt Property Management Program

· Information about buying or selling property Duck to Corolla

1-800-334-6315 Outside NC
1-919-261-3566 In NC

---

field for a septic system is necessary) and is surrounded by maintained common grounds; It's the condominium concept applied to single family homes. One reason for taking this approach is to ensure the preservation of as much of the property as possible, which includes a large number of oak trees and other exceptional physical features. There will be architectural controls, of course.

Amenities include controlled access to the development; the Claw Club, with outdoor pool, hot tub and other facilities; an on-site manager; 1300 feet of soundfront, and a soundside pier for fishing and crabbing.

OLD NAGS HEAD COVE

Rt. 158 For more information call Cove Realty
Nags Head, NC 27959 919-441-6391

This is a single family community started in the late 60s, built on a system of canals that gives many homes in the development direct access to the sound. Boat ramps into the canals are provided for those owners who don't have canalfront property. Many homes here

The Light Keeper's house at Currituck Beach Lighthouse casts interesting shadows with its turn-of-the-century architecture.
© '88 D. Westner

have both ocean and sound views. There is a clubhouse with swimming pool and tennis courts, as well as a small soundside beach. With the exception of a few lots on the market, Old Nags Head Cove is completely developed. Property values have benefited from the Village at Nags Head golf course which now abuts south side lots in the Cove.

THE VILLAGE AT NAGS HEAD

Rt. 158 For more information, call Village Realty
Nags Head, NC 27959 919-441-8533

Duck and points north may be hot, but there is no real estate anywhere on the Outer Banks hotter than The Village at Nags Head, started just three years ago. This classy development by the Ammons Corporation has taken over the old Epstein tract and turned it into one of the showiest spots on the beach. Centered around an 18-hole golf course, the development offers single and multi-family homes, soundside and oceanside -- including oceanfront property -- and almost everything has views of both the ocean and sound be-

---

Some people have it all

The Village at Nags Head

Village Realty
Rental Info: 919-480-2224 or 1-800-548-9688
Sales Info: 919-441-8533
Call for Free Brochure

Nags Head Golf Links   **Village Beach Club**
919-441-8074   919-480-2222

An Ammons Community

Village Realty Rentals
P.O. Box 1807 · Nags Head, NC 27959
158 By-Pass, Milepost 15

cause of the lay of the land. Other amenities include the golf course clubhouse and restaurant, an oceanfront beach club with an olympic-size pool, tennis courts, and soundside beach areas.

PIRATE'S COVE

Manteo-Nags Head Causeway

Manteo, NC 27954

For more information, call Pirate's Cove Sales Center
919-473-1451

Pirate's Cove is another luxury single and multi-family community, but with a focus on boating and sports fishing. Deep water canals provide all property owners with a dock at their door.

The marina sponsors big game fish tournaments throughout the season that draw hundreds of sports fishing aficionados and give the community a festival ambience throughout most of the summer.

A ships store and restaurant are part of this controlled-access development, along with a clubhouse, swimming pool, hot tub and tennis courts. See the chapter on "Manteo" for more information.

KINNAKEET SHORES

Hwy. 12

Avon, NC 27915

For more information, call Sun Realty
919-995-5821

On Hatteras Island, Kinnakeet Shores is the place to buy, says Eddie Goodrich, sales manager of the Avon office of Sun Realty. This is the largest development on Hatteras Island -- 500 acres stretching ocean to sound in an area that has become the windsurfing capital of the East Coast. Amenities will include tennis courts, swimming pools, a clubhouse with Nautilus equipment, and a restaurant and lounge, according to Goodrich.

JACKSON DUNES

Ocracoke, NC 27960

Sharon Miller Realty

Ocracoke Island Realty

For more information, call:
919-928-5711
919-928-6261

Developments on Ocracoke are characterized by their lack of development. None offer any recreational facilities, few have more than sand tracks for road access. Jackson Dunes, at close to ten years old, is one of the newest subdivisions. "We just don't have the land for any new subdivisions," says Sharon Miller, an Ocracoke real estate broker. "Right now, the most activity and more creative beach design is happening at Jackson Dunes," she explains, "but it's all resale."

The subdivision has town water and septic system waste treatment. All the lots are interior, though many border on marsh land and most have a sound view.

CONDOMINIUMS

Almost everyone is familiar with condominium ownership now. It's been the darling of city development and renewal for two decades, and middle America's ticket to the good life of back yard swimming pools and tennis courts. Basically, you own your own space -- be it apartment or townhouse -- and share ownership of all common grounds and facilities.

There are dozens of condominiums already built on the Outer Banks and dozens more in the works. While still relatively affordable, this type of ownership offers most of the advantages of owning resort property. David Watson of Resort Realty Co. points out that owners can expect to get a "higher yield on the rental of a condominium, but less appreciation" than on a single family home. "It depends on where you want your gains," he says when asked which is the better investment.

Tax advantages are the same as owning any vacation home and, unlike with co-ownership, because you own the condo for the entire year, in addition to using at as income property, you'll be able to get some personal use out of it as well without jeopardizing your tax write-offs.

Another thing to consider is that condos are not making the headway in the Hatteras market that they have to the north. One agent suggests that the typical Hatteras vacationer prefers single family housing. Another factor may be the lower prices on Hatteras mean single family homes are still affordable vacation choices. As property becomes more scarce and more expensive, condominium development will undoubtedly grow.

Condominiums are generally sold through real estate agents, without the gimmicks and "tours" that dominate time share. Consult one of the real estate agents listed in the next section for more information about condominium availability.

SINGLE FAMILY HOMES AND LAND

Our first piece of advice about buying a house on the Outer Banks -- or any piece of real estate -- is to use a real estate agent. There is far too much to know about the area market to not put this major investment in the hands of a professional.

We're going to look at these houses as a piece of resort real estate: an investment in a second home that will be used to build equity for your financial portfolio and, most likely (since close to 90% of all real estate properties sold end up in a rental program), to generate rental income.

If you could buy anything, what do the real estate pros recommend? Almost every one we asked said "Oceanfront." David Watson of Resort Realty put it this way, "With oceanfront property you have some assurance that the financial plan you set out will happen." He cited the higher occupancy rates for vacation rentals in oceanfront properties, as well as land value increases of 10-20% per year. Sherri Mason, rental manager for Britt Real Estate, confirms that oceanfront homes rent better and for more money. From the renters' point of view, she said, "oceanfront is most attractive."

Oceanfront may be the best all around investment -- but only if the property is safe from erosion. You need to keep in mind that sections of our shoreline have had severe erosion problems. In 1989 storms alone, the ocean claimed more than a dozen cottages between Kitty Hawk and South Nags Head and did serious, and sometimes irreparable, damage to over a hundred others. Before you buy, talk with town and county planners who are dealing with the erosion and storm damage problems and get their assessment of the property. A substantial barrier dune between the house and ocean is some of the best insurance you can have.

Owning a house on the sound can be a wise choice, too. Doug Twiddy, of Twiddy & Co. real estate in Duck, says "Get as close to the water as you can afford to get." Soundfront gets you there for less than oceanfront. While the property may give you water access, don't count on being able to build a boat dock, if one's not already in place. The Coastal Area Management Act (CAMA) and other governmental regulations protecting the shoreline and marsh make permission for any sort of construction on the sound difficult to obtain.

If you can't buy on the water, property in a planned community like Corolla Light, or oceanside in South Nags Head, could be a good investment, especially if the development gives you ocean and sound access. It all depends on what your financial and living needs are.

If you're interested in generating rental income, new construction rents better than old; three bedrooms will rent more weeks than 5; and anything with amenities -- the magic word in real estate these days, swimming pools, tennis courts, etc.-- will bring higher rents and more weeks of income.

If you're buying the house as an investment in your retirement, there are other factors you should consider such as convenience of shopping and services and long term condition of the neighborhood.

When looking at oceanside homes (that aren't oceanfront), an important factor is ocean access. A private access boosts property value but, from a rental standpoint, a public entry to the beach close by is just as good. If you don't have convenient access, the rentability of your property drops considerably.

Land -- raw land -- has been the ticket to financial success for more than a few people on the Outer Banks. Land appreciation over the past twenty years has often provided better yields than savvy stock market investments. Eddie Goodrich of Sun Realty says buying land is the "easiest and simplest way to make money on the Outer Banks. Buy it, keep it five years, and sell it."

It may not be quite that simple, but, as Woody West of Brindley & Brindley put it, "It's hard to miss on the Outer Banks."

Land from South Nags Head north through Duck is fully developed -- over developed, some might say. The Epstein tract in Nags Head, now host to the Outer Banks Mall and The Village at Nags Head, was the last bastion of open space in the area. While property values in this area will almost certainly continue to rise as long as visitors keep vacationing here, the days of really quick profit are probably gone.

Zoning and planned development on this section of the beach, though relatively new, is an accepted fact of life. Most likely -- and we hope we're right -- the beach will hang on to the character that has made it a successful family resort. The community, so far, has seemed willing to forgo immediate wealth for quality of life.

But even so, there are opposing forces at work. Some see financial advantages of large-scale development of other resort communities like Virginia Beach and Ocean City, Maryland. These proponents of progress feel that visitors to the area want the facilities and services this sort of development brings. Should these people have their way, there will be large profits to be made as individuals sell to corporations.

Hatteras Island now represents the investment opportunity that its northern neighbor offered ten years ago. "I believe in ten years the most valuable land [on the Outer Banks] will be Hatteras Island," states Eddie Goodrich. It's a belief that is well-grounded in hard fact.

Nearly 80% of Hatteras Island is part of the Cape Hatteras National Seashore. Every village on the island is surrounded by park service land, limiting its growth, providing natural barriers and the undeveloped beaches that Hatteras Island visitors prize. Dare County zoning was in place before serious development of the island started, also limiting growth. Mary Dickens of Outer Beaches Realty in Avon predicts continued appreciation of property (it averages close to 12% annually now). "There's no way to go but up," she says.

The area north of Corolla, "beyond the end of the road," (also known as the Currituck Banks) may be the place where investors find the best deals of all. Real estate agents who specialize in this area of the beach report increased activity as people realize the potential for profit. "People can afford to invest here," says Bill Hogan, one of the owners of Re/Max Island Realty in Corolla. "Even without a road, property has appreciated in the 25-50% range over the last few years."

In fact, it has. Values for oceanfront lots at Carova increased at roughly the same percentage as oceanfront lots in Whalehead Beach -- only at about half the price. This area, maybe even more so than Hatteras, has benefited from being a late bloomer. Taking its cue from Dare County's missteps, Currituck County has enacted zoning to strictly limit development. "The planning has been better," says Hogan. "There will be better control of growth."

If a road is put in, the people who are buying now have a lot to gain financially. Although it seems an impossibility now due to control of key land by the Fish and Wildlife Service, the road also seems inevitable. The county has platted 1000 lots above where the road currently stops. As more and more people purchase property, the demand for services -- and a road -- will have to be heard.

A FEW TIPS FOR BUYING OUTER BANKS PROPERTY

1. We'll say it again: Use a licensed real estate agent.
2. Educate yourself about the zoning ordinances and restrictive covenants of the community you're looking at. Doug Twiddy, Twiddy & Co., says good controls and an active property owners' association (needed to ensure upkeep of roads, undeveloped areas and water accesses) play an important part in long term property value.

PLAN NOW FOR FUN!

Sun Realty

It's time to start planning now for your much deserved vacation to the Outer Banks of North Carolina. Sun Realty has just the place for you! Call or write today for our 1990 rental brochure, featuring over 600 beach cottages and condominiums. Let us help you to make your next vacation the best yet!

FREE 1990 BROCHURE IG90
Sun Realty
P.O. Box 1630
Kill Devil Hills, NC 27948
800-334-4745
(IN & OUT OF NC)
919-441-7033
(LOCAL)

Name

Address

City   State   Zip

3. If the lot is undeveloped, call the local CAMA (Coastal Area Management Act) agent. He'll be the starting point. For a final determination, you may need to hire on the private firms that do land evaluations. While we don't like to think Outer Bankers are in the business of selling "swamp" land, federal regulations protecting the wetlands and shore areas have become increasing stringent. Someone who bought a lot 20 years ago may be unaware that his or her lot is unbuildable today.

4. Mary Dickens at Outer Beaches Realty suggests that you start by considering what area resources you are most likely to use. If you're a boating enthusiast, for example, there are very few places offering public access for boats at the present time. And, there are even fewer private communities with docks and/or canals. If you like to play golf, the closest golf course to Hatteras is an hour's drive north. The Outer Banks is spread out. Facilities that city dwellers take for granted can be miles away.

5. Ask your real estate agent to show you the rental history for any house, as well as information about surrounding properties.

6. If you're buying a lot, pay attention to the elevation. It can mean the difference between a good water view and none at all, especially if the property isn't waterfront.

7. "Look for amenities," said every single real estate person we spoke with. Community recreation facilities like a pool add value to the property and bring a higher rental income. And, if you're counting on rental income to help pay for your investment, don't overlook the amenities you can provide in the house. "Where people used to be satisfied with air conditioning," says Woody West, Brindley & Brindley, "now they want Jacuzzis and decks with a view."

8. For a wise investment when you're buying a lot to build on, pay attention to the ratio of property value to improvement value, recommends David Watson of Resort Realty.

Listed below are just a few of real estate companies you could call for help in finding the Outer Banks property that fits your needs:

Atlantic Realty, 261-2154, Rt. 158, MP 2 1/2, Kitty Hawk. Handling single and multi-family homes from South Nags Head to Corolla.

Beach Realty, 261-3815, Rt. 158, MP 2, Kitty Hawk. Single and multi-family homes from South Nags Head to Corolla.

414   OUTER BANKS REAL ESTATE

Brindley & Brindley, 261-2222, Offices on Hwy. 12 in Duck and in Corolla. Single and multi-family homes from Hatteras Island to Carova, specializing in the Corolla and Rodanthe areas.

Britt Real Estate, 261-3566, Hwy. 12, Duck. Single and multi- family homes in the Duck to Corolla area.

Coldwell Banker Twenty-Twenty Realty, 473-2020, Hwy. 64, Manteo. Single and multi-family properties, specializing in Roanoke Island.

Cove Realty, 441-6391, 105 E. Dunn Street, Nags Head. Single family homes in Nags Head and South Nags Head, specializing in Old Nags Head Cove properties.

Hudgins Realty, 261-4646, Rt. 158, MP 2-1/2, Kitty Hawk. Properties from South Nags Head to Corolla and on Roanoke Island.

"Your family's vacation matters to us"

SALVO
REAL ESTATE, INC.

Sales · Rentals · Property Management · Custom Built Homes

ON HATTERAS ISLAND
SALVO, NORTH CAROLINA 27972
(919) 987-2343

For All Your Insurance Needs

Mollie A. Fearing and Associates, Inc.

P.O. Box 939 - 415 Agona Street
Manteo NC 27954
(919)473-3476

Sharon Miller Realty, 928-5711, Ocracoke. Ocracoke Island properties.

Midgett Realty, 986-2141, 441-7887, Hatteras, Rodanthe, and Kill Devil Hills offices specializing in properties in northern and southern beach area.

Ocracoke Island Realty, 928-6261, Ocracoke. Ocracoke Island properties.

Outer Beaches Realty, 995-5252, Hwy. 12, Avon. Single and multi-family homes on Hatteras Island.

Re/Max Island Realty, 453-8181, Corolla. Homes from Nags Head to Carova, specializing in Currituck beaches property.

Southern Shores Realty, 261-2000, offices in Southern Shores and Grandy. Specializing in Currituck mainland and Southern Shores properties, but also handling homes in the Duck area.

Sun Realty, 441-7033, Rt. 158, MP 9, and 4 or 5 other locations from Hatteras to Duck. This is the areas largest real estate agency. They handle multi- and single family homes up and down the beach.

Surf or Sound Realty, 995-5801, Hwy. 12, Avon. Hatteras Island properties.

The Young People, 441-5544, Beach Road, MP 6, Kill Devil Hills. Homes from Corolla to South Nags Head, but specializing in the main beach area from Kitty Hawk south.

Twiddy & Company, 261-2897, Offices on Hwy. 12 in Duck and in Corolla. Specialty in homes in the area of Duck and north.

Williams Realty, 995-5211, Located next to the Avon Shopping Center, Hwy. 12, Avon. Properties on Hatteras Island.

BUILDING ON THE OUTER BANKS

North Carolina law requires that builders be licensed. This doesn't stop dozens of unlicensed construction-types from building homes or people from hiring them to do it. Unfortunately, for every one of those "bargain" homes that turned out right, we can tell you about two that were nightmares for the owners. Our advice is to hire a professional licensed builder. After talking with dozens of home owners, we can tell you the consensus is that it's worth the money.

Finding the right builder isn't always easy. Referrals from satisfied customers is probably the most reliable method. There is an Outer Banks Builders Association you can call for general information, and a check with the Chamber of Commerce wouldn't hurt, either, although they're not likely to tell you about any problems. Spend time talking with a builder before you hire him (there currently are no women builders in the area) to build your house. If he doesn't have time to talk with you ahead of time, you can pretty much bet he won't have time to talk with you while he's building your home, either. If you feel like he doesn't understand what you're looking for, call another builder. He's selling a product; you have the right to shop around.

There's no way we could go into all the building code and restrictions here. Virtually every square foot of the Outer Banks falls under some sort of zoning restriction, be it county or local. A good builder will know what's required. If you have any doubts, or you want a better understanding of how county and town ordinances affect your proposed home, call the county planning office or the appropriate town planning office. These people are there to help you and most are very willing to take the time to talk over your plans.

Bear in mind, too, that federal flood plain and CAMA regulations affect much of the property on the Outer Banks. Your friendly local planning department can steer you in the right direction for answers to any questions you may have.

A few of the builders that we've heard particularly good things about -- and whose work we've seen -- are listed below. The exclusion of anyone from this list doesn't mean we've heard anything bad about them. It's just not possible to list all construction companies.

Beach Realty & Construction, 261-3815, Kitty Hawk
Fulcher Homes, 261-3316, Kitty Hawk
Newcomb Builders, Inc., 441-1803, Colington
Newman Homes, 261-3844, Kitty Hawk
Tag Building Corporation, 441-7379, Kill Devil Hills
Bo Taylor Fine Homes, 261-2735, Rt. 1, Nags Head
Carl Worsley Company, 441-2327, Nags Head

HOME HELPERS

Once you've built a home, you'll want to have it furnished and we'd like to suggest a couple of companies that we know and think do a good job.

Carolina Casual, Rt. 158, Point Harbor, 491-2545. This company specializes in patio and deck furniture. Good prices and they deliver.

Island Interiors, 261-3614, Southern Shores. If you prefer the individual attention you get working with a small company, you'll enjoy the service you get from Marylu Martone, an interior designer who's been working on the Outer Banks for many years.

Manteo Furniture, Sir Walter Raleigh Street in downtown Manteo, 473-2131. They have a surprisingly large selection of furniture and appliances and will gladly do custom orders. Free delivery from Corolla to Ocracoke and good service.

Moyock Furniture, Duck, 261-1175. Interior designers on staff will help you select everything for your home. Or, you can do your own shopping. They can sell you everything from drapes to beds.

A&B Carpets, Southern Shores, Manteo, and Buxton, 473-3219. They have wallpaper, carpets, tile, flooring, and lots of helpful advice.

ISLAND INTERIORS

Furnishing fine homes on the Outer Banks for over 10 years.

✧ *QUALITY DOESN'T ALWAYS MEAN HIGHER PRICES* ✧

Specializing in customized furniture plans to meet your individual needs and budget.

Wicker by Henry Link, Bernhardt, Stanley, Lane, Lea, Bassett, Broyhill, Knob Creek, Lexington, and hundreds more.

Call for free on-site consultation
919-261-3614

BIRDS, FISHING, AND A TOUCH OF SOLITUDE
GOLD & SILVER SEASONS

To every thing, says Ecclesiastes, there is a season. And to things on the Outer Banks, there are seasons too.

Not everything happens in the summer. As Insiders, some of our best times on the Banks haven't been in the three sun-and people-filled months of June, July, and August. We have fished the Stream offshore in the warm smoky days of late September and October; seen the snow geese and ducks whistle by overhead in long vees almost from horizon to horizon; slept in lonely cottages in the depth of winter, the gas stove hissing and the mad booming of the surf shaking the night; watched the spring come suddenly as a shot, turning the forests green almost in a day. There are times in January that are almost like April, and times in April that are almost like July.

We call them the "gold and silver" seasons of the year, and you too can drink their crisp sweetness long before and after the hectic heat of summer.

Many of the Outer Banks' most faithful lovers find fall the time they like best. Temperatures are actually more comfortable (considering the human physiological range of activity) in September and October than they are during the summer proper: highs in the upper sixties to mid-seventies, lows in the low sixties. These are air temperatures; the sea temperatures sound even better, for the ocean acts as a giant heat reservoir, storing up all those rays and keeping them well into the autumn. Water temperatures are still in the seventies through these months, though there is a slow decline as time goes on. It's all a question of how hardy you are.

But you don't have to be *in* the ocean to enjoy it. The fishermen know this, and that's why the autumn is their favorite time of all along Hatteras and offshore. Late September, October, November, and early December (see "The Outer Banks Fishing Guide") are the prime seasons for blue, trout, croaker, and king mackerel. Late October is the most exciting of these times, for this is the season of the blues. Fish like colder water than human beings, and as the sun wheels towards winter the sea off the Banks comes alive with the small food fish these predators love. We've seen some fantastic blues blitzes on the crisp, high-ceilinged days when the gulls cry overhead and the wind has just a touch of bite..

And in the autumn the birds go by. Thousands, millions of them, heading south on the great fly ways that stretch from Canada to South America. Snow geese, every variety of duck, pelicans -- you can stand on the shore in northern Hatteras with binoculars and fill your sighting book. Take a look at our "Pea Island Wildlife Refuge" section, in the chapter on Hatteras Island, for a taste of what you can expect in the fall.

Winter in the Banks is usually snowless, but it gets cold, and windy as well. January and February see some nights dip below freezing. We've used the cottages of Nags Head and Kitty Hawk to hole up during the winter and write, think, just get away. The crowds are gone this time of year and the year 'round folks have more time to relax and visit with you -- if you want the company. There are plenty of restaurants, shops, and bars that stay open all year now, so finding diversions is easy -- if you want them. But, the beauty -- and quiet -- of these outer islands really show through during the cold months. It's a time of year we love to call the Banks home.

Spring comes early to the Outer Banks. We've been there on days in mid-January when the sun was warm and high and pine needles crunched underfoot in green grass, and all you wore was a sweater. By late March the temperature is already back up to the mid-sixties. Surf fishing begins, after a winter hiatus, with the arrival of the channel bass. April is the best spring month for these guys. Through March and April the pace slowly builds, and as May begins the whole tawny crescent of the barrier banks is once again ready for the summer.

To sum up, we think the term "Off Season," although descriptive, is not exactly accurate. There's really no "Off Season" for the Outer Banks the way there is for resort areas with wider swings in climate. If you choose to miss the hot months, or to make an additional visit outside of the most popular times, you can take advantage of lower rates, smaller crowds at your favorite diversions, and an entirely new range of enjoyments, recreations, and natural moods. In fact, we see (and predict) a lengthening of the active season on the Outer Banks. Already, in the last three years, the permanent population on the islands has doubled. More people are choosing to make this their year-round home, and as a direct consequence the occasional visitor will be able to take advantage of a longer, and in many ways a more enjoyable, season.

We call them the seasons of silver and gold. Maybe we've kept them to ourselves too long, but we've enjoyed them. You should too.

A graceful great blue heron heads into the twilight.

THE OUTER BANKS
FISHING GUIDE

Fishing is, beyond any doubt, the number one participant and spectator sport of the Outer Banks. In its various forms -- surf fishing, sound fishing, pier fishing, and full-scale Gulf Stream billfishing -- it is available for most of the year, with temporary but fierce booms when the season arrives and the big ones begin to bite. It's available right through the Banks, from Corolla down to Portsmouth, and on to Cape Lookout, but Hatteras Island is the true mecca of fishermen. Off Cape Point, beyond the lighthouse and Diamond Shoals, is the point where the warm blue waters of the Gulf Stream collide with the cooler, food-rich Virginia Coastal Drift. The combination provides a long fishing season and a variety of species matched by few if any other places in the world. Kitty Hawk and Nags Head have their piers and charter boats, but this special fishing guide will concentrate on Hatteras...because the fish seem to!

The island's heavy dependence on, and concentration on, sport fishing, along with its relative isolation, have made it the testing ground for many of the rigs and ideas that are now common in salt water fishing. Probably 60 to 65% of the terminal gear used in North Carolina has traditionally been made by various small subcontractors on the Outer Banks, who sit around in the off season and manufacture instead of fish. This has, in turn, led to the development of specialized rigs for the different types of fishing found on the Banks.

"We basically get two kinds of fishermen here on the Banks," says Ken Lauer. "The first are the tourists, who like to 'play' on a pier, or in the surf. They're happy with a six or twelve- inch fish. We see them between May and Labor Day. After that, the serious fishermen start to arrive."

Though the techniques overlap at places, there are basically three ways to fish on the Banks. These are from the surf (or a pier); from a boat, in the sounds; or from a larger boat, out in the Stream.

SURF AND PIER FISHING

Surf fishing is a sport and an art form all its own. It involves, much of the time, the use of four-wheel-drive vehicles and guides. Armed with specialized gear and up to seven rods apiece, the hard core surf fisherman spends September and December roving the Hatteras beaches at low tide to read the configuration of the sand bars. Where is it shallow? he asks himself, his guide, and every other fisherman he meets. Where are the bars? Where are there offshore holes at high water, where the fish will lurk?

On the Banks, the surf fisherman will find distinct species of fish around at different times of the year. Surf fishing really begins in early to mid-March, for those migratory fish (such as croakers and trout) that 'hibernate' offshore in winter and then move inshore and head north in the spring.

The next class is perhaps the most sought after: the drum family, or channel bass, as the largest are called (to clarify: a *Sciaenops ocellata* weighing, say, one pound, is known on the Banks as a 'puppy drum'. A little older, a little bigger, and it becomes a 'yearling drum'. One from 35 to about 70 lbs. will be called a red drum, or sometimes an 'old drum'. The really big ones, and it takes from forty to sixty *years* out there for them to attain this seniority, are 'channel bass', for which the world's record is 94 pounds, caught Avon off in 1984). The drum and channel bass have two seasons: mid-March to mid-May, as they move north, and then again mid-October to early December, as they move south again.

Another popular surf and pier fish is the blue, or bluefish, a vicious, toothy little fellow who's found at his best around here from mid-October to late November. There's a spring run for blues, too, but they tend to be emaciated. These, along with flounder, are the most popular fish available to the serious surf or pier fisherman. By the end of May surf fishing begins to taper off. In May to July about all the surf holds is one-pound blues, sea mullet, and Spanish mackerel in about the same size range. There are some summer fish, available mainly from the piers, and good for fun; spot, croaker, grey trout -- nice pan fish, but nothing to write home about. The pompano, also available then up to four lbs., are very tasty. And then there are the miscellanea: skate, blowfish, dogfish, rays, tarpon in late summer, and assorted sharks -- none all that common, but don't be surprised if one shows up on your hook.

Most fishing from piers and in the surf is done with casting lures or rigs using a sinker that will anchor in the sand and one or two hooks arranged to keep the bait away from the bottom. Hooks are usually size 4 to 6 for the smaller species and 6/0 to 9/0 for the larger. Bait is generally cutbait, cut mullet, shrimp, minnows, bloodworms, squid, or flounder and shark belly. Trout are commonly caught on a medium to large plastic lure; mackerel and large bluefish on metal casting lures; channel bass on mullet heads, cut menhaden or spot. As far as tide and time, low and incoming tides are often more productive than high water. Trout are best taken near dawn in clear water, while smaller drum are most likely found in the morning or evening in rough, murky water.

To try for the really big fish, you've got to haunt the ends of the piers, with a long rod (most often custom made), live-lining bluefish or spot with a heavy cork float and a four-foot wire leader.

Sounds too complex for you? The novice *can* catch fish on the Banks, if he uses his head. The tackle shops listed at the end of this section are stocked up not only with equipment but with information. All too often the visiting fisherman brings equipment that is too light and not suited to unique Banks conditions. It can make sense to leave your stuff at home and buy equipment here -- it will certainly be better suited to conditions, and may (since it's made here) be cheaper as well. A second option is renting. Most Banks tackle shops and piers rent rod, reel, terminal gear, and sometimes even foul weather gear and waders, and most can direct you to a local guide service.

Frank Merillat is a local guide who specializes in surf fishing. He has 26 years of fishing under his belt, the last eleven in Hatteras. Here are his surf fishing tips. "The first thing you have to realize is that all these fish are transitory. It's not like inland fishing where they hang around a tree or a rock. Off Hatteras it changes from tide to tide. This makes for more risky fishing, in terms of getting a predictable catch.

"It also means you have to work a little -- study the habits, or patterns, of the fish. The hard part is not catching them, it's finding 'em. Very few surf fish are difficult to catch. They bite readily at a variety of bait. Again, it's not like freshwater fishing, where you have to feed them the proper fly, place it just right, et cetera. Blues and drum are aggressive eaters and will readily bite.

"To find the fish -- the hard part -- you've got to learn to read the water. To understand what the bottom looks like; where the bars and sloughs are. The coast here has features something like this:

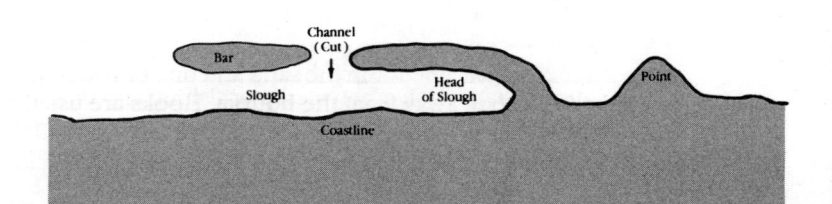

"The point is that this structure is rapidly changing. Day to day. So if you fish at the Point, for example, all the time -- just because it's been written about so much -- you may not get consistent catches.

"How do you read the water? Look at it. At low tide you can see the distinguishing marks: breaking waves, smooth water where the channels run. So it's very important to do your homework.

"Also, if you want to catch fish at Hatteras you need to spend time actively fishing. Not sitting in your motel room, not watching from your truck. You have to stand out there with a bait in the water. It's no mystery: these fish pass in migratory groups, and if you have a bait in the water when they're there you'll catch one.

"It's also important to vary your methods. If you're not catching anything with mullet you might try a lure or shrimp. Fish are changeable characters! Fish far out; fish close in. Jiggle the bait, vary the speed and motion of your retrieve. Hold your rod, then you can feel a bite. When the rod's in the rod holder you may be missing fish.

"Much of the time you catch nothing. You wait. Then suddenly there's a burst of action. You just got to be ready.

"Don't depend on the tackle shop people for *all* of your information. They talk to hundreds of people a day, so even when they give you a good spot it'll be crowded. A guide obviously can aid a fisherman. If you want to learn about gear, methods, habits, places to fish, then a guide's the way to go. Somebody who knows all this stuff doesn't need one. Or if it's not important to you to catch a fish. It's important to me to catch fish, and I'm a good fisherman. But if I went to Florida, I'd hire a guide. I don't like to waste the money and time. There's no way in the world a guide can guarantee you a fish, but I can guarantee you'll be better prepared to fish on your own afterward.

"Another subject. The time is here that fishermen need to be aware of our impact on the beach. If you drive on the dunes, or leave trash, you're ruining the island. Throw back fish you don't want. And if you do catch a beautiful forty-pound drum, use it! Eat it or give it to some old-timer on the island. There are lots of people who'll take a nice fish off your hands. Don't throw it in the dumpster. If I came to your home town and treated it the way some people treat this island I'd be thrown in jail. If we don't conserve and behave thoughtfully, we'll lose these beaches and our sport with them."

HEAD BOATS

An excellent intermediate choice between pier fishing and chartering a big boat yourself is the head boat, so called because it takes all comers on a regular schedule and charges X dollars "a head" (usually from fifteen to twenty dollars per person for a half-day, morning or afternoon). A lot of experienced fishermen enjoy head boating, but beginners especially love them. There's no pressure to bring home a big one, though certainly you can, and there's lots of fun and camaraderie for a small amount of cash.

Banks head boats generally cruise the sounds and inlets. In the spring and fall, however, they often head out to sea. Croaker, flounder, spot, and sea trout are the mainstays, depending of course on the season and your luck. Head boats generally provide fishing tackle, ice, bait, snack facilities, restrooms, and soft drinks, and the crew will help you bait your hook and deal with the fish once it's aboard, if you really aren't sure how it's done.

Oregon Inlet Marina, Hatteras Harbor Marina, Pirate's Cove, and several other locations on the Banks run head boats, especially during the season. See entries on individual marinas for more information on times, prices, and itineraries.

FRESH WATER FISHING

The fresh water fishing on the Outer Banks isn't nearly as well known as the salt water fishing, but it's there, as Dick Baker told us, and it's good. Kitty Hawk Bay and Currituck Sound offer "super bass fishing," and there are white and yellow perch and some nice catfish in the brackish sounds too. Numerous bass clubs fish this area, and the Master's Bass Classic has been held at Kitty Hawk. In early spring, Baker recommends crank and spinner baits, and worms in the summer, of course; go back to spinner and crank baits in the fall. For Kitty Hawk Bay, the public boat ramp west of the bypass opposite Avalon Pier offers the easiest access.

Don't say we didn't warn you, though, that fresh water licenses are required. North Carolina has carefully drawn lines between prominent points, and state fish and wildlife commission patrols will take *you* if you fish inside them or north of the Wright Memorial Bridge. Licenses are available at Tatem's, The Tackle Box, The Fishing Hook, Virginia Dare Hardware (Kitty Hawk), and Colington Creek Marina, among other agents.

BOAT FISHING: THE SOUNDS

Pamlico, Albemarle, Roanoke Sounds -- the small boater excels in these broad, shallow, brackish waters between the Banks and the mainland. The sounds in summer are crammed with fourteen-to-twenty- four footers after the hordes of gray trout, croakers, spot, flounder, tarpon, and at night even channel bass. Another popular fish in the sounds is cobia, which seems to hit its peak about the third week in May; this is a dramatic fish, a hard fighter, and good eating as well.

But in general, sound fishing is a more relaxed, family type of recreation than either surf or ocean fishing. You can hire a guide and a boat; or just set out on your own from a handy ramp in your own rig. A long, carefree day of summer fishing in the calm sound, maybe a case of beer...who needs to fight a marlin?

OCEAN FISHING

The ocean fisherman, that's who. He (and a lot of shes) revels in the Hemingwayesque challenge of a big, fighting billfish. And they're out there...**big** ones; in 1974 the IGFA all-tackle record blue marlin, 1,142 lbs., was taken off Oregon Inlet, and this was no fluke...hundreds are regularly taken off Hatteras during the summer months. Read our interview with Captain Ernal Foster of the *Albatross'* who started the Gulf Stream charter business in Hatteras in 1938.

Most of the Gulf Stream charter boats operate out of Oregon and Hatteras Inlets, plus a couple from Ocracoke and Roanoke Island. The Stream lies about an hour out, some 25 to 40 miles offshore. This is the closest the Stream comes to the coast north of Florida. Black and white marlin, dolphin, tuna, and wahoo are taken primarily by trolling. The blue marlin begin to show in mid-April, and peak in June; during July and August they taper off, but they're still there. By then the white marlin is getting plentiful, with a normal catch being one per boat per day. August is a good month for sailfish. Just beginning to catch on is the technique of long-lining for swordfish at night. There is a little wreck fishing off the Banks coast, but not as much as elsewhere along the Atlantic coast; skippers seem to prefer trolling to wreck-fishing. Certainly there are enough wrecks.

An excellent introduction to Stream fishing is the annual Sport Fishing School, held every June since 1950. This six-day course takes groups into the Gulf Stream on local boats for some exciting fishing. Most "students" are retirees or professional people, including families, who regard it as a vacation. Cost is about $600, lodging not included. For a brochure write North Carolina State University, Division for Lifelong Education, Box 7401, Raleigh NC, 27695-7401.

AUTUMN AND WINTER FISHING

Most Banks fishermen look forward to autumn. As the water cools in September, the larger fish begin to come inshore once again. The bluefish reappear, in larger sizes; Spanish mackerel show from four up to possibly nine pounds; puppy drum arrive in the surf. In November begins the return of the bluefish, now fat at ten and fifteen pounds. There is generally a terrific run of spot in September and October, averaging around a pound apiece, but copious, easy to catch, and tasty. As autumn goes on, the 'pier jockeys' begin to pull in channel bass again, especially from the two piers on the east face of the island (Hatteras Island and Avon).

November is the most looked-for month in terms of both quality and quantity of fishing, with Thanksgiving traditionally the peak (channel bass, bluefish, loads of two to five-pound flounder, and gray trout). This may continue on into December if the weather is warm. October and November see several team and individual tournaments, the Anglers Club, the Red Drum, The Capital City 4WD Club, and others.

The winter is a lull, it's very cold, there is little fishing from mid-December to mid-March. But the fish are there; big trout, croakers, and bluefish. As it gets colder they move offshore, to 80-100 feet of water. The commercial fishermen take them there, and many of the charter captains of Hatteras are commercial fishermen in the winter. Few sport fishermen can muster much enthusiasm for the Hatteras winter weather.

All in all, the Banks, especially Hatteras, offer the best year- round saltwater fishing to be found for a long way up or down the Atlantic coast.

OFF-ROAD VEHICLES -- THE CONTROVERSY

The use of Off-Road Vehicles (ORVs) on the beaches of Hatteras, Ocracoke, and Bodie Island has been limited. A 'zone' concept governs beach driving now, with these zones being opened or closed by National Park Service officials depending on erosion, nesting season, high visitor use areas, etc.

Though no permit is required to drive on the beach in the Park area, it is smartest to check with a ranger before you venture out to make sure you understand their guidelines and assure you are not entering a closed zone. Not knowing is no excuse, especially if you've wound up in some ecologically sensitive area.

One tip, there is NO beach driving allowed on the Pea Island National Refuge.

Once you're safely and legally on the beach, having reached it only by using one of the clearly marked and numbered ramps, you should remain on the portion of the beach between the water and the foot of the dunes, in other words, DO NOT drive on the dunes. The same goes for sound side driving: you should stay on the marked routes only. Your speed should be reasonable and prudent. And please pick up your trash -- not just to be a nice person, but to avoid the access-limit laws that have closed much of Cape Cod, for example, to any 4WD traffic at all. Vehicles must be state registered and street legal, the driver must also be licensed.

For current information on open zones and guidelines, you may contact the Headquarters, Pea Island National Wildlife Refuge, any National Park Service visitor contact facility, or you may write to: Cape Hatteras National Seashore, Route 1, Box 675, Manteo, N.C. 27954.

Each township on the Banks has its own requirements for permits to allow beach driving during certain times of the year. To get information or permits, contact the town administrative offices individually.

CITATIONS AND TOURNAMENTS

The Official North Carolina Saltwater Fishing Tournament is held annually to recognize outstanding angling achievement. The Department of Commerce, Travel and Tourism Division, awards citations for eligible species caught at or over certain minimum weights. Regulations on eligibility and boundaries may be obtained at these locations, which are also weighing stations for fish presented for citation:

Avalon Fishing Pier, Kill Devil Hills
Avon Fishing Pier, Avon
Bob's Bait & Tackle, Duck
Cape Hatteras Fishing Pier, Frisco
Dillon's Corner, Buxton
The Fishin' Hole, Salvo
Frisco Rod & Gun, Frisco
Hatteras Fishing Center
Hatteras Harbor Marina, Hatteras
Hatteras Island Fishing Pier, Rodanthe
Hatteras Marlin Club, Hatteras
Hatteras Tackle Shop, Hatteras
Island Marina, Manteo
Jennette's Pier, Nags Head
Kitty Hawk Fishing Pier, Kitty Hawk
Nags Head Fishing Pier, Nags Head
Nags Head Ice & Cold Storage, Nags Head

O'Neal's Dockside, Ocracoke
Oregon Inlet Fishing Center, Manteo
Outer Banks Pier and Fishing Center, Nags Head
Outer Banks Fishing Unlimited, Buxton
Pelican's Roost, Hatteras
Pirate's Cove, Nags Head-Manteo Causeway
The Red Drum Tackle Shop, Buxton
Salty Dawg Marina, Manteo
TW's Bait & Tackle, Duck, Kitty Hawk
Teach's Lair Marina, Hatteras
Tradewinds Tackle Shop, Ocracoke
Village Marina, Hatteras
Whalebone Tackle, Nags Head
Willis Boat Landing, Hatteras

ELIGIBLE SPECIES AND MINIMUM WEIGHTS FOR CITATIONS, 1990

Species	Minimum
Amberjack	50 lbs., or 50" with release
Barracuda	20 lbs.
Bass, Black Sea	3 lbs.
Bass, Channel/Red Drum	45 lbs., or 40" with release
Black Drum	40 lbs.
Bluefish	17 lbs.
Cobia	40 lbs.
Croaker	3 lbs.
Dolphin	35 lbs.
Flounder	5 lbs.
Grouper (any)	20 lbs.
Jack, Crevalle	20 lbs.
Mackerel, King	30 lbs.
Mackerel, Spanish	6 lbs.
Marlin, Blue	300 lbs.*
Marlin, White	50 lbs.*
Sailfish	30 lbs.*
Sea Mullet	1.5 lbs.

Shark (any)	100 lbs.
Sheepshead	10 lbs.
Snapper, Red	10 lbs.
Snapper, Silver (porgy)	4 lbs.
Spot	1 lbs.
Tarpon	30 lbs.*
Tautog	8 lbs.
Triggerfish	7 lbs.
Trout, Gray	6 lbs.
Trout, Speckled	4 lbs.
Tuna, Bigeye	100 lbs.
Tuna, Bluefin	80 lbs.
Tuna, Yellowfin	70 lbs.
Wahoo	40 lbs.

*Citation for release regardless of size

CURRENT ALL-TACKLE N.C. SALTWATER GAME FISH RECORDS

Fish	Weight	Location	Date
Amberjack	125	Off Cape Lookout	1973
Barracuda	67-7	Off Cape Lookout	1985
Bass, Black Sea	8	Off Oregon Inlet	1979
Bass, Channel	94*-2	Hatteras Island	1984
Bluefish	31-12*	Off Hatteras Island	1972
Cobia	103	Off Emerald Isle	1988
Croaker	5	Oregon Inlet	1981
Dolphin	77	Off Hatteras Island	1973
Drum, Black	84	Cape Fear River	1980
Flounder	20-8	Carolina Beach	1980
Grouper, Warsaw	245	Off Wrightsville Beach	1967
Mackerel, King	79	Cape Lookout	1985
Mackerel, Span.	13*	Off Ocracoke	1987

Marlin, Blue	1142	Off Oregon Inlet	1974
Marlin, White	118-8	Off Oregon Inlet	1976
Pompano	5	Oregon Inlet	1987
Sailfish	100	Off Ocean Isle	1987
Sea Mullet	3-8	Bogue Banks	1971
Shark, Tiger	1150	Yaupon Beach	1966
Sheepshead	18-7	Carolina Beach	1982
Snapper, Red	40	Off Cape Lookout	1970
Snapper, Silver	13	Off Cape Lookout	1987
Spot	1-13	Manns Harbor	1979
Tarpon	164	Indian Beach	1978
Tautog	12-14	Gulf Stream	1987
Triggerfish	10-8	Off Cape Lookout	1987
Trout, Gray	14-14	Nags Head	1980
Trout, Speckled	12-4	Wrightsville Beach	1961
Tuna, Bigeye	282	Off Oregon Inlet	1988
Tuna, Bluefin	732-8	Off Cape Hatteras	1979
Tuna, Yellowfin	237	Off Cape Lookout	1979
Wahoo	127	Off Oregon Inlet	1973

*World All-tackle record

To make application for all-tackle record recognition, write Suzanne Hill, Coordinator, N.C. Division of Marine Fisheries, P.O. Box 769, Morehead City, N.C. 28557.

Call 1-800-682-2632 for information or to report violations. Information current as of date of publication. Check at a tackle shop for latest update.

Wind surfing has become a top choice of visitors to the Outer Banks. DCTB

THE OUTER BANKS
SURFING, WINDSURFING, & OCEAN SWIMMING

Surfing has been around on the Banks since Bob Holland first began coming down from Virginia Beach in the late 50's. Word of the good surf here has spread; the East Coast Surfing Championships started here in the late 70's, and in 1978 and 1982 the U.S. Championships were held here.

"The best spot is at the lighthouse," says Scott Busbey, a resident pro and owner of the Natural Art surf shop. "Waves there usually break from the left, and the three jetties they built for erosion control formed a good sand bar."

Local surfers look forward to the hurricane season, from about the first of June to the end of November. This is when they begin to watch weather reports, hoping for the big northern swells. Waves get up to eight feet, and sometimes larger, but over about eight feet it tends to be "victory at sea."

Cape Hatteras (not just the Lighthouse beach) is always a popular spot. It has the advantage of having two beaches, facing in different directions; one faces south, the other east by southeast, so that when wind and swells are unsuitable at one, the other may be surfable. But when the wind comes from the southeast, which it often does in midsummer, be prepared to go swimming; surfing is poor. Two to three feet tends to be summer average. There's no channel at the Cape, which means you've got to muscle your way out there in heavy weather. Beware of the current when the waves come up; it's often two knots or more to the south along the beach, faster than you can swim, though on a board you might fight it. Wet suits a must until about the first of June; after that skin is OK till late October, or even later, depending on the lateness of the summer.

The lighthouse is usually the best, but not the only good break. The sandbars off the Banks are constantly shifting and changing, and there's a continual migration of surfers along them to find the best spots, which are then kept more or less secret. Surf along the Banks is where you find it. Places to check: Ramp 41; Frisco pier (off Billy Mitchell airport stay at least 400 feet from the pier itself); Kitty Hawk Pier, south of Coquina Beach. But you can always find a crowd at the Lighthouse.

LEARNING TO SURF

A lot of people, many of them from far inland, have learned to surf at Hatteras. If you've never done it, but you suspect that riding those big Atlantic waves in to the Cape Point break might be your kind of thrill, here are some tips to help you get started.

First, a bit of traditional surfer lore: the younger you are, the easier it is to start. If you're old enough to swim, and feel confident a hundred yards off the beach, you can surf. Here's how.

You can't surf without a board (body surfing doesn't count). You can rent one, or borrow one if you can convince a surfer to let go of his custom-made. Fortunately, any of the surf shops will rent you one for around ten dollars or so a day, a reasonable price, we think. (There will also be a deposit.) If you rent yours, be sure to ask if it's been waxed; if it hasn't, you'll be sliding all over the wave.

Second, you've got to find a break. We suggest not starting off where all the others are surfing. Get off by yourself, so that you won't be in the way of the more skilled. The break won't be as good, but then, neither are you. Right?

Item number three. To surf, you've got to learn to paddle the board. Find your balance position. Your chest should go about at the thickest part of the surfboard. This is important, so try paddling about till you feel comfortable. Watch how the others do it, up the beach.

Now paddle out to sea.

To surf, you must realize that the wave is moving toward the beach at some speed, while the shallowing water forces it to crest. You won't be picked up by it unless you're moving in the same direction at almost the same speed (this is why paddling is so important). This is the hardest part of learning, getting your timing down, learning to watch and catch the wave at that exactly correct fraction of a second.

Once the wave has you, you'll know it. You'll be carried forward fast and effortlessly, part of the sea in motion. It's a thrill.

Finally, to get up: just stand up, just as if you were doing a pushup from the speeding board. Don't get to your knees first. Just stand up naturally. Place one or the other foot forward (most people do it left foot forward, but there's no shame in being a "goofy-foot"), about a shoulder-width apart.

If you can stand up, and ride a wave into the beach that way once, you've done pretty well for your first day; don't stay out forever and agonize with sunburn tomorrow. The rest, the turning, and the other advanced maneuvers you see the more experienced people doing, will come with practice.

When you feel more confident, when you want to try the good breaks with the others, remember your manners. Stay out of the way if someone's already on a wave. That's about the only point of etiquette that's really important. You'll find, after hanging around for a while, that most surfers are friendly, and with time you'll fit in with the others just fine.

"Awoo!"

WINDSURFING

Windsurfing, or board sailing, is unquestionably the fastest growing sport on the Banks -- perhaps nationwide. And it's well-known that the entire Outer Banks and, some think, especially Hatteras, is the best windsurfing location on the Atlantic coast.

Kitty Hawk Sports

"Windsurfing is our Specialty"

Windsurfing · Catamarans · Sailboats
SALES · LESSONS · RENTALS
We are the Mistral and North High Wind Center

Nags Head (919) 441-6800 · **Cape Hatteras** 995-5000
Write: P.O. Box 939 Nags Head N.C. 27959

Ted James came to Hatteras in '72 from Florida to surf and fish, "Looking for what Florida lost years ago." He runs a commercial fishing boat in the winter, and has been making his Fox boards here and in Florida since 1968. James was one of the first to put sailboards in big surf here, and he was instrumental in improving the boards and rigs to their present state of excellence. He was busy shaping a racing board in his Buxton workshop when we asked him to tell us a little about windsurfing.

"It's real simple why Hatteras is so popular for windsurfers. People have been cussin' the wind here since there was wind. But with sailboards, the more wind the better.

"The equipment you use is a board and a rig. The heart of the system is a 'universal' that swivels and pivots in every direction. That allows you to position the mast, boom and sail, and determine the direction you go. Basically, to sail cross wind, the mast is up and down. To sail downwind, tip the mast forward, and that turns the front of the board downwind. Mast back, that turns the boat upwind.

"Now, that sounds complicated, and that's why I recommend lessons. What we do is spend two and a half hours -- the first lesson -- on teaching people to sail short distances. The second lesson we practice, increasing sail area, smaller boards, switching rigs -- whatever challenges the individual. We also teach self-rescue and rigging in the second lesson. Self-rescue's important in case the wind dies, or something breaks. People are recreationally proficient after two lessons.

"Now, that's not experienced surfers; that's people who walk in the door. You don't have to be athletic. Though it's easier to teach people who sail, in a way, because they know the wind. Surfing is not as big an advantage. No, you don't have to know how to swim. We put a jacket on them.

"It's not *easy* -- you have to pay attention -- but we've had people uncoordinated, overweight, and they catch on. A lot of them, it's the first athletic success they've ever had. And it means a lot to me to help them succeed. Our students range from twelve to sixty. We've taught over 1000 people in the last three years and only had one person who couldn't do it. It's neat -- sometimes you get teen aged sons, and Dad outshines them. They kind of laugh a little bit then."

Ralph Buxton, owner of Kitty Hawk Sports, started teaching windsurfing in 1980 in the Nags Head area. He is well-known for his participation and promotion of the sport. He explains that while the Canadian Hole, as the favorite spot in Hatteras is known, is certainly a great place to sail, windsurfers also enjoy the many upper Banks windsurfing areas because the wind conditions are just as good and there are many other attractions available to them if the wind isn't cooperating. Kitty Hawk Sport's Windmill Point Sailing Site in Nags Head is an ideal place to learn because of the shallow and sheltered water.

The basic sailboarding season is year 'round. December to March is slow, though, simply because it's cold (there's plenty of wind out there if you want it). James runs competitive events, the Hatteras Wave Classic in October and the Pro-Am in spring. Kitty Hawk Sports runs the Easter Dash for Cash, the August Watermelon Regatta, and the Thanksgiving Classic Regatta. They're as much fun to watch as they are to participate in. This is a booming sport now, and it's still early enough to say you were one of the pioneers.

Kitty Hawk Sports gives away a 10 page windsurfing publication listing sites, weather, gear, and other helpful information. Call 441-6800 to get your copy.

SURF SHOPS

There are several surf shops on the Banks, scattered north and south, including: Fox Water Sports, Buxton, 995-4102 Natural Art, Buxton, 995-5682. For a 24-Hour surf report, call 995-4646.

Windsurfing Hatteras, Avon, 995-4970
Hatteras Island Surf Shop, Waves, 987-2296
Resin Craft Surf Shop, Whalebone Junction, 441-6747
Wave Riding Vehicles, Kitty Hawk, 261-7952
   For a 24-Hour surf report, call 261-3332
Secret Spot Surf Shop, Nags Head, 441-4030
Vitamin Sea Surf Shop, Kill Devil Hills (MP5), 441-7512
Bert's Surf Shop, Nags Head, 441-1939
Ride the Wind, Ocracoke, 928-7451
BW's Surf Shop, Ocracoke, 928-6141

OCEAN SWIMMING

If you've grown up around the sea, sailing as a kid, spending long days on surfboards, you probably know that Mother Ocean can sometimes be dangerous. Here are a few tips for those who haven't spent a lot of time around salt water.

RIPS

Rip currents can carry a child or a wader out into rough water in seconds. They generally move along the shore and then straight out to sea. They often occur when there's a break in a submerged sandbar. You can see a rip; it's choppy, turbulent, often discolored water that looks deeper than the water around it. If you are caught in a rip, don't panic, and don't try to struggle straight back to shore against its force. Remember that rip currents are narrow. Very few are wider than thirty feet across. So simply swim parallel to the beach until you're out of it, or let it carry you seaward till it peters out. Then move to one side or the other of it and swim back.

UNDERTOW

When a wave comes up on the beach and breaks, the water must run back down to the sea. This is undertow. It sucks at your ankles from small waves, but in heavy surf undertow can knock you off your feet and carry you out. If you're carried out, don't resist. Let the undertow take you out till it stops. It will only be a few yards. The next wave will help push you shoreward again.

LOSING CONTROL IN WAVES

If a wave crashes down on you while you are surfing or swimming, and you find yourself being tumbled in bubbles and sand like a sheet in a washing machine, don't try to struggle to the surface against it. Curl into a ball, or just go limp and float. The wave will take you to the beach or else you can swim to the surface when it passes.

PRECAUTIONS

If you're new to the ocean, remember: Never swim alone.
Don't go into the water without observing the surf first.
Look for currents.
Don't go in unless you can swim.
Don't stay on the beach during electrical storms.

Try to swim in guarded areas.

Observe warning flags near public accesses. If they're red, don't go in.

Protect yourself from the sun. Sunburns don't turn into tans. They peel off.

Keep non-swimming children well above the marks of the highest waves.

Don't swim near fishermen or deployed fishing lines.

THE OUTER BANKS
SCUBA DIVING

"Most divers who arrive on the Banks as tourists don't realize what we have down here," says Art LePage, dean of the Banks' commercial divers. "What we have is nothing less than the finest wreck diving on the Atlantic Coast."

Amen. The over 600 wrecks that have made Hatteras and the Banks area dreaded by mariners for centuries have also made the area a paradise for the hard-case wreck diver. Hard-case, because the waters offshore are often cold and have variable visibility and strong currents, as well as a sizeable shark population. The changeable weather of Hatteras itself is another hazard. The shifting sands cover and uncover new wrecks almost every year, and the divers of the area are busy discovering them, so any list of good spots can be only partial; check at local shops for the up-to-the-minute information that will assure you a safe and enjoyable dive. With that in mind, here is a partial list of Banks diving opportunities, to whet your appetite for salt water:

LST 471 sunk in 1949. About 1/4 mile north of the Rodanthe Fishing pier, 100 yds. offshore in 15 feet of water.

Oriental (Boiler Wreck) thought to be a Federal transport that sank in 1862. About four miles south of Oregon Inlet; the boiler of the ship is visible in the surf.

Triangle Wrecks Josephine (lost 1915), **Kyzickes** (1927), **Carl Gerhard** (1929). Off 7-mile post at Kill Devil Hills, about 100 yds. out and 200 yds. south of the Sea Ranch. Depth about 20 feet.

USS Huron Federal screw steamer lost off Nags Head in 1877. Now in 26 feet of water. Many artifacts.

Liberty Ship (Zane Grey) About one mile south of Oregon Inlet at eighty feet.

U-85 German sub sunk in 1942. Northeast of Oregon Inlet in 100 feet of water. Boat needed (see Bodie Island section).

York, Benson, Buarque Freighters and tankers sunk by U-boats during Operation Paukenschlag in 1942. They lie offshore, but within dive boat range, in from 100-120 feet. Good challenging dives.

Beach Diving -- There are over 12 wrecks in shallow water between Duck and Hatteras. Great for free diving (without scuba gear) and spear fishing. Ask local divers for locations.

Sound Diving -- If you don't mind shallow, murky water, you may enjoy groping around north and west of Roanoke Island, where old Civil War forts lie submerged. Local divers have found cannonballs, bottles, relics, etc. with metal detectors.

Numbers to keep handy:
  Oregon Inlet USCG station -- 987-2311
  Ocean Rescue Squad (helicopter available) -- 911
  Divers Alert Network (DAN) -- (919) 684-8111.

Shops and Facilities: Two full-service dive shops serve the Banks, Nags Head Divers, and Hatteras Divers.

NAGS HEAD PRO DIVE CENTER
MP 13 1/2   441-7594
Kitty Hawk Connection shops

This is the oldest dive facility on the Outer Banks offering a full line of services -- equipment sales and rentals, airfills to 5,000 psi, service, and PADI and NAUI instruction. The Nags Head Divers also run their 50' dive boat, the *Sea Fox*, out of the Manteo Waterfront to the historic wrecks off the Outer Banks coast including the York, and the U-85. Open seven days a week, 9 a.m. to 9 p.m. from Memorial Day to Labor Day; open off-season on a regular schedule, hours 10 to 6. Call Phil Nutter for information.

HATTERAS DIVERS
Hatteras Village   986-2557

Hatteras Divers is owned by Donny Lang who plans charter trips to Tarpon, Abrams, Dixie Arrow, Proteus, box car reefs, other popular destinations. They're located just west of Hatteras Harbor Motel on the harbor. Hours, June - October, 9 to 6, Monday through Saturday. For information call or write P.O. Box 213, Hatteras, NC 27943. They can arrange charters and fill your air tanks. They offer rental on full gear.

FERRY
CONNECTIONS

For information on the Hatteras-Ocracoke free ferry, see the Hatteras chapter.

FROM OCRACOKE:
SWAN QUARTER AND CEDAR ISLAND RESERVATIONS

To avoid possible delay in boarding the Cedar Island-Ocracoke Ferry and the Swan Quarter-Ocracoke Ferry, reservations are recommended. These may be made in person at the departure terminal or by telephone. For departures from Ocracoke, call (919) 928-3841; for departures from Cedar Island, call (919) 225-3551; and for reservations for departures from Swan Quarter, call (919) 926-1111. (Office hours 6 a.m.- 6 p.m., later in summer.)

Reservations may be made up to 30 days in advance of departure date and are not transferable. These reservations must be claimed at least 30 minutes prior to departure time. The name of the driver and the vehicle license number are required when making reservations.

GROSS LOAD LIMITS
All Crossings:

Any axle	13,000 lbs.
Two axles (single vehicle)	24,000 lbs.
Three or more axles	36,000 lbs.

(single or combination vehicle)

More information may be obtained from Director, Ferry Division, Morehead City, NC 28557, or by calling (919) 726-6446 or 726-6413.

FERRY INFORMATION

OCRACOKE-SWAN QUARTER TOLL FERRY
Crossing Time Approx. 2 1/2 hrs.
Capacity Approx. 30 Cars
YEAR-ROUND

Leave Ocracoke	Leave Swan Quarter
6:30 AM	9:30 AM
12:30 PM	4:00 PM

FARES AND RATES APPLICABLE (ONE WAY) Same as Cedar Island -- Ocracoke Ferry Rates.

CEDAR ISLAND -- OCRACOKE TOLL FERRY
Crossing Time Approx. 2 1/2 hrs.
Capacity Approx. 30 Cars

SUMMER SCHEDULE
April 15 thru Oct 31

Leave Cedar Island	Leave Ocracoke
7:00 AM	7:00 AM
9:30 AM	9:30 AM
12:00 Noon	12:00 Noon
3:00 PM	3:00 PM
6:00 PM	6:00 PM
8:30 PM	8:30 PM

WINTER SCHEDULE
Nov. 1 thru April 14

7:00 AM	10:00 AM
1:00 PM	4:00 PM

FARES AND RATES APPLICABLE (ONE WAY)

A. Pedestrian	1.00
B. Bicycle and Rider	2.00
C. Single vehicle or combination 20' or less in length and motorcycles (minimum fare for licensed vehicle)	10.00
D. Vehicles or combinations from 20' to 40' in length	20.00
E. All vehicles or combinations 40' to 55' in length having a maximum width of 8 feet and height of 13'6"	30.00

Albemarle Hospital

Providing quality healthcare to Northeastern North Carolina for more than 75 years. Located just north of Elizabeth City, the hospital is conveniently adjacent to Colonial Medical Village and Albemarle Professional Park.

We have a 24-hour physician-staffed Emergency Department with specialists on call 365 days a year.

Emergency Department 331-4610
Patient Information 331-4631
Public Relations 331-4455 or 331-4416

Hwy 17 North, P.O. Box 1587
Elizabeth City, NC 27906-1587
(919) 335-0531

Accredited by the Joint Commission on Accreditation of Healthcare Organizations

---

NORTH BEACH MEDICAL CENTER

Urgent Care and Family Practice
Physician on Duty 9am - 9pm
365 days a year
No appointment necessary
(919) 261-4187

General Surgery
Obstetrics/Gynecology
Orthopedics
Otorhinolaryngology
(Ears, Nose & Throat)
Pediatrics

Physical Therapy
Podiatry
Psychological Services
Radiology
(X-ray, Mammography)
Urology

Regional Medical Services
John J. Carvalho, Administration
2 Juniper Trail
Kitty Hawk, NC 27949
Milepost 1
(Southern Shores, next to the Marketplace)

OUTER BANKS
HEALTH CARE

Although the Outer Banks Hospital is still only in the planning stages, basic and emergency medical care is available here. A medical helicopter is also available to evacuate any emergencies that are better handled at a nearby hospital.

In case of emergency:	**911**
Ocean saving services as well as accidents on land:	911
South of Oregon Inlet Police, Fire, Rescue Squad:	986-2144
Coast Guard:	995-6410
Ocracoke Island:	928-4831

OTHER MEDICAL ATTENTION

OUTER BANKS MEDICAL CENTER
158 Bypass MP 11, Nags Head   441-7111

The only 24 hour facility on the beach. Walk-ins are welcome and they have x-ray equipment on the premises.

BEACH MEDICAL CENTER
158 Bypass MP 10 1/2, Nags Head   441-2174

Open 7 days 8 a.m. to 8 p.m. and staffed by Dr. Hurley, Dr. Davidson, and P.A.s, this office provides general medical care. You may call for an appointment or walk-in.

NORTH BEACH MEDICAL CENTER

Next to Marketplace, MP 1   261-4187

Affiliated with Regional Medical Services, this facility offers complete medical care and can also take x-rays for you. Dr. Wilkinson and Dr. Dunkle are the staff doctors.

MACDOWELL FAMILY HEALTH CENTER

U.S. Highway 64, Manteo   473-2500

Dr. Brian MacDowell provides complete family medical care at this office. X-ray is also available. Psychological counseling services are provided by Debra MacDowell, MA, NCC.

BEACH MEDICAL CARE SOUTH

Hwy. 12 Buxton, next to Beach Pharmacy   995-4455

Also known as Cape Hatteras Family Care, this is the place to go if you need a few stitches or come down with a bug during your visit to Hatteras. Call ahead as hours are limited. M, W, F 1:30 - 5:30 p.m.; Tue 8:30 -11:30 a.m;. Thurs. 9:00 - 3:00 p.m.

Other possibilities for doctors on Hatteras:
Dr. Jacobs   986-2756
Dr. Slagle, Frisco   995-4104

OCRACOKE HEALTH CENTER

Just past the firehouse   928-1511

This is also a clinic offering general medical care. Their hours are limited, so if you can't get them, and your concern is serious, call the rescue squad at 928-4831. They'll be glad to help.

DENTISTS

BUDDE AND BUEKER, DDS

158 bypass, 9 1/2 MP, KDH   441-5811

Family dentistry with emergency services available.

FRANK AUSBAND, DDS
158 bypass, 11 MP, Nags Head   441-0437

Another dentist who welcomes emergencies; or make an appointment to get your teeth cleaned.

GYNECOLOGY

OUTER BANKS WOMANCARE
158 bypass, 5 1/2 MP, KDH, Overseas Professional Bldg. 441-1155

Mark and Pegeen Eggleston opened this top notch facility specializing in high-risk pregnancy. Gynecological and infertility services are offered; pregenancy related emergency care also available.

VIRGINIA DARE WOMEN'S CENTER
158 Bypass MP 10 1/2, Nags Head
441-2144

Patty Johnson, a certified nurse midwife and a family nurse practitioner, heads up this office. She and her staff offer women-centered care, including Paps, maternity care, and baby care. Hours are Mon., Tues., Thurs., and Fri. from 9 a.m. until 1 p.m., then 2 p.m. until 5 p.m. Closed on Wednesdays. You should call for an appointment.

CHIROPRACTIC CARE

ACKLEY CHIROPRACTIC CENTER
158 Bypass, MP 2 1/2, Kitty Hawk   261-1444

B.L. Ackley DC offers complete care here. Call or walk-in.

DARE CHIROPRACTIC
158 Bypass, MP 3, Kitty Hawk   261-8885

Allen Krolands DC and Burt Rubin DC provide comprehensive care at this facility.

OUTER BANKS CHIROPRACTIC CLINIC
158 Bypass, MP 10, Nags Head   441-1585

Jan van Beelen DC and Craig Gibson DC are the "back docs" at this office, the oldest in the area. It's probably a good idea to call before you go.

OTHER SERVICES

Dare Vision Center, 473-2155 and 441-4872, run by Dr. Adams, provides complete eye care. Located on Highway 64 in Manteo near McDonalds and on the 158 Bypass in Kill Devil Hills.

Albemarle Eye Care Center, 441-3163, 158 Bypass in Kill Devil Hills, offers total eye care. They also have a toll-free number: 1-800-682-6978.

Terry Gardner at Shear Genius, 441-3571, offers European facials with neck and shoulder massage, as well as full body massages.

The Outer Banks Hotline, 473-3366 north of Oregon Inlet or 995-4555 south of the Inlet, is a 24-hour crisis counseling service that also provides shelter to victims of abuse.

Atlantic Counseling Services, 441-1372, 158 Bypass in Nags Head, is run by Robin Craven, MA, certified professional counselor. He offers individual and family counseling as well as psychotherapy. Call for an appointment.

Outer Banks Dialysis Center, 441-0424, 158 Bypass in Nags Head, offers kidney dialysis. Call for information.

Dare Hospice, 441-6242, offering help to the terminally ill, their families and friends.

Alcoholics Anonymous: Hatteras, 995-4240 or 995-4283; upper beaches area, 261-1681, 441-6020, 473-5389.

SERVICE AND INFORMATION DIRECTORY

Coast Guard
Buxton Village	995-5881
Hatteras Island	987-2311
Hatteras Village	986-2175
North of Oregon Inlet	987-2311
Ocracoke	928-3711

County Sheriff
Hatteras Island (Dare County)	986-2144
North of Oregon Inlet (Dare County)	473-3481
Northern Outer Banks (Currituck County)	232-2216
Ocracoke Island (Hyde County)	928-3701

Fire Department
Avon Village	995-5021
Buxton Village	986-2500
Corolla	232-2424
Duck	261-3929
Hatteras Village	986-2500
Kill Devil Hills	441-2531
Kitty Hawk	261-3552
Manteo	473-2133
Nags Head	441-5508
Ocracoke	928-4831
Salvo Village	987-2411

Police Department
(If one isn't listed for your community, call the sheriff's dept.)

Hatteras Village	986-2144
Kill Devil Hills	441-7491
Kitty Hawk	261-3895
Manteo	473-3481
Nags Head	441-6386
Southern Shores	261-3331

National Park Service Offices

North of Oregon Inlet	473-2111 or 441-6644
South of Oregon Inlet	995-4474
Ocracoke Island	928-4531

CRISIS HOTLINE

Outer Banks Hotline (confidential counseling and information for any crisis, and shelter for battered women.)

North of Oregon Inlet	473-3366
South of Oregon	995-4555

ANIMAL SERVICES

Kitty Hawk, Nags Head, Manteo and Hatteras Island all have established veterinary clinics. Check the Yellow Pages under Veterinarians for a complete listing.

Dare County Animal Shelter (9 to 5)	473-2143

KENNELS

Water Oak Kennel, Buxton Village	995-5663
Animal Hospital of Nags Head	441-8611
Salty Dog Grooming and Boarding, Colington	441-6501
North River Kennel, Powells Point	491-2284

AUTOMOTIVE SERVICES

The Banks have adequate service and parts outlets to keep standard American makes going and most imports. But, if you break down in a vintage 1952 MGTD, you might have a bit of a wait till parts arrive.

There are three full-service dealerships on the Banks:

R.D. Sawyer Ford, Manteo	473-2141
Coastal (formerly McLeod) Chevrolet/Buick, Manteo	473-2125
Outer Banks Chrysler/Plymouth/Dodge/Jeep, KDH	441-1146

Other recommended auto services and towing:

Kitty Hawk Exxon, Kitty Hawk	261-2720
Johnny's Towing Service (AAA), KDH	441-7473 or 441-7283
Berry Automotive, Manteo	473-3807
Autotech, Nags Head	441-5293
Jackson Auto, Manteo	473-5990
Manteo Wrecker Service (AAA)	473-5654
Farrow Brothers Automotive, Avon	995-5944
Ballance Gulf & Oil, Hatteras Village	986-2424

CAR RENTALS

It is possible to arrange for car rentals at several Outer Banks locations, including the airport and most marinas.

National Car Rental	441-5488
Rt 158 By pass, MP 5 1/2 KDH	
B&R Rent-a-car	473-2600
Dare County Regional Airport, Manteo	
R.D. Sawyer Ford	473-2141
Highway 64, Manteo	

FISHING REPORT

Provided by WOBR Radio	473-3373
Red Drum Tackle Shop, Hatteras	995-5414
Oregon Inlet Fishing Center (for their boats)	441-6301
Kitty Hawk Pier	261-2772
Nags Head Fishing Pier	441-5141

Hatteras Island Fishing Pier (Rodanthe)	987-2323
Frisco Pier	986-2533
O'Neals Dockside, Ocracoke	928-1111

HOSPITALITY SERVICE

Southern Hospitality, owned and operated by Nancy McWilliams, is a new service for 1990, and we think a great one. The primary function of the service is to welcome newcomers to the area. When a new person or family moves to the Outer Banks, Nancy makes an in-home visit to answer questions, provide literature about the area, and just give a friendly Outer Banks "welcome." Call her at 473-2042 if you're a new permanent resident.

LIQUOR LAWS & ABC STORES

After a long dry spell, mixed drinks are now being served in most restaurants in northern Dare County (Duck, Southern Shores, Kitty Hawk, Kill Devil Hills, Nags Head). Currituck County (Corolla), Manteo, Wanchese, and the beaches south of Oregon inlet do not have liquor by the drink. Some restaurants serve only beer and wine, some offer setups for brown bagging.

Restaurants with a brown bag license will allow you to bring your own bottle into the establishment where you surrender it at the table and have the house mix the drinks. You will be charged for mixes and setups.

Beer and wine are available in most convenience stores and supermarkets, but bottle liquor is available only in county-run ABC (Alcohol Beverage Control) package stores.

There are four ABC package stores on the resort strip, and one each on Hatteras and Ocracoke Islands.

Duck ABC Store	261-6981

Rt. 12 (at Wee Winks Square)

Kitty Hawk ABC Store	261-2477

MP 1, Rt. 158 (next to Three Winks)

Nags Head ABC Store	441-5121

MP 10, Rt. 158 (at 8th Street stoplight)

Manteo ABC Store	473-3557

Rt. 64/264 (just north of Wanchese turnoff)

Buxton ABC Store	995-5532

Just off Rt. 12 in Osprey Shopping Center

Ocracoke ABC Store   928-3281
Located on Rt. 12 near Ocracoke Variety Store
ABC stores are generally open 10 a.m. to 9 p.m., Mon. - Sat. No personal checks or credit cards accepted. You must be 21 years old to enter the store. The legal purchase is one gallon.

LIBRARIES

The main Dare County Library, 473-2372, is located in Manteo on Hwy.64/264 across from the Manteo Elementary School. Bookmobile service is provided throught the county. Call for schedule.

The Kill Devil Hills branch , 441-4331, is located off Bypass 158 between the Baum center and the water treatement center near Collington Road

The Hatteras branch of the Dare County Library, 986-2385, is located in the county recreation building across from Burrus' Red & White store.

The Ocracoke Library is located behind the Fire hall. The hours are posted on the door.

MEDIA INFORMATION

Newspapers

The OuterBanks has one local weekly paper: The *Coastland Times*, published by Times Printing with offices in Manteo on Budleigh Street and in Kill Devil Hills on the Beach Road (473-2105). *The Coastland Times* is published on Sunday, Tuesday and Thursday. It covers news in Dare and surrounding counties.

Daily newspapers from nearby cities (Elizabeth City, Raleigh, Tidewater area, Richmond) are carried at several locations. You will even find a place or two carrying *The New Times* and *The Washington Post*.

Television

Outer Banks Cablevision, Kill Devil Hills, supplies cable television service to most of the Outer Banks. Most motels and hotels are subscribers and many offer special stations like HBO or the Disney Channel.

Of particular interest to visitors will be Channel 12. Outer Banks Panorama, an informative program about things to see and do in the area, appears regularly throughout the day. There are usually four or five different versions, so don't assume you've seen it all if you only watch one. Between Panorama shows, there is other local programming.

Radio
The Banks' first native radio station was WOBR, Wanchese, FM 95 stereo, and is still owned by the same person who began it. The station plays Adult contemporary and has a great Sunday morning jazz show from 10 to noon. They stay in tune with what a majority of Outer Bankers want to hear.

WOBR now leases their AM (1530) station to the Outer Banks Worship Center for Christian programming.

WRSF 106 (FM 105.7 to be exact) is the former WWOK out of Columbia. One of America's most powerful stations, Surf 106 plays popular music. Hunt Thomas' "Hot 9 at 9" evening show is particularly popular with the local teens.

WVOD FM 99.3, "The Voices of Dare," Manteo, is a locally-owned station that began broadcasting in the spring of '86. They offer a lot of different sounds and a varied format centering around adult contemporary. If you're here on Sundays, they have some great programming, starting with Sunday Classics, playing classical music, then, in the evening, the nationally syndicated Music Americana, followed by Fritz on Jazz. This station is also very community-minded, offering air space and the support of their personnel to local groups with worthy causes

WNHW FM 92, " Carolina 92" is the Outer Banks' newest radio station. They play country music in all aspects, including modern, pop, traditional, folk and rockabilly. Carolina 92 also airs music features like a weekly count down on Sunday afternoons. They also feature CNN news and sports, local news and weather, and fishing and beach reports.

POSTAL SERVICE & PACKAGE SHIPMENT
POST OFFICES
Corolla (next door to Winks)   453-2552
Kitty Hawk (turn toward sound at Kitty Hawk Road stoplight. Post office is about a mile into the village on the right)
                                                                       261-2211
Kill Devil Hills (MP 8 on Rt. 158)   441-5666
Nags Head (MP 13 on Rt. 158)   441-7387

Manteo (downtown at corner of Queen
Elizabeth and Ananais Dare Streets) 473-2534
Wanchese (on Rt. 345) 473-3551
Rodanthe (on Rt.12, south of Joe Bob's Trading Post) 987-2273
Avon (on Rt. 12, between Outer Beaches Realty
and the Avon Shopping Center) 995-5991
Buxton (on Rt. 12, just south of Buxton Books) 995-5755
Hatteras (on Rt. 12, one mile before ferry) 986-2318
Ocracoke (on Rt. 12 in village, next to Bluff Shoals Motel)928-4771

Packages can be mailed at any United States Post Office during regular window hours. Hours vary from town to town, so you might want to call first.

United Parcel Service (UPS) now has a service center on Roanoke Island. They accept packages from the public, subject to size limitations, weekdays from 3:30 - 5:45 p.m. They offer overnight express shipment to many U.S. locations. For information, call 1-800-662-7506.

Federal Express has several drop box locations around the Outer Banks. Pickup service can also be arranged. Federal Express offers overnight service to most U.S. destinations. Call 1-800-238-5355 for information or pickup.

Outer Banks Transit (441-7090), Route 158 Bypass MP 9, Kill Devil Hills, is centrally located and serves as a U.P.S. and U. S. Postal Service pickup point. They sell packaging materials, as well.

RENTAL SERVICES

Did you forget that much-needed beach chair or stroller? Never fear. There are several good rental companies on the Outer Banks that carry more items than you could ever forget to bring.

Life Saver Rent-Alls, 441-6048, 261-1344, 1-800-635-2764, is located in the Three Winks Shopping Center in Kitty Hawk and at MP 9 on the Beach Road. They offer an endless inventory of any vacation-supply needs including baby equipment such as cribs, jogging strollers or car seats; beach supplies such as umbrellas, surf boards, fishing rods and tackle, and volley ball sets; and cottage items from VCR's to linens.

Ocean Atlantic Rentals has four locations throughout the area: in the Corolla Light Shops, 453-2440; on the Beach Road at MP 10, 441-7823; in Scarborough Faire in Duck, 261-4346; and on Hatteras Island in Waves, 987-2492. They also have a toll-free number to call ahead and make reservations, 1-800-635-9559. They carry a very complete stock of any item you might need to make your vacation complete.

SELF-SERVICE LAUNDRIES

Kitty Hawk Laundromat , Beach Road MP 4, Kitty Hawk
Superette Launderette , Rt. 158 Bypass MP 6, Kill Devil Hills
P & G Wash & Dry , Outer Banks Mall, Nags Heads
Speed Wash , Rt. 158 Bypass MP 16-1/2, Nags Head
Mr. Clean Laundromat , Chesley Mall, Manteo
The Wash Basket, turn off Hwy. 12 at Cape Pines Motel, Buxton
Frisco Launderette, Rt. 12 across from Scotch Bonnet, Frisco

There are no self-service laundries in Hatteras Village or on Ocracoke

STORM AND HURRICANE PROCEDURES

June through November is hurricane season in the Outer Banks. All of the southeastern U.S. is prone to hurricanes but the Banks, due to their low elevation, frontage on the ocean, and lack of shelter, are particularly vulnerable. A hurricane strikes the Banks about every nine years; a major one every 42 years; a tropical cyclone about every five years. The Dare County Civil Preparedness Agency promulgates the following Hurricane Safety Rules:

1. Enter each hurricane season prepared. Every June through November, recheck your supply of boards, tools, batteries, non-perishable foods, and the other equipment you will need when a hurricane strikes your area.

2. When you hear the first tropical cyclone advisory, listen for future messages; this will prepare you for a hurricane emergency well in advance of the issuance of watches and warnings.

3. When your area is covered by a hurricane watch, continue normal activities, but stay tuned to the local stations (see Media in this Service Directory), or the National Weather Service Station at Buxton for advisories. Remember, a hurricane watch means possible danger within 24 hours; if the danger materializes, a hurricane warning will be issued. Meanwhile, keep alert. Ignore rumors.

4. When your area receives a hurricane warning:

Plan your time before the storm arrives and avoid the last-minute hurry which might leave you marooned, or unprepared.

Keep calm until the emergency has ended.

Leave low lying areas that may be swept by high tides or storm waves.

Leave mobile homes for more substantial shelter. They are particularly vulnerable to overturning during strong winds. Damage can be minimized by securing mobile homes with heavy cables anchored in concrete footing.

Moor your boat securely before the storm arrives, or evacuate it to a designated safe area. When your boat is moored, leave it, and don't return once the wind and waves are up.

Board up windows or protect them with storm shutters or tape. Danger to small windows is mainly from wind-driven debris. Larger windows may be broken by wind pressure.

Secure outdoor objects that might be blown away or uprooted. Garbage cans, garden tools, toys, signs, porch furniture, and a number of other harmless items become missiles of destruction in hurricane winds. Anchor them or store them inside before the storm strikes.

Store drinking water in clean bathtubs, jugs, bottles, and cooking utensils; your water supply may be contaminated by flooding or damaged by hurricane floods.

Check your battery-powered equipment. Your radio may be your only link with the world outside the hurricane, and emergency cooking facilities, lights, and flashlights will be essential if utilities are interrupted.

Keep your car fueled. Service stations may be inoperable for several days after the storm strikes, due to flooding or interrupted electrical power.

Remain indoors during the hurricane. Travel is extremely dangerous when winds and tides are whipping through your area.

Monitor the storm's position through National Weather Service advisories.

5. When the hurricane has passed:

Seek necessary medical care at the nearest Red Cross disaster station or health center.

Stay out of disaster areas. Unless you are qualified to help, your presence might hamper first-aid and rescue work.

Do not travel until advised by the proper authorities.

If you must drive, do so carefully along debris-filled streets and highways. Roads may be undermined and may collapse under the weight of a car. Slides along cuts are also a hazard.

Avoid loose or dangling wires, and report them immediately to your power company or the nearest law enforcement officer.

Report broken sewer or water mains to the water department.

Prevent fires. Lowered water pressure may make fire-fighting difficult.

Check refrigerated food for spoilage if power has been off during the storm.

Remember that hurricanes moving inland can cause severe flooding. Stay away from river banks and streams.

Tornadoes spawned by hurricanes are among the storm's worst killers. When a hurricane approaches, listen for tornado watches and warnings. A tornado watch means tornadoes are expected to develop. A tornado warning means a tornado has actually been sighted. When your area receives a tornado warning, seek inside shelter immediately, preferably below ground level. If a tornado catches you outside, move away from its path at a right angle. If there is no time to escape, lie flat in the nearest depression, such as a ditch or ravine.

During the summer season visitors may be notified of hurricane watches or hurricane warnings. The hurricane watch means that a hurricane could threaten the area within 24 hours. Evacuation is not necessary at that point, but you should be alert and check on the storm's progress from time to time via radio. If a hurricane warning is promulgated, visitors should leave the Banks and head inland using Rt. 64/264 or U.S. 158, following instructions of local authorities.

SURF REPORT

Provided by Wave Riding Vehicles for surfing 261-3332

Beach Service, through Nags Head Fire Department 441-5853

TAXI SERVICE

Roy's Taxi, Manteo 473-2716 (days) 473-3207 (nights)

Provides year-round taxi and limousine service.

Outer Banks Limousine Service 261-3133

Offers 24-hour taxi and limousine service and also makes pickups and deliveries to the Norfolk International Airport.

Outer Banks Transit 441-7090

Scheduled trips to Norfolk International Airport and the Norfolk area.

DUI Cab   480-1300
Beach Cab   441-2500
Island Limo   441-8803

TICKS, CHIGGERS AND OTHER PESTS

Whenever you're in the woods or scrub anywhere on the Outer Banks in warm weather, it's possible to pick up ticks. Ticks are small, hard-shelled black or brown insects endemic to the South. Check yourself all over carefully within 3-4 hours after the walk. The ticks bury their heads beneath the skin and gorge themselves on your blood. They head instinctively for hairy, warm areas.

The Outer Banks Medical Center advises their removal with tweezers, using slow, steady traction to make them release. Or, put a little alcohol on them: that often makes them back out on their own. There are other folk remedies you hear, too. If the head breaks off and if left in the skin, just leave it. It's not alive and will gradually heal.

If within 2-14 days after a tick bite you have headaches, flu symptoms and a rash, see a doctor. Some ticks carry Rocky Mountain Spotted Fever. It's treated with antibiotics.

Chiggers are tiny reddish insects that live in dirt or fallen pine needles, as on a trail. To avoid them, spray your socks, shoes and pants with a chigger-specific repellant before your walk. Don't sit down. Chiggers, once on you, will migrate to where your clothes are tight and start biting. Locals use clear fingernail polish over the bites. Calamine lotion or Benadryl work for the itching (don't scratch!)

Watch out for poison ivy and poison oak in the Banks woods, as well. For any severe or extensive tick, chigger or poisonous plant symptoms, see a doctor.

WESTERN UNION

You can send cables or telegrams or get information by calling their toll-free number: 800-325-6000. There are three Outer Banks locations where you can pick up or send messages and money:

Outer Banks Transit   441-7090
Rt. 158 Bypass, MP 9, Kill Devil Hills

Island Pharmacy   473-5801
Highway 64, Manteo

OUTER BANKS
PLACES OF WORSHIP

It used to be that we could report on all the churches the Banks had to offer. But, as with so many other aspects of life here, the number of worship centers has grown to such a degree that listing them all is impractical. So, we're compromising and giving you information on some of the churches in all the denominations represented here. We'd suggest you pick up a copy of the Sunday edition of the Coastland Times where you'll find a comprehensive list of all services available.

ASSEMBLY OF GOD
Worship Center Ark, Rt. 158 Bypass MP 11-1/2, 441-5182
Manteo Assembly of God, 473-3767
Wanchese Assembly of God, 473-5646
Avon Assembly of God, 995-5111

BAPTIST
First Baptist Church, Rt. 158 Bypass MP 4-1/2, Kitty Hawk, 261-3516
Seashore Baptist, Beach Road MP 15-1/2 (meets at Surfside Motel) 441-2001
Manteo Baptist Church, 473-2840
Cape Hatteras Baptist, Buxton, 995-5159

CATHOLIC
Holy Redeemer, Kill Devil Hills MP 7, 441-7220
Our Lady by the Sea, Buxton (for information, call 441-7220)

CHURCH OF CHRIST
Roanoke Acres, Manteo, 473-5584

EPISCOPAL
St. Andrews by the Sea, Beach Road MP 13, Nags Head, 441-5382

FULL GOSPEL
Liberty Christian Fellowship, Colington, 441-6592
Rock Church, Rt. 158 Bypass MP 4, Kitty Hawk, 261-3500

LUTHERAN
Grace Lutheran, Rt. 158 Bypass MP 13, 441-1530

METHODIST
Duck United Methodist, Duck, 261-3813
Colington United Methodist, Colington, 261-3813
Kitty Hawk United Methodist, 803 Kitty Hawk Village Rd, Kitty Hawk, 261-2062
Bethany United Methodist, Wanchese, 473-5254
Mt. Olivet United Methodist, Manteo, 473-2089
Buxton United Methodist, Buxton, 995-4306

PRESBYTERIAN
Outer Banks Presbyterian Church, Rt. 158 Bypass MP 8-1/2, Kill Devil Hills, 441-5897

UNITARIAN
Unitarian-Universalist Congregation, 261-2801

OUTER BANKS
ANNUAL EVENTS

Early Jan.
Old Christmas celebration at Rodanthe. Dancing, oyster roast, appearance of 'Old Buck,' the Christmas bull.

February
Frank Stick Invitational Art Show, 441-6584

Easter Weekend
Easter Windsurfing Regatta, 441-6800
SpringFest, with German oompah band and folk dancers, at the Weeping Radish, 473-1157

Late April
Wilbur Wright Fly-In, Wright Bros. Memorial, Kill Devil Hills and Dare County Airport, Manteo, 473-2600

Early May
Ocracoke Crab Festival, 928-6711

Surf Fishing Invitational Tournament, Ocracoke, 928-6711

Mid-May
Hang Gliding Spectacular at Jockey's Ridge, 441-4124.

Late May
Nags Head Woods Run, 441-2525

Memorial Day Weekend
Arts & Crafts Fair, Ramada Inn, Kill Devil Hills, 441-2151

June

Kitty Hawk Kites and Sports Triathalon, 441-2124, 1st Saturday in June

Dare Day Celebration, Manteo. Crafts, street dances, entertainment, parade.

Early June

Rogallo Kite Festival, Nags Head, 441-4124.

Boogie Board Contest, 441-6800

Mid-June

Marlin Fishing Tournament, Hatteras. Sponsored by Hatteras Marlin Club. P.O. Box 218, Hatteras, NC 27943

The Lost Colony season opens, running through late Aug. Sponsored by Roanoke Island Historical Association, 473- 2127.

Late June

Annual Seafood Festival and Blessing of the Fleet, Wanchese, 473-5501

Blue Water Open Billfish Tournament, Hatteras, P.O. Box 537, Hatteras, NC 27943

Early July

Outer Banks Sand Sculpture Contest, Kill Devil Hills, 473-3493

July 4

Fireworks displays at several locations on the Outer Banks

Mid-July

Youth Fishing Tournament, Nags Head. P.O. Box 626, Kill Devil Hills, NC 27948

Mid-August

Pirate's Cove Bill Fish Tournament, 473-3906

Wacky Watermelon Weekend and Windsurfing Regatta, 441-6800

August 18

Virginia Dare Day. Celebration of first English child born in America at Fort Raleigh National Historic Site, 473-5772.

August 19

Observance of National Aviation Day, Wright Memorial, Kill Devil Hills, 441-3761

New World Festival of the Arts in downtown Manteo, 261-3165

Early September

Labor Day Weekend Arts & Crafts Fair, Ramada Inn, 441-2151
East Coast Surfing Association Championship, Buxton, 995- 5785.
Outer Banks Triathalon, Roanoke Island, 473-1101

Mid-Sept.

Oregon Inlet Billfish Release Tournament, Oregon Inlet, 441-6301
Marsh and Sea Fest, North Carolina Aquarium, Roanoke Island, 473-3493

Early Oct.

Nags Head Invitational Surf Fishing Tournament, P.O. Box 626, Nags Head, NC 27959
Marsh and Sea Fest, North Carolina Aquarium, Roanoke Island, 473-3493
North Carolina Waterfowl Weekend, Nags Head, P.O. Box 102, Kill Devil Hills, NC 27948

Early Nov.

Cape Hatteras Surf Fishing Tournament, sponsored by Cape Hatteras Anglers Club, Buxton, 995-4253.

Thanksgiving Weekend

Thanksgiving Funboard Regatta, Nags Head, 441-6800.

Dec. 17

Anniversary of First Flight, at Wright Brothers National Memorial, P.O. Box 1903, Kitty Hawk, NC 27949

Mid-December

Christmas Open House and Candlelight Tour of the *Elizabeth II*, at the state historic site in downtown Manteo

Christmas Tour of Homes sponsored by the Voluntary Action Center, 473-2400

PERFORMING ARTS

The Banks have no resident opera, ballet, or professional theater, although a bus is chartered each year to attend a selection of performances of both opera and the Virginia Symphony in Norfolk. For more information, contact Marian Best, 441-4809. The Dare County Arts Council, Outer Banks Forum and College of the Albemarle all sponsor performing arts events throughout the year. throughout the year.

DARE COUNTY ARTS COUNCIL
Manteo   473-2774

A Manteo-based cultural organization, the Council fosters development of visual and performing arts within the Banks. Symphonies, concerts, showing of artists' works, musicals, and dramatic works are presented at varying times throughout the year. Season tickets available. Call for schedules and information.

OUTER BANKS FORUM   261-2064

The Forum is a collection of mostly northern beach residents committed to promoting the arts. They sponsor 8 to 9 programs a year, ranging from lectures to musical programs to plays. An annual subscription is available. Events are held in varying locations around the beach. Call for information.

THE LOST COLONY
Manteo   473-3414

A continuing outdoor drama, written by Paul Green and performed during the summer season at the Waterside Theatre, near Fort Raleigh. Season from mid-June to late August. For more details see entry in Roanoke Island section.

Outer Banks breezes are as good for flying kites as they are for cooling sunbathers. DCTB

INSIDE
PORTSMOUTH ISLAND

Southwest of Ocracoke

It's deserted now, except for its "ghosts" in Park Service uniforms. Empty. If you've never had that eerie feeling...then maybe you'll want to take the trip that most Banks visitors never make, to quiet, roadless, unpopulated Portsmouth Island.

It wasn't always that way. Portsmouth, which was a "planned community" authorized by the Colonial Assembly in 1753, was for many years the largest (actually, the only) town on the Banks. The slow changes of geology and economics have left it behind, however, and now it is no more. Will New York go the same way?

There is no bridge to Portsmouth from Ocracoke. There isn't even a ferry. The only way to get there, unless you brought a boat with you, is to make an arrangement with someone to take you over. As of this writing the Cape Lookout National Seashore has negotiated commercial use agreements with two parties on Ocracoke, Dave Harless (928-1951) and the Austins, Rudy and Junius (928-4361/4281). You can contact them or the NPS for rate and schedule information; you'll probably pay between ten and forty dollars depending on how many are in your party.

As you cross the inlet, if you decide to go, reflect on the fact that this was once the channel for much of the trade of Virginia and North Carolina. You see, throughout the 1700s and up to the mid-nineteenth century, Ocracoke channel was deeper than it is now. And of course ships were of shallower draft then, too. Seagoing ships could enter the inlet, moor or anchor near the southwest side, and offload their cargo into smaller coasters. Then these took it up the sound to such early ports as New Bern and Bath. Portsmouth Village was established to facilitate this trade by providing piers, warehouses, other port facilities, and labor.

The new town grew rapidly. The British raided Portsmouth during the Revolutionary War; a steady flow of supplies moved through it to General Washington's embattled armies. The British captured the town again during the War of 1812, but this again was only a temporary interruption and the town continued to grow. At its peak, just before the Civil War (War between the States), it handled over 1,400 ships a year and had a total population of almost 600 -- no Boston, but definitely the largest town on the outer islands.

Two things doomed Portsmouth: war and weather. In September of 1846, a terrific storm had opened two new inlets (named Hatteras and Oregon), and these gradually deepened as Ocracoke Inlet began to shoal. The Federals didn't help matters by sinking several ships laden with rock in Ocracoke channel, but war merely hastened Portsmouth's end. Such seagoing traffic as was left to the Banks shifted to Hatteras Inlet, and the backcountry trade was carried more and more by the new railroads. After that it was a question only of time. Few villagers returned after the war ended, even when a fish-processing plant was built, and the population steadily declined. Its last male resident, Henry Piggott, died in 1971, and with that Portsmouth's last two residents, Elma Dixon and Marian Babb, finally left.

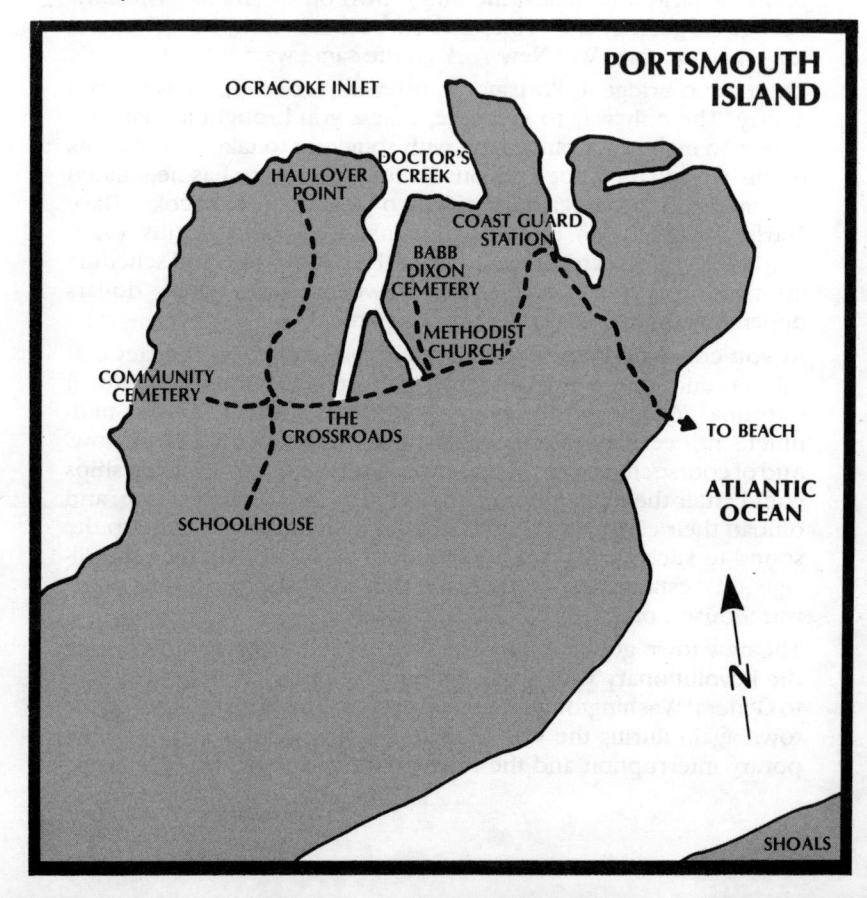

Now only the mosquitoes inhabit it. Portsmouth Island now belongs to the Cape Lookout National Seashore, and stabilization and preservation of the town is underway.

As you debark, at a newly-built dock at Haulover Point, you'll be able to look over the harbor from whence wharves, warehouses, and lighters once served the merchant ships anchored inside the Inlet. For a short tour, proceed southeast down the road. The first house on the right is the Salter-Dixon House, built around 1900. Part of this house is open as a visitor center, regularly in the summer months and intermittently in the spring and fall. Displays and more information, as well as restrooms and drinking water, are available inside. Down the main road you'll see a fence on the right and then a collapsed house. This is the Henry Babb house, built before 1875.

The small white building south of the Salter-Dixon house is the former Post Office. This was more or less the center of the village in its day. About forty yards west of it is the community cemetery, the largest in the village, with about 40 graves.

From the crossroads, follow the footpath south across the marsh to the former schoolhouse. Miss Mary Dixon taught classes in this one-room building until 1947. Now go back to the Post Office and proceed down the main road eastward. If you stop on the first little bridge and look to the north across the creek you will see a (now) yellow-painted cottage formerly owned by Henry Piggott, mentioned above. Continue across the second little bridge. To your left you will now see the Methodist Church. You may go in. The former congregation maintains a collection plate in the church. Proceeds are used for repair of the structure, but the National Seashore has paid for most of it. The rope operating the church bell, formerly functional, has been disconnected due to excessive use. Do not try to play the organ either. Behind the church is the Babb, Dixon plot where Mr. Piggott is buried.

Continuing east from the church, beyond the last houses you'll enter a stretch of open road. Beyond this lies the landing strip, the old Coast Guard station, watch tower, and outbuildings. Surf rescue boats were kept in the large building, as at Chicamacomico. The station was closed in 1937, though it was briefly reactivated for WWII.

About a hundred meters south of the station is the cistern of the old marine hospital, which was built in 1846 to serve sick and/or quarantined seamen. The Park Service has cut back the vegetation that threatened at one point to overwhelm it. The hospital proper burned down in 1894 and was not replaced.

To get to the Atlantic beach and the Wallace Channel Dock, walk on past the station; it's about another mile. If a northerly wind is blowing, there may be a few inches of water to wade through on the way.

A few notes of caution are in order. Prepare for mosquitoes in the summer. There's no mosquito control any more on the island and they get fierce. (Imagine what it was like living here before window screens and insect repellant were invented.) Take sunburn ointment too. Don't go inside any of the buildings other than the Salter-Dixon house and the church. They belong to the Park Service and are off-limits.

A note to fishermen: Portsmouth Island has great surf fishing, and you don't have to share it with a million other people. Don Morris, in Atlantic, N.C., has a car ferry that can take a limited number of four wheel drive vehicles over. He's at (919) 225-4261. NPS permits are required for all vehicles on Cape Lookout and Portsmouth Island; as of this writing they are free and available from the concessionaire and from any Cape Lookout Ranger Station.

NEARBY ATTRACTIONS

THE DISMAL SWAMP

The Great Dismal is one of the least known wonders of northeastern North Carolina and southeastern Virginia. Over two hundred thousand acres of it sprawl midway between the two states. This vast landscape of peat beds, vine and briar thickets, pines and hardwoods, cedar and cypress, canebrakes and canals hides in its heart a mysterious, deserted amber jewel of a lake, Lake Drummond.

The Indians knew and thinly inhabited what is now the Dismal long before the coming of the European settlers. The English, who were quick to snap up all available real estate in the area, avoided the Dismal Swamp, and Lake Drummond itself they did not discover until 1650, when it was found by a hunter who had lost his way. Little more was known about it until 1763, when George Washington decided to survey the area.

Washington discovered that the storied Dismal Swamp was not a swamp at all. Swamps are low-lying areas where surface water collects and cannot escape. The water stagnates and both land and water teems with parasitic, unhealthy life feeding on decay.

At first glance, the Dismal seems to be a swamp, simply because the ground is wet and there is lots of vegetation. But, in fact, the lake is twenty feet above sea level at its center, and the water is fresh; not stagnant, but drinkable. Washington said, "The Dismal Swamp is neither a plain nor a hollow, but a hillside with its lake at the top of the slope." What the Dismal is, in fact, is the only "live" peat bog in North America.

Peat is dead, preserved vegetable matter. Peat burns quite well, as the Irish have known for quite a while, and if it's given a few million years, it's apt to be even more burnable, as it can turn into coal. The Dismal Swamp produces peat. Its lush plant life, as it dies, falls into the dark water. Tannic acid in the water, from the roots of cypress roots, preserves this matter. It cannot rot, and peat is gradually formed.

Water is essential to peat formation, and unless the water table remains high, the peat will dry out and may catch fire. Where does the Dismal Swamp's water come from? Not from the sea, and not from runoff (water doesn't go uphill). Instead, deep springs feed Lake Drummond from underneath. Five rivers flow out of this area--none flow in. All the water is fresh, and the tannic acid, though it gives the water a dark color and flavors it, keeps the water clinically sterile and quite drinkable. (Tea is also rich in tannic acid.) In the days of sailing ships, this water was highly prized, as it stayed "sweet" in wooden casks for months longer than rainwater.

Another side effect of the amber water is that on sunny days it causes the lake to reflect like a mirror, creating a surreal effect in which a canoeist may begin to wonder which way is up. This and a variety of wildlife make the Dismal Swamp one of the undiscovered fun spots. It's sure to see much greater promotion in the future. But you can see it before it's spoiled! The Dismal Swamp Canal is administered by the U.S. Army Corps of Engineers, and the Wildlife Refuge by the Department of the Interior, so it's not a national park or anything like one. To reach the interior, and Lake Drummond, you will have to bring your own boat and travel the 3-1/2 mile long feeder ditch that supplies water to the Dismal Swamp Canal. (There is no road. Building any sort of road on a peat bog is hopeless.)

To reach the boat ramp maintained by the Corps of Engineers, just follow Rt. 17 until you see the signs. The ramp is about a half mile north from where the feeder ditch joins the canal. As you head toward the lake, grapevines and overhanging trees will brush the boat. You may also pass water moccasins, their heads craned above the water. The area is pretty wooly, and not at all for the camp-in-homelike-comfort set. Half a mile from the lake is a Corps of Engineers dam, where canoeists will need to tote their boats from one side to the others. Those of you with small, flat-bottomed boats, not over 1,000 pounds, may use a small railway provided. Others will probably not be able to make it.

Drummond is a wide, shallow lake, dotted with ancient twisted cypresses. The lake is only six feet deep, even in the center, and full of underwater stumps and logs. Canoes can explore the edges and probe up the drainage ditches, but we advise poor boaters to stay away from the edges of the lake and bring a spare prop, just in case.

Drummond is open from sunrise to sunset for boating and fishing. It's seldom visited, and is entirely unpopulated. Some will find that fact, alone, a special treat. About 10 primitive camping spots are available on a first-come basis at the Corps dam. There are toilet facilities, picnic tables and grills. The water, from wells, is safe to drink, but tastes awful -- better bring something in bottles. In fact, though camping is permitted here year-round, water is not provided at all in winter months.

For information, call Corps personnel at 421-7401.

MUSEUM OF THE ALBEMARLE
Elizabeth City   335-1453/2987

This small regional museum is devoted to the history of northeastern North Carolina. Area geography, Indian history, lumbering, farming, hunting, lifesaving, nautical history, wildfowl hunting -- this one-story brick building is crammed. Two fire engines delight children of all ages. Changing exhibits on a variety of topics are also featured on a quarterly basis. A Gift Shop with local crafts and memorabilia is available. Hours: 9 a.m. to 5 p.m. Tuesday through Saturday, 2 to 5 p.m. Sunday. Closed Monday and state holidays. No charge. To reach it, drive north from Kitty Hawk on Rt. 158 through Camden, across the Pasquotank River, and through Elizabeth City; it's on the right side of the road a few miles west of the city on Highway 17 South. Total distance from Kitty Hawk is about 47 miles.

HISTORIC EDENTON

Edenton, North Carolina is one of the oldest towns in America, and stands out still more by being one of the best-preserved. Settled around 1660, it was a center of colonial-era commerce and government. Joseph Hewes, a signer of the Declaration of Independence, lived here, as did Dr. Hugh Williamson, who signed the Constitution. Edenton had its own Tea Party in 1774, with the exception that the protesters were women -- one of the first female political actions on the continent. Later, Edenton became a backwater, as Williamsburg was for many years. And, like Williamsburg, this preserved it; the old houses and buildings were still standing years later when historians 'rediscovered' the town.

Today you can see such showpieces of colonial architecture as the Barker House, the Cupola House, the Chowan County Courthouse, the James Iredell House, and St. Paul's Episcopal Church. Together they are considered the state's most prestigious collection of 18th century buildings. Guided tours of town begin at the Barker House on South Broad Street, at the edge of Albemarle Sound. Open 10 a.m. to 4:30 p.m. Monday through Saturday, 2-5 p.m. Sunday, year round. A carriage tour leaves from the waterfront at the south end of Broad Street on weekends during the summer. The three-seater touring carriage is an adaptation of an original surrey and seats about nine. Two carriages are available for special events such as weddings and special parties. Call 482-2352.

Edenton has several good restaurants. One find is right off Broad Street, in Gaslight Square (follow the baker man, but you could just about follow your nose instead). Caroline's opens at 6 a.m. with just-made breads, pastries, doughnuts and rolls. They also serve traditional breakfasts if you are so misguided as to resist an occasional patisserie. Lunch specials are usually offered. Open Monday through Saturday; for lunches to go in advance call 482-2711. Another noteworthy restaurant is Boswell's, a family- owned eatery since 1947. Recently renovated, it's known in the area for its seafood specialties, ethnics and daily favorites. Billed as having "the best clam chowder in the world," it's satisfied visitors and locals for forty years. Lunch and dinner, open all week.

Three non-Holiday-Inn-type accommodations we recommend in Edenton are: The Governor Eden Inn, owned by C.Z. and Ruth Shackleford, 482-2072 (bed and breakfast, old home); The Trestle House, Hal and Louise Worthley, 482-2282 (modern inn, elegant in a rustic way); The Lord Proprietors Inn, Arch and Jane Edwards, 482-3641 (rooms in four restored old homes). Call for rates.

Edenton is most easily reached by crossing the Croatan Sound from Manteo on Rt. 64/264 and continuing forty miles west until turning right on Rt. 32 to cross the Albemarle. Turn left after you cross the bridge and go five more miles toward Edenton; Historic Edenton will be on your left.

SOMERSET PLACE

Pettigrew State Park   797-4560

We don't know who wrote the site press release, but its opening paragraph is worth quoting: "Passion, splendor and grim reality are all found in the epic story of Lake Phelps and the vast plantations carved from the haunting and mysterious coastal swamps on its banks by two extraordinary families. Here among majestic cypress and sycamore trees stands the elegant early nineteenth century home of Josiah Collins, III that once hosted the cultivated elite of North Carolina's planter aristocracy. Nearby, beneath sheltering limbs of great oaks, Charles Pettigrew, the state's first Episcopal bishop-elect, his congressman son and Confederate brigadier general grandson lie in eternal slumber beside rich, fertile farmland wrested from primeval nature by that potent combination of African slave labor and English immigrant ambition that has become the most enduring symbol of the "Old South."

That's a hard act to follow, but let's try. The plantation was one of the four biggest in North Carolina, with over 300 slaves growing corn and rice. The mansion, a 2 1/2-story frame building with fourteen rooms, was built in Greek Revival style circa 1830. It has been fully restored, with period furnishings. Six original outbuildings remain. The lawns and gardens alongside nearby Phelps Lake are especially beautiful in summer. A historically important collection of the plantations's slave records is open for genealogical research. A state historic site now, Somerset Place is open on the following schedule. April to October, Monday through Saturday 9 to 5 and Sunday 1 to 5. November to March, Tuesday through Saturday 10 to 4, Sunday 1 to 4, closed Mondays. Admission is free, but groups planning to visit should write Box 215, Creswell, NC, 27928 to make reservations. To reach it take Rt. 64/264 west across the Croatan Sound from Manteo and follow it west for about 40 miles. Turn left at the little town of Creswell and another five miles will bring you to Pettigrew State Park and Somerset Place.

CAPE LOOKOUT NATIONAL SEASHORE

Low, unpopulated, almost forgotten even by North Carolinians, more barrier islands stretch southwestward for 55 miles from Ocracoke Inlet. North Core Banks with Portsmouth Village, South Core Banks and Cape Lookout, and Shackleford Banks were incorporated into the Cape Lookout National Seashore in 1966.

These low, sandy islands have been untouched by either development or by stabilization. (Remember that the Outer Banks were stabilized by the CCC in the 1930s with dunes and plantings.) As a relatively recent NPS acquisition, and a remote one, there are relatively few facilities available for the visitor. But if you don't mind roughing it a little bit (dear ticks, chiggers, deerflies, mosquitoes, gnats, squalls, hurricanes, rip currents, sharks, and jellyfish), these islands are a great place for primitive camping, fishing, boating, and bird watching. A no-kidder: gnats may annoy you, but really stay alert for storms, as there is little shelter on most of these islands. You can call Coast Guard weather at 726-7550 for a forecast before you leave the mainland. Here's some helpful information for you "naturalists":

1) Two concessions operate out of Davis and Atlantic, NC, offering primitive cabins for overnight lodging.

2) There are no established campgrounds but primitive (back pack style) camping is allowed.

3) There are no paved roads but 4-wheel drive vehicles can operate on the beach front.

4) Water is available from pitcher pumps in the Cape Point area.

At Cape Lookout itself are located the lighthouse, erected in 1859, and a small Coast Guard Station, no longer active.

access: if you have your own boat, you will find launching ramps at marinas throughout Carteret County, though the easiest access to Cape Point is from Shell Point on Harkers Island. Concession ferry services (privately run, federally overseen) are available from Harkers Island to the Cape Lookout Light area, from Davis to Shingle

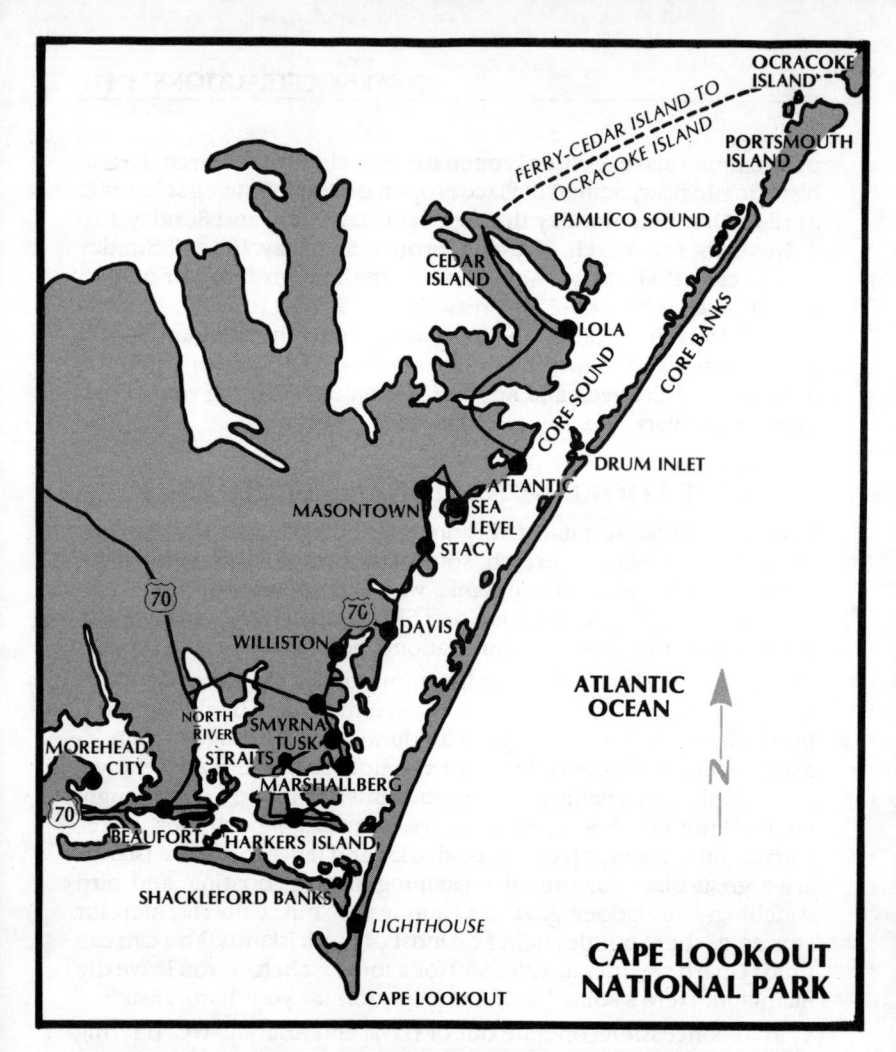

Point, from Atlantic to an area north of Drum Inlet, and from Ocracoke to Portsmouth Village. For current rates and more information, write or call the Park Service, Cape Lookout National Seashore, PO Box 690, Beaufort NC 28516; (919)728-2121.

HOPE PLANTATION

Windsor, NC   794-3140

Hope Plantation began as a grant from the Lord Proprietors of the Carolina Colony to the Hobson family in the 1720s. David Stone, a delegate to the North Carolina Constitutional Convention of 1789 and later judge, representative, senator, and governor (1808-1810), built an impressive home on the site circa 1800. The Hope Mansion is an outstanding Federal Period residence and is reminiscent in some ways of Monticello and is other ways of Scarlett O'Hara's Tara. Historic Hope Foundation acquired the mansion and land in 1966. Now restored, it and two smaller houses (the King-Bazemore and the Samuel Cox Houses) are open to the public as a furnished house-museum. There are also restored 18th century gardens. Hope is on the National Register of Historic Places.

Hope Plantation is outside of the town of Windsor, roughly a two hour drive west of Manteo. Take 64 out of Roanoke Island west to its intersection with 13; go north on 13; Hope is on NC 308 four miles west of US 13 bypass. Open March 1 through December 23, Mondays through Saturdays; holiday Mondays 10 a.m. to 4 p.m.; Sundays 2 p.m. to 5 p.m. Closed January and February. Adult admission is $5 for all three houses. Picnic facilities are available.

BE AN INSIDER

You can become one of the Insiders by sharing your Outer Banks travel experience. What you tell the authors of this guidebook will be weighed seriously in the editing of a revised edition.

Tell us about the good and the bad as you follow our recommendations. If enough of you are disappointed in a restaurant or motel, and our investigation confirms your experiences, we promise to drop the offending place out of our book. Your opinion has power.

On the positive side, share the happy times with your fellow vacationers. What places provided exceptional service, or helped you in an unusual way? Let's use *The Insiders' Guide* to recognize and reward excellence on The Outer Banks.

What about the organization of the book, itself? If you discovered a defect, or have a suggestion to improve its usefulness, write us about it.

The authors of *The Insiders' Guide* intended that this book should save you time, money, and a lot of exasperation and frustration. We travel a great deal ourselves, and in making this book, we tried to put in it all the things that we would want to know if we came to your city or town. Now that you'e used our book, help us to refine it and make it serve you better on your return visit.

Share your experiences with us and become one of the Insiders. Write us collectively, or as individuals. We'll be grateful to hear from you. Send your letters to: Insiders' Guides, Inc., P.O. Box 2057, Manteo, NC 27954.

THE INSIDERS' GUIDE COLLECTION

THE INSIDERS' GUIDE TO GREATER ORLANDO
Written by Cynthia Gross and Catharine Coward

Orlando, Florida, is the vacation capital of the South as well as one of the fastest growing areas in the country. This indispensible 700+ page guide will tell you everything you'll want to know about the sunny city and its surrounding neighbors. There's plenty of information on the major attractions, plus facts and insights into other enjoyable sites and activities the area has to offer. Newcomers will feel as if they know the quickly-changing region better with the Insiders' Guide in hand. $12.95

THE INSIDERS' GUIDE TO THE TRIANGLE
Written by Dee Reid and J. Barlow Herget

Whether you are planning a vacation, a business trip, or to relocate to the Triangle area of North Carolina -- Raleigh, Cary, Durham, Chapel Hill, Carrboro, or the Research Triangle Park -- this book will be an invaluable companion. It contains over 750 pages, over 80 pages of detailed maps and informative sections on topics such as neighborhoods, schools and child care, shopping, restaurants, accommodations, recreation, arts, colleges and universities, sports, worship, and much more. There's also a major relocation section with information on realtors and builders, buying a home, and renting. $9.95

THE INSIDERS' GUIDE TO SOUTH HAMPTON ROADS
Written by Nancy Venable and Sam Martinette

Anyone who has ever been to the Hampton Roads area of Virginia for business, travel, or as a new resident knows that a good guide is not only helpful, it's almost necessary! This guide to Norfolk, Virginia Beach, Suffolk, Portsmouth, and Chesapeake will answer your questions ranging from what the best child care is in the area to where you'll find a great nightspot. You'll also get authoritative information on relocating, the arts, universities, neighborhoods, the media, hospitals, the Chesapeake Bay, sports and recreation, the Military, history of the area, and much, much more. $9.95

THE INSIDERS' GUIDE TO WILLIAMSBURG
Written by Susan Bruno and Donna Quaresima

Another great Insiders' book that helps visitors to this colonial capital city get the most out of their stay. Written by two insiders, it gives information on accomodations, restaurants, attractions, campgrounds, shopping and more on Williamsburg, Jamestown, and Yorktown. $5.95

THE INSIDERS' GUIDE TO CHARLOTTE
Written by Bea Quirk and Carol Timblin

Here's a complete newcomer/business/visitor's guide to North Carolina's largest city, filled with information on accommodations, neighborhoods, restaurants, shopping, schools, surrounding smaller towns, places of worship, attractions, homes, and more. Informative maps, too. It's the only guide you'll need to get the most out of Charlotte. $9.95

Coming in early 1991, The Insiders' Guide to Buffalo/Niagara Falls.

Use our convenient order form on the following page to add to your collection of Insiders' Guides.

Order Form

Use this convenient form to place
your order for any of Insiders' Guides'
books -- fast and simple!

**INSIDERS' GUIDES, INC.
P.O. Box 2057, Highway 64
Manteo, North Carolina 27954**

**Call to place your order
with VISA or Mastercard
1-919-473-6100**

Name: _____

Address: _____

City/State/ZIP: _____

Quantity	Title/Price	Shipping	Total
	Insiders' Guide to Orlando, $12.95	$2.00	
	Insiders' Guide to the Triangle, $9.95	$2.00	
	Insiders' Guide to Charlotte, $9.95	$2.00	
	Insiders' Guide to South Hampton Roads, $9.95	$2.00	
	Insiders' Guide to the Outer Banks, $9.95	$2.00	
	Insiders' Guide to Williamsburg, $5.95	$2.00	
		NC residents add 5% sales tax.	
		GRAND TOTAL	

Payment in full (check or money order) must accompany order form.
Please allow 2-3 weeks delivery.
(Canadian deliveries, please add $3.00 per book)

NOVELS BY DAVE POYER

If you enjoyed *The Insiders' Guide to the Outer Banks*, be warned: Dave Poyer, author of the historical and recreational sections, is hitting the streets with novels, too.

STEPFATHER BANK

This mega-SF story is set in the year 2110 -- when The Bank owns everything and everyone. Except Monaghan Burlew, the chubby, self-styled poet and con artist who finally decides to revolt. Can one man and woman overthrow the worldwide financial monolith of the Greatmother Corporation? Why has the Bank kept everyone working without sleep for forty years? And what was "Docktor" Gnath Greatmother's final and most desperate invention? Find out in *Stepfather Bank*, in paperback from St. Martin's Press.

THE MED

This huge novel of the Navy and Marine Corps in action in the Mediterranean was compared by Publisher's Weekly to *From Here to Eternity*. Poyer's first official best seller, it follows five major characters through a hostage rescue in Cyprus, Syria, and at sea. Stephen Coonts, author of *Flight of the Intruder*, says "David Poyer pulls no punches. *The Med* is an honest, gritty tale of the real Navy. I loved it." Now in paperback from St. Martin's Press.

HATTERAS BLUE

A rubber raft with the bones of three people is unearthed from a sand dune at Cape Hatteras. Shortly thereafter, Lyle "Tiller" Galloway -- a salvage diver with a criminal record, the black sheep of a distinguished Coast Guard family -- is approached with a lucrative deal. An enigmatic man named Keyes wants to explore the wreck of a U-boat sunk in 1945, two days after the end of WWII. The boat contains a hoard that may make both of them rich. But there's a greater secret still at large after forty years, a plot as treacherous as the currents off the coast of Hatteras. Available in hardcover from St. Martin's Press, at bookstores on the Banks and everywhere.

INDEX OF ADVERTISERS

Albemarle Hospital	446
All Decked Out	226
Anchorage Inn	374
Avon Shopping Center	220
Awful Arthur's	279
Back Porch Restaurant	310
Beach Bowling Center	96
Berkley Center	383
Birthday Suits	75
Blackbeard's Treasure Chest	104
Boyette House	378
Britt Real Estate	404
Browning Artworks	223
Bubba's Barbecue	307
Buccaneer Motel and Apartments	342
Cape Hatteras Motel	365
Cape Pines Motel	370
Carolina Casual	46
Carolina Moon	43
Chalet Gift Shop	101
Christmas Shop	108
Comfort Inn	340
Country Time Cycle	100
Crockett's Seafood	142
Dare County Tourist Bureau	11
Daydreams	221
Day's Inn	340
Duchess of Dare	138
Ebbtide Motel	353
Emily's Soundside Restaurant	303

INDEX OF ADVERTISERS

Etheridge Seafood Restaurant	285
Falcon Motel	368
Frisco Shopping Center	224
Glenn Eure's Ghost Fleet Gallery	85
Hatteras Outdoors	221
Honey Bear	226
Island Inn	240
Island Inn Restaurant	240
Island Interiors	418
Jewelry By Gail	89
Kelly's	289
Kitty Hawk Pizza	277
Kitty Hawk Sports	437
Lifesaver Rent Alls	329
Lighthouse View Motel	367
Lost Colony	24
Manteo Booksellers	139
Mollie Fearing and Associates	415
Newby's	281
Ocracoke Island Realty	255
Oregon Inlet Fishing Center	Insider Back Cover
Outer Banks Cablevision	318
Outer Banks Chamber of Commerce	11
Outer Banks Mall	98
Outer Beaches Realty	394
Pea Island Resort	178
Penguin Isle	289
Pony Island Restaurant	313
Princess Waterfront Motel	374
Rascal	247
Regional Medical Services	446
Rudee's	297
RV's	Inside Front Cover

SPCA	332
Salvo Realty	414
Save the Horses	33
Scarborough House Inn	7, 141, 362
Seamark Foods	105
Sea Holly Square Merchant's Asso.	76
Sea Shore Stuffe	101
Shallowbags	138
Sharon Miller Realty	247
Shear Genius	74
Silver Lake Motel	380
Snaps	78
Southern Hospitality	18
Souvenir City	102
Splash, Too	77
Stack 'em High	278
Summer Stuff	227
Sun Realty	412
Surf or Sound Realty	327
Surf Side Motel	357
Village at Nags Head	406
Weeping Radish	8
Yellowhouse Annex	99
Young People	8

Index

A

A Life On Hatteras, 231
A Life On The Northern Banks, Oral History, 49
AAA Service, 453
ABC Stores, 454
Accommodations
 Anchorage Inn, 375
 Atlantic View, 372
 Beacon Motor, 354
 Berkley Center, 382
 Blue Heron, 358
 Bluff Shoal Motel, 381
 Boyette House, 377
 Buccaneer Motel, 343
 Cape Hatteras, 364
 Cape Pines, 369
 Cavalier, 346
 Chart House, 346
 Comfort Inn, 348
 Days Inn, 343
 Duke of Dare, 363
 Durant Station, 371
 Ebbtide, 352
 Econo Lodge, 351
 Edwards Motel, 376
 Elizabethan Inn, 361
 Falcon Motel, 368
 General Mitchell, 371
 Harborside, 381
 Hatteras Marlin, 372
 Hatteras Island, 365
 Howard Johnson's, 345
 Island Inn, 378
 Islander Motel, 358
 John Yancy Motor Hotel, 353
 Lighthouse View, 366
 Mariner, 345
 Nags Head Inn, 355
 Ocean Reef, 349
 Ocean Veranda, 355
 Oscar's House, 377
 Outer Banks Motel, 366
 Owens' Motel, 359
 Pirate's Quay, 379
 Pony Island Motel, 375
 Princess Waterfront Motel, 376
 Ramada Inn, 351
 Sanderling Inn, 341
 Scarborough Inn, 361
 Sea Foam Motel, 359
 Sea Oatel, 360
 See Sea, 350
 Ships Timbers, 382
 Silver Sands, 356
 Silver Lake, 379
 Surf Side, 356
 Tan-A-Rama, 344
 Tanya's Ocean House, 352
 The Chart House, 346
 The Mariner, 345
 The Sanderling, 341
 Tower Circle, 369
 Tranquil House Inn, 363
 Wilbur & Orville Wright, 349
 Ye Olde Cherokee Inn, 348
Accommodations, Hatteras Island, 364
Accommodations, Kill Devil Hills, 344
Accommodations, Kitty Hawk, 343
Accommodations, Nags Head North, 354
Accommodations, Ocracoke, 375
Accommodations, Roanoke Island, 361
Accommodations, Sanderling, 341
Accommodations, South Nags Head, 356
Added Touch, 143
Airlines, Outer Banks Airways, 27
All Decked Out, 225
Altoona Wreck, 195
Anchorage Inn, 375, 382
Andrew Cartwright Park, 126
Animal Services, 452
Animals, Lost and Found, 452
Annual Events, 464
Argyle Bake Shoppe, 142
Atlantic View Motel, 372
Atlantis, 320
Attractions, Bodie Island, 159
Attractions, Hatteras Island, 185
Attractions, Kill Devil Hills, 70
Attractions, Kitty Hawk, 57
Attractions, Nags Head, 84
Attractions, Ocracoke, 246
Attractions, Roanoke Island, 114
Attractions, So. Shores, Duck, Sanderling and Corolla, 38
Aunt Mary's Kitchen, 61
Austin Fish Co., 105
Automotive Services, 453, 458
Avalon Fishing Pier, 74
Avon, 179
Avon Shopping Center, 220
Avon Waterside Shops, 220
Awful Arthur's, 280, 316
Aycock Brown Welcome Center, 57

B

B.W.'s Surf Shop, 256
Back Bay National Wildlife Refuge, 34
Back Porch, 310
Barrier Island Sailing Center, 41
Barrier Island Station, 36, 397
Bay Cliff, 403
Beach Bowling Center, 97
Beach Hardware, 99
Beach Medical Care South, 448
Beach Medical Center, 223, 447
Beach Pharmacy, 223, 229
Beachcomber Campground, 392
Beacon Motor Lodge, 354
Belk's, 75
Ben Franklin Store, 140
Bequa, 76
Berkley Center, 382
Billy Mitchell Air Field, 202
Billy's Fish House Restaurant, 305
Billy's Seafood, 79
Birding on Pea Island, 189
Birthday Suits, 45, 78

INDEX 489

Bizarre Duck, 44
Blackbeard's Treasure Chest, 104
Blue Heron Motel, 358
Blue Point Oyster Bar & Grille, 273
Bluff Shoal Motel, 381
Bodie Island Lighthouse and Center, 162
Boyette House, 377
Browning Artworks, 223
Bubba's Bar-B-Q, 307
Buccaneer Motel, 343
Building on the Outer Banks, Builders, 416
Burrus Red and White, 229
Buxton, 179, 184
Buxton Village Books, 222
Buxton Woods, 184
Buxton Woods Nature Trail, 201
Buying Real Estate, Agencies, 413
Buying Real Estate, Tips, 411

C

Cafe Atlantic, 314
Caffey's Inlet Lifesaving Station, 36
Campgrounds, 385
Beachcomber, 392
Cape Hatteras KOA, 387
Cape Point Campground (NPS), 389
Cape Woods Camper Park, 388
Colington Park Campground, 385
Frisco Campground (NPS), 390
Frisco Woods Campground, 389
Hatteras Sands Camping Resort, 390
Kinnakeet, 390
North Beach Campground, 388
Ocean Waves Campground, 388
Ocracoke Campground, 393
Oregon Inlet Campground, 386
Pea Island Resort, 387
Stowe - A - Way, 389
Teeter's Campground, 392
Campgrounds, Hatteras, 386
Cap't. Ben's Restaurant, 311
Cape Creek Landing, 220
Cape Hatteras KOA, 387
Cape Hatteras Lighthouse, 199
Cape Hatteras Motel, 364
Cape Hatteras National Seashore, 198
Cape Hatteras Pier, 216
Cape Hatteras Sand-Alls, 222
Cape Pines Motel, 369
Cape Point, 198
Cape Point Campground, 389
Cape Woods Camper Park, 388
Capt'n Franks, 276
Car Rentals, 453, 458
Carawan Fish Co., 47
Carol's Seafood, 220
Carolina Moon, 45, 78
Carova Beach, 401
Carriage Rides, 254
Cavalier Motel, 346
Chalet Gift Shop, 103
Channel Bass Restaurant, 308
Chardo's, 285
Chart House, 346
Chef's Corner, 105, 290
Chicamacomico Life Saving Station, 194

Christmas Mouse, 99
Christmas Shop, 140
Clara's Seafood Grille, 299
Cloth Barn, 142
Co-Ownership, 398
Coast Guard, 451
Coastland Times, 455
Colington Harbour, 403
Colington Island, 71
Colony House Avon Cinema, 216
Colony House Cinemas, 97
Colony House Cinemas V & VI, 59
Comedy Club, 320
Comfort Inn, 348
Community Store, 256
Condominiums, 408
Conners Supermarket, 223
Coquina Beach, 159
Corolla Academy, 30
Corolla Light, 37, 401
Corolla Light Sailing Club, 41
Corolla Light Shops, 42
Corolla Lighthouse and Keeper's House, 39
Country Time Cycle, 100
Crisis Hotline, 452
Crockett's Seafood Market, 142
Crystal Dawn Evening Cruises, 323
Crystal Dawn Head Boat, 128

D

Dairy Mart, 291
Daniels Crab House, 107
Daniels', 47
Dare Centre, 75
Dare County Arts Council, 467
Dare County Library KDH Branch, 72
Dare County Regional Airport, 121
Dare County Tennis Courts, 97
Dare Shops, 104
Darrell's Restaurant, 300
Davis Clothing Store, 140
Daydreams, 220
Days Inn, 343
Deep Africa Mini Golf, 97
Dentists, 448
Diamond Shoals Light, 196
Diamond Shoals Restaurant, 304
Dillon's Corner, 222
Dockside 'N Duck, 45
Donetta, Donetta - The Waterfront Salon, 141
Dowdys Amusement Park, 322
Drinkwater Lounge, 317
Duchess of Dare Restaurant, 298
Duck, 35
Duck Blind Art Gallery, 43
Duck Deli, 45, 273
Duck Duck Shop, 44
Duck Soundside Shops, 45
Duck Woods Golf Course, 58
Duke of Dare Motor Lodge, 363
Dunes Restaurant, 294
Durant Motel, 371

490 INDEX

E

Ebbtide, 352
Ebbtide Family Restaurant, 287
Econo Lodge, 351
Edwards Motel, 376
Elizabeth II State Historic Site, 134
Elizabeth's Cafe and Winery, 274
Elizabethan Dinner Theater, 323
Elizabethan Gardens, 114
Elizabethan Inn, 361
Emergencies, 447
Emily's Soundside Restaurant, 302
Essex Square Shops, 140
Ethridge Seafood Restaurant, 284

F

Falcon Motel, 368
Farmer's Daughter, 45, 103
Fast Eddie's, 274
Fearings, 140
Federal Express, 457
Ferry Connections, Swan Quarter, Cedar Island, 444
Finely Ron's, 279
Fire Departments, 451
First Flight Air Strip, 71
Fisherman's Wharf Restaurant, 302
Fishing Guide, Outer Banks, 423
Fishing Report, 453
Fishing, Autumn and Winter, 428
Fishing, Boat -- The Sounds, 427
Fishing, Citations and Tournaments, 430
Fishing, Fresh Water, 427
Fishing, Head Boats, 426
Fishing, Ocean, 428
Fishing, Surf and Pier, 424
Food Lion, 78, 219, 220, 223
Food-A-Rama, 79, 142
Footsball Palace, 97
For Goodness Sake, 47
Forbes Candy and Carpet Golf, 97
Fort Raleigh, 115
Fox Water Sports, 222
Frisco, 179
Frisco & Co., 317
Frisco Campground, 390
Frisco Native American Museum, 202
Frisco Sandwich Shop, 306
Frisco Shopping Center, 225
Frisco Woods Campground, 389
Froggy Dog Restaurant, 304

G

Gallery Row, 87, 97
Gary's Restaurant, 308
Gathering Place, 256
General Mitchell Motel, 371
Geography, The Outer Banks, 17
Gingerbread House, 225
Glenn Eure's Ghost Fleet Gallery, 87

Go-Kart Grand Prix, 97
Gourmet Kitchen Emporium, 44
Graveyard of the Atlantic Museum, 202
Gray's Department Store, 44, 99

H

Hammock Hills Nature Trail, 247
Hang Gliding, 89
Harborside Gifts, 256
Harborside Motel, 381
Hatteras Divers, 443
Hatteras Harbor Marina, 216
Hatteras Inlet (Ocracoke) Ferry, 217
Hatteras Island Fishing Pier, 215
Hatteras Island Motel, 365
Hatteras Island Restaurants, 302
Hatteras Island Visitor Center, 198
Hatteras Library, 217
Hatteras Marlin Motel, 372
Hatteras Outdoors, 221
Hatteras Sands Camping Resort, 390
Hatteras Village, 179
Health Care, 447
History, Bodie Island, 159
History, Hatteras Island, 177
History, Kill Devil Hills, 63
History, Kitty Hawk, 55
History, Nags Head, 81
History, Ocracoke, 241
History, Roanoke Island, 109
History, The Outer Banks, 17
Hobby Craft Harbor, 102
Home Port Gifts, 220
Honey Bear Country Store, 226
Hospitality Service, 454
Howard Johnson's, 345
Howard, Elizabeth Anne O'Neal, 259
Hunting, 29

I

Island Gallery and Christmas Shop
Christmas Shop, 124
Island Gallery/Christmas Shop, 140
Island Inn, 378
Island Inn Restaurant, 312
Island Nautical, 141, 142
Island Ragpicker, 257
Island Trading Company, 141
Islander Motel, 358

J

Jackson Dunes, 407
Jennette's Pier, 94
Jewelry by Gail, 88
Jim's Camera House, 78
Jockey's Ridge State Park, 84
Joe's Starvin' Shark, 305

John Yancey Motor Hotel, 353
John's Drive-In, 276
Just For The Beach, 44

K

Kathy's Gifts & Clothing, 256
Keeper's Galley Restaurant, 275
Kelly's, 320
Kelly's Restaurant, 288
Kennels, 452
Kill Devil Hills Restaurants, 278
King Smith Gallery, 76
Kinnakeet Campground, 390
Kinnakeet Shores, 407
Kinnakeet Tavern, 321
Kite Kingdom, 76
Kitty Hawk Aero Tours, 73
Kitty Hawk Fishing Pier, 58
Kitty Hawk Kites/Sports/Connections, 91
Kitty Hawk Pizza, 276
Kitty Hawk Restaurants, 275
Kitty Hawk Sports, 100, 220
Kitty Hawk Sports, Duck, 42, 45
Kitty Hawk Station, 34
Kitty Hawk Water Sports, 96

L

Lady Dare, 103
Lady Victorian, 44
Laundries, Self-Service, 458
Laura A. Barnes, 161
Lee Robinson General Store, 227
LegaSea, 257
Libraries, 455
Library, Dare County, 124
Lifesaving Service, U.S., 22
Lighthouse View Motel, 366
Lighthouse, Corolla, 34
Lighthouse, Currituck, 37
Liquor Laws and ABC Stores, 454, 458
Loblolly Pines, 44
Lost Colony, The, 117, 467
Lucky Duck Gift Shop, 44

M

MacDowell Family Health Center, 448
Madeline's, 319
Manteo Booksellers, 141
Manteo Walking Tour, 137
Manteo, Downtown, 129
Mariner Motel, 345
Marketplace, The, 46
Media Information, 455
Medical Care, 447
Medical care, Gynecology, 449
Medical Center, Outer Banks, 86
Merchant Mariner, 256
Mex-Econo, 283, 317

Michaelen's, 46
Miller's Seafood and Steak House, 286
Miss Hatteras, Head Boat, 217
Monkey Island, 30
Monterey Shores, 402
Motel Market, guidelines, 335
Mother Vineyard, 123
Motif's, 44
Mule Shed, 103

N

Nags Head Fishing Pier, 93
Nags Head Golf Links, 93
Nags Head Hammocks, 99
Nags Head Inn, 355
Nags Head North Restaurants, 287
Nags Head Pro Dive Center, 443
Nags Head Woods Ecological Preserve, 73
Narrows Island, 30
Nat's Fresh Seafood, 257
National Park Service Info. Center, 94
National Park Service, Offices, 452
Natural Art Surf Shop, 222
Natural Selection, 142, 299
Nature Trail, Jockey's Ridge, 86
Nautilus Athletic Club, 75
NC Aquarium, 120
Newby's, 278
Newman's, 102
Nick-E, 143
Night Spots, 316
Night Spots, Hatteras, 321
Night Spots, Kill Devil Hills, 317
Night Spots, Kitty Hawk, 316
Night Spots, Nags Head North, 320
Night Spots, Nags Head South, 321
Night Spots, Ocracoke, 322
Norbanks Sailing Center, 42
North Beach Campground, 388
North Beach Medical Center, 448
North Beach Sailing, 45
North Carolina Books, 77
North Pond Trail, 187
Northern Banks, 29
Northern Beaches Restaurants, 271
Northern Outer Banks, 29
Northpoint, 400

O

O'Neal's Dockside, 253
Oasis Restaurants & Lounge, 297
Ocean Annie's, 44, 103
Ocean Reef Hotel, 349
Ocean Swimming, Precautions, 440
Ocean Veranda Motel, 355
Ocean Waves Campground, 388
Ocracoke Art Co-Op, 255
Ocracoke Civic Club, 249
Ocracoke Coast Guard Station, 248
Ocracoke Ferry Schedule, 218
Ocracoke Health Center, 448
Ocracoke Lighthouse, 251

492 INDEX

Ocracoke Museum and Visitor Center, 248
Ocracoke Pony Pens, 246
Ocracoke Restaurants, 310
Ocracoke Trolley, 253
Ocracoke Variety Store, 255
Ocracoke Village, 249
Ocracoke Visitors Center, 247
Off-Road Vehicles, 429
Off-Season, Outer Banks, 419
Old Kill Devil Hills Lifesaving Station, 38
Old Nags Head, 86
Old Nags Head Cove, 404
Old Post Office Shop, 256
Oral History, Ocracoke, 259
Orange Blossom Pastry Shop, 223
Oregon Inlet, 164
Oregon Inlet Campground, 386
Oregon Inlet Coast Guard Station, 161
Oregon Inlet Fishing Center, 162
Ormonds, 221
Oscar's House, 377
Osprey Gourmet, 45
Osprey Island Grille, 286
Osprey Landing, 45
Outer Banks Chamber Welcome Center, 72
Outer Banks Fishing Pier, 94
Outer Banks Forum, 467
Outer Banks History Center, 137
Outer Banks Mall, 103
Outer Banks Medical Center, 447
Outer Banks Motel, 366
Outer Banks Music, 46
Outer Banks Restaurants, 267
Planning and Pricing, 270
Outer Banks Transit, 457
Outer Banks Woman Care, 449
Owen's Restaurant, 294
Owens' Motel, 359

P

Package Shipment, 456, 458
Paige's, 46
Papagayo, 280
Papagayo's Cantina, 317
Party Poopers, 47
Pea Island Lifesaving Station, 188
Pea Island National Wildlife Refuge, 185
Pea Island Refuge Headquarters, 188
Pea Island Resort, 387
Pelican Restaurant, 314
Penguin Isle, 320
Penguin Isle Soundside Grille, 292
People's Drug Store, 47
Peoples Drug Store, 107
Performing Arts, 467
Petrozza's, 79
Pets in cottages, 330
Piers, U.S. Army Coastal Engineering, 36
Pig and Phoenix, 140
Pilot House Restaurant, 305
Pine Island Sanctuary, 36, 38
Pirate's Cove, 128, 407
Pirate's Quay, 100, 379
Pirates Chest, 224
Police Department, 452
Pony Island Motel, 375

Pony Island Restaurant, 312
Port 'O Call Restaurant, 282
Port O 'Call Gaslight Saloon, 319
Port Trinitie, 399
Portsmouth Island, 469
Princess Waterfront Motel, 376

Q

Quagmire's Shellfish Bar & Restaurant, 290
Queen Anne's Revenge Restaurant, 301
Qwik Shot, 140

R

R.V.'s , 296
Radio Shack, 103
Radio Stations, 456
Ramada Inn, 351
Real Estate, Outer Banks, 395
Rearview Mirror, 87
Recreation, Hatteras Island, 215
Recreation, Kill Devil Hills, 74
Recreation, Kitty Hawk, 58
Recreation, Nags Head, 89
Recreation, So. Shores, Duck, Sanderling, and Corolla, 41
Red Drum Tackle Shop, 222
Rental Service, 457
Rental companies (cottages), 326
Life Saver Rent-Alls, 457
Ocean Atlantic Rentals, 458
Renting a cottage, 325
Residential Resort Communities, 400
Restaurants
Awful Arthur's, 280
Back Porch, 310
Billy's Fish House, 305
Blue Point Oyster Bar & Grille, 273
Bubba's Bar-B-Q, 307
Cafe Atlantic, 314
Cap't. Ben's, 311
Capt.'n Frank's, 276
Channel Bass, 308
Chef's Corner, 290
Clara's, 299
Dairy Mart, 291
Darrell's, 300
Diamond Shoals, 304
Duchess of Dare, 298
Duck Deli, 273
Dunes, 294
Ebbtide Family, 287
Elizabeth's Cafe & Winery, 274
Emily's, 302
Etheridge, 284
Fast Eddie's, 274
Finely Ron's, 279
Fisherman's Wharf, 302
Frisco Sandwich, 306
Froggy Dog, 304
Gary's, 308
Island Inn Dining, 312
Joe's Starvin' Shark, 305

INDEX   493

John's Drive In, 276
Kelly's, 288
Kepper's Galley, 275
Kitty Hawk Pizza, 276
Mex-Econo, 283
Miller's, 286
Natural Selection, 299
Newby's, 280
Oasis, 297
Osprey Island Grille, 286
Owens', 294
Papagayo, 280
Pelican, 314
Penguin Isle, 292
Pilot House, 305
Pony Island, 312
Pony Island Restaurant, 312
Port O' Call, 282
Quagmire's, 290
Queen Anne's, 301
R.V.s, 296
Rudee's , 297
Sam and Omie's, 295
Ship's Galley, 298
Ship's Wheel, 296
Sportsman's, 275
Stack 'em, 278
Sweetwaters, 287
Thai Room, 283
Weeping Radish, 300
Wharf, 290
Windmill Point, 291
Restaurants, Kill Devil Hills, 278
Restaurants, The, 271
Revco Drug, 143
Revco Drug Store, 79
Rips (ocean), 440
Risky Business Seafood, 229
Roanoke Island Restaurants, 297
Rodanthe, 178
Roses, 103
Rudee's Restaurant & Raw Bar, 297

S

Salvo, 178
Sam & Omie's, 295
Sanderling, 402
Sanderling Inn, 341
Sanderling Restaurant, 271
Scarborough Faire, 44
Scarborough Inn, 361
Schooner Ridge, 402
Scuba Diving, 442
Nags Head Pro Dive Center, 93
Sea Foam Motel, 359
Sea Holly Square, 76
Sea Isle Gifts and Lamp Shop, 77
Sea Oatel, 360
Sea Scape Golf Club, 59
Sea Shore Stuffe, 104
Seagate North, 76
Seamark Foods, 79, 103, 105
Second Time Around, 140
Secret Spot Surf Shop, 100
See Sea Motel, 350
Service Directory, 451

Shallowbags, 141
Shear Genius, 79
Sheriff, County, 451
Ship's Galley, 298
Ship's Timbers, 382
Shopping, Hatteras Island, 219
Shopping, Kill Devil Hills, 75
Shopping, Kitty Hawk, 59
Shopping, Nags Head, 97
Shopping, Northern Outer Banks, 42
Shopping, Ocracoke, 254
Shopping, Roanoke Island, 140
Sidney's, 142
Sidney's Him, 142
Silk Gardenia, 42
Silver Lake Marina, 253
Silver Lake Motel, 379
Silver Sands Motel, 356
Single Family Homes and Land, 409
Snaps, 79
Sound Feet Shoes, 103
Soundside Factory Stores, 104
Soundside Watersports, 96
Southern Exposure Clothing Company, 102
Southern Hospitality, 454
Southern Shores, 35, 403
Souvenir City, 103
Splash, Too, 76
Sportsman's Restaurant, 275
Station Keepers Lounge, 321
Stow-A-Way Campground, 389
Summer Stuff, 226
Surf Report, 458, 460
Surf Shops, 439
Surf Side Motel, 356
Surf Slide, 97
Surfing, 435
Surfing, Learning How, 436
Surfside Casuals, 102
Surfside Plaza, 100
Swan Island, 30
Sweetwaters Restaurant, 287
Swimming, Ocean, 440

T

3/4 Time Music, 322
Take A Gander, 225
Tan-A-Rama, 344
Tanya's Ocean House, 352
Tar Heel Trading Company, 76
Taxi Service, 460
Taxi Services, 458
Teach's Lair Island Yacht Club, 216
Teeter's Campground, 392
Television, 455
Tennis Center, Sea Ranch, 74
Thai Room Restaurant, 283
The Monitor, 196
The Ship's Wheel, 296
The Source, 100
The Village at Nags Head, 82, 406
The Villages at Ocean Hill, 401
The Waterfront, 129, 133
The Wharf, 290
Theaters, Colony House VII and VIII, 58
Three Winks, 47

494 INDEX

Tickled Pink, 140
Ticks, Chiggers and Other Pests, 461
Tommy's Market, 45
Tops 'n Bottoms, 44
Tourist Bureau, Dare County, 124
Tower Circle Motel, 369
Tradewinds, 277
Tranquil House Inn, 363
Transportation, Outer Banks, 26
Trappings, 44
TW's Bait & Tackle, 44, 61

U

U.S. Coast Guard Facility, Buxton, 195
U.S. Lifesaving Service, 202
U85, 166, 194
Undertow, 440
United Parcel Service, 457

V

Vacation cottages, 324
Village Craftsmen, 257
Virginia Dare Hardware, 59
Virginia Dare Women's Center, 449

W

Wanchese and Mill Landing, 126
Wash Woods Coast Guard Station, 40, 205
Waterfall Park, 215
Waterfront Shops, 45, 141
Waterworks, 97
Waterworks, Too Sailing, 41
Wave Riding Vehicles, 61
Waves, 178
Waves, losing control in, 440
Wee Winks, 45
Wee Winks Square, 44
Weeping Radish, 125, 300
Weirs Point and Fort Huger, 120
Western Union, 461
Whalebone Seafood, 105
Whalehead Club, 30, 39
Whalehead: Tales of Corolla, 37
Whittler's Bench, 256
Wilbur & Orville Wright Motor Lodge, 349
Wildflowers on Hatteras Island, 190
Windmill Point, 291
Windsurfing, 435, 437
Windsurfing Hatteras, 220
Windsurfing, Kitty Hawk Sports, 93
Winks, 43
WNHW Radio, 456
WOBR Radio, 456
Worship, 462
Wrecks of Northern Hatteras, 194

Wright Brothers Memorial, 70
WRSF Radio, 456
WVOD Radio, 456

Y

Ye Olde Cherokee Inn, 348
Ye Olde Ham Shoppe, 105
Yellowhouse Galleries, 99
Yesterday's Jewels, 44
Yvonne's, 142